CH00660467

THE
The Story of

THE FORGOTTEN FLEET
The Story of the British Pacific Fleet 1944-45

John Winton

THE FORGOTTEN FLEET
The Story of the British Pacific Fleet 1944-45

DOUGLAS-BOYD
BOOKS

First Published in Great Britain by Michael Joseph Ltd 1969.
Reprinted by Douglas-Boyd Books   1989.
        Stream Cottage
        Scrag Oak
        Wadhurst
        E. Sussex TN5 6NP

British Library Cataloguing in Publication Data
Winton, John.
    The forgotten fleet: the story of the British Pacific fleet
    1944/45.
    1. World War 2. Pacific campaigns. Naval operations
    during Pacific campaigns of World War 2. Great Britain,
    Royal Navy.
    I. Title
    940.54'26
    ISBN 0-9514480-0-5

Printed in Great Britain by
        Antony Rowe Ltd. Chippenham.

Contents

Illustrations

Maps

Maps drawn by R. E. Martin

Preface & Acknowledgments

I BELIEVE that many people, here and in the United States, are still quite unaware that the British had two large fleets operating against the Japanese in the last year of World War Two. The general assumption appears to have been that victory at sea in the Far East in 1945 was entirely the achievement of the United States Navy. I hope that this book will go a little way towards putting the record straight and, belatedly, giving credit where it is due.

The book is intended to be a record of the operations of the East Indies and British Pacific Fleets, with enough information on the political and strategic background to place those operations in perspective. I have omitted a full account of the Commander-in-Chief, British Pacific Fleet's relations and negotiations with the Australian and New Zealand Governments in 1944 and 1945, because I felt that this was better left to Lord Fraser's eventual biographer. However, I have included for the sake of completeness a chapter on the Navy's part in the third campaign in the Arakan, although unfortunately I was not able to find room for eye-witness comments and contributions. Perhaps this complex, fascinating and almost totally forgotten piece of naval history deserves a book of its own.

The book could not have been written without the help of a great many people who very kindly wrote and talked to me of their experiences, lent me books, documents and photographs, and corrected my drafts. Amongst them I would particularly like to thank Lady Rawlings; Admiral of the Fleet The Earl Mountbatten of Burma, Admiral of the Fleet Lord Fraser of North Cape, and the late Admiral of the Fleet Sir Philip Vian; Admiral Sir Charles Daniel, Admiral Sir Michael Denny, Admiral Sir Michael Le Fanu, Admiral Sir Richard Onslov, Admiral Sir Manley Power and Admiral Sir Peter Reid; Vice Admiral Sir Hilary Biggs, Vice Admiral Sir Edward Evans Lombe, Vice Admiral Sir Norman Dalton, Vice Admiral Sir Arthur Hezlet, and Vice Admiral Sir Charles Hughes Hallett; Rear Admiral J. G. C. Given, Rear Admiral Sir Alexander McGlashan, Rear Admiral A. D. Nicholl,

Rear Admiral R. W. Parker, and Rear Admiral W. K. Weston; Captain
Eric Bush, Captain Tom Harrington, Captain T. G. V. Percy, Captain
John Robathan, Captain Henry F. Waight and Colonel Peter Norcock,
Royal Marines; Commander Denis Calnan, Commander Michael
Crosley, Commander Graham de Chair, Commander D. Holt Wilson,
Commander C. A. Jenkins, Commander John Rennie and Major
V. B. G. Cheesman, Royal Marines; Lieut. Cdr. Leslie Ellis, Lieut. Cdr.
A. M. Tuke, Lieut. Cdr. David Swanston and Lieut. Cdr. Robert F.
Morris, USNR; Rt Rev. Gerald Ellison, Bishop of Chester; Rt Hon.
John Silkin, MP; Mr R. G. Auckland, Editor of *The Falling Leaf*,
Journal of the Psywar Society, Mr John Baggs, Rev. J. G. Barnish,
Mr Eric W. Beeny, Mr V. M. G. Bennett, Mr Richard Bigg-Wither,
Mr H. C. Caistor, of St Helens Public Library, Mr D. Cartin, Mr
Geoffrey Cook, Miss Rose Coombs and the Imperial War Museum
Library, Mr George Dennison, Mr David Divine of *The Sunday Times*,
Mr Richard Douglas-Boyd, Mr Tom Dyke, Mr Colin Facer, Mr W.
Fenwick-Smith, Mr Norman Hanson, Mr Alan Humphreys of Reuters,
Lieut. Cdr. P. K. Kemp and the Admiralty Library, Miss Anne
Mackenzie, Secretary of the Fleet Air Arm Officers' Association,
Mr Andrew Morgan, Mr Derek Parfect, Mr Bill Rawlings, Mr P. G. W.
Roome, Lieut. Cdr. Ken Talbot, Editor of *Flight Deck*, Mr A. M. Tritton,
Mr Francis Tufton, Mr G. G. Turnbull of NAAFI, Mr Jack Waterman,
and Chief Petty Officer B. J. Wilcock.

Acknowledgments are also due to Viscountess Cunningham of
Hyndhope and Hutchinson Ltd. for an extract from *A Sailor's Odyssey*,
by Admiral of the Fleet Viscount Cunningham of Hyndhope; the
Controller of Her Majesty's Stationery Office for extracts from *The
War At Sea, 1939–1945*, by Captain S. W. Roskill, *The War Against
Japan*, by Major General S. Woodburn Kirby, *Grand Strategy*, by John
Ehrman, the Report of the Supreme Allied Commander, South-east
Asia to the Combined Chiefs of Staff, and Supplements to the *London
Gazette*; to the BBC for an extract from an interview by Mr Dick
Gregson; to the South African Broadcasting Company for an extract
from an interview with Lieut. C. H. H. Knollys, RN; to Captain Donald
MacIntyre, for extracts from *Fighting Admiral* (Evans Bros.); to the
executors of the late Admiral of the Fleet Sir Philip Vian for extracts
from *Action This Day* (Muller); to Captain Eric Bush for an extract
from *Bless Our Ship* (Allen & Unwin); to the Royal United Services
Institution, for an extract from their *Journal*; to General Sir Bernard
Fergusson, for an extract from *The Watery Maze* (Collins); to *The New*

York Herald Tribune, The Cornish Guardian, The Times of Ceylon, and *Illustrated*; to Westland Aircraft for two paintings by Mr V. M. G. Bennett; to the Royal Naval College, Greenwich, for a painting by Sir Oswald Birley; to Purnell's *History of the Second World War*, for two paintings by John Batchelor; and to Commander Graham de Chair for his painting of *Haguro*.

ACKNOWLEDGEMENTS

My thanks are due to the following for permission to reproduce photographs in which they hold the copyright. The Imperial War Museum 2, 3, 4, 9, 10, 11, 13 and 16. National Maritime Museum 1. Westland Aircraft Ltd. 5 & 6. Parnell & Sons 7 & 8. Commander Graham de Chair 12. The Ministry of Defence (Navy) 14, and The United States Naval Forces, Europe 15.

CHRONOLOGICAL SUMMARY OF EVENTS, OCTOBER 1944 – SEPTEMBER 1945

	Central Pacific	South-west Pacific	South-east Asia
Oct. 1944		20. US 6th Army landing at Leyte. 21. First Kamikaze attack (on HMAS *Australia*). 23–25. Battle of Leyte Gulf.	17–19. Eastern Fleet attack Nicobar Is. (MILLET).
Nov.	26. Final Japanese resistance on Peleliu (Palaus) ends.		22. Admiral Fraser C-inC BPF, Admiral Power C-in-C East Indies Fleet. *Stratagem* lost. 14th Army establish bridge-head across the Chindwin.
Dec.		15. Landing at Mindoro, Philippines. 25. Organised resistance on Leyte ends.	10. Advance in Arakan begins (ROMULUS). 20. First BPF strike at Pangkalan Brandan (ROBSON). 14th Army advance towards the Irrawaddy.
Jan. 1945	4–5. 3rd Fleet strike Formosa. 9–20. 3rd Fleet sortie into South China Sea, strikes at Formosa, Hainan and Indo-China.	9. US 6th Army landing at Lingayen Gulf, Luzon.	3. 3rd Cdo. Brig. landing at Akyab (LIGHTNING). 4. Akyab occupied. Second BPF strike at Pangkalan Brandan (LENTIL). 11. 14th Army establish bridgehead across the Irrawaddy, north of Mandalay. 12. 3rd Cdo. Brig. landing at Myebon (PUNGENT). 16. *Porpoise* lost. 21. 26th Ind. Div. landing at Ramree (MATADOR). 22. 3rd Cdo. Brig. landing at Kangaw. 24. First BPF strike at Palembang. 26. Royal Marine landing at Cheduba (SANKEY). 27. Burma Road opened. 29. Second BPF strike at Palembang.
Feb.	16–17. 5th Fleet strike at Japanese home islands. 19. US Marines landing on Iwo Jima.	10. BPF arrive at Sydney. 26. Corregidor secured.	9–22. Operation BLOCK, Ramree. 13–14. 14th Army establish bridgeheads across Irrawaddy south of Mandalay. 16. 53rd Brig. landing at Ryuwa.

	Central Pacific	South-west Pacific	South-east Asia
Mar.	10. B–29 fire raid on Tokyo. 16. Organised resistance on Iwo Jima ends. 18–19. 5th Fleet strikes at Honshu, Shikoku. 26. US 77th Inf. Div. landing on Kerama Retto (Okinawa). 26. BPF begin operations against Sakishima Gunto (ICEBERG).	4. Manila captured. 7. BPF arrives at Manus.	1–31. 14th Army battle for Meiktila. 8–20. 14th Army battle for Mandalay. 13. 4th Brig. landing at Letpan (TURRET). 26. Japanese relief convoy for Andamans sunk by 26th D.F. (ONBOARD) in Andaman Sea.
Apr.	1. US 10th Army landing on Okinawa (ICEBERG). Kamikaze attack on BPF: *Indefatigable* and *Ulster* damaged. 6. First massed kamikaze (kikusui) attack on Okinawa. Kamikaze attack on BPF: *Illustrious* damaged. 7. Battle of East China Sea: *Yamato* sunk. 9. Battle for Shuri begins. 12–13. BPF strikes at Formosa. 16. US 77th Inf. Div. landing at Ie Shima. 23. BPF arrive at Leyte.	17. Landing at Mindanao. Philippines.	1. 14th Army begin advance to Rangoon. 30. Japanese evacuation convoy from Rangoon sunk by 11th D.F. (GABLE), in Gulf of Martaban.
May	4. BPF resume strikes at Sakishima Gunto. Kamikaze attack on BPF: *Formidable* and *Indomitable* damaged. 4–5. Japanese 32nd Army counter-attack defeated. 9. Kamikaze attack on BPF: *Formidable* and *Victorious* damaged. 25. Last day of BPF strikes at Sakishima Gunto. 27. Naha captured. 29. Shuri captured.	1. 1st Australian Corps landing at Tarakan. 8. VE DAY.	2. 26th Ind. Div. landing at Rangoon (DRACULA). 3. Rangoon occupied. 9. Sandoway captured. 13. Gwa captured. Third campaign in Arakan ends. 16. *Haguro* sunk by 26th D.F. (DUKEDOM) in Malacca Strait.
June	14–15. BPF strike at Truk (INMATE). 18. Gen. Buckner killed. 21. Organised resistance on Okinawa ends.	8. *Ashigara* sunk by *Trenchant*, Banka Strait. 10. 9th Australian Div. landing at Brunei Bay.	
July	10. 3rd Fleet strikes at Honshu. 14. 3rd Fleet bombard Japanese mainland. 16. BPF joins US 3rd Fleet at sea off Japan. 17. First combined fleet strikes and bombardment of Japan.	1. 7th Australian Div. landing at Balikpapan.	5–10. East Indies Fleet minesweeping off Nicobar Is. (COLLIE). *Plucky* lost. 19. Japanese breakout across Sittang. 24–26. East Indies Fleet minesweeping off Phuket (LIVERY). *Vestal* lost.
July	18, 24, 28. 3rd Fleet strikes at Japanese warships, Yokosuka and Kure.		31. XE–4 cuts cables at Saigon (SABRE). XE–3 attacks *Takao* at Singapore (STRUGGLE) XE–5 damages cables at Hong Kong (FOIL)

Aug.	6. 'Little Boy' dropped on Hiroshima. 8. Russia declares war on Japan. 9. 'Fat Man' dropped on Nagasaki. 12. Main body of BPF withdraws for lack of fuel. 14. Japanese Government surrenders.		
		15. VJ DAY.	15. SEAC enlarged.
	27. Allied ships enter Tokyo Bay.		
Sept.	2. MacArthur accepts surrender of Japan, on board *Missouri*, Tokyo Bay.		5. Singapore occupied. 9. 25th Div. landing at Port Swettenham and Port Dickson (ZIPPER). 12. Admiral Mountbatten accepts surrender of Japanese forces in S.E. Asia, Singapore.

Chapter One

THE PROMISE

'. . . the war with Japan is not one in which we in this country are playing the part of benevolent assistants. Even if we are compelled, for the time being, to devote the greater part of our human and material resources to the task of defeating Germany, we are still principals in the Far Eastern War.' *Anthony Eden, Foreign Secretary: House of Commons,* 14 December 1943.[1]

BETWEEN 11 a.m. and 1.20 p.m. on 10 December 1941, Force Z – comprising the battleship *Prince of Wales*, the battlecruiser *Repulse* and four destroyers – was attacked in the South China Sea by Japanese bombers and torpedo-bombers of the 22nd Air Flotilla operating from southern Indo-China. Lacking fighter cover, *Prince of Wales* and *Repulse* were both sunk. Admiral Sir Tom Phillips, C-in-C Eastern Fleet, Captain J. C. Leach, and 327 officers and men of *Prince of Wales* were lost, together with 513 of *Repulse*'s ship's company.

This appalling calamity was the end result of a train of unfortunate circumstances; of decisions taken in London, after prolonged disagreement between the Prime Minister and the Admiralty; the grounding, at Kingston, Jamaica, of the aircraft carrier *Indomitable*; underestimates, in London and in Singapore, of the offensive skill of Japanese pilots and the operational ranges of their aircraft; the false report, received in *Prince of Wales* late on 9 December, of a Japanese landing at Kuantan on the east coast of Malaya; the unlucky chance which led a returning Japanese striking force directly over the British ships; and last, Admiral Phillips's own insistence on radio silence and his evident belief that there were in Singapore staff officers with the almost psychic powers of insight needed to divine that Force Z would require air cover off Kuantan from dawn onwards on 10 December.

[1] *Parliamentary Debates* (Official Record of the House of Commons), Vol. 395, col. 1427.

These circumstances culminated in a disaster which was at once a severe strategic set-back for the Allies, a shocking tactical defeat for the Navy and a personal tragedy for the officers and men of Force Z. A quarter of a century later, the loss of *Prince of Wales* and *Repulse* was still a subject of conversation to be broached with caution in many wardrooms in the Fleet.

After the destruction of Force Z it was more than three years before major British naval units again operated east of Singapore. By that time, a whole war had gone by. By November 1944, when the British Pacific Fleet was formally in being, the United States Navy and Marine Corps, assisted by units of the Royal Australian and New Zealand Navies, had already won for the Allies virtually complete control of sea and air over most of the Pacific. They had developed new weapons and new techniques, and had evolved a new philosophy of sea power on an Homeric scale, deploying huge fleets over vast distances and maintaining them at sea for unprecedentedly long periods of time. Into the closing stages of this war at sea the Royal Navy eventually entered in March 1945 as junior partners of the American fleets, equal in spirit but greatly inferior in numbers of men, ships and material. It could be said that in the Far East in 1945 the Royal Navy had to learn, for the first time in its history, how to be a poor relation.

The British Pacific and East Indies Fleets were, by British standards, great gatherings of ships.[1] They were a magnificent contribution by a nation 10,000 miles from the action who had already fought a war at sea for five years and over five oceans. But both British fleets were almost totally overshadowed by the giant US 3rd/5th and 7th Fleets. The imbalance in size, striking power and in publicity, may in part account for the comparative lack of interest shown at home in the performance of the Fleet during the latter stages of the naval war in the Far East. Perhaps nobody wants to watch what they imagine to be a Second Fifteen.

To understand this remarkable – and irreversible – change in the Royal Navy's status, *vis-à-vis* the navy of an ally, it is necessary briefly to retrace events in the Far East from December 1941, when the Japanese onslaught began, to September 1944, when the offer of a British fleet in the Pacific was made, and finally accepted.

Force Z's ill-fated sortie was intended to disrupt the Japanese landings at Singora and Patani, on the Kra Isthmus of Thailand. Simultaneously the Japanese also attacked Khota Baru in Malaya, Hong

---

[1] See Appendixes A and B.

Kong, Guam, Wake Island and the Philippines. Quickly establishing command of the air and local superiority on the ground, and with the added advantages of surprise, mobility and a high morale, the Japanese rapidly ran up a string of smashing victories which began at Pearl Harbour and continued until their first set-back at the Battle of the Coral Sea in May 1942.

Hong Kong fell on Christmas Day 1941 after a grim but hopeless resistance by the garrison. Wake Island had surrendered a day earlier, after an outstandingly brave defence by United States Marines. The Japanese 25th Army took Malaya in seventy-three days (they had been allowed a hundred), General Yamashita accepting the surrender of Singapore on Sunday, 15 February 1942. In the Philippines two divisions of the 14th Army (Lt. Gen. Homma) began with a landing on Batan Island on 10 December, and by the end of March the Japanese had captured the whole of the Philippine archipelago except the peninsula of Bataan on Luzon, and the offshore fortress of Corregidor. General MacArthur left the Philippines on 12 March, on the orders of President Roosevelt. Meanwhile, the 15th Army after their landing in Thailand drove northwards into Burma, reaching the Sittang River on 23 February and taking Rangoon on 8 March.

On 10 January the Allies in the south-west Pacific set up a combined command: ABDA (American, British, Dutch, Australian), with General Sir Archibald Wavell as Supreme Commander.[1] ABDA Command extended from Okinawa to Darwin, and from the Western Carolines to the Andamans – an area which, in view of the Japanese conquests at the time and the forces available to the Allies, now seems optimistic, not to say unrealistic. A day later, on 11 January, Lt. Gen. Imamura's 16th Army began its attack on the Dutch East Indies, landing at Tarakan in Borneo, and Manado in the Celebes. In seven weeks the Japanese captured Macassar, Timor, Sumatra and Java. On 8 March, after a total campaign of sixty days (compared with the Japanese estimate of 150 days), the Dutch East Indies Government surrendered unconditionally. ABDA Command had already dissolved on 25 February, on General Wavell's irrefutable argument that there was now nothing left for ABDA to command.

Nevertheless, this period was distinguished by two very gallant naval actions fought by Allied ships in the Java Sea on 27 and 28 February, when mixed and makeshift forces of British, Dutch, American and

---

[1] On hearing of his new appointment, Sir Archibald was reported to have said: 'I've heard of holding the baby – but this is twins!'

Australian warships, who had had little opportunity to exercise together and whose movements were bedevilled by communications difficulties, engaged superior Japanese fleets escorting the troop convoys for the invasion of Java. Four cruisers and three destroyers[1] were sunk in these actions. Three of the surviving ships, a cruiser and two destroyers,[2] were also sunk, on 1 March. In spite of this sacrifice, the Japanese landings were delayed by barely twenty-four hours.[3]

For the Navy, as for the other services present, the fall of Singapore had been a dark and terrible episode, illuminated only by astonishing acts of individual bravery. The remnants of the Eastern Fleet retreated to Ceylon where, in March, Admiral Sir James Somerville arrived to take over as C-in-C, leaving the vigorous personality of Admiral Sir Geoffrey Layton to organise the defence of Ceylon.

Sir James acted like a tonic on the Eastern Fleet. He had a bright war record as Flag Officer Force H already behind him. He was bold, witty, and outspoken, an admiral with the common touch and, at times, a somewhat Rabelaisian turn of humour.

On first seeing his fleet at sea Sir James signalled: 'So this is the Eastern Fleet. Well never mind. There's many a good tune played on an old fiddle.' This rather rueful signal had some justification. The Eastern Fleet was the largest yet assembled by the Royal Navy in the war and it contained every ship a hard-pressed Admiralty could spare. On paper it looked convincing enough; five battleships, three aircraft carriers, seven cruisers, and fourteen destroyers. But four of the battleships were R Class ships dating from the First World War – old, slow and of short endurance.[4] One of the carriers was *Hermes*, old, slow and small, whilst the ships' companies and air groups of the two larger carriers, *Formidable* and *Indomitable*, both lacked training and battle experience. Outwardly radiating a confidence he could not have felt, Admiral Somerville set about preparing his variegated fleet for battle.

There was in fact no time to lose. The Eastern Fleet, whatever its shortcomings, was still a 'fleet in being'. As such, it was a threat to

[1] The Dutch cruisers *De Ruyter* and *Java*, HMAS *Perth* (Captain H. M. L. Waller, RAN), and USS *Houston* (Captain A. H. Rooks, USN), and the destroyers HMS *Jupiter* (Lt. Cdr. N. V. J. T. Thew), *Electra* (Cdr. C. W. May) and the Dutch *Kortenaer*.
[2] HMS *Exeter* (Captain O. L. Gordon), *Encounter* (Lt. Cdr. E. V. St. J. Morgan) and USS *Pope*.
[3] See Captain S. W. Roskill's *The War at Sea 1939–1945* (HMSO, 1956), Vol. II, pp. 13–18. For a personal account of HMAS *Perth*'s part, see also *Out of the Smoke* by Ray Parkin (The Hogarth Press, 1960).
[4] *Resolution, Ramillies, Royal Sovereign* and *Revenge*.

the flank of the Japanese advance in Burma. On 28 March intelligence reported a powerful Japanese raiding force entering the Indian Ocean and heading west. Flying his flag in the battleship *Warspite*, Admiral Somerville assembled his fleet at sea on 31 March and deployed it in two tactical units, a fast Force A under his own command and a slow Force B under Vice Admiral Algernon Willis, his second-in-command. Without information on the strength or position of the Japanese force, Admiral Somerville hoped to engage the enemy with Force A, preferably by a night torpedo attack with Albacore aircraft from *Indomitable*, while Force B remained in support.

However, short endurance forced the Fleet to return for replenishment and refuelling at the fleet base of Addu Atoll,[1] in the Maldive Islands, before the Japanese could be brought to action. It seemed to Somerville that a chance had been lost and it was characteristic of him that he should have been disappointed. 'I fear', he wrote, 'they have taken fright, which is a pity because if I could have given them a good crack now it would have been timely.'[2]

On the evidence, it now seems extremely fortunate that no encounter with the Japanese fleet took place. Barring a miracle, the outcome would almost certainly have been another shattering disaster to the Eastern Fleet, for the Japanese raiders were actually Vice Admiral Nagumo's formidable Striking Force, including five of the six carriers which attacked Pearl Harbour, four fast battleships, two cruisers and destroyers.

Nagumo failed to find the Eastern Fleet, but made short work of the targets available to him. Whilst Vice Admiral Ozawa, with one carrier, cruisers and destroyers, raided the east coast of India, Nagumo's aircraft fell upon Colombo on Easter Sunday, 5 April; on the same day dive-bombers surprised and sank the cruisers *Cornwall* and *Dorsetshire*, which had been detached from the main fleet. On 9 April, off the east coast of Ceylon, *Hermes*, the destroyer *Vampire*, the corvette *Hollyhock* and two tankers were also bombed and sunk. The Eastern Fleet's slow force withdrew to Mombasa, while the fast force steamed to Bombay. Admiral Somerville still had his fleet in being but from now on he would, in his own words '. . . have to lie low in one sense but be pretty

---

[1] 'Fleet Base' is a euphemistic term for Addu Atoll. The sailors of the Eastern Fleet called it 'Scapa, with —— palm trees'.

[2] For a full account of this period, and of Admiral Somerville's part in it, see Captain Donald MacIntyre's good biography of the man, *Fighting Admiral* (Evans Bros., 1961), from which this quotation is taken (p. 187).

active in another – keep the old tarts out of the picture and roar about with the others'.[1]

Meanwhile, on the day *Hermes* was sunk, the surviving American and Filipino forces on the Bataan peninsula surrendered. Corregidor, the last Allied stronghold in the Philippines, fell on 6 May. In the north, the British and Indian troops of Eastern Army in Burma were approaching the Assam frontier, after a retreat of 1,000 miles – the longest in British military history. Thus in six months the Japanese had seized an empire of 90,000,000 people, which stretched from Rabaul to Rangoon,[2] and contained 88% of the world's rubber, 54% of its tin, 30% of its rice, 20% of its tungsten, and the rich oilfields of the East Indies, at the cost of some 15,000 men, about 400 aircraft and a couple of dozen warships, none of them larger than a destroyer. The prestige and prospects of the Allied nations in the Far East had touched bottom.

Yet, it was at this point that Japan over-reached herself. On their own admission, the Japanese armed forces were by then suffering from a 'Victory Disease' (contracted in an especially virulent form by Admiral Nagumo's aircrews, who had proved irresistible from Pearl Harbour, to Darwin, to Colombo). It seemed that nothing could stand against them. However, to use a descriptive piece of American slang, they were all shortly to receive their 'comeuppance'. At Pearl Harbour the Striking Force had failed to find and destroy the American aircraft carriers, nor had it seriously damaged the oil storage tanks and repair facilities of the naval base. These seemingly trivial threads left uncut, of which only a few Japanese officers appreciated the significance at the time, were to prove the means whereby the whole fabric of Japanese conquests was unravelled.

After the unlamented dissolution of ABDA Command, the United States assumed strategic responsibility for the whole of the Pacific, including Australia and New Zealand. Great Britain retained responsibility for the Indian Ocean, Malaya and Sumatra. In April 1942 General Douglas MacArthur was appointed Supreme Allied Commander, South-west Pacific, while Admiral Chester W. Nimitz became Commander in Chief, Pacific Ocean Area. Mr Churchill and President Roosevelt had already agreed at the 'Arcadia' Conference in Washington in January 1942 that the Allies' first priority was the war against Germany. Allied strategy in the Pacific at this time was therefore defensive, intended to contain the Japanese wherever possible until a

---

[1] *Fighting Admiral*, p. 195.
[2] See map, p. 24–5.

turn for the better in the European war and the growing military power of
the United States enabled the Allies to take the offensive in the Pacific.

For their part, the Japanese had a choice of offensive strategies, all
most attractive. The first objectives, for which they had gone to war,
had been gained so swiftly and comprehensively that the Imperial
General Staff had not yet settled future strategy. Japan could strike in
the west, mounting invasions of Ceylon and southern India, while continuing her present advance through Assam into northern India; or she
could move southwards and invade Australia. Both these alternatives
were favoured by the Naval General Staff, though not by the Army.
The third choice was to strike in the east, at Midway and Hawaii and,
in the process, provoke a major fleet action in which the main American
fleet would be utterly and finally destroyed – with the possibility then
of a negotiated peace. The destruction of the American fleet was a
consummation dear to the hearts of Admiral Yamamato, the C-in-C
Combined Fleet, and his staff. The Naval General Staff preferred a
modified plan to isolate Australia from her allies by seizing the chains
of islands which ran south-east from the tip of New Guinea through
the Solomons, New Hebrides and the Fijis, to Samoa. They had
already begun to put this plan into effect with landings at Lae and
Salamua in New Guinea in March 1942.

It is possible that the Imperial General Staff were swayed by
Doolittle's Raid on Tokyo, which seemed to make Admiral Yamamato's
point that the United States Navy should be eliminated. Their eventual
decision was a compromise: to continue with the Naval General Staff's
plan, *and* to invade Midway, inviting an action against the American
fleet. The first part of the plan was to begin in May with landings at
Tulagi in the Solomons and at Port Moresby on the south-east tip of
Papua. The second part, the landing on Midway, was to take place in
June. The way to the crucial battles of the Coral Sea and Midway was
now clear.

On 20 April the Japanese invasion force for Port Moresby, escorted
by a Covering Group and including the light carrier *Shoho,* commanded
by Rear Admiral Aritome Goto, sailed from Truk for Rabaul and thence
into the Coral Sea.[1] A small detachment landed on Tulagi on 3 May,

[1] For full details of the Battle of the Coral Sea and other Pacific actions
mentioned in this chapter see the relevant volumes of *The History of United
States Naval Operations in World War II* by Samuel Eliot Morison (OUP).
For shorter but excellent accounts see also *The Great Sea War,* ed. by E. B.
Potter and Fleet Admiral Chester Nimitz (Harrap, 1961), and *The Battle for the
Pacific* by Captain Donald MacIntyre (Batsford, 1966).

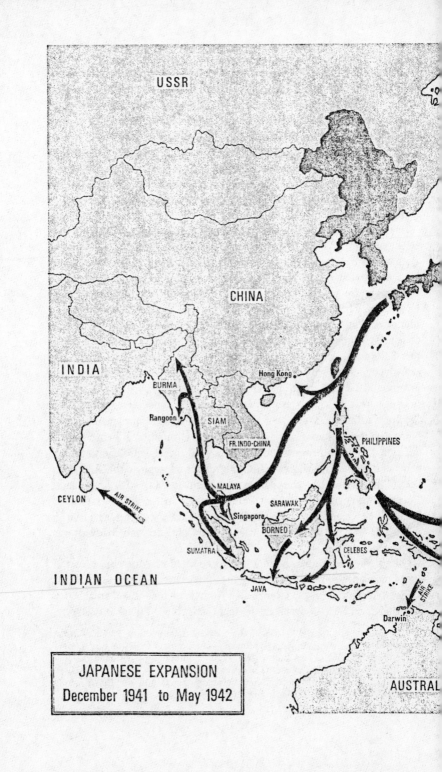

JAPANESE EXPANSION
December 1941 to May 1942

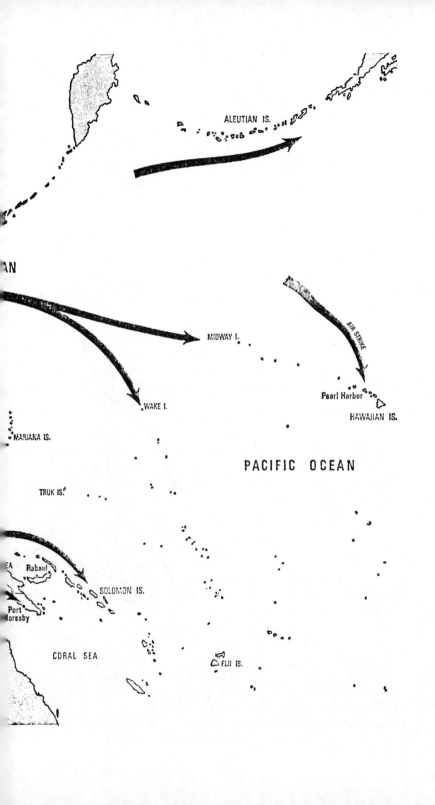

while the remainder headed for Port Moresby. At the same time a powerful Striking Force under Vice Admiral Takeo Takagi, including the fleet carriers *Shokaku* and *Zuikaku* (Rear Admiral Tadaichi Hara), passed north of the Solomons to enter the Coral Sea from the east. An Allied fleet attempting to molest the Port Moresby invasion force would be caught between Goto's Covering Group to the west and Takagi's Striking Force to the east. It was a promising plan and, but for errors by Hara's air groups, it might have succeeded.

At Pearl Harbour Admiral Nimitz had forewarning of the broad intention of the Japanese dispositions. Allied intelligence had succeeded in cracking Japanese naval codes and with this priceless advantage Nimitz assembled such naval forces as he had, formed them in two task forces around the carriers *Yorktown* and *Lexington*, and despatched them to the Coral Sea. The two task forces made a rendezvous west of Espiritu Santo on 5 May and were joined by a Cruiser Support Group from MacArthur's SW Pacific Command, under Rear Admiral J. C. Crace, RN. The Allied fleet was under the tactical command of Rear Admiral Frank Fletcher, USN, in *Yorktown*.

Neither side had definite knowledge of the other's position or strength, although Takagi was unknowingly only seventy miles from Fletcher late on 6 May, and the first contact was not made until the 7th, when bombers and torpedo-bombers from *Yorktown* and *Lexington* sank *Shoho*. On the same day, Hara's aircraft attacked the tanker *Neosho*, mistakenly identified as a carrier, and her attendant destroyers *Sims*, sinking them both. The main carrier action opened the next morning with simultaneous strike and counter-strike, in which the Allies damaged *Shokaku* and the Japanese damaged both *Yorktown* and *Lexington* – the latter having to be sunk later by Allied forces. At no time during the action had any ship on either side sighted an enemy ship; the Battle of the Coral Sea was the first naval engagement in history fought entirely between aircraft carriers.

When both fleets disengaged on 9 May, the Imperial Japanese Navy had apparently gained yet another victory. The light carrier *Shoho* was a fair exchange for *Neosho*, *Sims* and the valuable and experienced fleet carrier *Lexington*. But strategically, the Japanese had suffered a sharp reverse. The Port Moresby invasion force turned back. Japanese expansion in the Far East had received its first setback of the war. Furthermore, damage to *Shokaku* and losses inflicted upon *Zuikaku*'s air groups prevented either carrier taking part in the approaching battle at Midway.

Admiral Yamamato's design for Midway, again accurately forecast by Allied intelligence, included two favourite Japanese tactical devices: the diversionary decoy, and the pincer movement. The plan was bold, conceived upon the grand scale, but fantastically complicated, involving the deployment of no less than eleven separate groups of ships.

In essence, the plan required the Mobile Force of carriers to neutralise the defences of Midway preparatory to an invasion by the Occupation Force. The Main Body and the Second Fleet Covering Group lay in wait to trap the American fleet in the triple pincers of Nagumo's carriers, Kondo's battleships, and Yamamato's Main Body which included his flagship, the colossal 64,000-ton battleship *Yamato*. Far to the north, the Aleutian Occupation Groups would, Yamamato hoped, at the least serve to confuse the tactical issue and, at best, decoy a substantial part of Nimitz's fleet away from the main action.

Admiral Yamamato longed for the 'one decisive fleet action' and it is ironic that he should have dispersed his ships to pursue different objectives at the very time when he could have forced such an action. He could have collected together his whole fleet and simply advanced upon Midway. The American fleet, such as it was then, would have been bound to give battle and Yamamato's concentrated force of eleven battleships, eight carriers and innumerable cruisers and destroyers should have been more than enough to dispatch it.

Yamamato's complicated armada was opposed by two Task Forces: TF 16, consisting of the carriers *Enterprise* and *Hornet*, six cruisers and nine destroyers, and TF 17, with the carrier *Yorktown*, two cruisers and five destroyers. TF 16 was commanded by Rear Admiral Raymond Spruance who, as the war progressed, was to emerge as the greatest sea-captain of the Pacific.

For once indifferently served by his reconnaissance aircraft, Yamamato did not suspect the presence of American carriers at Midway, and the crucial moment of the battle was thus an excellent demonstration of the truth of an old principle of public-house brawls.[1] On the morning of 4 June aircraft from *Yorktown* and *Enterprise* arrived undetected over the Mobile Force and dive-bombed *Soryu*, *Kaga* and Nagumo's flagship *Akagi*. The three Japanese carriers were caught when at their most vulnerable, with their flight decks crowded with aircraft about to be launched to strike the American fleet. Subsequent explosions and fierce

[1] 'Thrice is he armed that hath his quarrel just,
But four times he who gets his blow in fust!'
Henry Wheeler Shaw (Josh Billings) 1818–85

petrol fires completed the work of the bombers and all three carriers later sank. Later the same day aircraft from *Hiryu*, the fourth and last of the Mobile Force carriers, badly damaged *Yorktown*, but *Hiryu* was herself then sunk by bombers from *Enterprise* and *Hornet*. By 5 June the Japanese fleet was in retreat, its air superiority in the Pacific lost for ever.

The four-day action off Midway, which began with the first sighting of part of the Occupation Force by long-range reconnaissance aircraft from Midway on 3 June and ended with the final torpedoing of the crippled *Yorktown* on 7 June, was the turning-point of the war in the Pacific. It was the Japanese Navy's first clear defeat since the Korean Admiral Yi Sun Sin in his Kwi-Sun 'Tortoise' ship sank 120 Japanese ships by fire and ram in 1592. It was, in Admiral Morison's words, the 'sockdolager'. The United States Navy, and the Marines on Midway, had won one of the decisive sea battles of history, a victory to rank with Salamis and Lepanto.

This brilliant flash of light, coming at a gloomy time for the Allies, naturally aroused thoughts of some form of defensive counter-attack in the Coral Sea area. But the decision was complicated by the fact that the area was in General MacArthur's South-west Pacific Command, whilst the ships, troops and transports necessary for such a campaign were administered by Admiral Nimitz's Pacific Ocean Command. General MacArthur proposed a direct frontal assault upon the Japanese stronghold of Rabaul, in New Britain. However, Admiral Nimitz was reluctant to commit his ships, and particularly his few and precious remaining carriers, to such an enterprise. A compromise was reached: Admiral Nimitz was to command an assault on the Santa Cruz islands and the seaplane base at Tulagi; as soon as a satisfactory base had been established, command was to be transferred to General MacArthur, who would then direct a dual assault through Papua and the Solomons, eventually converging upon Rabaul.

Plans were well advanced when the disturbing news was received from reconnaissance aircraft and from Australian coast-watchers that the Japanese were building an airstrip on the island of Guadalcanal in the Solomons.

Guadalcanal has been variously described as 'loathsome', 'fever-ridden', and a 'totally worthless piece of real estate'. But all commentators are agreed that it was strategically priceless and the US Joint Chiefs of Staff were quicker to appreciate its significance than were the Japanese. On 7 August 1942 the 1st Division of the US Marines under

Major General Alexander Vandergrift landed on Tulagi and on Guadalcanal. The Tulagi assault met fanatical resistance from the Japanese garrison (a foretaste of events to come) but the Guadalcanal landing was unopposed, which was fortunate, for the manner and organisation of the landing left room for improvement. In thirty-six hours the Marines had captured the airstrip. The battle for Guadalcanal virtually meant the battle for this airstrip, known as Henderson Field,[1] which was as tactically vital in the coming campaign as Maleme had been in Crete and as strategically important as the Motoyama airfields were to be on Iwo Jima.

Japanese naval reaction to the landings was swift and violent. On the night of 9 August Admiral Gunichi Mikawa, with a force of seven cruisers and a destroyer, made one anti-clockwise sweep at high speed around the small island of Savo, off Guadalcanal. The mixed force of Allied ships defending the troop transport anchorages, caught unaware and dispersed, and inexperienced in the neglected arts of night-fighting, lost four cruisers[2] shelled and torpedoed in a short but vicious engagement.

The Battle of Savo Island was a defeat for the Allies comparable to that inflicted upon the Italian fleet at Matapan. It also dispelled the legend that the Japanese were a myopic race with poor night vision. Yet the disaster might have been even worse. Mikawa withdrew, fearing an attack by American carrier aircraft at first light, although the transport anchorages off Tulagi and Guadalcanal were actually at his mercy.[3]

The Japanese High Command, still preoccupied with the capture of Port Moresby, were slow to realise Allied intentions on Guadalcanal. Two crushing defeats at the Tenaru River (21 August) and Bloody Ridge (12–13 September) awoke them. The struggle for Guadalcanal developed into a race by both sides to build up their resources on the island. At sea, there eventually came to be a curious state of balance. By day the Allies, with Henderson Field and Halsey's carriers,[4] controlled the air, and hence the sea. By night, the initiative returned to the Japanese who reinforced their troops on Guadalcanal with convoys

---

[1] Called after Major Lofton R. Henderson, US Marine Corps, who led a very gallant bombing attack on *Hiryu* during the battle of Midway on 4 June.

[2] USS *Astoria, Vincennes, Quincy,* and HMAS *Canberra.*

[3] Vice Admiral Frank J. Fletcher, USN, in tactical command of the Guadalcanal Expeditionary Force, had withdrawn the carriers from the Guadalcanal area on 9 August – a decision which is still controversial.

[4] Vice Admiral William F. Halsey Jnr. replaced Admiral Robert Ghormley as Commander, South Pacific, in October 1942.

of transports and destroyers – Rear Admiral Raizo Tanaka's famous 'Tokyo Express' – running down under cover of darkness from Rabaul to Guadalcanal through 'The Slot', as the passage between the two chains of Solomon Islands was called.

The sea-fights off Guadalcanal, when both sides sought to interrupt the flow of the other's reinforcements, made some of the most stirring history of World War Two at sea and proved that the Allies in the West might be opposed by a good navy, but in the Far East they faced a great one. So many ships were sunk in the waters off Savo Island that they were nick-named 'Ironbottom Sound', and the stretch of sea between San Cristobal and Espiritu Santo, 'Torpedo Junction'. Between August and December 1942, in a series of ferocious night engagements, two carrier actions,[1] and submarine attacks at Torpedo Junction, the Allies lost *Hornet* and *Wasp*, three cruisers and eight destroyers; many other ships were damaged, including *Saratoga* and *Enterprise* and the battleships *North Carolina* and *South Dakota*. These losses were counterbalanced by the sinking of the Japanese battleships *Hiei* and *Kirishima*, the carrier *Ryujo*, one cruiser and six destroyers.

On 23 and 24 October two further Japanese attempts to take Henderson Field were defeated and by the end of the year the tide on Guadalcanal was running against the Japanese. The Japanese Army were at first reluctant to abandon the island, although it had become a costly and 'open-ended' commitment, but by 7 February 1943, under the Allies' very noses, the redoubtable Tanaka's ships had spirited away the last Japanese from Guadalcanal. The Allies had gained the vital island.

Midway, Guadalcanal and subsequent campaigns in defence of the Solomons steadily drained away Japan's experienced and irreplaceable aircrews.[2] The air groups who took part in later Pacific operations were not the same formidable weapons Nagumo had commanded in the first six months of the war. Tactically, the United States Navy learned off Guadalcanal a lesson the US Army was to learn at Kasserine Pass in Tunisia: superior technologies were not enough against a skilful, determined and highly trained enemy. The US Navy were quick to take the point: more attention was paid to exercising task forces and flotillas together as units, and greatly improved ship's Combat Information

[1] Cape Esperance (11–12 October) 1st Guadalcanal (12 November) and 2nd Guadalcanal (15 November) and Tassafaronga (30 November); carrier actions Eastern Solomons (24–25 August) and Santa Cruz (26 October).

[2] It was estimated that Japan lost some 2,500 naval aircraft in the attempt to recapture Guadalcanal and in the subsequent defence of the Solomons.

Centres were designed, to enable a commander to assess more accurately the radar and visual action information presented to him.

Some months before Guadalcanal was taken the Japanese had already suffered their first defeat of the war on land – in Papua, where Australian troops (and notably the remarkable men of 'Kanga Force' at Wau) had proved that the Japanese were not invincible jungle-fighters. Despite an unhelpful commentary from General MacArthur,[1] the Australians in Papua counter-attacked in September 1942, forcing the Japanese to retreat along the Kokoda Trail; by 31 January 1943 the Australians had fought across the Owen Stanley mountain range and reached Buna, on the north coast of New Guinea (and suffering, in this little-known campaign, almost twice the casualties sustained by the US Marines on Guadalcanal).

The advance on Rabaul was sustained on two fronts – in the Solomons, and in New Guinea – throughout 1943 and was hastened by a brilliant success for Allied aircraft in the Battle of the Bismarck Sea. In the three days from 2 to 4 March 1943, bombers of the US Army and Royal Australian air forces attacked a Japanese convoy, sinking four escorting destroyers and all the eight troop transports carrying an entire infantry division.

Supported at sea by the Seventh Fleet[2] and transported by the Seventh Amphibious Force, MacArthur's forces carried out a succession of combined operations along the north coast of New Guinea, capturing Nassau Bay (30 June 1943), Lae (16 September), Finschafen (2 October) and, on 26 December, assaulting Cape Gloucester in New Britain. In the Solomons the Allied advance continued with the invasions of New Georgia (30 June), Vella Lavella (15 August) and Bougainville (1 November), being accompanied by another series of hard-fought naval actions.[3] By New Year's Day 1944, Rabaul had been partially neutralised and by-passed; the door of the Bismarcks, the Japanese outer defensive barrier, was ajar.

In the Indian Ocean, Admiral Somerville was pursuing – with the

---

[1] He is reported to have told General Marshall: 'The Australians have proven themselves unable to match the enemy in jungle fighting. Aggressive leadership is lacking.'

[2] In March 1943, General MacArthur's naval forces in the South-west Pacific became the US Seventh Fleet, commanded first by Admiral Carpender and later by Vice Admiral Thomas Kinkaid. The Seventh Amphibious Force was commanded by Rear Admiral Daniel Barbey.

[3] Kula Gulf (5–6 July 1943) Kolombangara (12–13 July) Vella Gulf (6–7 August) Vella Lavella (6–7 October), Empress Augusta Bay (2 November) and Cape St George (25 November).

greatest impatience – a policy of masterly inactivity. After the operations in Madagascar in May 1942 the Eastern Fleet was steadily depleted to provide ships for other theatres. *Indomitable* left in July, for the 'Pedestal' convoy to Malta. *Formidable* soon followed, to take part in the 'Torch' landings in North Africa. In January 1943 *Illustrious* went home for refit, and later in the year *Warspite*, *Valiant*, the cruiser *Mauritius* and several destroyers all left the station, leaving Admiral Somerville with barely enough ships to escort the Cape–Suez and Indian Ocean convoys. With his somewhat vestigial fleet remaining, Sir James bore the situation with good humour, recognising that 'in war it is sometimes hardest of all to refrain from activity; yet the need to conserve one's strength for concentration at the vital point remains paramount'.[1] For most of 1943 the vital paramount points for the Royal Navy were still the Mediterranean and the Atlantic.

Plans to send a major British fleet to the Pacific remained an academic exercise at least until the surrender of the bulk of the Italian fleet in September 1943, and the immobilisation of the German battleship *Tirpitz* by midget submarines in Altenfjord the same month. These two events released a number of ships, including most of the Mediterranean Fleet, for service elsewhere. Mr Churchill suggested that some of the ships should reinforce the Eastern Fleet, first operating for four months in the Pacific under American command, to gain experience and to assist in the war against Japan. The Admiralty reported that by 1 December 1943 they could send out a force of three capital ships, one or two carriers, and some cruisers and destroyers. This force, known as the 'British Pacific Ocean Force' was never actually formed, due to other commitments,[2] but 'its planning is of interest because it demonstrates British readiness to share the burden of the Pacific war at the earliest possible moment'.[3]

The evolution, in 1943 and 1944, of the Allies' strategy for the Far East was a long and a tortuous process. The disagreements, which lasted for most of 1944, between the Prime Minister and his Chiefs of Staff on the definition of the British role in the strategy became a dialogue of an almost Japanese complexity.[4]

On 25 October 1943, before the 'Sextant' conference in Cairo, the

[1] Roskill, Vol. II, p. 238.

[2] The resumption of the Arctic convoys in November 1943 and, ironically, the requirement to strengthen the Eastern Fleet for operations in early 1944.

[3] Roskill, Vol. III, Part 1, p. 239.

[4] The discussions are given in full in *Grand Strategy*, Vol. V, by John Ehrman (HMSO, 1956).

Combined Chiefs of Staff produced a study for the defeat of Japan twelve months after the defeat of Germany, assuming that to have taken place by October 1944. The study offered no prospect of the defeat of Japan within this period, but so far as a British fleet would be concerned, one of the study's most important conclusions was that the Allies should aim to capture Formosa from the Pacific in the spring of 1945 – with the option of an assault on northern Sumatra (Operation CULVERIN) if for any reason the Formosa operations were postponed. An invasion of the Japanese main islands might be attempted in the autumn of 1946. The study assumed that the British fleet, and particularly its aircraft carriers, would take part in the attack on Formosa. There was also one significant reservation: if the British aircraft carriers were thus employed in the Pacific, any major amphibious operation requiring strong air support (for example, CULVERIN) would not be practicable.

At Cairo, in November 1943, the Combined Chiefs of Staff agreed that the main effort against Japan should be in the Pacific and should be concentrated in two theatres: the South-west Pacific advance, along the axis of New Guinea/Dutch East Indies/Philippines, and the Central Pacific advance across the Japanese Mandated islands, both advances to converge and culminate in an assault on Luzon, or Formosa, or the south coast of China, in the spring of 1945. All offensives against Japan were to conform to these two main axes,[1] although the priority between the two was left open. It was also agreed that the British fleet would operate mainly in the Pacific and that the main British effort on land in South-east Asia in 1944 would be the recapture of upper Burma. The report setting out these conclusions was initialled by the Heads of Governments, including Mr Churchill.

The British Chiefs of Staff therefore came away from the conference with the British future in the Pacific, as they thought, now settled. They were anxious to get to work. Time was passing and there was much to be done. On 30 December they sent their programme for the Pacific to the Prime Minister for approval.

Although the programme was essentially the same as the report he had initialled in Cairo, Mr Churchill replied to the Chiefs of Staff on 11 January 1944, disagreeing strongly, in principle and in detail. He himself had always advocated that the centre of gravity of British strategy in the Far East should be in the Indian Ocean and should incorporate an advance through Burma to Malaya and the forcing of

[1] See map, pp. 40-1.

C

the Malacca Straits, beginning, if at all possible, with his old love –
Operation CULVERIN. In this 'Indian Ocean' strategy Mr Churchill was
supported by the other Ministers on the Defence Committee and by
the Foreign Office. There were, to be sure, excellent political reasons
for the appearance of a strong British fleet in the main operations against
Japan in the Pacific. But it was equally important, politically, that the
former British territories in South-east Asia, and especially the Malay
peninsula, should be recaptured by force of British arms. Remote islands
in the Pacific, of whatever strategic importance, had little meaning for
the peoples of Japanese-occupied South-east Asia. In other words, the
Japanese must not only be defeated, they must be seen to be defeated.

Mr Churchill therefore objected to the Pacific programme on the
grounds that it made no allowance for Russian entry into the Japanese
war; that the Americans themselves had not yet resolved the shape of
their final assault on Japan, and that it was by no means certain they
would welcome the assistance of a British fleet in the Pacific; and that
the programme left no outlet in 1944, before the defeat of Germany,
for the forces building up in South-east Asia. For this last, the solution
was clearly CULVERIN.

The Chiefs of Staff exerted themselves to answer the Prime Minister's
objections. The date, and the scale, of any Russian participation in the
war against Japan was still an enigma, and in any case could not affect
the immediate issues in 1944. Mr Churchill's point about the final
American strategy was, however, well taken.

It was true that the US Joint Chiefs of Staff had not yet decided
which of the two main axes, the South-west Pacific or the Central
Pacific, should have priority. The South-west Pacific advance became
known as the 'Army Plan' and its chief protagonist was General
MacArthur. He had promised the people of the Philippines that he
would return and he felt deeply that the United States were morally
bound to liberate the Philippines at the first opportunity. To the General,
an assault upon Japan which left the Philippines still occupied by the
Japanese would be unthinkable.

The Central Pacific strategy was known as the 'Navy Plan'. Its chief
advocates were Admiral Nimitz and his staff, and it was also favoured
by Admirals King and Leahy on the Joint Chiefs of Staff committee.
The plan had many advantages: it was a shorter route to Japan, and
would provide bases for very long-range bombing of the Japanese
mainland at a much earlier stage: it also avoided a series of protracted
land campaigns under very difficult geographical and climatic conditions

(the suicidal resistance of Japanese island garrisons in the Pacific was already showing just how protracted such campaigns were likely to be). Above all the Central Pacific strategy would make the full use of sea power, a department of war in which the Allies in the Pacific were growing stronger with every month.

It was unfortunate that the two strategies should have become so closely associated with the 'Army' and the 'Navy',[1] for the controversy tended to arouse all the worst aspects of the traditional rivalry between the two services. The dispute might never have arisen in this way had the entire Pacific theatre been under one command – a concept which had been considered but never set up, because of the vastness of the areas involved and because of General MacArthur's special position. At last, after careful thought, the US Joint Chiefs of Staff announced on 14 March 1944 objectives which clearly favoured Nimitz, who was to capture the Marianas, Carolines and Palaus, whilst MacArthur completed the isolation of Rabaul and captured Hollandia in New Guinea, and the Admiralty Islands. For these operations, Mr Churchill was informed, a British fleet would not be required in the Pacific in 1944, and probably not until the summer of 1945.

Mr Churchill's third objection, his misgivings about the sincerity of American desire for a British fleet in the Pacific, was thus proved well founded. The first doubts on this matter had arisen during the discussions on the 'British Pacific Ocean Force', which was primarily a political proposal, and recognised by the Americans as such. As the various conferences succeeded each other, the chief source of British unease about the prospects of a British fleet ever operating in the Pacific came to be identified in the austere personality of Fleet Admiral Ernest J. King, USN.

John Gunther once described Admiral King as 'a formidable old crustacean'.[2] The popular mythology of the United States Navy insisted that he shaved every morning with a blow-torch. Certainly, a more unlikely bearer of the homely Christian name 'Ernie' could hardly be imagined. Not surprisingly, one of the few British naval officers to achieve any kind of *rapport* with 'Ernie' was the irrepressible Somerville.[3]

---

[1] The terms 'Army' and 'Navy' plan are used for convenience. Not all General MacArthur's staff shared his emotional preoccupation with the Philippines, nor were all the naval staff at Washington and Pearl Harbour in agreement with the 'Navy' plan. But in general, the main combatants fell into these two categories.

[2] *Roosevelt in Retrospect* (Hamish Hamilton).

[3] He once told him: 'The trouble with you, Ernie, is that you try and pretend

A defensive note tends to creep into the writings of American historians on the subject of Admiral King's relations with the British in general and with the Royal Navy in particular. But nothing is gained by beating about the bush. Admiral King disliked the British, although the reason for his Anglophobia is obscure.[1] As Commander in Chief, United States Fleet, Admiral King had many qualities. Tact was not always one of them. He was reported as saying that he wished to have nothing to do with the Royal Navy. This was at least an historically original opinion. On the other hand, it must be said that Admiral King genuinely believed in the overall importance of the Pacific war and he had, very naturally, a wish to see his own service prosper. His attitude towards the Royal Navy was based upon an unpalatable but inescapable truth: unless a British fleet in the Pacific could be self-supporting, it would not only be a doubtful help, it might even be a definite hindrance in the war against Japan. In short, he could use a genuine weapon in the Pacific, but he had no time for a political paper-weight.

Uncertainties about a British fleet in the Pacific persisted until the Second Quebec conference in September 1944. In the meantime, the Chiefs of Staff addressed themselves to the Prime Minister's fourth objection, the dispositions of forces and the future in South-east Asia.

This question also involved Admiral Lord Mountbatten, Supreme Allied Commander in South-east Asia, and the 'Axiom' Mission he had sent to London in 1944. The 'Axiom' Mission and the Chiefs of Staff at first disagreed on the scale of forces required to mount CULVERIN. These differences had been largely resolved by the end of February and both sides agreed that CULVERIN could not be mounted without serious deficiencies in November 1944, as had been suggested; but assuming the defeat of Germany by October 1944, it could be mounted using British resources alone in March 1945.

Mr Churchill was alarmed at this long delay before any British offensive action in the Far East and he was also sceptical of the figures agreed for CULVERIN. He pointed out that CULVERIN would admittedly require a large part of the resources already earmarked for South-east Asia but if CULVERIN were abandoned and only the assault in northern Burma carried out, there would then be a considerable surplus of men

---

you are a bloody so-and-so, when you're not like that at all really.' *Fighting Admiral*, p. 257.

[1] In 1954, when Admiral Sir Charles Hughes Hallett was in Washington, he asked his American friends: 'What made him so anti-British?'. They replied: 'Well I don't know. I guess he just didn't care for you people.'

and materials. Mr Churchill proposed that all the resources in the area be used in a bold execution of the whole 'Indian Ocean' strategy (including, by implication, CULVERIN). The debate had thus moved through a full circle and returned to its starting-point.

Mr Churchill's case appeared to be strengthened by the arrival of the main Japanese fleet at Singapore on 24 February 1944. The Admiralty did not share the Prime Minister's concern, and he replied with some memorable sarcasm.[1] In fact, the Japanese had almost no offensive intentions in the Indian Ocean. They had moved to Singapore so as to be nearer to their supplies of fuel in the Dutch East Indies and because American bombing of Truk and Yap had made those bases impossible for large ships. However, their presence at Singapore did serve to distract the debate on British Far Eastern strategy.

Just when the deadlock seemed complete, a compromise strategy was evolved. Known as the 'Middle Strategy',[2] it proposed a British offensive based on Australia along the axis of Timor/Celebes/Borneo/Saigon, with the choice afterwards of either turning west and south to Malaya, or east and north to Hong Kong and the Chinese mainland. Middle Strategy had three advantages: it would place British forces in the Pacific, give the opportunity of assaulting Malaya from the east as well as the west, and it was a shorter route to Borneo than any undertaking such as CULVERIN.

But this strategy also had drawbacks. It made almost no contribution to the main Pacific strategy and no allowance for the speed of the American advance (as the Americans were not slow to point out). Also, it would obviously be more economical of forces to approach Borneo north of New Guinea, along the route already secured by General MacArthur's forces. A modified Middle Strategy was proposed, for a British offensive along the axis New Guinea/Halmahera/Borneo/Saigon, but with the same 'end-game' possibilities to Malaya or Hong Kong as in the original Middle Strategy. However, in June the Prime Minister rejected both the Middle Strategy and its modified version. The compromise had failed, and the final British strategy for the Far East was still undecided.

---

[1] 'They [the Admiralty] say that the British and American shore-based aircraft on the eastern shores of India and Ceylon are capable of defending India from attack without naval assistance. . . . These are new doctrines for the Admiralty and if our experience should make them good it is evident that wholesale transference of Naval strength to Air strength should be made after the war.' Memorandum to the Defence Committee, 29 February 1944. (Ehrman, p. 443.)

[2] See map, p. 38.

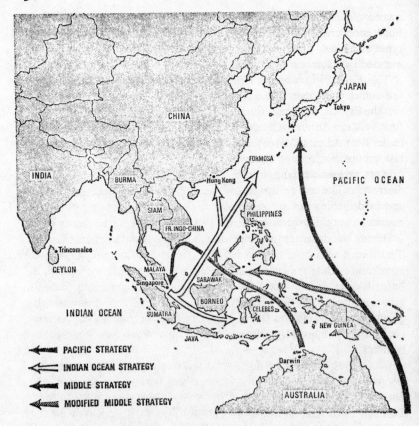

POSSIBLE BRITISH STRATEGIES IN THE FAR EAST, 1944

While the Prime Minister and the British Chiefs of Staff deliberated, the US Joint Chiefs of Staff, Admiral Nimitz, and General MacArthur were occupied with the more mundane matters of actually progressing the war in the Pacific. For most of 1943 there was a comparative lull in the Central Pacific. The theatre was awaiting the arrival of the queen of Pacific battles, the *Essex*-class aircraft carrier. These magnificent 27,000-ton, 32-knot vessels were designed primarily for the offensive, being lightly-armoured but carrying an impressive complement of ninety aircraft. The first of them arrived at Pearl Harbour on 30 May 1943, and by the autumn the Central Pacific Fleet had six heavy carriers including a new *York own* and a new *Lexington*, five new

11,000-ton *Independence*-class light carriers, twelve battleships, and a huge concourse of cruisers, destroyers and landing craft of various types and sizes. The fleet, later designated the Fifth Fleet,[1] was commanded by Raymond Spruance, now promoted Vice Admiral.

The Fifth Fleet was the largest, most powerful, most flexible and self-sufficient weapon that naval history had ever seen. Its striking tip was the Fast Carrier Task Force, designated Task Force 58, commanded first by Rear Admiral Charles Pownall and afterwards by its famous leader Rear Admiral Marc A. Mitscher. TF 58 was deployed in separate task groups, each group normally containing two heavy and two light carriers, and each having its own escort of fast battleships, cruisers and destroyers. The task groups could operate independently or in company and by detaching groups individually to refuel and rearm were able to maintain continuous pressure on the enemy.

During the drive across the thousands of miles of the central Pacific Task Force 58's brief was to seal off a target atoll from all enemy interference while the landings were in progress. This it accomplished by striking at distant islands to prevent the Japanese bringing up reinforcements, by pre-invasion strikes on the target atoll defences, by giving tactical support to the troops on the beaches during the assault phase, and by intercepting enemy attempts by sea or air to threaten the landings.

While Task Force 58 held the ring, the marine and army assault troops – the Fifth Amphibious Corps under Major General Holland Smith – were carried to the target beaches by Rear Admiral Richmond Turner's Fifth Amphibious Force, a further large fleet of transports, cargo ships and landing ships and craft, with its own escort of carriers, battleships, cruisers and destroyers. In addition, the Fifth Fleet had its own shore-based air force under Rear Admiral John Hoover. The Fifth Fleet used no permanent bases; a mobile Service Force of tankers, repair ships, tenders and floating docks set up floating bases in lagoons some distance to the rear of the operations. There could be no question of 'living off the land'; the targets, being mostly tiny coral atolls, held nothing of any assistance to an invading force. Every item of war supply had to be transported to the scene of the action. Thus to the art of warfare the Fifth Fleet added the science of logistics, on a titanic scale.

The Fifth Fleet began the 'Atoll War' with landings in the Gilbert Islands on 20 November 1943. The Japanese garrison on Butaritari in

[1] The Central Pacific Fleet did not officially become the Fifth Fleet until January 1944, but the term is used hereafter for convenience.

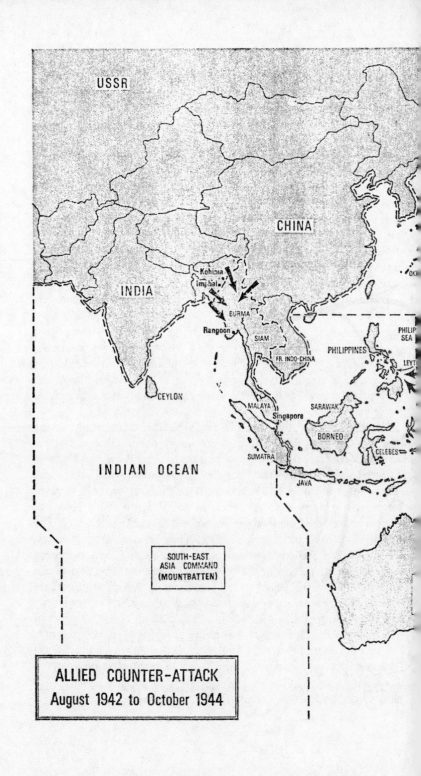

USSR

CHINA

INDIA

Kohima
Imphal

BURMA

Rangoon

SIAM

FR. INDO-CHINA

PHILIPPINES

PHILIP
SEA

LEYT

OKI

CEYLON

MALAYA
Singapore

SARAWAK

BORNEO

CELEBES

SUMATRA

JAVA

INDIAN OCEAN

SOUTH-EAST
ASIA COMMAND
(MOUNTBATTEN)

ALLIED COUNTER-ATTACK
August 1942 to October 1944

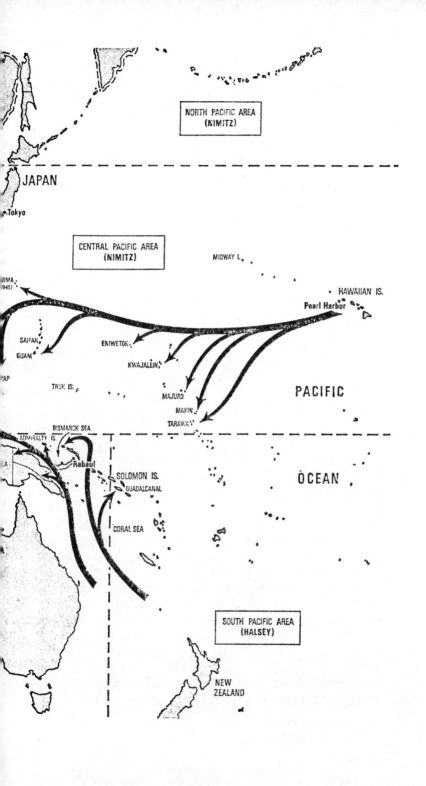

Makin atoll were overwhelmed by weight of numbers, but on the more strongly defended Betio Island in Tarawa atoll the United States Marines engaged in some of the bloodiest fighting of the whole war. When Tarawa was captured on 23 November at the cost of more than 3,000 Marine casualties, the Fifth Fleet had learned much about assaults on strongly defended beaches; in this limited sense, it could be said that Tarawa performed the same service for the Allies in the East as had Dieppe in the West.

The next objectives were the Marshall Islands, a similar archipelago of coral atolls some two hundred miles to the north-west. Admiral Nimitz chose to strike first at the major atoll of Kwajalein, by-passing the nearer atolls of Wotje and Maloelap. After an intense preliminary bombardment (a lesson learned from Tarawa) the Fifth Amphibious Corps landed on the islands of Roi-Namur and Kwajalein on 1 February 1944, capturing them by 4 February, both after fanatical resistance.

The remaining major atoll in the Marshalls was Eniwetok, to the west. Before the landings, Task Force 58 raided Truk, Saipan, Guam and Wake. Truk was heavily attacked on 17 and 18 February. Eniwetok atoll was invaded on 23 February, the islands of Parry and Engebi taken in one day, Eniwetok itself in three days.

The loss of the important atolls in the Gilberts and the Marshalls, and the progress being made by General MacArthur's forces in New Guinea, at last forced the Japanese High Command to abandon the concept of an outer defensive line extending to the Bismarcks and to set up a new inner line, more than a thousand miles to the west, running from the Marianas, to the Palaus, to western New Guinea. Many islands to the east of this line remained in Japanese hands until the very end of the war but their garrisons, by-passed by the Allied advance and cut off from all assistance except from submarines, were decimated by starvation, by disease, and by repeated air attacks from carriers of the Fifth Fleet who used these isolated Japanese outposts as 'live' practice targets for aircrews new to the Pacific.

In New Guinea, the South-west Pacific Command celebrated the New Year of 1944 with landings at Saidor on 2 January. The capture of the Admiralty Islands to the north followed in March. General MacArthur then planned to sidestep the main Japanese 18th Army at Wewak by landing further along the coast at Hollandia and Aitape. For this operation he received the help of the Fifth Fleet. Growing ever more confident of their ability to remain at sea within range of Japanese air bases, Task Force 58 steamed south and secured MacArthur's seaward flank in March and April with further attacks on Truk, on the Palaus and the western Carolines. The Hollandia landings were carried out successfully on 22 April, although remnants of the Japanese forces around Aitape continued their resistance until the end of the war. After another landing on the offshore island of Wakde on 17 May, MacArthur's next main objective was the larger island of Biak where, on 27 May, the Japanese opposition was much stronger than had been expected.

Biak was important to the Japanese. Its airfields were needed to provide land-based air support for the Japanese First Mobile Fleet during Operation A–GO – the plan devised by the new C-in-C, Admiral Soemu Toyoda,[1] to bring the American fleet to decisive action in the area of the western Carolines. A strong naval force, under Vice Admiral Matome Ugaki, was assembling at Batjan in the Moluccas for this purpose when, suddenly, the whole strategic position for the Japanese was changed by events 1,000 miles to the north.

On 11 June aircraft from Task Force 58 raided Saipan and Tinian, in the Marianas. Two days later, battleships of the Fifth Fleet began a heavy bombardment. Caught by surprise, the Japanese High Command realised that the Allies were about to assault the Marianas.

To the Japanese a threat to the Marianas overrode every other consideration. The Gilberts and the Marshalls could be lost. Even the fortresses of Truk and Rabaul could, if necessary, be abandoned to their fates. But the Marianas must be held. If Saipan fell to the Allies, then Japan's defeat was inevitable.

Ugaki's Southern Force sailed hurriedly from Batjan and met the Main Body of the Mobile Fleet, under Admiral Ozawa, on 16 June some three hundred miles east of the Philippines. Preceded by Vice Admiral Takeo Kurita's Van Force one hundred miles ahead, Ozawa's Mobile Fleet of nine carriers, five battleships, thirteen cruisers, twenty-eight destroyers and 450 aircraft, headed eastwards across the Philippine Sea. Between them and the Allied troops landing at Saipan lay Task Force 58, Spruance's armada, which covered over seven hundred square miles of sea and contained fifteen carriers, seven battleships, twenty-one cruisers, sixty-nine destroyers and 900 aircraft. Both sides knew that a climactic moment in the Pacific war was approaching. From Japan,

---

[1] Admiral Yamamato was killed when his aircraft was ambushed and shot down over southern Bougainville on 18 April 1943. His successor Admiral Miniechi Koga, was also killed in a plane accident in March 1944, and was succeeded by Admiral Toyoda.

Toyoda signalled to the Mobile Fleet: 'The rise or fall of the Empire depends upon today's battle. Let every man do his utmost'.[1]

The first Battle of the Philippine Sea, on 19 and 20 June 1944, was the last and greatest of the Pacific carrier battles. It was arguably Admiral Spruance's finest action. His orders were specifically and solely to 'capture, occupy, and defend Saipan, Tinian, and Guam'. He allowed nothing, neither the glorious but uncertain prospect of destroying the Japanese fleet, nor the danger of being himself caught on the 'anvil' between Japanese carrier-borne and shore-based aircraft, to divert him from his purpose.

His dedication was tested on 18 June when, after an enemy location report of dubious validity, Mitscher in *Lexington* suggested a sortie to the west and a strike on the Japanese fleet the next morning. Spruance, flying his flag in the heavy cruiser *Indianapolis*, rejected the proposal. His primary concern was Saipan and he decided to remain near the island, accepting the risk of being 'shuttle-bombed' by Japanese aircraft taking off from the carriers, striking the Allied fleet, and landing to refuel and re-arm on Guam or Tinian.

In the event, Spruance's caution placed Task Force 58 in the ideal position to receive and defeat the Japanese attack the next day. For eight hours on 19 June, Ozawa launched strikes against Task Force 58 (whose bombers and torpedo-bombers had been flown off, with orders to stay clear). Meanwhile, Task Force 58's fighter direction teams skilfully deployed the Hellcat fighters to engage the enemy.

It was not a fight, but a massacre. Including their aircraft losses on Guam, the Japanese lost more than 300 aircraft, with their irreplaceable crews, during the day. On 20 June Spruance at last set out in search of the Mobile Fleet but contact was not made until late in the day. Nevertheless, Mitscher at once flew off a strike which succeeded in sinking the carrier *Hiyo* and damaging *Chiyoda* and *Zuikaku*.

The successes of US submarines on 19 June were not then known[2] and there was disappointment at Pearl Harbour and in the Fifth Fleet that more Japanese ships had not been sunk. Even Admiral Spruance himself appears almost to have been persuaded that he might somehow have missed a great opportunity. In fact, by remaining on the defensive

---

[1] The same signal flown by Admiral Togo from his flagship *Mikasa* at Tsu-shima, almost forty years before.

[2] The carriers *Shokaku* and *Taiho* (Ozawa's flagship) later sank as a result of torpedo hits scored on 19 June by US submarines *Cavalla* and *Albacore* respectively.

on 19 June, he had won a smashing victory. Some Japanese carriers had escaped, but without their aircraft, they were neutered animals. Whatever the naval strategists' opinions about the battle, the men of the US Navy recognised the worth of the victory and, with their own inimitable talent for the apt phrase, nick-named it 'The Great Marianas Turkey Shoot'.

With the Japanese Mobile Fleet defeated and withdrawing to the north-west, the invasion of Saipan could proceed without distractions. The island was declared secured on 9 July but only after a frantic resistance by the Japanese, when the military and naval commanders had shot themselves and many of the Japanese civilian population, men, women and children, had committed a horrible mass suicide by throwing themselves off the cliffs at Marpi Point. The nearby islands of Guam and Tinian were invaded on 21 July and 24 July (Guam after a bombardment lasting thirteen days) and both islands secured by the middle of August – although isolated pockets of Japanese soldiers continued to resist for some time.[1] With MacArthur's forces at Sansapor, on the western tip of New Guinea, and already planning an assault on Morotai in the Moluccas, the two arms of the Allied offensive in the Pacific were thus only a thousand miles apart, poised to strike either at Luzon in the Philippines, or at Formosa.

At this stage, the dispute between the proponents of MacArthur's 'Army' and Nimitz's 'Navy' strategy reached its bitterest stage. Despite personal arbitration by President Roosevelt at Honolulu in July 1944, during which he showed himself in sympathy with MacArthur's case, the final shape of the assault on Japan was still unsettled by the time of the 'Octagon' Conference at Quebec in September.

For their part, the British Chiefs of Staff arrived for the Second Quebec Conference with the British strategy for the Far East at last resolved. During long and seemingly interminable discussions in the summer of 1944, involving the Prime Minister, the Chiefs of Staff, the Commonwealth Prime Ministers, the Defence Committee and Admiral Lord Mountbatten, the merits and demerits of CULVERIN, CHAMPION (advance in central Burma from the north), VANGUARD (sea-borne assault on Rangoon) and various combinations and permutations of all three had been debated almost to exhaustion. It was decided to carry out CHAMPION and to plan for VANGUARD – although the discussions were continually frustrated by two considerations: first, the American advance in the Pacific was progressing at a rate which surprised the

[1] The last Japanese on Guam did not surrender until 1960.

Americans themselves and made plans for British participation obsolete almost before they were suggested; and second, a major British contribution on land in the Far East presupposed the defeat of Germany by the winter of 1944. This event still seemed possible, though not probable, when the Octagon Conference opened, but became more and more unlikely, until the disaster at Arnhem and the German counter-offensive in the Ardennes in December 1944 removed the possibility entirely.

The hard truth was that by 1944 Great Britain had passed her peak in terms of war production and man-power. Whatever expedients might be tried, the country could physically produce no more. Her share of the Allies' war effort, and hence her influence on the forming of strategic policies, had declined steadily since the end of the North African campaign in May 1943. As the British contribution comparatively declined, so it became even more important that such resources as she did possess in the Far East should be used at the centre of the main operations against Japan. A direct invasion of the Japanese home islands, as opposed to air bombardment and blockade by sea, had always been implicit in the American Pacific strategy and the US Joint Chiefs of Staff gave it official approval on 11 July 1944, when they included in a restatement of their overall objectives the invasion and seizure of objectives in the industrial heart of Japan.

On one point at least the Prime Minister and his Chiefs of Staff were unanimous: the final main fleet operations against Japan would now certainly be in the Central Pacific and the British fleet must take part. The fleet must not, as the US Joint Chiefs of Staff proposed, be relegated to a minor role as an 'Empire Task Force' in South-west Pacific operations under General MacArthur's command. If this American proposal were accepted the British Chiefs of Staff evidently feared that the fleet would come to resemble Voltaire's derisive description of the Holy Roman Empire:[1] the British Pacific Fleet would be neither British, nor in the Pacific, nor even a fleet.

In Quebec, Mr Churchill offered the British fleet to President Roosevelt on 13 September, and received his famous reply.[2] It was also

---

[1] 'Le saint empire romain n'etait en aucune maniere ni saint, ni romain, ni empire': 'the Holy Roman Empire was neither holy, nor Roman, nor an empire.'

[2] 'No sooner offered than accepted.' See Churchill, Vol. VI, p. 136, and *A Sailor's Odyssey* by Viscount Cunningham of Hyndhope, p. 611 (Hutchinson, 1951). A complete transcript of the conversation is given in Ehrman, Vol. V, pp. 518–519.

decided at Quebec that Lord Mountbatten's South-east Asia Command should undertake the advance into central Burma, now called CAPITAL,[1] and follow it with DRACULA before the 1945 monsoon in March, or failing that, in November.

On his return to London the Prime Minister reported to the House of Commons on 28 September 1944: 'The new phase of the war against Japan will command all our resources from the moment the German War is ended. We owe it to Australia and New Zealand to help them remove for ever the Japanese menace to their homeland, and as they have helped us on every front in the fight against Germany we will not be behindhand in giving them effective aid.

'We have offered the fine modern British fleet and asked that it should be employed in the main operations against Japan. For a year past our modern battleships have been undergoing modification and tropicalisation to meet wartime changes in technical apparatus. The scale of our effort will be limited only by the available shipping.'

It was a noble promise. It now only remained to keep it.

[1] In August 1944 it was believed that the code names CHAMPION and VANGUARD had been compromised. They were changed to CAPITAL and DRACULA respectively.

Chapter Two

THE FLEET

'. . . It was quite clear that in the intensive, efficient and hard striking type of war that the US Fleet was fighting, nothing but the inclusion of a big British force would be noticeable and nothing but the best would be tolerated.' *Admiral Sir Bruce Fraser*.

THROUGHOUT 1943 circumstances had made the Eastern Fleet the 'Orphan Annie' of the service, neglected and starved of ships. But with the turn of the new year of 1944 reinforcements began to arrive from other stations. In January the Admiralty planned to send a total of 146 ships to join the Eastern Fleet in the next four months. On 27 January Vice Admiral Sir Arthur John Power, commanding the First Battle Squadron and Flag Officer Second in Command, Eastern Fleet, arrived in Ceylon with the battle-cruiser *Renown*, the battleships *Valiant* and *Queen Elizabeth*, the fleet aircraft carrier *Illustrious* and the repair carrier *Unicorn*, which was temporarily used as an operational carrier because of the shortage of aircraft carriers on the station.

There was also a shortage of destroyers. The Eastern Fleet did not have enough to escort both the Indian Ocean convoys and the fleet itself. The convoys took priority. It was not until April, when the Eastern Fleet had been reinforced by more destroyers, the escort carriers *Shah* and *Begum*, the French battleship *Richelieu* and most important of all, by the US carrier *Saratoga* and three American destroyers, that Admiral Somerville was able to attempt an offensive sortie against the Japanese. This was Operation COCKPIT, on 19 April, when aircraft from *Saratoga* and *Illustrious* attacked the harbour and oil storage tanks at Sabang, an island off the north coast of Sumatra. On 17 May, shortly before *Saratoga* and her escorts returned to the United States, a second strike (Operation TRANSOM) was carried out, on the Wonokromo oil refinery and the harbour of Sourabaya in Java.

The enemy appeared to be taken by surprise and neither strike met much opposition. However, both strikes demonstrated that in the theory and practice of operating carrier-borne aircraft *Saratoga* was in a class quite above *Illustrious*. Clearly the Fleet Air Arm had something more to learn before they could take their place alongside the Americans in the Pacific.

Two more fleet aircraft carriers, *Victorious* and *Indomitable*, joined in July and on 22 July Admiral Somerville led a considerable force of two battleships, one battle-cruiser, two carriers, seven cruisers,[1] and ten destroyers to sea for a more ambitious attack on Sabang (Operation CRIMSON), which in the event was 'James' Farewell Party'. Sir James had his 62nd birthday on 17 July and CRIMSON provided satisfactory birthday festivities: the capital ships bombarded the harbour, while aircraft from *Illustrious* and *Victorious* attacked airfields, and the destroyers led by Captain Richard Onslow steamed off the harbour entrance, firing guns and torpedoes at close range in a most spectacular manner.

On 8 August the new battleship *Howe* arrived at Trincomalee, but the capital ship *status quo* was restored the same day, when the huge floating dock in the harbour (AFD 28) collapsed; *Valiant*, in the dock at the time, was so badly damaged she was sent home. On 22 August Sir James was relieved as C-in-C Eastern Fleet by Admiral Sir Bruce Fraser. Sir James had hoisted his flag in the sombre days of March 1942, when it had seemed that nothing would stop the Japanese advance. He had shepherded the fleet through the weeks and months of weakness of 1943, and was now leaving when the fleet was gathering its strength and flexing its muscles for its part in the offensive against Japan. He went to Washington to relieve Admiral Sir Percy Noble as Head of the British Admiralty Delegation.

In the Pacific, events were hurrying towards the largest battle in naval history, the second of 1944 in the Philippine seas, known as the Battle of Leyte Gulf. Early in September, to support forthcoming landings in the Moluccas and the Palaus, aircraft of the Third Fleet[2]

[1] The battleships *Valiant* and *Richelieu*; battle-cruiser *Renown*; aircraft carriers *Illustrious* and *Victorious*; cruisers *Nigeria*, *Kenya*, *Gambia*, *Ceylon*, *Cumberland*, *Phoebe* and *Tromp*.

[2] Admiral Halsey relinquished command of the South Pacific Force and Area on 15 June 1944 and thereafter he, as Commander Third Fleet, and Spruance, as Commander Fifth Fleet, alternately commanded the Pacific Fleet. While Spruance and his staff were at sea, Halsey and his staff were ashore planning the next operation, and vice versa. The ships of the Third and Fifth Fleets were the same; only the fleet commanders and their staffs changed. Thus, the Fast Carrier Task Force was Task Force 58 under Spruance, Task Force 38 under

D

carried out strikes on Yap, the Palaus, Mindanao and on 12–14 September, the central Philippine islands. The latter strikes met startlingly feeble opposition; some two hundred enemy aircraft were destroyed and several ships sunk, for the loss of eight aircraft from the Fast Carrier Task Force. Admiral Halsey, excited and convinced that the central Philippines were just 'a hollow shell with weak defenses and skimpy facilities' urgently suggested to Nimitz that the planned assaults on Yap and the Palaus be cancelled and all Allied forces be concentrated for an assault on Leyte as early as possible.

In fact, the weakness of the Japanese defence was due to a planned withdrawal of their resources, until the Allies were plainly committed to a major offensive in the Philippines. However, Admiral Nimitz agreed to by-pass Yap but insisted on the landings in the Palaus. After the familiar and well-practised overture of air strike and bombardment by the Fast Carrier Task Force, the 1st US Marine Division assaulted the island of Peleliu, 470 miles east of Mindanao, on 15 September. The Japanese garrison of 10,000 troops, including the 14th Division, were ensconced in natural caves and strong interlocking fortifications. The battle was as bitter as any in the Pacific and organised Japanese resistance did not end until early in 1945. The neighbouring atoll of Ulithi had been abandoned by the enemy and was taken on 23 September without opposition. Ulithi atoll was a superb natural harbour and quickly became the main advanced base of the Third Fleet. Ulithi's restricted exits had disadvantages, however, in typhoon weather.

Meanwhile, MacArthur's forces in the south-west Pacific by-passed the strong Japanese garrison in Halmahera, in the Moluccas, and landed virtually unopposed on the more northerly island of Morotai. Thus by the beginning of October 1944 the Allies held an inner ring of islands running from the Marianas, south and west to the Moluccas, and were in an excellent position to launch an attack on the Philippines.

The Joint Chiefs of Staff, at Quebec, considered the implications of Halsey's news. With MacArthur's agreement, they cancelled the landings on Yap, the Talauds, and Mindanao. Nimitz and MacArthur were ordered to join forces for a landing at Leyte on 20 October – two months before the date originally set for an invasion of the Philippines. The 24th Army Corps, then actually on their way to the assault on Yap,

---

Halsey. Spruance commanded the operations in the Gilberts, Marshalls, Marianas, Iwo Jima and Ryukyus, while Halsey commanded the operations in the western Carolines, the Philippines and the strikes against the Japanese mainland in July–August 1945.

were diverted to Manus in the Admiralty Islands to join MacArthur's forces for Leyte (a remarkable example of the flexibility of planning in the Pacific war). After Leyte, an invasion of Luzon would inevitably follow. Thus, the long argument between the 'Army' and 'Navy' plans was finally resolved by the pressure of events.

The loss of the Philippines would effectively cut off the Japanese home islands from the resources of the Dutch East Indies and Malaya. The Japanese had anticipated the attack and prepared a plan – SHO 1 – for the defence of the Philippines which, in the Japanese tradition, inevitably called for both a complicated command structure, and the use of a decoy.

Since February 1944 the surviving Japanese battleships and most of the heavy cruisers had been based at Singapore, so as to be near their supplies of oil fuel. The surviving carriers were stationed in Japan attempting to re-equip with fresh air groups to replace those decimated in the Philippine Sea in June.

On 10 October Admiral Halsey's carriers began the preliminary strikes in support of the Leyte landings. The attacks were so widely spread, from the Ryukyus down to the northern Philippines, and so violent, with up to 1,000 aircraft taking part, that the Japanese were convinced that the main assault was under way. Admiral Soemu Toyoda, commander of the Japanese Combined Fleet, prematurely committed hundreds of naval aircraft to the Philippines in execution of their part of SHO 1. They were severely mauled by the Third Fleet aircraft, and in a week the Japanese had lost some 600 aircraft in trying to stop an invasion which had not yet begun.

On 18 October Vice Admiral Takeo Kurita sailed from Lingga Roads, off Singapore, with the First Striking Force, calling at Brunei for fuel on 22nd. After leaving Brunei, the force split into two, Kurita keeping five battleships under his command, while two battleships made up a separate force under Vice Admiral Shoki Nishimura. At the same time Vice Admiral Jisaburo Ozawa sailed from Japan with the Main Body, including four carriers. This was only a shadow force. The carriers were short of aircraft and experienced aircrews. Ozawa was sailing on a voyage of self-sacrifice, offering his weak force as live bait, hoping to draw Halsey's fleet away from Leyte whilst the Japanese capital ships penetrated the Philippine archipelago – Kurita through the San Bernardino and Nishimura through the Surigao Strait – to emerge on the eastern side and fall upon the troop anchorages at Leyte.[1]

[1] See map, p. 52.

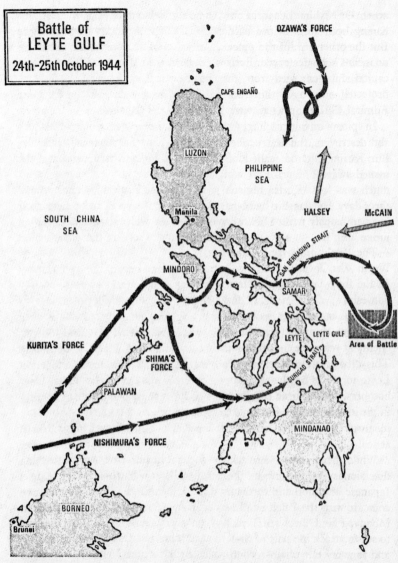

Battle of
LEYTE GULF
24th-25th October 1944

OZAWA'S FORCE

CAPE ENGAÑO

LUZON

PHILIPPINE
SEA

HALSEY   McCAIN

SOUTH CHINA
SEA

Manila

SAN BERNADINO STRAIT

MINDORO

SAMAR

KURITA'S FORCE

LEYTE   LEYTE GULF

Area of Battle

SHIMA'S
FORCE

PALAWAN

SURIGAO STRAIT

NISHIMURA'S FORCE

MINDANAO

BORNEO

Brunei

This time the bait was taken – hook, line, sinker and very nearly the angler too. Misled by over-optimistic aircrew reports, Halsey believed Kurita's force had been destroyed and on the evening of 24 October led the major part of the Third Fleet away from the entrance to San Bernardino to attack Ozawa's force which had been reported to the north. Of Nishimura's force only one destroyer remained, the remainder having been sunk in the battles in the Surigao Strait on 24th–25th. But the other arm of the pincer, Kurita's First Striking Force, had by no means been destroyed. Early on the morning of 25 October, Kurita's capital ships emerged from the San Bernardino Strait. Before them, protected only by a thin screen of light escort carriers under Rear Admiral Clifton Sprague, were the Leyte troop anchorages.

In spite of an outstandingly gallant defence by Sprague's little carriers and destroyers, the destruction of the invasion force seemed inevitable. But Kurita faltered, called off the chase of Sprague's carriers, and turned away. The prize for which the Japanese Navy had sacrificed so much was lost. Kurita himself had been under air attack for nearly three days. His flagship had been sunk under him. As Winston Churchill magnanimously wrote: 'Those who have endured a similar ordeal may judge him.'[1]

The Battle of Leyte Gulf, which has been called the 'Trafalgar' of World War Two, ended the effectiveness of the Japanese fleet at sea.[2] In the four days of action from 23 to 26 October they had lost three battleships, four carriers, ten cruisers and nine destroyers, with numerous other ships badly damaged. Substantial units, including six battleships, remained after Leyte, but for the rest of the war the principal enemy at sea were the shore-based Japanese army and navy air forces. This change was underlined in a most ominous manner during the Leyte invasion by the first appearance of organised kamikaze suicide bombers. By the time the British Pacific Fleet arrived to play its part in the invasion of the Ryukyus the Japanese were using suicide bombers in a way which could almost be described as a substitute for a fleet at sea.

While these events were taking place, the Eastern Fleet carried out diversionary operations in the Indian Ocean, attempting to distract Japanese attention and forces away from the Pacific. In September, to coincide with the Peleliu and Morotai landings, Rear Admiral Clement Moody, Flag Officer (Air), took the carriers *Victorious* and *Indomitable* to sea to attack the port of Sigli in northern Sumatra (Operation LIGHT) and to carry out photo-reconnaissance flights. On 17 and 19 October, the eve of the Leyte landings, Admiral Power himself sailed with the main Eastern Fleet to carry out a series of air strikes and bombardments on the Nicobar Islands (Operation MILLET).

[1] Winston Churchill, *The Second World War.*
[2] The bibliography on Leyte is extensive. See Morison, Roskill or MacIntyre.

There was now a new spirit, a sense of anticipation, in the Eastern Fleet. It was common knowledge throughout the fleet that the newest and fastest ships would soon form a British task force to take part in the main Pacific war at sea. Although *Victorious* had served with the American fleet in 1943, and the minelayer *Ariadne* had contributed to the Leyte landing, the Pacific had been an American war. For the Eastern Fleet the events in the Coral Sea, at Midway, Guadalcanal and Saipan had been like the distant rumble of thunder on the eastern horizon. Now, some of them would be joining that war.

In October Admiral Fraser was recalled to London to discuss the formation of the new fleet which he would command. At the Admiralty he met two officers who were to play important parts in supporting the fleet at sea. They were Rear Admiral Charles Daniel, who had already visited the United States the previous January to examine the requirements of a fleet train and who, in April, had led the British Naval Liaison Party to Australia to lay the foundations of fleet support based in that continent; and Rear Admiral Douglas Fisher, who had an appointment hitherto unknown in the Royal Navy, that of Rear Admiral Fleet Train.

Admiral Fraser returned to Colombo in November and on 22nd hoisted his flag in *Howe* as Commander in Chief, British Pacific Fleet. Admiral Sir Arthur John Power, who had been Flag Officer Second in Command of the Eastern Fleet, hoisted his flag as Commander in Chief of the newly-designated East Indies Fleet.

The Commander in Chief, British Pacific Fleet, faced immense and quite unprecedented difficulties. His responsibilities were unusually complicated: for the conduct of the fleet he was answerable, in the traditional way, to the Admiralty in London; for fleet operations he was responsible to Admiral Nimitz at Pearl Harbour; for the supply and shore support of the fleet he negotiated directly with the Australian and New Zealand authorities. He presided over the affairs of the Royal Navy's largest fleet of the war, with the longest line of communications of any British fleet in history. As the fleet grew, the C-in-C BPF and his staff began to operate what was virtually a miniature Admiralty, 12,000 sea miles from home.

Bruce Fraser was an officer whom more than one senior admiral between the wars had shrewdly 'tipped for the top'. His appointment as C-in-C was an extraordinarily fortunate one. The new fleet needed a commander who not only had great experience as a naval administrator in war-time but who also had a touch of glamour, the property known in show business as 'star quality', which could only be gained through some successful and widely-publicised action against the enemy. Not less important, he had to secure the co-operation and goodwill of men and women of several nationalities and at all levels. Above all, he had to be a man who could work with the Americans.

Admiral Fraser fulfilled these requirements brilliantly. For the first three years of the war he had been Third Sea Lord and Controller, an appointment which, though there is no exact army equivalent, could be defined as 'Quartermaster of the Navy'. As Commander in Chief afloat, flying his flag in the battleship *Duke of York*, he had led the ships of the Home Fleet in the dramatic ambush and destruction of the German battlecruiser *Scharnhorst*, off the North Cape on Boxing Day 1943. He had a way with the press, and a natural flair for public relations. But his greatest service to his country and his fleet was the cordial relationship he established with Admiral Nimitz. The two men became firm friends. Theirs was a friendship founded on mutual respect, as Lord Fraser himself recalls:

'I remember very well when I first went over to see Admiral Nimitz in Honolulu. At the end of our talks I was congratulating him on what the American fleet had done. He said, "Yes, I think we have done very well. There's only one thing we envy you, and that is your British traditions." I was very surprised and said, "Do you really think so, Admiral?" "Yes," he said, "it's the one thing you've got which can neither be bought nor sold. Guard it with your lives." I always remember that. Wonderful thing for an American admiral to say.'[1]

As his Chief of Staff Admiral Fraser chose his old friend and colleague Edward Evans Lombe, who had served with him for most of the previous ten years. Evans Lombe had served as Fraser's Executive Officer before the war and had been naval assistant when Fraser was Third Sea Lord. He had commanded a cruiser under Fraser in the Home Fleet. Like the other senior officers of the British Pacific Fleet, Evans Lombe saw in the Pacific a marvellous professional opportunity: 'It was the sort of job I might dream of. I was quite a young man in my early forties, and one had half the world to play on.'[2]

Admiral Fraser's task as C-in-C kept him at Sydney for much of the time. Afloat he would have been senior to any of Nimitz's sea commanders. Vice Admiral Sir Bernard Rawlings was therefore chosen to

---

[1] Admiral of the Fleet Lord Fraser of North Cape. Conversation of 12.10.67.
[2] Vice Admiral Sir Edward Evans Lombe. Conversation of 8.11.67.

lead the fleet at sea, being appointed Vice Admiral Second in Command, British Pacific Fleet, and Flag Officer Commanding the First Battle Squadron.

For such a distinguished and devoted officer, Bernard Rawlings remains curiously unknown outside the service. He abhorred personal publicity, and this obscurity is probably just what he would have wished. Yet his was the personality which moulded the fleet at sea, and he was the man who led them into battle. Perhaps now it is time to give credit where it is due.

In the conditions of the Pacific, where ships were often out of sight of each other for days at a time, the fleet commander inevitably tended to become a remote figure. Many men in the fleet never met Rawlings, and the ship's companies of the aircraft carriers in any case owed their first allegiance to the fiery personality of Admiral Vian. But amongst those who knew him well, Bernard Rawlings inspired the most fanatical loyalty. Nearly a quarter of a century later, the surviving members of his personal staff still speak of 'Uncle B.' in terms of the greatest affection and respect. Rawlings's Chief of Staff in the Pacific, Captain Peter Reid (who had also been his Executive Officer in *Valiant*) perhaps knew him best of all:

'He was a Cornishman, tall, spare and very alert. The twinkle in his eye and his approachable manner combined with a tremendously strong sense of purpose and of duty. He had *vision*, and this combined with a quick mind and originality of thought. He always rather preferred an unconventional answer, and I soon found that whatever we were required to do, his reaction was to see whether we could not "contrive" to do rather more than was thought possible.'[1]

Rawlings's sense of humour was remarked by all who knew him. The chaplain who served with him in the battleship *Barham* in the Mediterranean writes:

'He was one of the most charming people and he had a pleasant freedom from red tape. He used to enjoy sitting up to all hours talking with his friends in the Admiral's cabin. In *Barham* he had the ship's painter do a large version of the words from Holy Writ "The letter killeth but the spirit giveth life", and had this put over the door. It was all the more pointed since Geoffrey Cooke, Captain at that time, was a person

---

[1] Admiral Sir Peter Reid. Letter of 29.10.67.

devoted to the exact interpretation of King's Regulations and Admiralty Instructions!'[1]

Sir Bernard's Reports of Proceedings were written in a style worthy of a professional literary gentleman. For a regular naval officer he was unusually well-read, indeed his erudition startled his flag lieutenant, Lieutenant Geoffrey Cook, RNVR:

'I had to do a crash reading course in everything from Marlowe to Freud just to keep up with Uncle B.'[2]

He was a man of wide interests, though no hobbies in the accepted sense of the word. '*Hobbies*?' his Secretary, Commander John Rennie, used the word as though it were somehow unimaginable. 'Uncle B. didn't have *hobbies*. He was interested in everything.'[3] But Sir Bernard did have a weakness for songs, sung to piano and accordion accompaniment late at night, usually in the company of his American Liaison Officer, Captain E. C. Ewen, USN, who had an unexpectedly large repertoire of British music-hall ditties. One officer in Rawlings's flagship *King George V*, who had some talent on the accordion, often received the summons:

'Several occasions in harbour I was bidden to the Cuddy to accompany the pair of songsters. The Admiral's Coxswain used to knock on my cabin door and say "Admiral's compliments, sir, and would you bring your machine?" '[4]

When the BPF was formed, Admiral Rawlings had already had a long war and a hard war. In October 1939 he took command of *Valiant*, then completing a three-year modernisation, and commanded her during the Norwegian campaign and in Force H. He was promoted Acting Rear Admiral in October 1940 and commanded a cruiser squadron in the Mediterranean. During the evacuation of the army from Crete in May 1941 his flagship the cruiser *Orion* was attacked and badly damaged by the Luftwaffe. There were many casualties amongst the soldiers and the Flag Captain was killed. Rawlings himself was wounded. Captain Reid later visited him in hospital. 'He was in great spirits, but it was a shattering experience.'[5] One of *Orion's* officers wrote to his family at

[1] Rt Rev. Dr Gerald Ellison, Bishop of Chester. Letter of 6.1.68.
[2] Geoffrey Cook. Conversation of 20.9.67.
[3] Commander John Rennie. Conversation of 20.9.67.
[4] Mr Tom Dyke (ex-Lt. RNVR). Letter of 14.8.67.
[5] Reid. Ibid.

the time: 'My wretched Admiral never closed his eyes for forty-eight hours on end and really had an awful time. He was absolutely marvellous and I think he did magnificently.'[1]

But in even those desperate days Bernard Rawlings retained his sense of humour. 'He saw no reason why the dullest, most difficult, or possibly dangerous situation should be approached with a long face. His infectious ability to see the funny side was a constant inspiration to those around him.'[2]

To Rawlings, his Commander in Chief in the Mediterranean, Admiral Sir Andrew Cunningham, was the greatest sailor of all time. In Rawlings's opinion, Cunningham had accomplished more in the Mediterranean than Nelson, with less forces. For his part, Admiral Cunningham thought very highly of Rawlings:

'. . . Our greatest loss at this period was Rear Admiral H. B. Rawlings, who struck his flag in *Ajax* on January 15 and went home to England for a well deserved rest. He was a man of fine qualities, and no failings that I ever discovered. Rather quiet and retiring, he never obtruded himself; but was quite fearless in discussion and in expressing his occasionally unorthodox opinions. Full of imagination, he thought in a highly original way, largely no doubt as a result of the great knowledge and experience acquired outside the usual naval orbit in Poland and Japan.[3] A man of high ideals, he was quite fearless in action. Highly strung, I feel sure he had difficult moments and had sometimes to drive himself relentlessly; but with his capability of rapid and courageous decision in tight corners he seemed instinctively to do the right thing. With his great sense of humour and very human understanding, he was a grand and inspiring leader much liked, respected and trusted by those who served under him. As for me, I have the greatest affection for his great qualities as a leader and fighting seaman.'[4]

The Mediterranean in 1941 was the supreme period of trial in Admiral Rawlings's career. He gave all he had. When Admiral Cunningham was considering the appointment of the Second in Command, British Pacific

[1] Francis Tufton (then Assistant Secretary to Admiral Rawlings). Letter to his mother.

[2] Vice Admiral L. N. Brownfield (Rawlings's Chief of Staff in the Mediterranean). The *Cornish Guardian*, October 1962.

[3] Admiral Rawlings was a member of the Foreign Office and Military Missions in Poland from 1918 to 1921, and was Naval Attaché in Tokyo from 1936 to 1939.

[4] Viscount Cunningham of Hyndhope, *A Sailor's Odyssey* (Hutchinson, 1951), p. 444.

Fleet, he suggested Rawlings to Admiral Fraser but wondered whether, after his hard war, Rawlings was fit enough to take on such arduous duty in the Pacific. He asked Admiral Fraser to call in at Cairo (where Rawlings was Flag Officer, Eastern Mediterranean), on his way out to Ceylon and report. Admiral Fraser did so, and reported that Rawlings 'was fit and well and I was delighted to have him. Afterwards Rawlings told me he knew he was being vetted!'[1]

In the Pacific, Admiral Rawlings's greatest achievement was the respect and affection he won from the American operational commanders. The happy relationship at the top had a benign and helpful effect throughout the fleet. To the Americans, Rawlings actually looked his part:

'Rawlings was not only a great tactician and able leader in the Royal Navy but for we Americans he fitted the traditional image of a magnificent British admiral and cultured English gentleman of the old school. It was my good fortune to be with him when our admirals Nimitz, Halsey and Spruance were also with him and I observed unmistakably their liking for him, both on social occasions and in the grim prosecution of the war.'[2]

Admiral Rawlings seized on the fact that it was vital for him, as the sea-going commander of the British task force, to be on good terms with the Americans. He handled the situation with the utmost skill and delicacy, not only in his personal meetings, but in small, neat touches, the wittily appropriate signal and the inspired gesture. After the Japanese had surrendered and the combined fleets were at sea off Japan waiting to enter Tokyo Bay, Admiral Halsey, prompted by his British Liaison Officer, signalled his fleet: 'Splice the main-brace' and a few minutes later, ostensibly as an afterthought (American ships being 'dry') signalled again, cancelling the order for the American task groups. The British units in the Third Fleet duly and gratefully spliced the mainbrace. But next day, when Rawlings transferred at sea to Halsey's flagship *Missouri*, he told the fleet commander that he had studied that signal carefully and had noticed that he had cancelled the order for all American groups except his own. Whereupon Rawlings produced a jar of Navy rum; Admiral Halsey and all hands present in the Admiral's cabin spliced the main-brace.

[1] Lord Fraser. Letter of 25.10.68.
[2] Lt. Cdr. Robert F. Morris, OBE, USNR (Ret.), USN Liaison Officer *King George V*. Letter of 28.6.68.

Rawlings himself looked back on his service in the Pacific as the peak of his career. 'When I last saw him at his home near Bodmin, he had to have oxygen in his room: he looked back on the Pacific as the greatest time in his life, and we recalled so many things. He was most certainly the right man for that command.'[1]

There could only be one possible choice of officer to command the aircraft carrier squadron, the striking tip of the fleet. Rear Admiral Sir Philip Vian had first achieved fame as Captain of the destroyer *Cossack* during the *Altmark* affair, and he could be described as the 'stormy petrel' of the service in World War Two. He had served at sea wherever the fighting was fiercest: as Captain (D) of the 4th Destroyer Flotilla during the *Bismarck* chase; as a cruiser admiral defending the Malta convoys against, in his own phrase, 'all known forms of attack', and notably in his greatest action, the Second Battle of Sirte; as the assault force commander for the invasion of Sicily; and as the naval commander of the Eastern Task Force for the landings in Normandy.[2] Vian arrived in Ceylon in the new carrier *Indefatigable* on 10 December 1944. When he hoisted his flag in *Indomitable* as Flag Officer Commanding First Aircraft Carrier Squadron, the fleet needed no further reassurance that the game was once more afoot.

Admiral Vian did not trouble to establish good relations with the Americans. His attitude evidently was that they could take him as they found him. Admiral Vian did not, in fact, bother to endear himself to anyone. The opinions of all who served with him can be summed up in one sentence: 'By God, he could be an awkward bastard.' Yet he was universally admired and respected as the Navy's greatest fighting admiral of the war. He thrived in action, and only in action: the detailed trivia and administrative routine of non-operational service wearied him. 'You only know Philip Vian when you've seen him in a fight.'[3] He inspired his air groups, who would have flown anywhere and done anything for him. Vian's somewhat sardonic sense of humour and his air groups' belief that no aircraft took off nor landed on one of his carriers unseen by him are well illustrated in a neat anecdote from the carrier squadron engineer officer, whose duties often took him from carrier to carrier.

[1] Reid. Ibid. Admiral Rawlings died on 30 September 1962 after a long illness. He was buried at sea to the southward of the Cornish coast. His memorial in the parish church of St Petroc's, Bodmin, has the epitaph he himself chose: 'One of Cunningham's Captains.'

[2] Admiral Vian has written his memoirs of his war career in *Action This Day* (Muller, 1960).

[3] Evans Lombe. Ibid.

'Owing to the lack of wind, we had to be catapulted off *Indomitable*'s flight deck. Normally the aircraft's own natural speed is so assisted by the catapult that she is practically airborne in the short length of the catapult stroke. However, this time the engine cut just before the end of the stroke and we dipped alarmingly towards the sea over the ship's bow. Fortunately, just in time, the engine picked up and we turned away towards *Victorious*, our objective. But it wasn't to be so easy. At the crucial moment, down came a tropical storm and blotted out sea and ships and sky. What was worse, the wireless homing apparatus simultaneously went unserviceable. So there we were, stooging around completely blinded. I had never before appreciated the exact significance of that word so beloved of airmen – "stooging". After an hour of this unhappy experience I'm bound to admit to becoming a little worried. We were hundreds of miles from any land. The fleet, zigzagging on its course below, might just as well have not been there at all. Suddenly, the homing beacon picked up, we got our bearings, and in half an hour I was relieved to see a friendly deck ready to receive us. As I climbed out, a signalman doubled up to me with a signal from the Admiral, who never missed a trick. It read simply – "I hope you didn't get your feet wet".'[1]

In December 1944 two more able and experienced admirals were appointed to the fleet, to complete the sea-going team. Rear Admiral E. J. P. Brind was appointed Flag Officer Commanding Fourth Cruiser Squadron (CS 4) and Rear Admiral J. H. Edelsten, who had been Cunningham's Chief of Staff in the Mediterranean, to command Destroyer Flotillas (RA(D)). The command structure of the British Pacific Fleet at the outset was therefore: (see diagram p. 62).

At its peak, the BPF was a truly representative Commonwealth fleet. Two cruisers, *Gambia* and *Achilles*, were manned by New Zealanders. Another, *Uganda*, was Canadian manned, while the Australians contributed the 7th Destroyer Flotilla, part of the 4th Flotilla, and many of the minesweeper escorts for the Fleet Train. There were many Canadians and South Africans in the squadrons, and an astonishingly high proportion of New Zealanders; sometimes as many as one in four of a squadron's aircrew were from New Zealand.[2] At that stage of the war the ship's companies naturally contained mixtures of inexperience

---

[1] Rear Admiral Sir Alexander McGlashan. Letter of 11.12.67.

[2] There was local recruiting in New Zealand for naval aircrew, whereas New Zealanders who wished to fly with the RAF had to go to England for selection. Therefore a great many New Zealanders who wanted to fly joined the Fleet Air Arm.

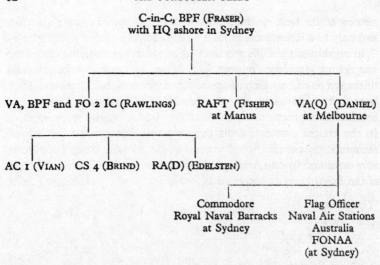

C-in-C, BPF (Fraser)
with HQ ashore in Sydney

VA, BPF and FO 2 IC (Rawlings)   RAFT (Fisher)   VA(Q) (Daniel)
                                   at Manus   at Melbourne

AC 1 (Vian)   CS 4 (Brind)   RA(D) (Edelsten)

Commodore   Flag Officer
Royal Naval Barracks Naval Air Stations
at Sydney   Australia
                     FONAA
                     (at Sydney)

and maturity. There were many young men in the fleet fresh from school in war-time who were serving in their first ships. But the majority, particularly the petty officers and chief petty officers, were veterans who had served in the Navy for years. Some, like Admiral Rawlings himself, had been in the war since the day it began. Cdr. C. L. G. Evans, Commander (Air) of the carrier *Implacable*, which joined the fleet in 1945, had led the flight of Skuas which shot down the first German aircraft of the war in September 1939. Captain E. D. G. Lewin, the Fleet Fighter Direction Officer, had flown *Ajax*'s Sea Fox spotting aircraft at the Battle of the River Plate, and Captain H. G. Maclean, Master of the Fleet, had been Vian's navigating officer in *Cossack*. A Prince of the Romanovs was serving in the fleet as an engineer officer. The future consort of Queen Elizabeth II was First Lieutenant of the destroyer *Whelp*. The aircrews included men who had been sheep-farmers, opticians, solicitors, sewage inspectors and the pianist of Guy Lombardo's band. Amongst the ship's companies were farm labourers, chauffeurs, actors, cartoonists, and a former lightweight champion of Great Britain.

Reserve officers and men overwhelmingly outnumbered the regular RN in every ship. When the escort carrier *Ruler* with a ship's and air-crew officer complement of more than sixty joined the fleet her Commanding Officer, Captain H. P. Currey, was the only regular RN officer on board. Of thirteen air squadron commanders in the fleet in December 1944, nine were RNVR officers. Whole squadrons with not a single RN aircrew officer were no rarity; on VJ Day, in August 1945, *Implacable* had only two RN officers in an air group of over 150 officers.

In no ship of the BPF was there at any time any suggestion that the war against Japan was 'not our war'. When the fleet reached Australia, this was a point on which the press were understandably curious. They were quickly reassured. The fleet shared with the Prime Minister the conviction that they must go on until the last enemy had been defeated. In the United States, although there were still some last pockets of resistance, the generally prevailing opinion was most soberly and charitably expressed by one American newspaper under the headline 'Return of the Royal Navy to the Far East':

'There is even a disposition in some American naval circles, which have spent the intervening three years in learning all the intricate lessons of Pacific sea-air warfare in the hard way, to doubt whether British naval power trained under the very different European conditions, would be any great help in the Pacific. That, however, seems a rather narrow view and one which insufficiently honours the great and loyal co-operation which the Royal Navy and Royal Australian Navy have given our forces in the Pacific – from the tragedy of the Java Sea, when *Exeter* and *Perth* were lost along with our *Houston*, through the lean days in 1943, when *Victorious* helped our still scanty carrier forces, down to the battle around Leyte in which *Shropshire* and *Australia* played distinguished roles. None can yet afford to look askance at any reinforcements; the one question is only how to secure that integration and flexibility of command which can make the maximum use of all forces available.'[1]

On one point the Prime Minister and the men of the fleet disagreed. Mr Churchill used the expression 'a fully-tropicalised fleet' to give the impression that ship's companies would have living conditions of an almost Byzantine luxury. The phrase may have referred to air-conditioning and improved ventilation in certain compartments containing electronic or other special equipment, but it emphatically did not mean comfortable living conditions on the messdecks in tropical weather. Heat, shortage of fresh water, overcrowding and general discomfort, with outbreaks of prickly heat, rashes, boils and periodic gastro-enteritis amongst the ship's company were a constant source of anxiety to all commanding officers.

The British Pacific Fleet was a fast, heavily armed, balanced force

[1] *New York Herald Tribune*, 12 December 1944.

of capital ships and aircraft carriers, screened by cruisers and destroyers, of a kind which would have changed the course of the war in the Far East had it been available to Admiral Phillips or Admiral Somerville. There were some famous names in the battle line: *King George V,* Rawlings's flagship, had chased *Bismarck* and pounded her into help-lessness, had searched for *Tirpitz* in March 1942, covered Arctic con-voys and supported the landings in Sicily and Salerno, and had escorted the remnants of the Italian Fleet to surrender in Malta. She was the first British battleship to be fitted with a properly equipped fighter direction room, designed from the experience gained by the RAF in the defence of Britain. Amongst the carriers, too, there were some names which were household words. From *Illustrious* had flown the Swordfish which carried out the epic strike on the Italian fleet at Taranto in November 1940; the ship herself had endured a savage attack by the Luftwaffe off Pantelleria in January 1941. After repair in the United States, *Illustrious* had taken part in the Madagascar operation and in the Salerno landing. *Victorious* had served in every ocean from the Arctic to the South Pacific; her aircraft attacked *Bismarck,* and *Tirpitz* in March 1944, and had escorted the 'Pedestal' convoy to Malta and the 'Torch' convoys for the landings in North Africa. In October 1942, after *Hornet* had been sunk and *Enterprise* damaged, the Americans asked for the loan of a British carrier. *Victorious* arrived at Pearl Harbour the following March and began to retrain her ship's company and aircrew in US methods and procedure; in May she relieved *Enterprise* in Halsey's Third Fleet and operated in company with *Saratoga* in the South Pacific for some months in the summer of 1943.

The majority of the aircraft flown by the East Indies and British Pacific fleets were American designed and built.[1] The pre-war planning and design of British naval aircraft was a sorry tale of indecision and inter-service squabbling between the Navy and the Royal Air Force. The Navy did not regain control of its own air arm from the RAF until 1937 and entered the war without a modern high-performance single-seat fighter. The very names of the fleet fighters in the first years of the war, Sea Gladiator, Sea Hurricane and Seafire, betray the several – and only partly successful – attempts to convert to carrier flying fighters which had been designed primarily for the RAF. The torpedo-bomber Swordfish, one of the most successful naval aircraft of all time, was first built as a private speculative venture by the Fairey Aviation Co.

[1] See Appendix C.

Two torpedo-bombers, the Albacore and the Barracuda, were later designed for the fleet but neither was entirely satisfactory in service.

One of the features of the British carrier operations in the Far East was the long-lasting 'love–hate' relationship between the fleet and the Seafire. After the strikes at the Palembang oil refineries in January 1945, Admiral Vian concluded: 'My most particular impression from this operation is that Seafire aircraft are unsuitable for sustained ocean warfare',[1] and after the BPF's operations against the Sakishima Gunto in April, the American liaison officer in *Illustrious*, Lt. Cdr. H. A. Rowe, USN, observed that from what he had seen of the Seafires they were not worth carrying in a carrier force. Yet at the end of the war, when the fleet was operating off Japan, the two Seafire-equipped carriers, *Indefatigable* and *Implacable*, both operated Seafires most successfully, using them as fighter-bombers and ground-strafing aircraft. The plain truth was that Seafires were too well-bred for the rough-house of the flight deck. They were beautiful aircraft, in every sense of the word, but had the most appalling deck-landing accident rate. Their under-carriages were too fragile, their tyres too liable to burst, their long propellers too prone to strike the steel flight deck and they had a tendency to 'float' on their final approach, missing the arrester wires and taking the crash barrier. Their normal range was so short that they could only be employed for the defence of the fleet, flying combat air patrols[2] above the task force.

The two best fleet fighters, the Corsair and the Hellcat, were both American and both custom-built for their purpose, which was carrier warfare in the Pacific. The BPF had two Hellcat squadrons at the outset, both embarked in *Indomitable*. Some 350 Hellcats saw service with the Fleet Air Arm and their qualities are best described by *Indomitable*'s Hellcat fighter wing leader, and one of the most distinguished fighter pilots in the Navy, who remembers the *marque* very kindly:

'As Manager of the Hellcats, I recall their extreme reliability as well as their great flexibility for attacking anything from a high CAP right through the machinations of ground attack by gun and rocket; their usefulness as both a night-fighter without radar and a camera-carrying vehicle for photo-reconnaissance work. My own No. 5 Wing undertook all these roles fairly successfully and indeed we had the highest number

[1] Supplement to the *London Gazette*, 5 April 1951, p. 1804.
[2] Known hereafter in this book as CAPS.

E

of kills during this period. Because of the Hellcat's wonderful and docile flying qualities, our accident rate on the deck was extremely small and they were particularly adept at landing-on regularly in a very short space of time. The only drawback the old Hellcat had was that the wings had to be spread manually and this really rather knocked points off our ability to get into the air quickly. A further comforting feature of this splendid aircraft was that it was very ruggedly built and would absorb a great deal of enemy fire from astern. Our excellent maintenance ratings were able to repair and replace parts more swiftly than any of the other aircraft types engaged in this particular war.'[1]

The Corsair was a fearsome-looking aircraft. With its long engine cowling, its crooked inverted 'seagull' wing, and its general air of scarcely controlled menace, it inspired almost as much fear in the hearts of those who were to fly it as in the enemy. One pilot, who later commanded 1833 Corsair squadron, recalled his first sight of the 'monster' at Quonset Point:

'The sentry on the hangar which held our Corsairs showed us into a side-door and we went up a staircase on to a balcony overlooking the hangar. There were these monsters. Really, they looked killers to me. They were the most dangerous bloody looking things I had ever seen. I'm not ashamed to admit it, that night I made a will.'[2]

The Corsair was an advanced design, with a complicated hydraulics system which spread and folded the wings, lowered and retracted the arrester hook, loaded and cocked the guns and 'did everything but cheer when you got a hit'. The Corsair's long nose gave very poor visibility forward while landing on, and the under-carriage on earlier versions tended to 'bounce' on landing, but the Fleet Air Arm persevered and grew very fond of Corsairs. The US Navy temporarily discarded them for carrier work and during the July–August operations off Japan Captain Denny in *Victorious* commented upon the wonder occasioned in *Shangri La* by the landing thereon of a moth-eaten Corsair Mark II with "bouncing under-carriage" from *Victorious*, the like of such a museum piece never having been seen in a Fleet Carrier of the US Navy. *Victorious* and *Illustrious* each had two squadrons of Corsairs, with experienced pilots, many of whom had been embarked for over a year.

Each carrier in the fleet had one squadron of bombers which, at the

[1] Captain Tom Harrington RN. Letter of 16.5.68.
[2] Mr Norman Hanson. Conversation of 22.7.68.

time of the formation of the fleet, were discarding the British Barracudas and re-equipping with American Grumman Avengers. The Avenger, a robust, reliable, three-seater torpedo-bomber-reconnaissance (TBR) aircraft, was the standard bomber of the BPF, from Palembang to Japan.

The only British-designed aircraft to undertake regular strikes on Japanese-held territory was the Firefly, which replaced the Fulmar in the fleet.

The Firefly had a good range, firepower and deck landing safety but lacked speed, largely because it carried a crew of two. The BPF had one very experienced Firefly squadron who had embarked in *Indefatigable* in May 1943 and had taken part in the attacks on *Tirpitz* at Altenfjord in July and August 1944. Lastly, for air–sea rescue purposes, one carrier in the squadron normally carried two amphibious Walrus aircraft, commonly known as the 'Shagbat' or 'Steam Pigeon'.

On hoisting his flag, Admiral Fraser was in no doubt about where his fleet should operate – in the central Pacific, in the main naval offensive against Japan. The best policy was to employ the largest possible forces against the centre of the enemy's power and not to dissipate it in side-shows. Provided the supply situation could be satisfactorily resolved, Admiral Fraser was sure his fleet would be a real asset in the Pacific. He did not preclude the possibility of a British task group operating as an integral part of an American task force; if that was the best way to bring the maximum force most effectively against the enemy, then so be it.

National pride was also involved. It would be disastrous for British prestige in the eyes of the Dominions if the British Pacific Fleet, assembled in the face of so many difficulties, was then diverted into 'side-shows' in the South-west Pacific, as the Australians suspected their own ships were being diverted.

There was a third and professional reason. The United States Navy had evolved this new type of naval warfare in the Pacific. It was essential that the Royal Navy have first-hand experience of it, in combat, and not merely read about it in American instruction manuals and admirals' memoirs after the war was over. Carrier-borne warfare as practised in the Pacific may never now be repeated and even if it were the Royal Navy, though possibly still having the expertise, no longer has the capability to take part. But at the time, it seemed essential that the Navy should perform this new musical score in concert with its composers, and in front of a live audience, rather than interpret it later from old recordings.

Admiral Fraser's first duty was therefore to meet his operational superior, Admiral Nimitz, and discuss with him the future of the British fleet. The C-in-C flew to Australia on 4 December 1944, and thence to Pearl Harbour taking with him Evans Lombe, his Secretary, the Assistant Chief of Staff, and the Fleet Wireless Officer.

Admiral Nimitz was cautiously enthusiastic about the prospect of a British fleet in the Pacific. His caution was realistic rather than political. While he would welcome any effective addition to his fighting strength he also had the usual American misgivings over the British ability to keep the fleet supplied. Nevertheless, there seems no doubt that Nimitz would have liked to have been able to say to Fraser, in effect: 'You're on the team. Start tomorrow.' But that decision still rested in Washington.

The discussions concluded with the signing by Nimitz and Fraser of the Agreement N/F.1, known as the 'Pearl Harbour' Agreement. The Agreement actually committed the Americans to very little: Admiral Fraser was to report his fleet for duty to Admiral King, Chief of Naval Operations, in Washington, who would assign the British either to Nimitz or to MacArthur: the British Task Force Commander at sea would have the same status as an American Task Force Commander, but could be placed under American orders if the immediate tactical situation demanded it. After some detail about the impending operations against the Ryukyus, the Agreement descended to cryptographic information and minutiae on the numbers and ranks of liaison officers, and the censorship of press material. It was also agreed that the British fleet should have an intermediate base anchorage and facilities at Manus, in the Admiralty Islands (and not, as had been tentatively debated, at Espiritu Santo, in the New Hebrides). The British fleet would adopt American communications methods and procedures, just as US ships with the Home Fleet were already conforming to British practice. Admiral Fraser had evidently made up his mind that the British fleet would, by hook or by crook, operate under Nimitz, for no similar agreement was ever signed with MacArthur, although theoretically the British fleet was at that time just as likely to be assigned to the Southwest Pacific.

At the end of the year, Admiral Fraser dispatched a signal to the Admiralty setting out his operational policy. He intended no less than to do as the Americans and keep his fleet at sea in the operational area indefinitely. This would mean far more sustained use of the fleet than had been envisaged, or had been allowed for in the preparation for the fleet train.[1] It would also involve the setting up of an intermediate base between Australia and the operational area, and some means of replenishing the fleet with fuel and stores at sea in advance of the intermediate base. The size of the fleet train, as planned at that time, would not permit this. Instead of calculating the fleet train on the basis of the fleet required, and the distances between bases, Admiral Fraser perforce had to make the calculation the 'other way about', and decide what forces could be supported in the forward area by the existing fleet train. The fleet could only increase as at the same rate as the fleet train.

While most of his staff returned to Sydney, Admiral Fraser flew to Leyte for informal discussions with General MacArthur and Vice Admiral Kinkaid, Commander of the US 7th Fleet. The outcome of this visit almost terminated the Commander in Chief's appointment in the most violent manner, on 6 January 1945:

'MacArthur asked me if I would like to go up and see the Lingayen Gulf landings in the Philippines. So I went. I took my flag lieutenant and my secretary with me. We embarked in this American battleship [*New Mexico*] and went up with the landing party. About halfway there, these kamikazes started to come down. One sank an American carrier just alongside us. Having no armoured flight deck, of course, she went up in flames. Then next morning a kamikaze came down on us, on to the front side of the bridge. I was standing the other side. General Lumsden[2] was up on top, with the captain. They were both killed. One of my young chaps was killed. Fortunately, the Admiral [Oldendorf] and I had just been talking on one side of the bridge and he called me across the bridge to the other side, to look at something. This thing came down just where we had been standing.'[3]

At the C-in-C's headquarters in William Street, Sydney, the news of the kamikaze attack caused some understandable consternation. 'We were told there had been this smash up in the *New Mexico*, but we couldn't get any details of what had happened. For about twenty-four hours I didn't really know whether we had a Commander in Chief or not.'[4]

The Eastern Fleet's operations in 1944 had been intended to divert enemy resources to the Indian Ocean, but from Japanese records it is

[1] For a fuller history of the Fleet Train, see Chapter Nine.
[2] The Prime Minister's representative on MacArthur's staff.
[3] Fraser. Ibid.
[4] Evans Lombe. Ibid.

now clear that the Japanese were at full stretch in the Pacific and nothing short of a full-scale sea-borne invasion of Rangoon or Singapore would have forced them to make any strategic redisposition of their naval forces. The Eastern Fleet's activities were excellent training and good for morale but were only minor nuisances to the enemy. As one war correspondent expressed it:

'It could be said, and with a certain amount of truth at one time, that British naval strikes against the Japanese were of the tip and run variety, and that certain individual efforts amounted to little more than banging at tne back door of the Japs and running away before the door was opened.'[1]

At the meeting with Fraser in Pearl Harbour, Admiral Nimitz had asked that on its way from Ceylon to Australia the British Pacific Fleet make a series of strikes on the oil refineries in Sumatra. These were important strategic targets. Putting them out of action would involve not only banging on the back door but punching the nose of whoever opened it.

Japan had entered the war with a tanker tonnage of only 575,000 tons. New construction had taken the total tanker tonnage to 834,000 by November 1943, but new construction and tonnage captured or salvaged were never able to outpace the rate of losses. By the end of 1944, 156 Japanese tankers of 934,000 tons had been lost to American submarines, aerial mines, strikes by shore-based and carrier-borne aircraft, and other causes. Because of convoy delays and shipping shortages, the total tonnage of oil imported into Japan dropped from a peak of nearly two million in 1943 to only 625,000 tons in 1944. The Sumatran oil-fields had a potential yearly production of three million tons of crude oil and their refineries were by far the largest producers of aviation spirit for the Japanese war effort. The refineries at Pangkalan Brandan, in the north of the island, and at Soengei Gerong, the smaller of the two refineries at Palembang, were together capable of producing three-quarters of Japan's total requirement of aviation spirit.

The Sumatran oil fields had already received some attention from Allied forces. On 11–12 August 1944, B-29 bombers flying from Ceylon had bombed Palembang and mined the Musi river. The same month, the submarine *Porpoise* mined the entrance to Belawan Deli, the port of Medan, and closed the harbour. The British Pacific Fleet operations against the oil fields were given the code-name OUTFLANK, and the first

[1] A. W. McWhinnie, *Illustrated*, 24 February 1945.

of a series of strikes was intended to be on Pangkalan Brandan (Operation ROBSON).[1]

Pangkalan Brandan is in north-eastern Sumatra, fifty miles north-west of the town of Medan, and eight miles inland of the small port of Pangkalan Soe Soe. Dutch and American refinery personnel had fired the oil wells at Pangkalan Brandan and had blown up much of the installations at Pangkalan Soe Soe in the spring of 1942, but the Japanese had succeeded in resuming production by the end of the year. Refined oil was piped from Pangkalan Brandan to Pangkalan Soe Soe, where there was tank storage capacity for thirty million gallons. There was a second pipe-line to Belawan Deli, where there was deeper water for large tankers.

Force 67,[2] commanded by Admiral Vian, left Trincomalee on 17 December, 1944, and made a rendezvous with Force 69,[3] the oiler group, the next day. After *Argonaut*, *Black Prince* and the destroyers had refuelled, Force 67 sailed for the flying-off position, which was some sixty miles north-west of Diamond Point, at the northern entrance to the Malacca Strait, and reached it undetected early on the morning of 20 December.

The order of battle for Operation ROBSON was:

Strike
12 Avengers from *Indomitable*
16 Avengers from *Illustrious*
Each armed with four 500 lb bombs
4 Corsairs from *Illustrious*, each armed with two 500 lb bombs

Escort
Top Cover: 8 Hellcats from *Indomitable*
Middle Cover: 12 Corsairs from *Illustrious*
Close Cover: 8 Hellcats from *Indomitable*

The weather at the flying-off position was bad, with poor visibility, low clouds and intermittent but heavy rain squalls, and the launch was delayed for twenty minutes before Admiral Vian ordered the strike to proceed at 0636. One Avenger from *Indomitable* crashed in the sea

---

[1] See map, p. 72.
[2] The aircraft carriers *Indomitable* (flagship) and *Illustrious*; cruisers *Newcastle*, *Argonaut*, and *Black Prince*; and destroyers *Kempenfelt*, *Wrangler*, *Wessex*, *Whirlwind* and *Wakeful*.
[3] RFA *Wave King*, and destroyers *Whelp* and *Wager*.

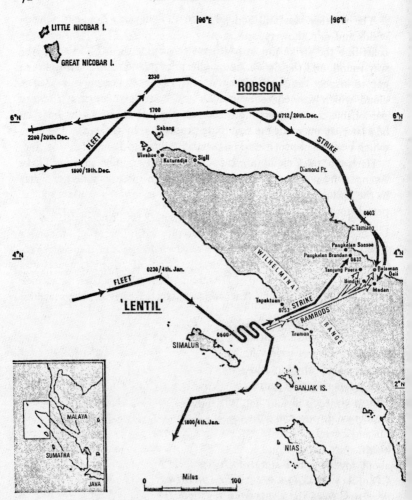

BPF STRIKES at SUMATRAN OIL REFINERIES
20th December 1944 (ROBSON) and 4th January 1945 (LENTIL)

shortly after take-off, but the crew was recovered uninjured. The remaining twenty-seven Avengers with escort took departure from the fleet at 0715. The four Corsairs, the first to take off from a British carrier with long-range tanks and 500 lb bombs, followed to catch up the rest of the strike.

The weather was still bad on the way to the target, with squally winds and rain showers, and about fourteen miles from the Sumatran coast-line the strike ran into a barrier of thick cloud. There was no way round, and the Strike Leader, Lt. Cdr. W. Stuart, led through a gap to inspect the target. But target and coast-line were shrouded in cloud which seemed to extend down to sea-level and, 'after some pardonable confusion among the clouds' as Captain Eccles in *Indomitable* later commented, the strike diverted to attack the secondary target which was the port of Belawan Deli.

Here, too, thick cloud hindered the strike and prevented many of the Avengers from seeing their target properly. Avengers bombed the quay in the harbour from 1,500 feet, while Corsairs strafed and set on fire petrol storage tanks and warehouses in the town, and a goods train and buildings at Kocala Simpang. Two Corsairs became detached from the main body and somehow found their way through dense cloud to either Pangkalan Brandan or Pangkalan Soe Soe, where they strafed and set on fire a large oil tank. Meanwhile, Hellcats of top cover surprised and shot down a Sally.[1] After nearly three years of comparative peace and tranquillity, the defences of Belawan Deli were clearly taken off guard. Anti-aircraft fire, both heavy and light calibre, was scattered and inaccurate, and no Japanese fighters were seen.

The absence of enemy fighters was very fortunate, for in the excitement of the bombing and strafing runs, radio discipline deteriorated, with pilots shouting instructions and advice to each other over the air. Ultimately the radio bedlam over the target was such that the Strike Leader could not make his instructions heard, the strike became split up and eventually strike and escort made a rendezvous at the same height, just under cloud level, and all fifty-five aircraft began to mill about together in a state of chaotic confusion. Lt. Cdr. Mainprice, CO of 854 Sq. *Illustrious'* Avengers, formed up his squadron and took departure from the rendezvous on his own initiative. The rest of the strike and escort composed themselves and returned without opposition to the fleet. The four Corsairs armed with bombs had been unable to find the target and returned without making an attack. All aircraft were landed on by 1050, and Force 67 retired to the west.

In the afternoon a somewhat ingenuous message from a Japanese wireless operator ashore 'Am closing down now, will call you later' was intercepted and on the suggestion of Captain C. E. Lambe, commanding *Illustrious*, eight Corsairs from *Illustrious* and eight Hellcats from

[1] Sally: Allied code name for Japanese Mitsubishi army bomber.

Indomitable carried out a low-level sweep on airfields at Sabang and Oleelhoe, the harbour of Kota Raja, in northern Sumatra. Once again there was no enemy fighter opposition and no aircraft were seen on any of the airfields. Force 67 arrived at Trincomalee on 22 December.

ROBSON had been largely thwarted by the weather, and the fleet at once began preparations for a second attempt at Pangkalan Brandan (Operation LENTIL). Admiral Vian once more led the fleet, now designated Force 65,[1] to sea on 1 January 1945. It was now a period of full moon and it had been decided that it would be unwise for the fleet to enter the Malacca Strait. Another flying-off position was therefore chosen, some thirty miles north-east of Simalur Island, on the western or Indian Ocean side of Sumatra. The strike would have a more difficult flight to the target, of eighty miles overland crossing the 10,000 foot peaks of the Wilhelmina Range, but the force could remain longer in the area if necessary. The order of battle for LENTIL was:

Strike
16 Avengers from *Indomitable*
16 Avengers from *Victorious*
Each armed with four 500 lb bombs
12 Fireflies from *Indefatigable* each armed with eight 60 lb rockets

Escort
Top Cover: 8 Hellcats from *Indomitable*
Middle Cover: 16 Corsairs from *Victorious*
Close Cover: 8 Hellcats from *Indomitable*

Fighter Ramrods[2]
8 Hellcats from *Indomitable*
8 Corsairs from *Victorious*

Force 65 reached the flying-off position early on 4 January and this time the weather was excellent, with visibility up to fifty miles, sunshine and a brisk wind. The fighter Ramrods took off at 0610 to strafe the airfields around Pangkalan Brandan, and the main strike and escort took departure at 0740. Twelve miles from the target the Fireflies were detached to rocket and strafe the town of Pangkalan Soe Soe, and claimed to have set on fire a small tanker in the harbour (although this was not acknowledged in the Japanese reports).

[1] The aircraft carriers *Indomitable* (flagship), *Victorious* and *Indefatigable*; cruisers *Argonaut*, *Black Prince*, *Ceylon* and *Suffolk*, and eight destroyers.
[2] RAMROD: code name for offensive fighter sweeps against specified targets, normally airfields, harbours and shipping.

The main strike had been unmolested on their flight to the target but the defences had been thoroughly warmed up by the attack of 20 December, and there was heavy and accurate anti-aircraft fire on the approach over Pangkalan Soe Soe. When the Avengers deployed to attack their targets the fighter escort were at once engaged by up to a dozen Japanese fighters. Overjoyed by their first real taste of aerial combat in the Far East, many of the escort broke off to take part in furious dog-fights all over the target area and succeeded in shooting down five Oscars.[1] Meanwhile the Avengers, feeling somewhat neglected, continued with their bombing runs, against light and inaccurate flak over Pangkalan Brandan. Some oil tanks were bombed prematurely and much of the oil refinery area was soon obscured by smoke and flame, but the bombing inflicted considerable damage.

The Ramrods sighted twenty-five aircraft on the ground at Medan and Tanjong Poera airfields, and destroyed seven of them, as well as shooting down a Dinah[2] and a Sally. Meanwhile, five 888 Sq. Hellcats from *Indefatigable* flew photo-reconnaissance flights and 62,000 leaflets were dropped.

The Avengers were weakly escorted as they came out of the target area and headed for the rendezvous, but fortunately there were no Japanese fighters. One Avenger had been damaged by an enemy fighter during the approach and a second force-landed in the sea twelve miles off Tapa Tuan with engine failure. Destroyers were sent to pick up the crew. A Firefly ditched, out of fuel, close to *Indefatigable*. The rest of the strike and escort landed on without incident.

In the afternoon, while Force 65 was retiring south of Simalur Island a 'bogey' was detected over the fleet, but the height was estimated incorrectly and the intruder, a Japanese reconnaissance aircraft, escaped the CAP. Force 65 arrived at Trincomalee on 7 January.

At the 'postmortem' after LENTIL, the Avenger squadron commanders complained, quite rightly, that they had been left virtually unprotected during the vulnerable period between making their bombing runs and reaching the rendezvous; too many fighters had been detached to strafe ground targets or had allowed themselves to be lured away into attractive dog-fights. It transpired that three of the fighter escort, including the escort leader, had had R/T failures and, unknown to the rest of the escort, had returned to the fleet. The fighter escort had thus lacked co-ordination. However, Lt. J. B. Edmundson of 1836 Squadron, who

[1] Oscar: single-engined Nakajima Japanese army fighter.
[2] Dinah: twin-engined Mitsubishi Japanese army reconnaissance bomber.

took over leadership of the escort, excused himself and his fellow fighter pilots in the most disarming manner: 'What always seems to happen is that someone sees a 'bogey', makes a hasty report, and chases off, followed by everyone else who is anywhere near. The fault is actually that it's not even every month of the year that you see a Zero in the Fleet Air Arm, so you can hardly blame a fighter pilot for making the most of his opportunities.' Edmundson added, reassuringly: 'I think Avengers are a pleasure to escort, and the more we do it, the better protection they will get.' The Avenger aircrews had to be satisfied with that assurance.

The two strikes against Pangkalan Brandan had achieved a fair success, against moderate opposition. The bad R/T discipline and over-eagerness of the fighter pilots were errors of inexperience and happily there had been no Japanese fighters to take advantage from them. But ROBSON and LENTIL had only been rehearsals. The air groups would not be so lucky in the third and largest operation in the OUTFLANK series – the attack on Palembang.

Chapter Three

PALEMBANG

THE two strikes on the Palembang oil refineries which took place on 24 and 29 January 1945 (Operations MERIDIAN ONE and TWO) were among the most competent performances of the Fleet Air Arm during the war. Yet they were nearly still-born. When the OUTFLANK programme was first debated, there was some opposition to a Palembang strike in certain sections of the Admiralty who had apparently assumed the attitude of unusually solicitous boxers' managers, anxious not to over-match their boys too early in their fighting careers. The Palembang refineries were more than 150 miles from the nearest point on the western or 'Indian Ocean' coast of Sumatra and were strongly defended by a ring of fighter airfields and anti-aircraft batteries. They were a formidable proposition for any attacking force and the BPF aircrews' state of training, it was said, was not equal to such a task. If, as was suggested, there were heavy losses, the fleet's morale would suffer. From experience of the air war in Europe it would seem that the refineries would be better attacked by large fleets of heavy bombers. Lastly, and as always in the affairs of the British Pacific Fleet, there were political considerations. The Australian Government had been assured that the fleet would arrive in Australia by the end of 1944; if the fleet delayed to attack Palembang, the date could not be kept.

Admiral Fraser answered all objections. He disbelieved the gloomy forecasts of heavy aircrew losses; in his view, the Japanese were hard pressed in the Pacific and were not as strong in the Indian Ocean as was feared. Furthermore, an oil refinery consisted of a few vital vulnerable points set in a vast insensitive field which would be more economically and efficiently attacked by precision bombing by carrier-borne aircraft than by area saturation bombing from heavy bombers. A feature of the air war in the Pacific was the way in which raids by carrier-borne and heavy bombers were now to be planned to complement

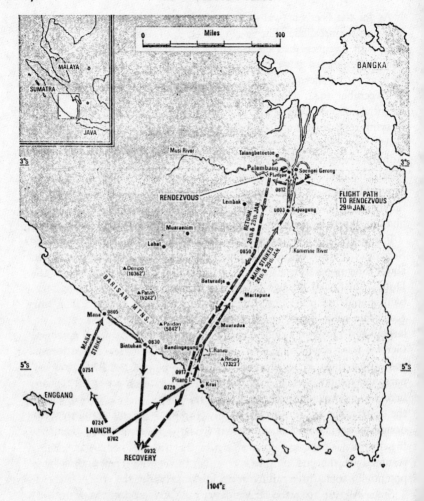

BPF STRIKES at SUMATRAN OIL REFINERIES,
PALEMBANG, 24th and 29th January 1945

(Times are given for 24th. Times were similar on 29th)

each other, each arm attacking targets most suitable to its peculiar talents (although, it must be said, later raids on Japan by the US Army Air Force appeared to be more in competition than collaboration with the US Navy).

As for the fleet's arrival in Australia by the end of 1944, that date was simply unrealistic. The re-equipping of the carrier bomber squadrons with Avengers had taken much longer than expected and would take longer still if it were to be completed in Australia, where there were as yet no shore facilities. Even if the fleet had arrived in Australia in December 1944, it could not have operated against the enemy. The essential support ships, and particularly tankers and escort carriers for ferrying replacement aircraft, had not arrived.

At Pearl Harbour, Admiral Fraser had been at pains to convince Admiral Nimitz of the British Pacific Fleet's worth, and Admiral Nimitz had been so far impressed as to ask the fleet to attack Palembang. It would look very bad if the fleet refused at the first time of asking. 'Eventually,' as Admiral Fraser has said, 'everyone at headquarters gives in, when the man on the spot insists.'[1] The strikes were on.

Palembang is an important road and rail junction in south-eastern Sumatra.[2] Palembang town lies on the north bank of the Musi river, about forty miles from its mouth. The two refineries of Pladjoe (Royal Dutch Shell) and Soengei Gerong (Standard Oil) lay on the south bank, about five miles downstream of the town and either side of the Komerine river where it enters the Musi. In 1945 Pladjoe was the largest and most important oil refinery in the Far East and Soengei Gerong was second only to it. Both refineries had been in Japanese possession since February 1942, when Palembang was captured by parachute troops. As at Pangkalan Brandan, refinery personnel had fired the oil wells and carried out some demolition but unfortunately the destruction was not complete; the refineries were of such advanced design for their time that the Japanese, as they later admitted, had not the technical expertise to repair them. However, production was resumed by the end of the year and at the time of the raids was potentially some three million tons of crude oil a year.

Since August 1944 the air defence of Sumatra had been entrusted to the 9th Air Division of the Japanese 7th Area Army. In January 1945 there were six fighter squadrons and one reconnaissance squadron based in Sumatra;[3] three of the fighter squadrons, equipped with Oscars and Nicks,[4] had been transferred from the Philippines in

---

[1] Lord Fraser. Conversation of 12.10.67.
[2] See map, p. 78.
[3] The 21st, 26th, 33rd and 87th Air Regiments, the 24th and 71st Independent Air Squadrons; and the 74th Independent Air Reconnaissance Squadron. A bomber squadron, the 58th Air Regiment, was also based in Sumatra.
[4] Nick: Japanese Army Kawasaki twin-engined fighter.

December 1944, and one from the Celebes in January 1945. Palembang itself was defended by four fighter squadrons, operating from a ring of airfields – normally dusty red strips, carved from the jungle, with a handful of wooden hangars and huts – of which there were four within forty miles of the refineries and others in use or under construction at Lahat, Lembak, Talangbetoetoe and Martapura. The refineries and the airstrips were also defended by batteries of heavy and light calibre anti-aircraft guns.

It was estimated that the destruction of the two refineries would require three strikes: the first on Pladjoe, the second on Soengei Gerong, and a third to 'mop up' any remaining targets left untouched on either refinery. On each occasion the attack would be made by a striking force of Avengers, strongly escorted by Corsairs, Hellcats and Fireflies, whilst Corsair Ramrod sweeps forestalled enemy fighter interference by ground-strafing the nearby airstrips. The remaining Corsairs and Hellcats, and all *Indefatigable*'s Seafires would meanwhile provide CAPS over the fleet. A subsidiary strike on the coastal airstrip at Mana, and photo-reconnaissance flights over Sumatra were also planned.

A scale model of the refineries had been built and briefing officers had the assistance of former members of the refinery staff. The fleet carried out a full rehearsal at sea off Ceylon on 13 January, with a combined strike and escort exercise on Colombo in the morning and fighter sweep exercises off Trincomalee and Sigiriya in the afternoon, and sailed on 16th to rendezvous with the oiling force.

The fleet, designated Force 63, and commanded by Admiral Vian,[1] was virtually the British Pacific Fleet as it was first constituted, less the battleship *Howe* which had already gone ahead to Australia:

1st Aircraft Carrier Squadron: *Indomitable* (flagship), *Illustrious, Victorious* and *Indefatigable*: battleship *King George V*;
4th Cruiser Squadron: *Argonaut, Black Prince, Euryalus,* and *Ceylon*;
25th Destroyer Flotilla: *Grenville* (Captain D), *Undine, Ursa, Undaunted*;
27th Destroyer Flotilla: *Kempenfelt* (Captain D), *Wakeful, Whirlwind, Wager, Wessex,* and *Whelp*.[2]

Force 63 carried the largest complement of aircraft fielded by the Fleet Air Arm so far in the war, made up as follows:

[1] Admiral Rawlings had caught pneumonia after flying out from England. He took passage in *King George V*, but was not flying his flag.

[2] *Ceylon* and *Wessex* had stayed, to embark mail and radar spares, and sailed after the fleet.

	Indomitable	Illustrious	Indefatigable	Victorious
He	39			
Co		36		34
Av	21	14	21	19
Fi			12	
Se			40	
Wa		2		
TOTAL: 238	60	52	73	53

Force 63 made a rendezvous with the oiling group Force 69[1] on the morning of 20 January, and *King George V*, the cruisers and the destroyers fuelled during the day. The weather was bad, with gusting winds and a troublesome swell, and the oilers complained of much gear being damaged by the destroyers. After fuelling, Force 63 proceeded towards the flying-off position, leaving *Ceylon* and *Urchin* to accompany the oilers.

Force 63 approached the flying-off position, which was off the coast of Sumatra some seventy miles east of Enggano Island, during the night of 21-22 January and again on the night of 22-23 but an inter-tropical front lay obstinately against the Sumatra coast; the weather was unsuitable on each occasion, with low cloud and persistent downpours of rain. When the force tried for the third time, the weather brightened. By 0600 on 24 January the cloud level had lifted, there was a moderate north-westerly breeze and it was the beginning of a fine day. The peaks of the Barisan range, which the strike had to cross, were visible sharp and clear to the east, and so, at 0615, Admiral Vian ordered the strike to be launched.

The Order of Battle for MERIDIAN ONE, the Pladjoe strike, the first of the two largest strikes undertaken by the Fleet Air Arm during the Second World War was:

Air Co-ordinator: Major R. C. Hay, Royal Marines (*Victorious*)

Strike: No. 1 Bomber Wing
11 Avengers from *Indomitable* (857 Sq.: Lt. Cdr. W. Stuart, RNVR, Strike Leader)
12 Avengers from *Victorious* (849 Sq.: Lt. Cdr. D. R. Foster, RNVR)
No. 2 Bomber Wing
12 Avengers from *Illustrious* (854 Sq.: Lt. Cdr. W. J. Mainprice)

[1] *Urchin* (Senior Officer), RFAs (Royal Fleet Auxiliaries), *Echodale*, *Wave King* and *Empire Salvage*. RFA *Arndale* sailed from Fremantle on 15 January to join Force 69.

F

12 Avengers from *Indefatigable* (820 Sq.: Lt. F. L. Jones, RNVR)
All Avengers armed with four 500 lb bombs

Escort: Top Cover
16 Corsairs from *Victorious* (1834 Sq. and 1836 Sq.: Lt. Cdr. C. C. Tomkinson, RNVR, Top Cover Leader)
Middle Cover
8 Corsairs from *Illustrious* (1830 Sq.: Lt. P. S. Coles, Senior Pilot) and 16 Hellcats from *Indomitable* (1839 Sq.: Lt. Cdr. M. S. Godson, and 1844 Sq.: Lt. Cdr. T. W. Harrington, Middle Cover Leader)

Strike and Bow Close Escort
12 Fireflies from *Indefatigable* (1770 Sq.: Major V. B. G. Cheesman, RM)
Armed with eight 60 lb rocket projectiles
Stern Close Escort
8 Corsairs from *Illustrious* (1833 Sq.: Lt. Cdr. N. S. Hanson, RNVR, Close Escort Leader)

Mana Strike and Escort
5 Avengers of 857 Sq. and 4 Hellcats of 1844 Sq. all from *Indomitable*

Fighter Ramrod Sweeps 'X Ray' and 'Yoke'
12 Corsairs from *Illustrious* (1833 Sq. and 1830 Sq.: Lt. Cdr. M. R. Tritton, RNVR, 'X Ray' leader) and 12 Corsairs from *Victorious* (1834 Sq. and 1836 Sq.: Lt. Cdr. R. D. B. Hopkins, 'Yoke' Leader)

Whilst the strike was in progress, two of *Indomitable*'s Hellcats flew photo-reconnaissance flights and two Walrus amphibians ('Darby' and 'Joan') were available in *Illustrious* for air–sea rescue sorties. Thus a total of 144 aircraft were concerned in MERIDIAN ONE, not including those flying CAPS over the fleet.

Flying-off was full of incident. In *Indefatigable* one Avenger surged forward on the flight deck and crashed into its neighbour. Both were damaged, causing a delay. The ten remaining Avengers of 820 Sq. had taken off by 0638 and were led by their Senior Pilot, Lt. F. L. Jones, the squadron CO being medically unfit. In *Victorious* one Avenger failed to start, another returned early to make an emergency landing, and three more returned prematurely.[1] The surviving seven were led by

[1] Captain Denny, in *Victorious*, attributed this high unserviceability rate to the fact that the ship had four Corsairs and one Avenger embarked over normal complement, with a consequently larger number of aircraft parked on deck, where they had been subjected to prolonged downpours of rain and showers of spray.

their CO, Lt. Cdr. Foster. In *Indomitable* and *Illustrious* the first Avengers were catapulted at 0619 and the whole strike component airborne by 0636. The thirty-two Corsairs and sixteen Hellcats of the strike escort were all away from their carriers by 0631.

In the second range, of Fireflies from *Indefatigable* and Ramrod Corsairs from *Victorious* and *Illustrious, Indefatigable*'s troubles persisted. One Firefly could not lower its flaps and, by 'Murphy's Law', it had to be that of Major V. B. G. Cheesman, Royal Marines, CO of 1770 Sq. ranged at the head of his squadron. The first Firefly was not in the air until 0710, and 1770 Sq. might never have caught up the rest of the strike had not the departure been delayed. In the event, they overtook the strike a few miles short of the target. The Ramrod Corsairs had all taken off by 0709, soon overhauled the main strike, and went ahead to strafe their target airfields.

Strike and escort had formed up and after some circumnavigation of the fleet by the Strike Leader – later criticised by the Air Co-ordinator – the eighty-seven Avengers, Corsairs, and Hellcats[1] took departure from the fleet at 0704, nine minutes later than scheduled, followed hot-foot by *Indefatigable*'s Fireflies. They crossed the Sumatran coast at 0718 at 4,500 feet, climbing for the mountains. The weather was now excellent for their venture, with visibility more than sixty miles and a layer of high thin cloud enabling the pilots to look up-sun. Climbing to 12,000 feet over the mountains, the aircrews could see stretched below them the broad jungle plain of eastern Sumatra, a vivid green, and ahead the line of the Komerine River which would lead them to Palembang. Far away, in the misty haze, lay the Banka Strait and beyond that the South China Sea, where no British warships or aircraft had operated since 1942.

The original strike plan had called for the strike to lose height after crossing the mountains but because the strike had already flown rather higher than planned, the Strike Leader decided to maintain height – a decision which caused some confusion amongst the Top and Middle Cover fighters overhead, none of whom were certain what height they were expected to be keeping.

The strike had been detected by the enemy air-raid warning system as it crossed the coast-line. Fifteen miles from the target the first cry of 'Bandits!' was heard as some fifteen or twenty Tojos and Nicks which

[1] Of the 47 Avengers, 32 Corsairs and 16 Hellcats in the Pladjoe strike and escort, two Avengers did not take off and five Avengers and one Corsair returned early.

had been orbiting south-west of Palembang at heights between 15,000 and 30,000 feet broke through Top and Middle Cover, diving steeply out of the sun. The Japanese pilots had been briefed to concentrate upon the Avengers and they conducted their attacks with great determination. Palembang was the training centre for the 7th Area Air Army and a proportion of the attacking Japanese pilots were instructors. Their standard of flying was generally high – 'except for one laddie, who made an awful shambles of it. I saw loads of stuff coming over my wing, someone firing dead astern of us. I looked in my rear view mirror and there was this Oscar as big as a house. Everything happened in split seconds, I was going to shout "break" one way or another but before I could get the words out of my mouth or press the button the fellow disappeared and shot underneath me. Then, to my amazement, he appeared right in front of us, in absolute plan view. We all heaved back on our sticks and belted him. When you hit someone with point-fives something goes. Chunks flew off him and he fell off sideways in a sort of tail glide. He was only the length of a room away from us. We damned nearly ran into him.'[1]

A wild air battle had begun, in which the enemy fighters were driven off; one Tojo and a Nick were claimed shot down during the engagement, but S/Lt. R. J. A. Shaw of 1833 Sq. was lost. His Corsair was last seen heading northwards with a Tojo on its tail. All Top Cover Corsairs and at least twelve of Middle Cover Hellcats were engaged in dog-fights all over the target area, leaving eight Corsairs of Close Escort the unenviable task of escorting four squadrons of Avengers on their last lap to the target.

Meanwhile, the refinery anti-aircraft defences had opened an intense barrage of heavy and light flak, growing ever more accurate for height, so that the airbursts were deafeningly audible in the Avenger cockpits, but happily failing to track the aircraft for bearing. By now, the Avenger pilots could see their target plainly below: the great expanse of the oil refinery set in the bright green jungle, the blue and grey storage tanks, a few striped with red, and some attempt at camouflage. On the refinery perimeters, a number of khaki or olive-coloured balloons, estimated at about thirty, were flying at 2,000 feet and ascending.

The balloons were an alarming and most unusual obstacle, and a sure sign of the importance the enemy attached to the refineries. Previous reconnaissance photographs taken by USAAF aircraft from

[1] Norman Hanson (ex-Lt. Cdr. RNVR) CO of 1833 Sq. Conversation of 22.7.68.

Ceylon had indicated the possibility of balloons at Palembang but the strike had no prepared plan to deal with them. The Strike Leader requested the Fireflies, who had just joined, to go ahead and strafe the balloons, but the request was not acknowledged and in any case the Fireflies were not armed with the most suitable tracer ammunition for the purpose.

At this time, three or four twin-engined Japanese aircraft, probably Nicks, on the fringe of the air-battle were exercising what appeared to be some form of air-to-ground control of either AA fire or fighters. However, as the Air Co-Ordinator drily remarked, 'No noticeable difference was observed after three of these twin-engined aircraft had been shot down'.[1]

The Fireflies flew down with the Avengers. Their squadron CO had been a survivor of *Cornwall* and had a personal score to settle:

'On our journey through the morning sky all thoughts are on the action to be taken if visibility should deteriorate still further, when on arrival over the mainland, we suddenly emerge into a brilliantly clear sky. This is exactly what we wanted. So we press forward towards the target. "Starboard thirty, target thirty miles, formation 'B' for Baker, go!" as the squadrons deploy to their attack formations. There are the barrage balloons all round the target. "Bandits left thirty up ten miles" comes a report over the R T as our fighters wheel to attack the Japanese fighters sent up to intercept us. "Bandits right ninety level closing" – bandits here and bandits there. The battle is on.

'Now we approach the target, and what a target, sitting there in the morning sunrise! 'Attack, attack, attack!' and in we go. Now don't rush it. Take careful and accurate aim. Remember how those bombs hit *Cornwall*. Don't muck it up at the last minute by being over-enthusiastic. Down we go, 300 knots, closing fast, sights on, hold it hold it fire! I hear my rockets go. Switch to cannon and a burst of cannon shells all on their way to the target, a tower of machinery known as a 'cracking plant' which should be full of petrol. And by Jove, it is! An enormous explosion takes place and sheets of flame reach up into the sky.

'Watch out. A Jap fighter trying to get on my tail. Avoiding action and try to get on to his, but he's away now. The whole place is flame and smoke and chaos.'[2]

---

[1] Supplement to the *London Gazette*, 5 April 1951. Admiral Sir Arthur Power's Dispatch 'The Carrier-Borne Aircraft Attacks on Oil Refineries in the Palembang (Sumatra) Area in January, 1945', p. 1809.

[2] Major V. B. G. Cheesman, 'I Was There': III *Avenged!*, in manuscript.

Though harassed by flak, and disconcerted by the balloons, the Avenger squadrons deployed for their attack and ran in on their targets with the greatest skill and courage. The squadrons deployed at 0811 and attacked at 0814, No. 1 Wing leading, in steep glide-dives of about forty-five degrees with six-second intervals between aircraft, descending from around 8,000 feet to drop their bombs.

For one Avenger crew of 857 Sq. in No. 1 Wing, almost everything that could go wrong, did so. It simply was not their day:

'During the briefing we had been told that W/T silence would be observed until we reached the target, and that we would bomb at about 3,000 feet. If a balloon barrage was spotted, the CO would issue new instructions about bombing. Everything went smoothly during the flight there – I didn't hear a sound over the radio and it wasn't until later that I learned that our radio was U/S [unserviceable].

'As we approached the target at about 12,000 feet we could see a carpet of bursting shells at about 10,000 feet. We saw the CO begin his dive and so followed. When we were down to about 7,000 feet we were somewhat alarmed to see four 500 lb bombs whizz by just in front of our nose. It was the Senior Pilot letting go his bombs (apparently they had been told at the target not to fly lower). Knowing nothing of these altered plans we continued down, only to see a couple of balloon cables flashing by. Down to 3,000 feet now, we spotted our target and pressed the tit to release the bombs, only to find we had a hang-up. Preparing to go round again, the air gunner warned that an enemy fighter was approaching. Taking evasive action and trying to find some cloud and being several thousand feet below our formation, we were on our own. The Tojo was still attacking and the air gunner, thinking at last he had him in his sights, pressed the button – and the gun jammed!

'Fortunately, for us, the CO of one of the fighter escort squadrons had spotted us and the Tojo, and had given him a good burst and winged him. But the Jap wasn't quite finished yet. He next tried to ram us and was actually flying level with us when his tank caught fire and he rolled over and crashed just by his own aerodrome.

'We made our way safely back after that and then had to land on with four 500 lb bombs still aboard. Only one other thing could have gone wrong and that would have been if the bombs had been nose-fused. Fortunately they weren't.'[1]

[1] Mr Eric W. Beeny (ex-Lt. RNVR). Letter of 12.9.68.

Some storage tanks were bombed too early and smoke was obscuring the target when No. 2 Wing attacked, but subsequent photography showed that the bombing was remarkably accurate. The damage to the refinery was assessed in Admiral Vian's report as:

Crude distilleries and run down tanks: hits.
Reforming unit, redistillation unit, cracking unit and distillation units: hits in area – probably about 30% destroyed.
Main boiler and electric power house: probably one hit and two transformers destroyed.[1]

The attack was over by 0822 and the Avengers emerged from the target area in a long straggling procession. The bombers flew north of Palembang town, encountering intense AA fire, and headed towards the rendezvous, which was a small island in the Musi river some miles to the westward. The Fireflies were patrolling the air-lane from the target to the rendezvous and the Close Escort with some remnants of Middle Cover were still in company but most of the escorting fighters were still engaged in combat up to thirty miles away and many of the Avengers were unprotected at this critical time in the raid. A number of enemy fighters were apparently lying in wait for them. Several Avengers were attacked and were unable to call for help because of radio chatter (the R/T discipline was later described as 'atrocious' and 'would not have been permitted at a training school'). It was here, in the flight between target and rendezvous, that the Avenger squadrons sustained most of their damage and one Avenger from *Indomitable* was lost. The Japanese Tojo pilot who was responsible has described his success:

'At 1500 feet two Avengers were flying southwards, their leader trailing smoke. Sitting ducks. I carefully turned in behind them, concentrating on the damaged Avenger which still had its bomb doors open. Probably its hydraulics had been damaged. Six hundred yards, five hundred yards. Suddenly its ball-turret gunner opened fire. Red tracer slipped past my Shoki,[2] but I held my fire. Two hundred yards. I could clearly see the gunner in the ball-turret. Now I was flying in the wash of my quarry and my aircraft was bouncing around like a mad thing. Steadying up the Shoki I fired at point-blank distance. The bullets from my four 13 mm. guns ripped into the Avenger, its

---

[1] Admiral Vian's report, Supplement to *London Gazette*, 5 April 1951, p. 1808.
[2] The Tojo was known to the Japanese as the 'Shoki' (Demon).

green-house canopy bursting into fragments, like leaves in a gale. Flames seared back from the port wing roots and the Avenger rolled on to its back and then fell away into the jungle below.'[1]

The strike left the rendezvous at 0826 and began the flight homewards. After numerous alarms, when Fireflies were reported as 'bogeys', the strike crossed the coast at 0916 and broke up into individual carrier groups for landing on at 0928.

One Avenger of *Indefatigable*'s 820 Sq. failed to reach the fleet. It had been damaged in the raid and earlier *Illustrious* had heard an aircraft, evidently this one, using the wrong call-sign and asking for directions. Courses to fly were passed by *Indefatigable*, and *Indomitable* and by *King George V* but without response and the aircraft was presumed to have crashed into the sea. The crew were not recovered. The pilot, Chief Petty Officer Pilot H. Mitchell, had left his maps of southern Sumatra behind in the ship; it was probable that his Observer, S/Lt. A. Hemington, RNVR, had been killed or seriously wounded and was unable to prompt him. A Hellcat from Middle Cover was also lost during the raid; it was last seen by 854 Sq., going down in the distance. The pilot, S/Lt. J. K. Haberfield, RNZNVR, of 1839 Sq., was captured by the Japanese.

The presence of so many Japanese fighters over the target showed that the Ramrod sweeps had not been fully effective. Flown off in the second range, they had arrived over the enemy airfields too late to prevent many of the defending fighters taking off. The Ramrod sweeps themselves had heavy losses and indeed lost more aircraft than either strike or escort – five Corsairs, four of them to flak. Over Lembak airfield S/Lt. A. H. Brown, RNVR, of 1830 Sq. was killed when his Corsair was hit, crashed upside down in front of the hangars and cartwheeled in flames through a line of parked aircraft. From Lembak the sweep flew via Palembang to Talangbetoetoe, an airstrip to the north, entirely surrounded by jungle and heavily defended by AA guns. Here, Lt. A. W. Sutton, RCNVR, Senior Pilot of 1830 Sq. disappeared after the third strafing run and was not seen again by his flight; S/Lt. E. J. Baxter, RNZNVR, of 1833 Sq., was hit over Talangbetoetoe but successfully baled out and was seen to land safely near Simpang, a few miles from Lake Ranau. Over one of the Palembang airstrips S/Lt. I. L. Grave of 1834 Sq. collided with another aircraft and his Corsair

---

[1] Major Hideaki Inayama, of the 87th Air Regiment; *The Royal Air Force Flying Review*, Volume XV, No. 8.

crashed into the ground and burst into flames. The Japanese fighters had rightly concentrated over the refineries and left the defence of the airstrips to the guns. Out of range, the Ramrods were able to fly almost at will. While a few aircraft flew CAPS overhead, the main body of the Ramrod worked over the airstrips, strafing parked aircraft and any other targets which presented themselves. They destroyed about twenty aircraft of various types, including several dummies, on the ground as well as a power station, control towers, hangars, motor vehicles and rolling stock. The Ramrods returned to their carriers and had landed on by 1015.

The last to return, at 1130, were the two photo-reconnaissance Hellcats from *Indomitable* who had flown off at 8 o'clock and covered eleven airfields and the target, and had discovered six new airfields.

The Mana strike had taken off at 0709 and, after one Avenger had returned with engine trouble, bombed the airfield and buildings, claiming one Dinah destroyed on the ground. A Hellcat pilot of the escort was wounded by flak.

Meanwhile, with the fleet, the Seafire CAPS had been having an eventful but discouraging forenoon. *Indefatigable*'s ill luck had continued. The day had been a tale of Seafire disasters and deck landing crashes, with Seafires smashing their under-carriages, bursting tyres, ditching in the sea, slamming their tails on the flight deck and breaking their backs. After lunch the fighter protection of the fleet was taken over by the other carriers because, *Indefatigable* was informed, of their slowness in operating Seafires. Captain Graham noticed sadly that No. 24 Fighter Wing finished their day in a very low state of spirits.

The fleet had lost two Avengers, six Corsairs and a Hellcat, and many other aircraft had been damaged by flak or by fighters. One Seafire pilot ditched and was recovered by *Whirlwind*. The Close Escort Leader, Lt. Cdr. Hanson, crashed into the sea astern of *Illustrious* whilst attempting to land on, and was picked up by *Wessex*.

After all aircraft had been landed on, Force 63 withdrew south-westward at 22 knots. At 1415 that afternoon a small group of 'bogeys' estimated at 'four plus' was detected by radar but the eight CAP Hellcats sent to intercept could not make contact and the enemy echoes faded north of Enggano Island. The destroyer *Ursa* fuelled from *King George V* on 25 January and in the evening was detached from the fleet for Cocos Island with despatches for transmission (Force 63 keeping radio silence off the enemy coast). She rejoined on 27 January, while the fleet was fuelling.

The fleet fuelling from 26-27 January was an ominous portent for the future when (the fleet hoped) it would be operating in the Pacific. The fuelling was very slow, through parted hoses, erratic station-keeping and general lack of expertise in the evolution. *Indefatigable* fuelled from *Echodale* with no troubles, but *Illustrious* found on closing *Empire Salvage* that the tanker had only her aviation petrol hose streamed; Captain Lambe remarked on the strain of station-keeping for some twelve hours on a tanker whose course and speed were continually varying. *Indomitable*'s fuelling was also slow, because of parted hoses. But worst of all, the fuel state remaining in the tankers showed that there was only enough fuel for one more strike at Palembang.

For the strike on Soengei Gerong (MERIDIAN TWO), the operational plan was changed. Only Pladjoe had so far been attacked and the enemy must surely guess that another strike was probable; they might even have taken prisoner aircrew who had revealed under duress that another strike was imminent. It was unlikely that the Japanese could fly in fighter reinforcements to Palembang but they could be expected to make a much more determined attempt to attack the fleet. The strike was reduced, and four fighters each from *Illustrious*, *Indomitable* and *Victorious* reinforced *Indefatigable*'s CAPS over the fleet (the memory of the Seafires' adventures in MERIDIAN ONE might also have influenced Admiral Vian in this decision). The Fireflies would be used as close escort throughout the raid. The fighter Ramrods would be flown off in two parts, timing their flights to arrive simultaneously over the two most formidable airfields, at Lembak and Talangbetoetoe. An alternative flying-off position, north of Enggano Island, was selected but was not used.

The strike plan also had an important alteration. After bombing Soengei Gerong, the Avenger pilots were briefed to break away to starboard and fly in a wide half-circle to the south of the refineries, forming up at the same rendezvous as before. The route from target to rendezvous would be longer but would avoid the intense flak from the north of Palembang town. The wing leaders held a conference in *Indomitable* during the fuelling period. Lt. Cdr. Mainprice, CO of *Illustrious*' Avengers, returned from it reassured that a plan had been devised to deal with the balloons.

The Air Co-ordinator, Strike Leader, and Avenger armament were the same for Soengei Gerong as for Pladjoe, and the main strike consisted of twelve Avengers from each of the four carriers. The Order of Battle for the rearranged escort and Ramrods was:

Escort: Top Cover
12 Corsairs from *Illustrious* (1833 and 1830 Sqs. Lt. P. S. Cole, Top Cover Leader)
Middle Cover
16 Hellcats from *Indomitable* (1839 and 1844 Sq.: Lt. Cdr. T. W. Harrington, Middle Cover Leader)
Close Escort
12 Corsairs from *Victorious* (1836 Sq.: Lt. Cdr. C. C. Tomkinson, Close Escort Leader) and 10 Fireflies from *Indefatigable* (1770 Sq.: Major V. B. Cheesman)

Ramrod 'X-Ray' (Talangbetoetoe)
12 Corsairs from *Illustrious* (1833 and 1830 Sq.: Lt. Cdr. A. M. Tritton)

Ramrod 'Yoke' (Lembak)
12 Corsairs from *Victorious* (1834 Sq.: Lt. Cdr. R. D. B. Hopkins)

Armed Reconnaissance (Mana)
Two Fireflies from *Indefatigable*

Two of *Indomitable*'s Hellcats were to fly photo-reconnaissance flights, and 'Darby' and 'Joan' were once again available for air–sea rescue.

After fuelling, Force 63 approached the Sumatran coast for the fourth time and reached the flying-off position on 29 January. The weather was very bad, with heavy rain-storms, squally winds, and a low cloud ceiling, although the mountains to the east were clear. Flying off was postponed twenty-five minutes to 0640.

While strike and escort were taking off rain squalls sometimes reduced the visibility to under half a mile. The form-up was described by the Close Escort Leader, Lt. Cdr. Tomkinson, as 'something of a nightmare'. There were some anxious moments as the carrier air groups collected in their waiting positions in very poor visibility. By 0710 visibility had improved and the Air Co-ordinator chafed at what seemed to him an unconscionable delay. Exasperated, he noticed the Strike Leader making a second full circuit of the fleet although all units had joined up. 'The result of this extra unnecessary circuit was that three Avenger squadrons were hopelessly out of position and the fighter escort was all jumbled up . . . making aviation in the area extremely hazardous.'[1]

[1] Supplement to *London Gazette*, p. 1810.

In spite of Major Hay's strictures, the form-up in those conditions was a fine flying achievement and the strike eventually took departure from the fleet at 0732, only two minutes late. An Avenger from *Indomitable* ditched almost at once, and Major Hay commented, somewhat heartlessly: 'It seemed a little early in the day to start losing aircraft.'[1] The crew were picked up by *Undine*.

After the customary early returns (of three Avengers and four Corsairs) strike and escort crossed the coast at 0740 and began to climb for the mountains. The Strike Leader continued to climb to 10,000 feet, embarrassing the escort overhead, who were forced into cloud. The Strike Leader maintained his height, ignoring repeated requests to fly lower, and there were some hard feelings between strike and escort on this point.

The Japanese had established a patrol over the Sumatran plain south-west of the refineries. The first 'bogies' were reported at 0814, when the strike was still more than fifty miles from Palembang, but were dispersed by Top Cover, one Tojo being shot down by Lt. A. H. Churchill, RNZNVR, of 1833 Sq. The Avengers sighted their target at 0840 and began their deployment for attack. The fires at Pladjoe had been extinguished. The balloon barrage was still flying.

The Japanese fighters struck again at the worst time for the Avengers, when they were in the act of deploying for their attack and when it was most difficult for their own fighters to escort them closely. The rear squadron of No. 1 Wing, 849 of *Victorious*, was attacked by several Tojos five miles short of the target and suffered severely.

The Avengers continued through fighter attack, through two intense flak box barrages at 3,000 and 11,000 feet and through the balloons to drop their bombs. A few balloons were shot down but almost the whole barrage still remained when Mainprice, leading 854 Sq. Avengers, decided to attack under the balloons. His Avenger and that of his wingman S/Lt. R. S. Armstrong, RNVR, both hit balloon cables. Both aircraft were lost, with their complete crews.

More Avengers were attacked and damaged in their final dives and on their bombing runs over the target, but the bombing was more accurate than at Pladjoe, until the inevitable smoke from burning oil storage tanks began to obscure the refinery. The damage to Soengei Gerong was summarised in Admiral Vian's report:

Boiler and electric power houses: direct hits claimed, but not shown

---

[1] Ibid., p. 1810.

on photographs; photography ceased about half-time because of smoke.

1000 lb cracking plant, fractionating columns, coke stills, pipe stills and re-run stills: All hit.

Depropaniser and 750 lb cracking plant: probably hit.[1]

After bombing, the Avengers straggled out in ones and twos from the target and headed for the rendezvous. As in the first strike, they were inadequately escorted and were once again attacked by Tojos and Oscars lying in wait. Two Avengers of 849 Sq., those of Lt. K. M. Burrenston and S/Lt. W. E. J. Lintern, were shot down. Lt. Levitt of 1770 Sq. shot down an Oscar but was himself then shot down, with his observer Lt. J. F. Webb, RNZNVR. Two more Japanese aircraft, a Hamp and another Oscar were shot down by S/Lts. G. E. Pugh, RNVR, and V. J. Redding, RNVR, both of 1770, in the flight between target and rendezvous.

The Avenger pilots defended themselves with great panache, handling their aircraft like single-seater fighters. S/Lt. W. Coster, RNVR and Lt. Jones, Senior Pilot of 820 Sq. had a prolonged engagement with a Tojo which made several runs on them from starboard to port. Jones took skilful evasive action until the Tojo had apparently exhausted its ammunition and broke away to port immediately in front of Coster who followed it round, firing with his Avenger's front gun until he too had expended all his ammunition. The Tojo spun off and was last seen flying on its back twenty feet above the trees, with smoke and flame billowing from its fuselage. At about the same time, on his way to the rendezvous, Lt. G. J. Connolly, RNVR, of 854 Sq., noticed one of *Victorious*'s Avengers flying low over the jungle and under attack by two Tojos. Connolly surprised and shot down one Tojo and on being engaged by the other coolly shook it off. He remained in company with the damaged Avenger and his CO Mainprice having been killed, took over the leadership of *Illustrious*' Avengers. Many of the Avengers afterwards complained thst they had seen no escorting fighters below 7,000 feet between target and rendezvous, and they had not been able to summon help because of radio interference.

The strike left the rendezvous at 0901 and crossed the coastline at 0955, R T discipline was once more described as 'appalling'. 'Crossing the coast,' wrote Major Hay, 'seemed to be the signal for complete radio chaos. Primarily the Avengers giving their damaged friends

---

[1] Supplement to *London Gazette*, p. 1808.

extracts from pilot's handling notes. It is about time everybody knew their emergency drill without having to talk about it.'[1] Some lapses might be excused: it was only human for the Avenger crews to feel a sudden upsurge of relief and thankfulness, and a desire to swap reminiscences after a time of considerable peril. Unforgivable, however, were serious breaches of security during the flight to the target; more than one Avenger crew had compromised the whole strike with careless talk by transmitting, in clear, such questions as 'How far to go now?'

Strike and escort returned to the fleet with no further opposition and broke up into carrier groups for landing at 1015. The battered Avenger squadrons barely reached the fleet and the last survivors were still arriving more than an hour after the main strike had landed on. Six badly damaged Avengers ditched near the fleet. The crews were recovered safely with the exception of one Observer, S/Lt. M. J. Gunn, RNVR, of 849 Sq. who died in *Whelp* from his injuries – in spite of the tourniquet applied in flight by his Air Gunner PO A. N. Taylor.

The X-Ray and Yoke Ramrod sweeps were over their targets fifteen minutes before the arrival of the main strike, but once again they were just too late. Most of the Japanese fighters were already airborne. There were few chances for strafing, although X-Ray Ramrod destroyed three Tojos on the ground at Lembak including 'one very highly polished Tojo; must have been the commanding officer's'. The Ramrods vented their frustration by strafing and setting on fire a Japanese barracks on the north bank of the Musi river. Whilst Yoke Ramrod were returning to the fleet, Lt. L. D. Durno, RNVR, of 1834 Sq., whose Corsair had been hit in an oil tank over Talangbetoetoe, was forced to bale out. He was not picked up.

At Mana, the armed reconnaissance of two Fireflies found no activity except a football match. The players immediately broke off their game and ran to man their defences, which appeared to be one light AA gun.

The photo-reconnaissance flights landed on *Indomitable* at 1030, having surveyed the target, airfields at Lahat and Palembang, and a new airfield at Pajajaman. Twenty-five thousand leaflets were distributed over southern Sumatra.

During the day the enemy made several attempts to locate Force 63. At 0917 CAP Seafires sighted a Tojo, but it escaped into cloud. Twenty minutes later, a small group of enemy aircraft approached from the north. Seafires intercepted and S/Lt. J. W. Hayes, RNVR, of 894 Sq.

[1] Supplement to *London Gazette*, p. 1810.

shot down a Sally – whereat there was much balm in *Indefatigable*. Hayes was himself shot down but was found in his dinghy, all smiles, and recovered by *Undine*. At 1026 a much larger formation was detected to the north. Seafires and Corsairs were vectored out, but the enemy force moved away without attacking the fleet; when that CAP returned, however, the Corsair of S/Lt. S. G. Maynard, RNVR, of 1836 Sq. was missing. Ten minutes later, another small group of Japanese aircraft passed some forty miles to seaward of the fleet.

It was inevitable that sooner or later the enemy would find the fleet, and a serious attack developed at 1150, when seven Sallys were detected twenty-five miles south-east of the fleet. They were later identified by the Japanese broadcast as aircraft of the Shichisci Mitate Unit of the Army Special Corps, led by Major Hitoyuki Kata, of the Special Attack Corps.

The enemy were sighted about fourteen miles on *Illustrious'* port beam and two Corsairs from CAP were visually directed and intercepted, S/Lt. J. A. O'N. Shaw of 1830 Sq. shooting down one Sally about eight miles from the fleet. The enemy approached the fleet low at about fifty feet and it was at first thought that they were torpedo aircraft. The fleet turned together to the north-west to present a more difficult stern-on target. The enemy's behaviour showed that they were suicide aircraft and that they were heading for *Illustrious* and *Indefatigable*. The enemy were taken under fire by *King George V*, *Illustrious* and *Indefatigable*, and finally by most of the fleet with 6 inch, 5·25s, bofors and pom-poms. *Indomitable* launched three Hellcats which were in action immediately after take-off, S/Lt. K. A. McLennan, RNZNVR, shooting down two Sallys, assisted by gunfire from *King George V*. Another Sally approached *Illustrious* very low and fine on the ship's port quarter; chased by a flight of Seafires led by Lt. Cdr. J. Crossman, RNVR, CO of 894 Sq., and engaged by *Illustrious'* gunfire, the enemy narrowly missed the flight deck and crashed in the sea 1,500 yards off the starboard bow, after releasing what appeared to the alarmed watchers on *Illustrious'* bridge to be a torpedo but was more probably a section of the fuselage.

Indefatigable's Seafires were making up for all their frustrations. Seafires were seen to engage five out of seven of the attacking force. S/Lt. K. E. Ward, RNVR, pursued a Sally through the fleet AA barrage until it crashed in the sea only three hundred yards on *Indefatigable*'s port beam. A second Sally was shot down close astern of *Illustrious*, on *Indefatigable*'s starboard beam, and a third on *King George V*'s starboard beam by the battleship's gunfire. All seven enemy aircraft were destroyed in an action lasting four minutes. Their attack was determined but did not damage any ship and in Admiral Vian's words 'a plan of attack appeared to be lacking and the aircraft offered easier targets than I have ever seen'.[1] *Indefatigable*'s Seafire squadrons were jubilant and Captain Graham was glad to see that No. 24 Fighter Wing ended their day in a very high state of spirits.

However, when the smoke and excitement of the battle had cleared, it was found that the fleet had suffered a self-inflicted injury. Two shells from *Euryalus* had hit *Illustrious*' flight deck and island, causing casualties of twelve killed (including Lt. Walker, pilot of Walrus 'Joan'), and twenty-one wounded.

At 1530 Admiral Vian signalled 'Meridian completed'. Enemy aircraft continued to shadow the fleet as it withdrew. Shortly before sunset, two of *Victorious*' Corsairs from CAP were vectored out to a 'bogey' north of the fleet but were recalled without making contact.

Admiral Vian was unable to report that the Palembang refineries had been destroyed, but production at Soengei Gerong was at a standstill until the end of March, when both refineries were producing at about one-third capacity. Production had improved to only half by the end of May and the refineries were a greatly reduced asset to the Japanese for the rest of the war. Ironically, the Japanese could have repaired more than they did; the necessary tools and materials for repairs were at the refineries and had not been damaged in the raids. Sixty-eight enemy aircraft had been destroyed: thirty-eight on the ground and thirty in the air (with another seven 'probables').

In the carriers, jubilation at the success of the raid was tempered with sadness. It was known that the bombers had done well, but the cost had been high. Four more Avengers, two Corsairs and a Firefly had been lost to the enemy in MERIDIAN TWO. The Japanese claimed 206 British aircraft shot down by aircraft, anti-aircraft and coastal batteries, and thirty-three probables. The figures were exaggerated, but actual losses were high enough. Force 63 had lost sixteen aircraft in combat, eleven ditched near the fleet, and another fourteen from deck landing crashes, a total of forty-one aircraft for 378 sorties. This was a proportion of about one aircraft for every ten sorties - a casualty rate which would have made even Bomber Command flinch. Thirty aircrew had been lost: nineteen Avenger aircrew (six complete crews

---

[1] Supplement to *London Gazette*, p. 1804.

and S/Lt. Gunn); the pilots of one Hellcat and eight Corsairs; and the two-man crew of a Firefly. Three pilots were seen to make apparently safe landings in enemy territory. Four were wounded and five more unfit to fly for some time afterwards.

The two carriers hardest hit were *Victorious* and *Illustrious*. In the two days' flying *Victorious* had lost eleven aircrew, seven of them from one squadron, 849 Avengers. Ten of her nineteen Avengers were missing, ditched, or unserviceable through combat damage. *Illustrious* had lost ten aircrew, including her Avenger wing leader, and the Senior Pilot of 1830 Corsairs. Every one of her returning Avengers had been damaged by flak and/or enemy fighters. The ship was now short of a quarter of her full complement of Corsairs and Avengers, 8% of Corsair pilots and 10% of Avenger crews. The Palembang strikes showed that the fleet urgently needed spare air groups and a reserve aircraft carrier.

There were other lessons to be learned. Palembang had proved the BPF in battle. The ships would now reach the Pacific with at least one notch in their belts. Yet the OUTFLANK series had demonstrated in advance all the problems which were about to beset the fleet. A third strike had been feasible and quite clearly called for: enemy fighters had largely been defeated, the weather still held, and the fleet's position still unknown to the enemy. But MERIDIAN THREE had had to be abandoned because 'there was not enough oil' – the eternal cry of the British Pacific Fleet. The Oiling Group had only just enough fuel for the fleet to reach Australia. Furthermore, fuelling between strikes had occupied two whole days, when the fleet could have been at great risk.

The fleet's anti-aircraft gunnery defence was poor. The Special Attack Corps had been shot down to the last aircraft but they had still penetrated perilously close to the carriers. Fire discipline and aircraft recognition were also poor. In addition to the needless tragedy in *Illustrious*, one Hellcat had been taken under fire by *King George V* as it broke off its attack, and Crossman's Seafires had actually been damaged by 'friendly' gunfire (although it should be said that the Seafires took their own risks by pursuing their enemy so close to the fleet).

The fragility of the Seafire in carrier work and the contrasting ruggedness of American types of aircraft had been proved once more. The need for discipline in the air had been underlined again and again. The bombers' interests would not always have been best served had the fighter escort remained rigidly beside them. Nevertheless, Avengers

G

had been lost because they had been left unescorted and had been unable to make their appeals for help heard.

The operational conditions of the Fleet Air Arm did not lend themselves to the creation of 'aces', in the RAF sense of the word, but two aircrew personalities emerged from the OUTFLANK series in Harrington, the Hellcat leader, and Hay, the Air Co-ordinator. The Air Co-ordinator's duty was to accompany the strike, and control the approach to the target and the withdrawal, the Avenger squadron commanders being responsible for the conduct of their individual attacks. This concept had been borrowed from the US Navy and tried out, with success, for the first time in OUTFLANK. Apart from his co-ordinating duties, Major Hay found time to take excellent photographs of the bombing results and, in spare moments, he and his flight shot down three Tojos and an Oscar.

Careful arrangements had been made for air–sea rescue. Fleet destroyers picked up the crews of seven Avengers, two Corsairs and two Seafires. The submarine *Tantalus* was in position in the Malacca Strait and one aircraft is known to have ditched within twenty-five miles of her, but the submarine had no calls for help and the crew were not recovered. Walrus 'Darby' with an escort of two Corsairs took off on the morning of 24 January to search off Pisang Island for C. P. O. Mitchell and his crew. On 29th, urged by Captain Lambe who felt the loss of his aircrews deeply, 'Darby' and 'Joan' both made air–sea rescue sorties, one of them to search Lake Ranau, whence survivors had been briefed to make their way if possible.[1] Nothing was seen of S/Lt. Baxter or of any other survivor and no rescue attempt was made, somewhat to Admiral Vian's relief: 'I felt that we were overstepping the limits of reasonable risk to the rescuers. It remained ever a problem where to draw the line.'[2]

The pilots of damaged aircraft were determined at all costs to ditch in the sea rather than bale out over land. Their fears of being captured by the Japanese were well founded. At least nine survivors of the Palembang raids were taken prisoner by the Japanese. In February they were taken to Outram Road Gaol in Singapore for interrogation by the Kempei Tei, the Japanese secret police. The Outram Road Gaol records were destroyed and many of the cells, with their revealing

---

[1] Whether by coincidence or by editorial clairvoyance, the January 1945 issue of the Fleet Air Arm magazine *Flight Deck* carried an article on survival techniques for aircrew forced down in jungle. The editor was Lt. A. P. Herbert, RNVR.

[2] *Action This Day*, p. 167.

graffiti, were white-washed. The details of the Palembang survivors' fate will probably never now be known. From the evidence of other prisoners of war, and from the statements of three Japanese officers who admitted the crime, it seems likely that between 4 and 5 p.m. on a day between 18 and 20 August 1945 (after the Japanese surrender) the nine survivors were blindfolded and driven in a closed bus to a beach north of Changi. Five of them were named. They were S/Lt. J. K. Haberfield, RNZNVR, of *Indomitable*, Baxter and Shaw of *Illustrious*, Burrenston and Lintern of *Victorious*. There were also two unidentified sub-lieutenants and two unidentified petty officers. They were all beheaded with Japanese ceremonial swords. Their bodies were weighted, taken out in a boat and dropped in the sea. Major Toshio Katoako, Captain Tateki Ikede and Lieutenant Tsuyoshi Miyashita admitted the murders but committed *sepporo* (honourable suicide) before they could be brought to justice.[1] Another more senior Japanese officer was implicated but there was not enough evidence for a conviction. With the after knowledge of this atrocity, Major Hay's demand after LENTIL, that all Japanese aviators who after being shot down have a chance of rejoining their own lines should be destroyed, can be seen in its proper perspective.

Force 63 fuelled on 30 January and, after *Ursa* had again been detached with despatches, steamed southwards towards Australia. On 31 January King Neptune's herald came on board and on the next day, the Monarch himself. The fleet reached Fremantle on 4th and Sydney on 10 February, there to meet an Australian welcome still remembered with awe and gratitude by all who experienced it.

Australia had been under 'American occupation' since 1942, when the United States began to use Australia and New Zealand as spring-boards for their drive up through the Solomons and New Guinea. The Americans had been welcome, but now it was high time for some new faces. The Australians were delighted to see the British fleet, and exerted themselves to be hospitable. The people of Sydney raised £A200,000 by public subscription to build the British Centre, which was the focus of the city's hospitality and was staffed by more than 4,000 voluntary workers. The Centre had beds for 1,200 and at its peak was serving 6,000 meals every day. Three hundred young Australian women (chosen from a roster of 63,000) attended the dances every night as hostesses. Day to day hospitality was offered to sailors in 12,500 homes all over New South Wales. But statistics can only go a

[1] See also *The Times* of 16 January 1946.

little way to describe the warmth and scale of Australia's welcome to the British Pacific Fleet.

For their part, the staff of the Commander-in-Chief were anxious that the fleet should miss no nuance of the Australian way of life, and published several information sheets explaining Australian idiosyncracies. One of them is perhaps worth recalling:

'The Australian is a friendly chap and has few inhibitions about formal introductions. He likes to chat on the tram or train with the fellow next to him. In fact, he's a bit hurt if you refuse to join him in conversation and is apt to regard you as a bit "stand-offish" if you don't accept a proffered cigarette. His slang is colourful. In addition to the usual abbreviations in common use you will find that a pound is a *fiddly* (rhyming slang – fiddly did); five shillings is a dollar, an Oxford (scholar) or a Caser; a shilling is a bob or a deaner; sixpence is a *zac*, and threepence a *trey*. Here are a few expressions chosen at random:

"You Beaut"	This can mean good or bad according to circumstances. Words with the same general meaning are *bonza, bobby dazzler, humdinger*.
"Fair Cow"	"Ain't it a Fair Cow" simply means that the worst has happened.
"Wouldn't It?"	This is a shortened form of wouldn't it give you a pain? Wouldn't it tear you to ribbons? etc., and means that things have gone wrong and there's little that can be done about it.
"Dinkum"	All right, honest, reliable. The "Dinkum Oil" is synonymous with "straight from the horse's mouth".
"Too Right" } "My Oath"	Yes (emphatically).'

Meanwhile, the British Pacific Fleet's future was still unsettled. Rear Admiral Fisher (Rear Admiral, Fleet Train) had arrived in Sydney and sailed on 24 February for Manus, where the embryonic Fleet Train was assembling. Admiral Fraser had obtained permission at least to move the fleet nearer to the war zone and the main fleet sailed from Sydney on 28 February, with Vice Admiral Sir Bernard Rawlings flying his flag in *King George V*, arriving at Manus on 7 March.

There the fleet stayed, while the world passed it by. The British ships were expecting to take part in the forthcoming operations against the

Ryukyus, but the executive order from Admiral King did not arrive. While General Krueger's 6th Army were driving back the remnants of Yamashita's troops on Luzon, while the United States Marines were enduring their month's ordeal for the airfields of Iwo Jima, Slim's 14th Army in Burma were crossing the Irrawaddy and preparing to take Mandalay, and in Europe Bradley and Montgomery were driving towards the Rhine, the British Pacific Fleet lay at Manus, exercising, refuelling and swinging to their anchors. The ships had arrived and were ready, but nobody had any use for them. They had brought their instruments twelve thousand miles across the world, but it seemed that nobody was going to ask them to play.

Chapter Four

ICEBERG ONE

This old Pacific Ocean had inspired a strange devotion;
   It was bitter and at intervals it stank;
It was tough and it was risky; it was full of rotten whisky;
   It was rugged -- but goddammit, it was YANK!
Until there came invasion, on that memorable occasion
   When towards the TBS we turned an ear,
And a voice both arch and skittish, and indubitably British,
   Said: 'Rogah! Thenks, old boy! You're loud and cleah!'[1]

'I AM left wondering', wrote Admiral Rawlings, 'under what circumstances and by whose whimsical conception these islands should have been named in honour of Their Lordships.'[2] The British Pacific Fleet (designated Task Force 113) was at Manus, in the Admiralty Islands. It had arrived on 7 March 1945 on its way up to the combat area where, it was devoutly hoped, it would take part in the impending assault on Okinawa (Operation ICEBERG). On passage from Sydney the fleet had carried out air, gunnery and replenishment at sea exercises and for the first time had practised US Navy tactical fleet formation and manoeuvres.

The fleet had adopted American signalling methods and procedures. This had been a considerable undertaking but in practice had caused no serious difficulties. The Royal Navy had already had some experience of American methods from the 'General Signal Book' which was used by both RN and USN ships in the Atlantic and Russian convoys. This experience was useful in the Pacific. Once RN communications personnel

[1] 'Home Thoughts from Abroad', from *Limey Rhymes*, by the British Naval Liaison Officer to Com. 3rd Fleet, printed in USS *Missouri*, November 1945. Reproduced by permission of Admiral Sir Michael Le Fanu. TBS: 'Talk Between Ships', short-range radio.

[2] Captain S. W. Roskill explains the origin of the name in *The War At Sea*, Vol. III, Part II, p. 333. Captain Carteret named the islands the Admiralty Islands in 1767, after a hostile reception by the natives.

accustomed themselves to American phraseology and terms of speech, they quickly learned to use the new signals in the USN publications. USN officers and ratings were loaned to RN Ships on arrival in the Pacific and served on board as liaison teams for the first three months. Rates of sending and receiving morse, and volume of signal traffic, both increased after the change to the USN system. The telegraphists were able to increase their speed but the volume of traffic was a heavy burden on fleet communications staff throughout the fleet's existence.

Manus was a huge anchorage and a most uncomfortable one. The equatorial climate was hot and humid. The armoured steel flight decks of the carriers acted as giant heat absorbents; an egg placed on a flight deck assumed a 'fried appearance' in a few minutes. Members of the ship's company who slept on deck often had to wait until 11 p.m. before the flight deck was cool enough to place their camp beds. Aircraft handlers who had worn gym shoes in home waters quickly reverted to stout leather soles in the Pacific. At Manus the myth of the 'fully-tropicalised' fleet was finally exploded. Breathless sweltering calms alternated with sudden violent squalls which disrupted boat routines and training schedules, and shortened the fleet's notice for steam. Many of the auxiliaries of the Fleet Train (Task Force 112), of which twenty-seven had arrived at Manus, were anchored miles from the fleet. It was difficult to reach them or even to communicate with them. There was a shortage of boats; the need for extra boats had actually been foreseen and they had arrived, but were still in Australia. The long heavy swell in certain parts of the harbour prevented ships berthing alongside each other without suitable catamarans. The fleet had no suitable catamarans. There was no properly equipped waterboat and the fleet was short of nearly 200,000 gallons of fresh water a day.

At Manus the fleet waited and wilted. The days passed, with no operational assignment, and morale sank. Inactivity is the severest test of a fleet's temper and there were incidents of insubordination, born of frustration, even in Vian's flagship *Indomitable*. The fleet's stay at Manus was, as Admiral Fraser said, 'a period of most unpleasant suspense'.

Admiral King's reluctance to commit the British Pacific Fleet to its projected role in ICEBERG was not – or only very slightly – due to Anglophobia. There were in fact excellent arguments for deploying the British fleet elsewhere, in the South-West Pacific under MacArthur. These arguments arose out of the shape of American strategy in the Far East, leading to the final defeat of Japan. The crucial question in this strategy was: would it be necessary actually to invade the main islands of Japan, or might Japan be reduced by a combination of sea blockade and air bombardment, without invasion?

The United States War Department appear to have reconciled themselves to the necessity of an invasion, with its likelihood of frightening casualty rates, at an early stage. On 11 July 1944 the US Joint Chiefs of Staff proposed the invasion and seizure of objectives in the industrial heart of Japan. At the end of the month, at Roosevelt's Pearl Harbour meeting with his two Pacific commanders, Nimitz and MacArthur both pressed their points of view – Nimitz, with Admiral King behind him, advocating the invasion of Formosa, and MacArthur insisting on the invasion of Luzon. Formosa was the better launching pad for an invasion of Japan, but Luzon lying squarely across the route between Japan and the resources of the East Indies, was too large and too dangerous to be neglected. The result of the meeting was an agreement that Luzon should be invaded. However, these conclusions do not appear to have disturbed the main stream of planning in Washington for on 9 September, before the Octagon Conference, the US Joint Chiefs of Staff proposed to defeat Japan by blockade *and* by invasion, with an assault on Luzon in February 1945 or an invasion of Formosa in March.

MacArthur's case was eventually brought about by events in the field. The acceleration of the Leyte invasion made a subsequent invasion of Luzon almost inevitable, but there would not be sufficient troops or assault shipping in the Pacific to invade Formosa until a later date. An invasion of Luzon lessened the need for an invasion of Formosa. Admiral Nimitz proposed an alternative: a landing on Iwo Jima in the Bonin Islands in January 1945, followed by invasion of the Ryukyus in March. On 3 October 1944 the US Joint Chiefs of Staff directed Nimitz to invade Okinawa on 1 March 1945. Finally, on 22 January 1945, the Joint Chiefs defined their revised objectives which were: an assault on Kyushu, followed by an invasion of the Tokyo plain. The immediate objectives for the US Armed Forces in the Pacific were, the assault on Iwo Jima on 19 February, and the invasion of Okinawa on 1 April.

Iwo Jima was secured on 16 March, Manila on 4th. Okinawa (some people believed) would not withstand for more than about a month. It would be some time before Allied resources could be redeployed in the Pacific after the defeat of Germany and in the meanwhile, other operations must be mounted to keep the Japanese under pressure and to contain the largest possible numbers of their forces until the final assault on the Japanese mainland. In these circumstances the British Pacific Fleet was in an extraordinary position. All the currently planned operations were expected to be over before the British fleet was fully operational, while the final invasion of Japan, in which it might well play a part, was still some way in the future. In the meantime, what was the fleet to do?

The British Pacific Fleet was no longer a hypothetical collection of ships nominated in a planner's docket. Though not yet at full strength nor in a full state of training, it existed. It was actually there in the Pacific and was the only flexible naval reserve in the whole theatre. When Admiral King and the other Joint Chiefs cast around for intermediate operations to maintain pressure on the Japanese it was natural that they should wish to withhold their naval reserve from the Ryukyus and employ it meanwhile in the intermediate operations. In short, the situation was developing exactly as Admiral Fraser had feared: the British fleet to be used in 'side-shows' while the Americans prosecuted the main war in the Pacific.

The US Joint Chiefs of Staff considered three 'intermediate' operations: an attack on the island of Hainan, off the south China coast, to threaten Japanese sea communications and to open a new air-route to China; an attack on the Chusan-Ningpo area of China, south of Hangchow and the Yangtse estuary to threaten Japanese river communications and provide another base for air attack on Japan; and an attack on North Borneo, to provide a base for the British Pacific Fleet at Brunei, to capture the valuable oil and rubber resources of Borneo, and again, to threaten Japanese sea communications.

Of the three possibilities, the Joint Chiefs of Staff and General MacArthur were much attracted to the last. Borneo was a convenient starting-point for future operations in the South China Sea. Rubber and oil were vital to the Japanese war effort. The British Pacific Fleet would, surely, welcome a base on former British territory. The British fleet carriers could provide air cover for the assault stages of an attack by Commonwealth troops.

The Borneo suggestion was coolly received in London. True, it had superficial attractions, especially by bringing British warships so near to the former British colonies in Malaya and Hong Kong. But the whole conception tended to reopen all the old wounds of the Middle and 'Modified' Middle Strategies. The British Chiefs of Staff replied that Brunei was too far from Japan and from Australia. It could not be furnished as a base until the beginning of 1946, when Singapore itself might have well been recaptured. The Chiefs of Staff were at pains to explain that if the Brunei attack were being undertaken mainly on their behalf, they would be glad to see it abandoned. Admiral Fraser later wrote that the notion of basing the British Pacific Fleet at Brunei was obviously disconnected from any existing plan of strategic employment.

But while the British Chiefs of Staff had been composing their reply Admiral King had at last relented. He may have succumbed to pressure from Nimitz and others who suspected that Okinawa was to be a far more formidable proposition than anyone anticipated; he may have been influenced by a spate of press reports that the British fleet was about to be relegated ignominiously to a 'back area'; or he may simply have tired of the whole argument. On the night of 14 March when Commodore Evans Lombe was working late at the Williams Street headquarters; 'a signal finally came through to say "You are to operate under Nimitz". So I was able to send a signal straight on, saying "Report to Nimitz". I must say that gave me a lot of pleasure. The fleet had been hanging about at Manus for some days and really it was a little bit tiresome not knowing wl.at to do next. Then I rang Admiral Fraser and told him what I'd done.'[1]

And so, on the morning of 15 March, at Manus, Admiral Rawlings received the signal for which the British Pacific Fleet had been waiting:

'Commander Task Force 113, repeated to Commander Task Force 112 [Fisher], from C-in-C, BPF; In accordance with instructions received from COMINCH (King) you are to report Task Force 113 together with Task Force 112 to C-in-C Pacific [Nimitz] forthwith for duty in operations connected with ICEBERG.[2]

But the victory was not quite complete. There was a reservation in the 'small print' of a second signal, timed three minutes later: COMINCH has directed that employment of Task Force 113 and Task Force 112 must be such that they can be disengaged and reallocated at seven days' notice from him.

To Admiral Rawlings and the fleet, only the first signal mattered. All exercises were cancelled and all ships recalled to harbour, where the

[1] Admiral Sir Edward Evans Lombe. Conversation of 8.11.67.
[2] The text of this and other signals are the paraphrased versions from Admiral Sir Bruce Fraser's despatch 'The Contribution of the British Pacific Fleet to the Assault on Okinawa, 1945'. Supplement to the *London Gazette* of 2 June 1948.

admiral's staffs were occupied by a nice calculation: how long would the fleet take to re-embark the squadrons who had been training ashore, and to top up with fuel and stores, bearing in mind the shortage of boats and the swell? And when should the first Tanker Group (who could make only nine knots, in fine weather) be sent on ahead, and how best to organise and position them for an operating period which was likely to last for at least three weeks? Later on 15 March, Rawlings signalled to Nimitz that the fleet was reporting for duty and would be ready to sail at noon, local time, on 17 March. Rawlings added: 'it is with a feeling of great pride and pleasure that the British Pacific Force joins the US Naval Forces under your command.' Admiral Nimitz replied next day, with typical generosity: 'The British Carrier Task Force and attached units will greatly increase our striking power and demonstrate our unity of purpose against Japan. The US Pacific Fleet welcomes you'.

The Tanker Group[1] sailed on 17 March, the main fleet following the next day, en route for the combat area, via Ulithi. It had 'come on to blow' the night before, but the 18th was a bright day and the fleet was beginning on a merry note. The Royal Marine band played on the flagship quarterdeck and there was a general air of 'We're off to see the Wizard'. All the frustrations of the past were for the time being forgotten. That great enterprise for which they had come so far and waited so long was at last under way.

Task Force 113 arrived at Ulithi on 20 March where, in that huge atoll harbour, the most uninformed ordinary seaman in the fleet could see with his own eyes the scale of the battle in which he was about to take part. The harbour was jammed with warships and assault shipping, assembled for the assault phase of ICEBERG, and this huge concourse of shipping was only part of Admiral R. K. Turner's Joint Expeditionary Force of more than 1,400 ships and craft,[2] carrying 182,000 assault troops, which were at that moment converging upon Okinawa from Seattle and from San Francisco, from Guadalcanal and Espiritu Santo, from Oahu, from Leyte and from Saipan.

Okinawa,[3] the main island of the Ryukyus archipelago (or Nansei

---

[1] Task Unit 112.2.1: escort carrier *Striker* (with replacement aircraft), tankers *San Ambrosio, Cedardale,* and *San Adolpho,* destroyer *Whirlwind,* frigate *Findhorn,* and sloop *Crane.* Task Unit 112.2.5: escort carrier *Speaker* (for CAP duties), destroyer *Kempenfelt,* and sloop *Pheasant.*

[2] 385 warships, 828 assault ships. The total with landing craft carried on board ships was 1,400.

[3] See map, p. 108.

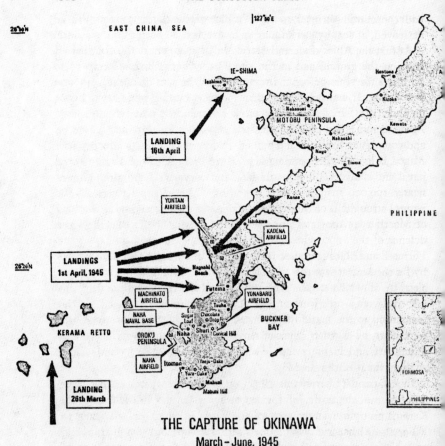

THE CAPTURE OF OKINAWA
March – June, 1945

Shoto) had been in Japanese possession since 1879. It is a mountainous island sixty-one miles long and varying from three to eighteen miles in width, and is only 350 miles from Kyushu. Possession of Okinawa would give the Allies a good harbour (at Naha, on the west coast), airfields for long-range bombers within fighter range of the Japanese mainland, and an excellent strategic base lying directly across the Japanese lines of communication with the resources in the south.

After the collapse of the Sho-Go plan for the defence of the Philippines the Imperial Japanese Staff recast their defence planning. In January 1945 they decided that the final battle would be fought in Japan. The defence of the Ryukyus would be only a holding operation. The remaining Japanese air strength would be husbanded until the Allies had committed themselves to a landing, whereupon they would be destroyed, at sea, by sea and air suicide units.

At first the Allies underestimated the Japanese strength on Okinawa, both on the ground and in the air. The Ryukyus had been closed to outsiders for years before the war and accurate intelligence information was scanty. It was believed that the Japanese had about 50,000 troops on the island. In fact, Okinawa was defended by the Japanese 32nd Army, commanded by a very able officer, Lt. Gen. Mitsuru Ushijima, and comprising the 24th and 62nd Divisions and the 44th Independent Mixed Brigade, with a strength of some 70,000 men. With additional naval and native Okinawan personnel, the total garrison strength was nearly 100,000 men, the majority concentrated in the south, in the natural stronghold of Shuri, the ancient capital of Okinawa. At the end of March 1945 the Japanese had nearly 6,000 aircraft devoted to the defence of the approaches to Japan, most of them based in Japan and Formosa and about 4,000 of them suicide aircraft. Of the suicide units by far the largest was the 10th Air Fleet, based in Kyushu, with 2,000 aircraft, of which 1,300 were in training but were to be ready for combat by 30 April. In the event the total number of Japanese aircraft committed to the battle for Okinawa was nearer ten thousand. There were four all-weather airfields on the island, at Yontan, Kadena, Machinato and Naha, a fifth under construction at Yonabaru, and a sixth on the offshore island of Ie Shima. Japanese naval strength in the Ryukyus consisted only of small craft but there were nearly three hundred suicide boats, of the type used in the Philippines, in the Kerama group of islands, west of Okinawa.

For the Allies, the task of capturing Okinawa was given to the US 10th Army, commanded by Lt. Gen. Simon Bolivar Buckner Jr., who had spent the previous four years organising the defences of Alaska. The 10th was a newly formed Army, but its two Corps were veterans: the 24th Corps (Maj. Gen. John R. Hodge) had captured Leyte, and the 3rd Amphibious Marine Corps (Maj. Gen. Roy S. Geiger, USMC) had captured Guam and Peleliu. The total strength of 10th Army was 182,000 men (although more than half a million men were to take part in the battle for Okinawa before it ended). L-Day, for the main landing, was fixed for Easter Sunday, 1 April, an ironical choice, remembering the Japanese taste for such dates. General Buckner's troops were to be preceded and accompanied by all the air and sea bombardment support which Admiral Nimitz could command. The structure of the Central Pacific Task Force, which carried out the invasion of Okinawa.

and the British Pacific Fleet's place in it, is best shown in a diagram.

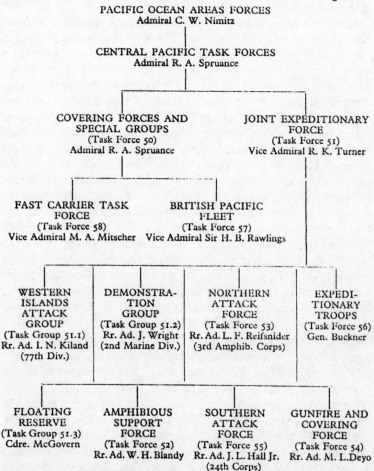

PACIFIC OCEAN AREAS FORCES
Admiral C. W. Nimitz

CENTRAL PACIFIC TASK FORCES
Admiral R. A. Spruance

COVERING FORCES AND
SPECIAL GROUPS
(Task Force 50)
Admiral R. A. Spruance

JOINT EXPEDITIONARY
FORCE
(Task Force 51)
Vice Admiral R. K. Turner

FAST CARRIER TASK
FORCE
(Task Force 58)
Vice Admiral M. A. Mitscher

BRITISH PACIFIC
FLEET
(Task Force 57)
Vice Admiral Sir H. B. Rawlings

WESTERN
ISLANDS
ATTACK
GROUP
(Task Group 51.1)
Rr. Ad. I. N. Kiland
(77th Div.)

DEMONSTRA-
TION
GROUP
(Task Group 51.2)
Rr. Ad. J. Wright
(2nd Marine Div.)

NORTHERN
ATTACK
FORCE
(Task Force 53)
Rr. Ad. L. F. Reifsnider
(3rd Amphib. Corps)

EXPEDI-
TIONARY
TROOPS
(Task Force 56)
Gen. Buckner

FLOATING
RESERVE
(Task Group 51.3)
Cdre. McGovern

AMPHIBIOUS
SUPPORT
FORCE
(Task Force 52)
Rr. Ad. W. H. Blandy

SOUTHERN
ATTACK
FORCE
(Task Force 55)
Rr. Ad. J. L. Hall Jr.
(24th Corps)

GUNFIRE AND
COVERING
FORCE
(Task Force 54)
Rr. Ad. M. L. Deyo

The British Pacific Fleet's task in ICEBERG was important, but was subsidiary to the main operation. The British carriers were not yet considered experienced enough to operate in close company with the Fast Carrier Task Force. The fleet was stationed semi-independently, on the left of the 5th Fleet battleline, off the islands of the Sakishima Gunto, south-west of Okinawa.[1] Its duty was to prevent the Japanese staging aircraft reinforcements through the Sakishima islands, which ran like a chain of convenient stepping stones between Okinawa and

[1] See map, p. 111.

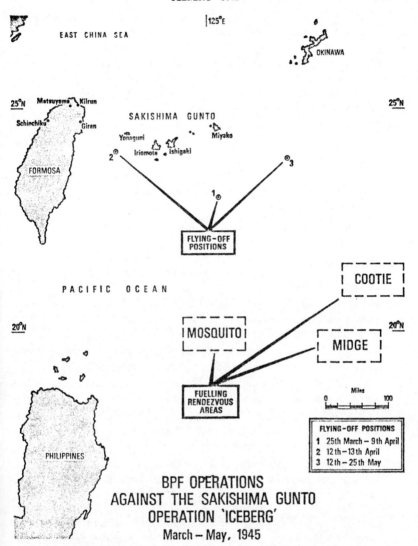

EAST CHINA SEA

OKINAWA

SAKISHIMA GUNTO

FLYING-OFF POSITIONS

PACIFIC OCEAN

COOTIE

MOSQUITO

MIDGE

FUELLING RENDEZVOUS AREAS

FLYING-OFF POSITIONS
1 25th March – 9th April
2 12th – 13th April
3 12th – 25th May

BPF OPERATIONS
AGAINST THE SAKISHIMA GUNTO
OPERATION 'ICEBERG'
March – May, 1945

Formosa, by neutralising the airfields on the two roughly saucepan-shaped islands of Miyako and Ishigaki – two names which still haunt the memories of all who served in the BPF at that time. This was a necessary, but an unglamorous task. Off the Sakishima Gunto the British Pacific Fleet stood no chance of glory and every chance of being attacked.

At Ulithi the fleet fuelled from US tankers and some technical officers made unobtrusive use of US logistical services. Final operational orders and details were circulated. Admiral McMorris, Nimitz's Chief of Staff, had flown from Guam to confer with Rawlings and his staff. US photo-reconnaissance aircraft had taken more than 100,000 photographs, and the BPF were deluged with intelligence information on every subject from the estimates of Japanese air strength to the natural history of the *habu*, a poisonous snake indigenous to the Ryukyus. In *Victorious*, Captain Denny carried out an experiment: 'Serial orders issued by the numerous British authorities, the American manuals, the operation orders, the intelligence material all relevant to the operation, reports and returns due, when piled on my sea-cabin desk reached to the deck-head.'

The man under whom the British Fleet was now to serve was Raymond Spruance, the victor of Midway and the Philippine Sea. Spruance was both a naval officer and a statesman. He was a man of brilliant intellect and sound tactical judgment; he was a gifted staff officer and an outstanding commander at sea – a rare combination of talents. An abnormally shy man, he hated personal publicity and would go to great lengths to avoid it, but as Professor Morison has remarked 'he went on winning battles for his country'. In his personal habits he was ascetic, a frugal eater and drinker. His favourite recreation was walking; at sea, he would walk for hours on the quarterdeck (or 'fantail') of his flagship and, as he had only a small and consequently overworked staff, his usual walking companion was his British Liaison Officer who acted as sounding board and hobby-horse for the admiral's theories and opinions (it could be that in rendering this small service the Royal Navy contributed another vital part to the victory in the Pacific). Rawlings and Spruance were not able to meet before ICEBERG, but this proved to be no great handicap; as Admiral Spruance recalled after the war:

'In spite of the fact that Admiral Rawlings and I had had no chance for a personal conference before the operation, Task Force 57 did its work to my complete satisfaction and fully lived up to the great traditions of the Royal Navy. I remember my Chief of Staff remarking one day during the operation that if Admiral Rawlings and I had known each other for twenty years things could not have gone more smoothly.'[1]

Off Okinawa, Spruance was to be a good friend of the British Pacific

[1] Royal United Services Institution *Journal*, Vol. 91 (1946), p. 554.

Fleet and an understanding leader, always ready with the appreciative (and much appreciated) signal of encouragement.

While the British fleet was at Ulithi, the Fast Carrier Task Force was already at sea, at work on the strategic isolation of Okinawa. On 18 and 19 March aircraft from Task Force 58 struck at airfields in Kyushu and Honshu and at shipping in the Inland Sea. The Japanese retaliated with suicide attacks. The carriers *Enterprise*, *Yorktown* and *Wasp* were hit and *Franklin* very badly damaged, nearly eight hundred of her ship's company being killed. By superb damage control *Franklin* was saved and eventually reached the United States.

Speeded by a 'good hunting' signal from Admiral Spruance on 22 March, the BPF sailed from Ulithi, bound for the Sakishima Gunto, at 0630 on 23rd, assuming the designation Task Force 57 on clearing the harbour.[1]

Task Force 57 at that time consisted of:

1st Battle Squadron (Task Unit 1)
  King George V (Flag of CTF 57), *Howe*

1st Aircraft Carrier Squadron (Task Unit 2)
  Indomitable (Flag of AC 1 and Second in Command TF 57), *Victorious*
  Illustrious, Indefatigable

4th Cruiser Squadron (Task Unit 5)
  Swiftsure (Flag of CS 4), HMNZS *Gambia, Black Prince, Argonaut*

Destroyers (Task Unit 8)
  Euryalus (Flag of RAD temporarily), 25th Destroyer Flotilla,
  Grenville (Captain D.25), *Ulster, Undine, Urania, Undaunted*; 4th
  Destroyer Flotilla, *Quickmatch* (Captain D.4), *Quiberon, Queenborough,
  Quality*; 27th Destroyer Flotilla, *Whelp, Wager*

TF 57's aircraft complement was:

Indomitable: 29 Hellcats, 15 Avengers
Victorious: 37 Corsairs, 14 Avengers, 2 Walrus
Illustrious: 36 Corsairs, 16 Avengers
Indefatigable: 40 Seafires, 20 Avengers, 9 Fireflies

[1] The British fleet used American force designations. Thus in Task Force 57, the first number, 5, referred to the Fifth Fleet; the second number 7, to the British Pacific Fleet. The Fast Carrier Task Force was Task Force 58. Their commanders were designated CTF 57 and CTF 58. A task group in a task force had an extra numeral, e.g. TG 58.1, 58.2, etc. A unit of a group received yet another numeral, e.g. TU 52.1.1, TU 52.1.2, etc.

H

This total aircraft strength of 218 was barely equivalent to a single task group of TF 58, but the British fleet was nevertheless given the status of a Task Force.

After gunnery and communications exercises on passage, TF 57 made a rendezvous with TUs 112.2.1 and 112.2.5 in position ANT (18°30′N, 129°08′E) by 0600 on 25 March and began to refuel. As before off the Sumatran coast the fuelling did not go well. Mr David Divine, war correspondent for Kemsley Newspapers Ltd., who had served with Allied fleets since Dunkirk, was a witness of that fuelling.

'I had just come from the USS *Lexington* – the second *Lexington*. I'd been living in her for a long time. *Lexington* would fuel quite willingly in a wind of Force 6, provided the sea wasn't up to the wind yet. The American tankers would take a ship on either side in that sort of weather. They would have everything aboard, three lines pumping, in twenty minutes. They would be switching stuff on the jackstay and so on, in that time. *KGV* went up astern of one rusty old tanker, which appeared to be manned by two Geordie mates and twenty consumptive Chinamen and it took us, I think, an hour and a half to pick up a single buoyed pipe-line, fiddling around under our bows.'[1]

The big ships of the British fleet were still refuelled by the 'astern' method: the tanker streamed her messenger line and hoses astern, to be grappled, picked up and connected by the following ship. It was a much slower and more difficult method than the American practice of fuelling abeam, where ships steamed alongside each other; but, to be fair, the British ships had not had the chance to practise fuelling at sea as often as *Lexington* and neither the fleet nor the Geordie mates and the consumptive Chinamen were assisted by the weather on 25 March. There was a stiff north-easterly wind and a heavy swell, with parted messenger lines, broken and straying hoses, and frayed tempers. Rear Admiral Edelsten in *Euryalus*, Senior Officer of the oiling group, tried to speed up the operation by having some of the destroyers fuelled from *King George V*, *Howe* and *Striker*. Nevertheless Admiral Rawlings was forced to abandon the fuelling at 1450, when several destroyers were still 30% short of their full capacity. *Quality* and *Whelp*, both with defects, were replaced by *Whirlwind* and *Kempenfelt* from the oiling force screen. *Wager* was left behind, rejoining TF 57 next day.

[1] David Divine, Defence correspondent of the *Sunday Times*. Conversation of 21.3.68.

At 1530 Admiral Vian assumed tactical command of the fleet,[1] and TF 57 steamed at 23½ knots through the night towards its first strike assignment.

Meanwhile, the Allies had won the first round of the struggle for Okinawa. On 24 March battleships and cruisers from TF 58 under Vice Admiral Lee and Rear Admiral Morton Deyo's Gunfire and Covering Force began the preliminary naval bombardment of Okinawa. The Japanese had transferred their 9th Division from Okinawa to Formosa in late 1944 and had insufficient troops to defend all the outlying islands off Okinawa; on 26th the US 77th Infantry Division landed almost unopposed on the Kerama Retto, a small group of islands fifteen miles west of southern Okinawa. Two hundred and fifty Japanese suicide motor-boats were captured. More important, the Keramas were a first class site for a logistic support and repair base in the immediate operating area; fleet tenders, oilers, and repair ships of the US Service Squadron 10 had gratefully occupied it within four days.

Before dawn on 26 March 1945, TF 57 approached the flying-off position, 100 miles due south of Miyako. There were six principal airfields in the Sakishima Gunto,[2] three each on Ishigaki and Miyako, to be neutralised, and kept neutralised, by cratering the runways with bombs, by strafing installations and aircraft on the ground, and by maintaining CAPS over the targets to prevent the Japanese staging in fresh aircraft. The first CAPS and anti-submarine patrol were off at 0605 followed at sunrise half an hour later by a strong fighter Ramrod of Corsairs and Hellcats to sweep over Ishigaki and Miyako.

The enemy's response was only luke-warm and the Ramrods reported little activity, although one Corsair ditched twenty miles off Tarima Shima, between Ishigaki and Miyaki; the pilot was picked up by Walrus. Perhaps the enemy were surprised, for later that forenoon and again in the afternoon when two squadrons of Avengers with top, middle and close fighter cover bombed Ishigaki, and Hirara and Nobara on Miyako, they met accurate heavy flak. One Avenger of 854 Sq. was shot down over Ishigaki; the pilot, Lt. H. L. Taylor, RNVR, and his crew[3] were

---

[1] While aircraft were operating, it was logical for the carrier admiral to have immediate tactical control of the fleet, to synchronise turning in and out of the wind, etc., but to conform to the fleet commander's overall intentions.

[2] On Ishigakishima: Miyara, Hegina and Ishigaki. On Miyakoshima: Nobara, Hirara, and Sukhama. There was also a seaplane base at Karimata, on Miyako, and a little-used airstrip on Iriomoteshima.

[3] Observer: S/Lt. W. R. Slade, RNVR; Air Gunner: PO J. Brown.

lost. On the same strike, *Victorious'* air group suffered a serious set-back when Lt. Cdr. C. C. Tomkinson, RNVR, an experienced Corsair pilot and CO of 1836 Sq., failed to return, His Corsair was seen to ditch correctly but Tomkinson did not get out; his death may have been to a faulty life-jacket. By the end of the day all airfields on Ishigaki and Miyako had been bombed and strafed, and small craft strafed and damaged in Hirara and Ishigaki harbours. Twenty-three enemy aircraft were claimed destroyed on the ground (although all but one of them were later judged to be dummies or non-operational).

There had been several air-raid alerts in the fleet during the day. At 0940 a Dinah was intercepted by Seafires from the fleet CAP but escaped. One 'bogey' was found on investigation to be a USAAF search Liberator – 'a most unwelcome intrusion'. TF 57 had not been warned of this aircraft's flight and the Liberator was fired on by at least one ship in the screen. The technical difficulty of differentiating between friendly and enemy aircraft was already a problem – which was never properly solved.

The Dinah had almost certainly reported TF 57 and as the night was fine with bright moonshine, Admiral Rawlings expected an attack. At 0245 on 27th a shadowing aircraft was detected by radar to the east. TF 57 altered course, but the shadower was persistent. Just after 3 a.m. Japanese radar transmissions were picked up and the fleet began electronic countermeasures by jamming. *Euryalus* opened out from the screen and fired at the intruder who then 'remained at a respectful distance for a time'. A Hellcat was launched from *Indomitable* and the pilot Lt. N. G. Mitchell, RNVR, of 1839 Sq. nearly brought off a spectacular interception by moonlight, but the moon passed behind cloud just as he was about to fire. A successful interception here might have had a desirable psychological effect on the enemy, convincing them that TF 57 had radar-equipped night fighters which, of course, it had not. Lt. Mitchell reported that he had been called up by an aircraft which claimed to be American and warned him of its presence; evidently this was a Japanese trick to allow the shadower to close TF 57 unsuspected.

At dawn on 27th TF 57 was once again at the same flying-off position. A fighter Ramrod was launched over Ishigaki, followed by the morning and afternoon 'bomber runs' of two Avenger squadrons and Fireflies, with fighter escort, to bomb and strafe shipping, harbour installations, the wireless station at Hirara, and Sukama airfield. In the forenoon strike the Avenger of Lt. Cdr. F. C. Nottingham, RNVR, who had taken Mainprice's place as CO of 854 Sq., was hit by flak over Hirara and one wing caught fire. Nottingham flew out to seaward and dived to extinguish the fire, but soon afterwards the wing disintegrated. His observer and air gunner[1] had no chance, but Nottingham himself baled out and was sighted in his dinghy by an Avenger from *Indomitable*. The US submarine *Kingfish*, on air–sea rescue duties, was asked to look out for ditched British crews, but replied that 'she would have to ask her boss first'. After a battle of wills in the flagship between Admiral Vian and his American Liaison Officer[2] the situation was clarified on appeal to Admiral Spruance. Assisted by a CAP flight of Corsairs of 1833 Sq., *Kingfish* picked up Nottingham after an anxious search lasting nearly three hours:

At about 5.45 I said to the CO of the submarine that I would definitely have to go at six, because I had no earthly idea how far we had to fly. The fleet were heading out to the replenishment area by this time. I certainly didn't want to risk a night landing with my boys. We were no night landers in Corsairs. He said, 'One more search'. I said, 'It'll have to be just one, and we'll make an all-out effort, just one fighter to stay with you, the rest will go and search'. I was worried because it was getting duskish and I didn't like my boys floating out there on their own, on an open sea with no other ships. The other three went off and I stayed with the submarine. They'd just gone when, suddenly, way down on the starboard side, I saw a flare come up, about a mile and a half to the south of us. The submarine saw it at the same time and it turned on a sixpence. I recalled the boys and screamed off down and there was old Freddie, sitting in his dinghy, waving his paddle furiously at me as I went over. The submarine came tearing down and – terribly efficient – long before she got to Freddie she had a couple of lads in bathing trunks with life-lines round them out on the hull. Immediately they drew up alongside Freddie the two lads jumped into the water and helped him up on to the pressure hull.[3]

Returning from the same strike that morning, the Strike Leader, Lt. Cdr. Stuart ditched some fifty miles from the flying-off position. He and his crew were picked up by *Undine* (who also, on the same sortie, rescued an American Corsair pilot who had been adrift in his dinghy for forty-eight hours). One Corsair, that of S/Lt. P. C. J. H. Spreckley,

[1] Observer: Lt. F. W. Squires, RNVR; Air Gunner: PO P. H. Firth.
[2] See *Action This Day*, p. 176.
[3] Norman Hanson. Conversation of 22.7.68.

RNVR, of 1834 Sq. was shot down over Ishigaki during the day, and two Seafire pilots, S/Lts. A. G. Cooper and S. C. Yarde,[1] were killed in deck-landing accidents.

In the first two strike days TF 57 had lost nine aircrew, six aircraft in combat and another eleven operationally. 273 strike and 275 CAP sorties had been flown. The Avengers had dropped sixty-four tons of bombs and the Fireflies had fired 151 rockets. It was a start.

Further strikes and a battleship and cruiser bombardment had been planned for 28th but a typhoon report from Guam made Admiral Rawlings pause. If the programme were carried out and the replenishment were subsequently delayed by bad weather, TF 57 might not be back in position in time to attack the Sakishima Gunto on 1 April, L-Day, and if there was one time above all when Spruance would require the Sakishima Gunto airfields neutralised, it was the three-day period from L − 1 to L + 1. Admiral Rawlings decided that a replenishment in the hand was worth two in the future; the strikes and bombardment were cancelled, TF 57 withdrew, and met the Tanker Group in Area Midge at 0730 on 28 March.

Replenishment occupied the fleet until the afternoon of 30th. TF 57 divided into two groups for fuelling, disengaging from the Tanker Group for the night. *Quality* and *Whelp*, with defects made good, relieved *Kempenfelt* and *Whirlwind* who rejoined the Tanker Group screen. Rear Admiral Edelsten transferred from *Euryalus* to *Whirlwind* and, with *Striker* and *Crane*, went back to Leyte, while *Euryalus* rejoined the other cruisers in TU5.

By dawn on 31 March TF 57 was in its flying-off position for another strike day, consisting of fighter Ramrods and target CAPs over Miyako and Ishigaki and two escorted Avenger strikes on Ishigaki barracks and airfields. S/Lt. R. C. Sheard, RNVR, of 849 Sq. and his crew[2] were lost when their Avenger crashed on Ishigaki airfield and burst into flames. Ishigaki town was well strafed by rocket-bearing Hellcats, Corsairs and Fireflies. Lt. Cdr. Stuart was forced to ditch for a second time. On this occasion he and his crew were recovered by the ubiquitous USS *Kingfish*, whose wardroom by now must have begun to resemble a home for Fleet Air Arm gentlemen in reduced circumstances.

A strike day was a long day's activity for the fleet, and particularly

---

[1] The ghost of Sam Yarde was later supposed to haunt *Indefatigable*. Singing was heard in the showers, and shower-stalls were wet, although there was nobody there.

[2] Observer: S/Lt. A. R. Legge, RNVR; Air Gunner: Ldg. Airman N. Hewkin.

for the ship's companies of the aircraft carriers. Their day began before 4 a.m. when those not already on watch were roused by the bugle calls 'Flying Stations' and 'Range aircraft'. In the darkness, while the flight deck was still damp with overnight dew and the island super-structure a shadowy shape against the Pacific sky, the aircraft handling parties were on deck to range some twenty or thirty aircraft, spotting them on the flight deck in the order in which they would fly off. Meanwhile, Admiral Vian and the carrier captains studied meteorological and intelligence reports and the aircraft serviceability states in the carriers. Before dawn the ship's companies went to action stations, most of them to remain at or near their action stations until dark, their meals being brought to them. The radar picket, normally *Argonaut*, who had the most suitable radar, and an attendant destroyer, opened out from the fleet to a distance of about thirty miles in the likeliest direction of an enemy counter-attack. The first fleet and radar picket CAPs and anti-submarine patrols (ASPs) flew off, followed at sunrise by the first fighter Ramrod sweeps. By breakfast time the Avengers and fighter escort of the morning strike were on deck and warming up for their flight of more than a hundred miles to bomb the runways of Ishigaki and Miyako. So on, throughout the day, the fleet wheeled and turned in and out of the wind, for the carriers to land on and fly off strikes and escorts, and to relieve CAPS and ASPs. Every aspect of life in the carriers was subordinated to, and ruled by, the flying programme; even the sailors' daily rum issue, traditionally a noon-day ritual, was deferred until the evening, when flying was over for the day. When the last aircraft had landed on at dusk, the air engineering and ordnance departments worked all night to repair, rearm and refuel aircraft for the next day's strikes.

Replenishments were hardly less strenuous. The fleet carrier air groups were generally able to recuperate, CAPs, ASPs and target-towing duties in the replenishment area being carried out as far as possible by the replenishment carriers. But for most of the ship's companies replenishment was in no sense synonymous with rest and recreation. The fleet had to fuel and the carriers to top up with aviation spirit, fly on replacement aircraft, and fly off flyable 'duds'. As the number and variety of ships in the Logistic Support Group increased, ships were able to reammunition with shells, bombs and rockets, replenish with stores of all kinds, and transfer casualties to a hospital ship which lay, by international convention easily distinguishable by day and fully illuminated by night, at some distance from the remainder of the

Support Group. A 'postie' destroyer distributed mail and official correspondence which had been brought up by the Support Group. The fleet also had a full training programme, under the control of Rear Admiral E. J. P. Brind, of air warning and engaging exercises, Kamikaze defence, bombardment procedures, close-range sleeve target firing and fighter direction exercises. In general, the men of the fleet were almost thankful to return to the striking area.

The fleet was playing itself in, and beginning to grow accustomed to the operational cycle of strike and replenishment when, on 1 April, the enemy jerked the routine sharply out of joint. At 0650, when the first Ramrods were already on their way in to Ishigaki, several bogeys were detected to the westward, height 8,000 feet, range seventy-five miles, closing the fleet. This was part of a group of some twenty aircraft, probably of the Japanese First Air Fleet, from Formosa.

At forty miles, the group split up and were soon afterwards engaged by the fleet CAP, one Zeke[1] being splashed by a Corsair from *Victorious*. The Ramrods had been recalled and a flight of Hellcats, led by Lt. Cdr. Harrington, shot down an Oscar, by means of a little cunning. Harrington insisted that his Hellcats carried a special 'cocktail' of ammunition, made up of five ball, one tracer, and one armour-piercing; with this loading, the Hellcats could attack any sort of target. The sight of the tracer often surprised the enemy into a mistake:

'. . . He was flying out of killing range and I carefully fired a good long blast over his port wing. He very kindly obliged by executing rather a difficult turn to port, which enabled me to close and shoot this unhappy amateur down.'[2]

The remainder of the enemy penetrated to the fleet and one Oscar machine-gunned *Indomitable*'s flight deck, causing seven casualties, one fatal, and then flew on to attack *King George V*, but without any casualties. An officer in *Indomitable* witnessed the remarkable *sang froid* of the driver of one of the small trucks used for towing aircraft:

'He was driving his little truck across the flight deck when the attack began. There was a terrible noise and you could see the marks of machine-gun bullets popping along the deck. The truck was hit and the wind-screen shattered. But he drove on and was unhurt. Either he

---

[1] Zeke: Japanese Army Mitsubishi or Nakajima single-engined fighter.
[2] Captain T. W. Harrington, RN. Letter of 16.5.68.

was very brave or more likely, he hadn't the first idea of what was happening.'[1]

S/Lt. R. H. Reynolds, RNVR, of 887 Sq. engaged a Zeke over the fleet which, at 0727, dived on *Indefatigable*. The ship's Deck Landing Control Officer was on the flight deck:

'I was on deck with Sub. Lt. Roger Green of 820 Sq. Two Fireflies were ranged waiting with crews in them for take-off. The Jap aircraft came straight for *Indefatigable* from five or six thousand feet and passed her to starboard. It then pulled straight up and looped off the top to come vertically into the ship. I imagine the pilot intended to go down the funnel but missed and hit the flight deck alongside the flight deck sick bay and into one of the barrier stanchions. As it made its first pass Roger and I decided on discretion and leapt over the port side into the cat walk and immediately after the bang went back to the flight deck. The remaining bits of aircraft were burning and there was damage in the island sick bay. There was a lot of what I at first thought was smoke filling the entrance to the island and Lt. Cdr. Pat Chambers, Lieutenant Cdr. (Flying), emerged bleeding and shocked. I put him in the care of one of the aircraft handling party members and he was taken to sick bay. The aircraft handling party was soon assembled and the remains of the Jap aircraft were manhandled over the port side. One man produced an object for my scrutiny which turned out to be a piece of finger. That was all that was found of the pilot.'[2]

The Japanese aircraft crashed on the flight deck abreast the island superstructure where its 500 lb. bomb detonated, wrecking both flight deck barriers, the flight deck sickbay and the briefing room. The armoured flight deck was dented to a depth of three inches and a small fire started in the roof of the hangar below. Eight men were killed instantly and the final casualty total was four officers and ten ratings killed, and sixteen wounded. The casualties included Lt. Cdr. Chambers, an air engineer officer, and half the operations room crew.

The fires were soon extinguished, jury barriers rigged, and the first Seafire landed on at 0816, less than an hour after the explosion – a very fine achievement by *Indefatigable*'s ship's company. With its own experience of the devastation caused by kamikazes, the United States

---

[1] This story was told towards the end of a reunion dinner and I cannot now remember the officer's name.
[2] P. G. W. Roome (ex-Lt. RNVR). Letter of 9.7.68.

Navy was profoundly impressed by this demonstration of British armoured flight decks. As *Indefatigable*'s own USN Liaison Officer succinctly expressed it: 'When a kamikaze hits a US carrier, it's six months repair at Pearl. In a Limey carrier it's a case of "Sweepers, man your brooms".'

S/Lt. Reynolds later shot down two Zekes, but another Seafire, diverted to *Victorious* while *Indefatigable*'s flight deck was out of action, crashed into a barrier on landing and the pilot, S/Lt. W. G. Gibson of 894 Sq., was killed.

At about 0755 a Zeke pursued by a Seafire over the fleet jettisoned what appeared to be a 500 lb. bomb very close to the destroyer *Ulster* in the screen. The force of the explosion breached the ship's hull and collapsed the bulkhead between the after boiler-room and the engine-room. Two of the engine-room personnel were killed and one seriously wounded. *Ulster* was unable to steam but remained afloat with her armament intact and after the raid was over *Gambia* took her in tow for Leyte.

A strike of sixteen Avengers escorted by three flights of Corsairs was launched at 1215 to bomb airfields and runways at Ishigaki. They reported no enemy reaction but later in the afternoon target CAPs noticed increased activity on Hirara and Ishigaki. Ramrods were flown off which destroyed three enemy aircraft on the ground. The Corsair of S/Lt. H. J. H. Roberts of 1834 Sq. was damaged by flak. He was seen to ditch correctly and make a 'normal water landing' but by some mischance he was not picked up by the ASR Walrus.

At 1730 on this eventful day radar detected a low-flying bogey to the north-west. Hellcats tried to intercept but the enemy force, four suicide bombers of the 8th Air Division from Schinchiku in Formosa, slipped past them in cloud and were soon sighted and taken under fire by the fleet.

One aircraft, probably a Jill[1] or a Zeke, dived on *Victorious*. The fleet was altering course at the time and *Victorious* tightened her turn, swinging to starboard under full helm: 'Actually the kamikazes were much more frightening than they need have been because in a big aircraft carrier, with enormous horse power on the engines, I reckoned I could dodge them.'[2] The aircraft banked but appeared to be out-turned by the ship and missed, striking its wing-tip against the port flight deck edge and plunging into the sea where its bomb detonated under-

---

[1] Jill: Japanese Navy Nakajima single-engined reconnaissance aircraft.
[2] Admiral Sir Michael Denny: Conversation of 27.11.68.

water some eighty feet clear of *Victorious*' port side. Tons of water, quantities of petrol and fragments of the aircraft were blown on the flight deck. Amongst the debris was a manuscript giving target priorities and other instructions for suicide pilots. This document was welcomed by the fleet intelligence staff, but was received without enthusiasm by Captain Denny: 'The only unmistakable feature of it was its reek of cheap scent.'

On Okinawa itself, L-Day had made an encouraging start. At 0406 Vice Admiral Richmond Turner made the traditional signal: 'Land the Landing Force'. Shortly before dawn ten battleships, nine cruisers, twenty-three destroyers and 177 gun-boats opened the pre-assault bombardment. The first waves of assault troops touched down on the beaches of Hagushi at 0830, against only token resistance from special units left in the area. The Japanese had guessed correctly the Allies' probable landing point but General Ushijima had decided not to contest the beach-head. By 1000, units of 24th Corps had captured Kadena airfield and on the left flank the Marines overran Yontan airfield at 1300. By nightfall on 1 April, 10th Army had 50,000 troops ashore and had established a beach-head between two and three miles deep and eight miles long.

With the Allied landing on Okinawa an accomplished fact, the Japanese could expect to begin staging aircraft through the Sakishima Gunto in earnest. Admiral Rawlings regretfully cancelled battleship and cruiser bombardment of Ishigaki and Miyako which had been planned for 2 April. Bombardments by heavy guns, with all their sound and fury, were good for morale and Admiral Rawlings was well aware that his fleet contained many raw, untried young men. But he was convinced that 'once enemy aircraft begin staging through an aerodrome the most profitable means of destroying them is by air and not by guns'.[1] The veil of the ark of the tabernacle at Whale Island must have been rent from top to bottom at that moment.

2 April was a disappointment. The lack of activity on Ishigaki and Miyako early on 1st had suggested that perhaps the enemy aircraft were leaving the airfields at first light. A search of four Hellcats was flown at 0510 by moonlight, but the mission was a failure: the two Hellcats for Miyako returned early with radio defects and those which reached Ishigaki found nothing. A Ramrod of Hellcats and Corsairs launched at 0630 also found nothing except one aircraft on the ground which was destroyed and one Zeke which Hellcats shot down over

[1] Supplement to *London Gazette* of 2 June 1948, p. 3294.

Ishigaki. At 1045 TF 57 withdrew to refuel in Area Midge, an American task group from TF 58 covering the Sakishima Gunto in its absence.

TF 57 had generally acquitted itself well in the 1 April suicide attacks but there was no doubt that the American criticism of our ships, that they 'were not able to look after themselves', was fair. Ships of the Royal Navy tended to be designed and equipped for action against other ships and since the Mediterranean actions against the Luftwaffe and Regio Aeronautica fleets had had little opportunity to practise against airborne targets. TF 57's AA armament contained a high proportion of two-pounder pompoms and 20 mm. bofors guns which did not have the 'stopping power': the Zeke which dived on *Victorious* had almost certainly been hit by the ship's gunfire but had been able to carry through its attack.

The other main problem was aircraft identification. Hellcats and Seafires had been fired on by the fleet:

'This matter of differentiating between our own aircraft and the enemy's becomes daily of more importance. With the suicide attack, and, as is inevitable with our own fighters pursuing the enemy right on to the Fleet's guns, there is only a matter of seconds in which to act. Presented at certain angles there is very little difference between the suicide-equipped Japanese single-engined aircraft and some of our own fighters. On the other hand, the means of controlling, particularly of stopping, the fire of the innumerable small guns that are now scattered about ships, often with poor communications, make the problem very difficult.'[1]

Admiral Rawlings asked Commodore R. P. Carne of *Striker* to examine the problems of recognising friendly fighters, when close in: several methods were tried and a Fleet Aircraft Recognition Officer was later appointed, but the fleet's record in the Pacific was marred by several tragedies, and a proper solution was never found.

Replenishment lasted three days and was another unhappy experience. The weather was too bad for fuelling on 3rd and TF 57 steamed westwards to Area Mosquito where better weather had been forecast. On 4th, with a heavy swell still running, fuelling began at 0730 and continued with an overnight break and numerous delays until 1930 on 5th. *King George V* and *Howe* left the fuelling area nearly 50% short of full capacity, while the four carriers had embarked only enough aviation fuel for the next two day's operations. Admiral Rawlings had taken a

[1] Supplement to *London Gazette*, p. 3294.

calculated risk. He was determined to keep his promise to Spruance and accepted the chance that a change of programme, or action damage, might place his ships in a very awkward situation.

By steaming at 20 knots all night TF 57 was in position for flying off early on 6 April and the flying programme began: 0450, four Hellcats for pre-dawn surveillance of Ishigaki and Miyako; 0530, four Seafires for CAP over the radar pickets *Argonaut* and *Urania*; 0625, Corsairs and Seafires for fleet CAPs, and Avengers for anti-submarine patrols; 0635 Hellcats and Corsairs for target CAPs. At 0905 a Hellcat pilot, S/Lt. J. R. Northeast, RNVR, of 1844 Sq. returning from Miyako chased a Frances[1] for thirty miles and shot it down.

The Japanese had industriously filled in the craters on the runways overnight. This was to happen again and again; TF 57 had no squadron of night intruder aircraft and it was impossible to keep the airfields out of action permanently. In this sense the Avenger squadrons were like housewives doing the same chore, on morning after morning.

An accident on deck prevented three of *Victorious'* Avengers taking off, and one Avenger of 849 ditched after take-off, but the remaining bombers, with fighter escort, were launched early in the afternoon. The weather was bad and the strike became separated while returning to the fleet but they had succeeded in bombing Hirara town and airfield, Nobara, Sukhama, and Miyara airstrips, barracks and local government buildings, while the fighters strafed radio and radar stations and small craft offshore.

At about 1700 that afternoon a group estimated at four bogeys was detected and although Lt. Cdr. M. S. Godson and S/Lt. E. T. Wilson, SANF(V) intercepted and shot down one Judy,[2] a second broke through cloud and dived on *Illustrious*, who took 'radical avoiding action.' The aircraft was in sight for about ten seconds in which time *Illustrious'* gunners shot away its port wing and part of the tail. The starboard wing-tip passed through a radar aerial cage above the compass platform, spinning the aircraft into the sea close aboard on the starboard side abreast the funnel, where its bomb exploded. The blast destroyed two Corsairs ranged on the flight deck and lodged a rubber dinghy – unexpected equipment for a suicider – on the ship's transmission aerials, but caused no casualties amongst the ship's company. Portions of the pilot's anatomy were blown on board; part of the skull and the eye-balls were picked up on the flight deck and the Captain's Secretary,

[1] Frances: Japanese Navy Yokosuka twin-engined torpedo bomber.
[2] Judy: Japanese Navy Yokosuka single-engined dive bomber. Reconnaissance.

commanding a pompom crew, was horrified to find a piece of 'bacon', a sliver of burned human flesh, sticking to the gunsight.

Almost immediately afterwards the Seafire which had been pursuing the suicider was shot down by the gunfire of the fleet. The pilot, S/Lt. N. V. Heppenstall of 894 Sq., was not recovered.

More enemy aircraft were discovered skirting the fleet. A Jill was shot down by Corsairs from *Illustrious* and a Judy by Hellcats and Corsairs and the gunfire of the 4th Destroyer Flotilla. Another unidentified aircraft was hit and seen in flames on the horizon and was also credited to the 4th Destroyer Flotilla.

Although no use was being made by the enemy of the Sakishima Gunto airfields it is almost certain that some aircraft of the 8th Air Division passed north of TF 57 on their way to Okinawa. Admiral Nimitz had already signalled to his operational commanders to 'expect all out enemy reactions'. Off Okinawa the ships of the Expeditionary Force were enduring the first massive Japanese airborne retaliation. 660 aircraft, 355 of them suiciders,[1] had launched the first of ten massed attacks in the picturesquely-named 'kikusui' or 'floating chrysanthemum' campaign.

The *kikusui* attacks began at about 1500 on 6th and lasted intermittently for two days. Fighters from TF 58 and from Admiral Turner's TF 51 shot down some 380 of the attackers but sheer weight of numbers overwhelmed the defence. The initial blow fell on the radar picket destroyers. *Bush* and *Calhoun* were both sunk. Two ammunition supply ships were sunk in the Kerama anchorage, leaving 10th Army short of certain types of mortar ammunition for most of the campaign. In all, six ships were sunk and twenty-one damaged including the carrier *Hancock*, which was knocked out of the battle line.

On 5 April the C-in-C of the Japanese Combined Fleet had signalled to the fleet: 'I order the Special Sea Attack Force to carry out on Okinawa the most tragic and heroic attack of the war.' This force, commanded by Vice Admiral Seiichi Ito, consisted of the giant battleship *Yamato*, the light cruiser *Yahagi* and eight destroyers. They had embarked 7,000 tons of fuel, all that had been allotted to the Navy for the defence of Okinawa, and sailed on 6 April, committed to what was nothing more than a kamikaze sortie on an Homeric scale, in aid of the defences of Okinawa. After firing their last shell the ships were to be beached, and the ship's companies were to join General Ushijima's forces.

---

[1] 660: 406 from 5th Air Fleet, 209 from 6th Air Army, 45 from 8th Air Division. Of the 355 suicide aircraft, 230 were Navy, 125 Army.

The Special Sea Attack Force was first reported on 6th by the US submarines *Hackleback* and *Threadfin*, on patrol off the east coast of Kyushu, as it cleared the Bungo Strait. It was sighted again on the morning of 7th by reconnaissance aircraft south-west of Kyushu. TF 58 was then some 250 miles south-east of *Yamato*, off the Amami Gunto. Between 1000 and 1030, 380 dive-bombers and torpedo-bombers were launched in three strikes. *Yamato* had no air support and her predicament oddly resembled that of *Prince of Wales* and *Repulse*. *Yamato* capsized and sank at 1425, after five bomb and ten torpedo hits, taking with her Admiral Ito, Captain Ariga and all but 269 of her company of 2,400. *Yahagi* and four of the destroyers were also sunk; the four remaining destroyers, two badly damaged, reached Japan. TF 58 lost ten aircraft and sixteen aircrew. This Battle of the East China Sea was the Imperial Japanese Navy's last action at sea in the Pacific.

Admiral Rawlings and his fleet had followed these events 'with admiration and at the same time, it must be admitted, with envy'.[1] For TF 57, 7 April had been what might be described as a routine day off the Sakishima Gunto. The Japanese had once more filled in the bomb craters and made the airstrips serviceable. Three Avenger strikes were launched against Ishigaki, Hirara and Nobara airfields: 'all runways in the islands were left well cratered and unserviceable. All visible aircraft had been attacked and there was no activity on any airfield.'

However, the day cost the fleet three Corsair pilots, whose deaths in their respective ways illustrate combat conditions of the time. Lt. A. H. Churchill, RNZNVR, a gallant and experienced New Zealand pilot of 1833 Sq., had been expressly warned to make only one, or at most two, strafing runs on Ishigaki airfield. He made a third, and was shot down by flak; it could be that he lost his life through overconfidence or foolhardiness.

The death of S/Lt. H. Marritt of 1830 Sq. was a cautionary tale. The ground-strafing Corsair pilots had discovered from experience that arracks in what they called 'Hendon Air Display style', flying in 'high, wide, handsome and *dead*', were suicidal against the Japanese gunners on Ishigaki and Miyako. He survived longest who flew lowest, with the propellor a yard from the ground, not from any spirit of bravado but for self-preservation. At Hirara, for instance, the safest

---

[1] Supplement to *London Gazette*, p. 3295.

approach to the airfield was through the town, below roof-top level. Marritt was flying in a flight led by a very experience ground-strafing pilot, Lt. P. S. Cole, Senior Pilot of 1830 Sq. when he 'raised his head above the sheets', rising momentarily above the roofs of Hirara. At once a Japanese shell smashed through Marritt's windscreen and decapitated him.

S/Lt. J. H. Burns of 1836 Sq. was lost in unexplained circumstances from the fleet CAP. He was reported to have lost his way and ditched. He was sighted in the water about seventy miles from the fleet by an American Privateer, who dropped dinghies and circled above until relieved by Fireflies. *Urania* was sent to the sighting position and found Burns, but he was already dead. There was a possibility that his death was due to oxygen failure. The accident caused some misgivings and the fighter pilots' faith in air-sea rescue waned to some extent after the loss of Roberts [on 1st] and Burns. The most careful and conscientious arrangements were made for rescue, but they were not infallible.

On the evening of 7th, TF 57 withdrew and set course for fuelling area Cootie, while US carriers from TF 52 covered the Sakishima Gunto. The fleet refuelled in good weather from 8 to 9 April. The tanker group included reinforcements, the Canadian-manned cruiser HMCS *Uganda* and the destroyers *Urchin* and *Ursa* who had completed docking at Manus. *Gambia* also rejoined, having towed *Ulster* to Leyte.

TF 57's original programme had called for two more strike days on the Sakishima Gunto, on 10 and 11 April, and then a return to Leyte for replenishment. However, on 9th, Nimitz proposed that TF 57 attack airfields in Formosa instead.

The task of neutralising the airfields in Formosa had been assigned to General MacArthur's South-west Pacific Air Force. Nimitz and MacArthur, both considerable personalities, were not intimate friends. British officers who served in the Pacific have remarked that the two commanders were waging what almost amounted to separate wars and passing between their respective war theatres was like crossing the frontier between two autonomous feudal kingdoms. Many of the aircraft oppressing the Allied fleets off Okinawa were undoubtedly staging through Formosan airfields, but despite Nimitz's repeated requests for action, the South-west Pacific Air Force had so far paid them very little attention.

Admiral Spruance agreed with Nimitz' suggestion and signalled to Rawlings to cancel his Sakishima operations for 10th and 11th and to strike at Schinchiku and Matsuyama airfields in Formosa instead, in an operation codenamed ICEBERG OOLONG.[1]

To TF 57, this was a welcome change. By now the whole fleet was weary of the very names Ishigaki and Miyako. As for the aircrew, the patterns of the towns and airstrips of the Sakishima Gunto seemed likely to be imprinted on their brains for ever.

The flying-off position for OOLONG was thirty miles south-west of Yonakuni Shima, where TF 57 arrived early on 11 April, only to find continuous low cloud at 1,000 feet, intermittent rain and drizzle, with visibility sometimes reduced to a mile. TF 57 reversed course, hoping that the weather would improve but when meteorological reports showed similar weather over Formosa, the operation was postponed for twenty-four hours. Admiral Vian had considered launching a small Ramrod hoping they would find Schinchiku, but 'their return journey would be a considerable gamble and surprise lost'.[2]

The next day the weather had improved and two strikes of Avengers with strong fighter escort were launched at 0715 arriving over their targets just after 0900. 820 Sq. and 857 Sq. bombed Schinchiku successfully; there was no enemy fighter opposition, but intense and accurate flak. At Matsuyama, 849 Sq. and 854 Sq. found their target weathered in by cloud and, making a circuit out to sea, attacked their alternative target of Kiirun harbour from the north. Docks, shipping, and a chemical plant were bombed, whilst Hellcats and Corsairs strafed a factory, railway station and lines, shipping at Tansui, and destroyed a bridge near Matsuyama. S/Lt. D. Maclachlan, of 849 and his crew[3] failed to return from the Matsuyama strike.

At 0920 two Fireflies of 1770 Sq. piloted by Lt. W. Thomson, RNVR, and S/Lt W. P. Stott, RNVR, who were flying CAP for an American Marine 'Dumbo'[4] aircraft off Yonakuni Shima, surprised a flight of Sonias and in what Admiral Vian described as a 'brilliant little encounter'[5] shot down four Sonias[6] and damaged the fifth.

Meanwhile, the fleet fighters and direction teams were enjoying their best day of the year. *Indefatigable*'s Seafires began by splashing a Zeke from a group of four at 0704. Later, Corsairs from *Illustrious* jettisoned

---

[1] Oolong: a kind of China tea.
[2] Supplement to *London Gazette*, p. 3297.
[3] Observer: S/Lt. D. McAleese, RNZNVR; Air Gunner: Ldg. Airman G. Claughan.
[4] 'Dumbo': air–sea rescue aircraft.
[5] *Action This Day*, p. 180.
[6] Sonia: Japanese army single-engined bomber.

their drop tanks to chase a shadowing Dinah from 19,000 feet down to sea level and destroyed it at 1115. At 1410 a second Dinah escorted by two Oscars escaped the CAP but at 1530 a Hellcat pilot, S/Lt. W. H. I. Atkinson, RCNVR, shot down a Zeke north-west of the fleet.

But the most competent performance was to come. The enemy sortied from Ishigaki that evening and the fleet CAP intercepted. In a brisk action lasting ten minutes, three Hellcat pilots Lt. D. M. Langdon, RNVR, and S/Lts. W. Fenwick-Smith and W. M. C. Foster, RNVR, shot down four Oscars and a Tony[1] – Fenwick-Smith being personally credited with two of the Oscars. One Hellcat was badly damaged in this combat and the pilot, S/Lt. J. D. S. Smithwick, RNVR, was killed attempting to land on *Indomitable*. Meanwhile, Corsairs from *Victorious* and *Illustrious* shot down a Val[2] and another Oscar. Fourteen enemy aircraft were destroyed in the air that day, and one on the ground – a Tess[3] at Matsuyama. Earlier, S/Lt. A. T. Millard, RNVR, of 1833 Sq. was forced to ditch a few miles north of Formosa while escorting a strike. Although Dumbo aircraft searched for the rest of the day, Millard was not sighted.

That evening, Admiral Rawlings received signals showing that the Allied fleets off Okinawa were under very heavy air attack. He reached a characteristic decision.

'I came to the conclusion during the evening that we must contrive to remain for a further period; even if we could do little more than occasionally strike at the Sakishima Gunto, we should anyhow provide an alternative target to take some of the weight.'[4]

Admiral Vian fully agreed with the suggestion. It was decided that if losses over Formosa the next day were light, TF 57 would contrive a fifth strike period off the Sakishima Gunto.

A second *kikusui* attack had been timed to coincide with a counter-attack by the Japanese 32nd Army in the southern half of Okinawa. The Marines were steadily advancing up the northern half but in the south the American 24th Corps advance had lost momentum on the approaches to the Japanese defensive stronghold of Shuri. The front line stretched from Machinato in the west to Tsuwa on the east coast. On the night of 12/13 April, the Japanese 62nd Division attempted to

---

[1] Tony: Japanese army Kawasaki single-engined fighter.
[2] Val: Japanese navy Aichi single-engined dive bomber.
[3] Tess: Japanese navy reconnaissance aircraft.
[4] Supplement to *London Gazette*, p. 3298.

penetrate the Allied lines by infiltration and to spread out in the rear areas as far north as Futema. The attack was a failure and was over by dawn on 14th. At sea, despite their hideous losses – TG 51 alone claimed 147 Japanese aircraft shot down – kamikaze pilots sank the destroyer *Mannert L. Abele*, damaged the battleships *Idaho* and *Tennessee* and ten other ships.

Friday 13 April began with another self-inflicted tragedy for TF 57. At 0540, before dawn, a group of four bogeys was detected and one Val dive-bombed *Indomitable* but missed, having first confidingly switched on navigation lights and fired a recognition cartridge (which was incorrect). A second Val was shot down by gunfire of the Fleet. Four Hellcats had been launched but they were too late to intercept and were ordered to stay clear. Three did so, but the fourth flew low across the centre of the fleet. In the darkness it was mistaken for an enemy and shot down. The pilot, Lt. Thurston, was killed. An hour later, a second group of bogeys was detected twenty-five miles to the north-west. The CAP intercepted and S/Lts. G. S. P. Salmon and D. A. Baldwin, RNVR, of 1830 Sq. shot down two Zekes.

The Avenger strikes were flown off at 0645 and incredibly – because they were made by the same aircraft, on the same targets, at the same time of day as before – they met no enemy fighters and no aircraft were lost. Runways and installations at Schinchiku and Matsuyama, a petrol dump, barracks and a ceramic factory north-west of Matsuyama were all bombed. The fighters strafed a variety of targets including grounded aircraft at Giran and Major Hay 'caught a passenger train which was skulking in a tunnel but rather carelessly had left the engine sticking out'. Fireflies flying CAP for a Dumbo aircraft rocketed and destroyed the radar station at Yonakuni Shima.

In the evening Admiral Spruance signalled his appreciation of TF 57's co-operation and initiative, and accepted Admiral Rawlings's offer of two more strike days on 16th and 17th. It is possible that the real respect Admiral Spruance and the 5th Fleet had for the British fleet began with this offer.

The same day, the fleet was grieved and shocked to hear the news of the death of President Roosevelt. On 14th, Admiral Rawlings ordered colours to be half-masted for the last hour before sunset.

'Since United States ships do not, I understand, fly their colours in the operational areas and the half-masting of our colours at sea in war is I believe only done when convoying or burying the deceased, the position was not clear as regards TF 57. I felt it fitting, however, and in keeping with what I knew to be the feeling of the Fleet for this great leader and sincere friend of the British Empire, to mark the occasion irrespective of precedent.'[1]

British officers serving with the American fleet noticed, with the great shock and grief, an extraordinarily ambivalent, almost schizophrenic attitude towards Roosevelt amongst some of their American colleagues. The American career naval officers, the 'Academy men' who had attended Annapolis, were Republicans almost to a man and could be relied upon, if they voted, to vote the straight GOP ticket. Roosevelt the President, and C-in-C of all American armed forces, commanded their whole loyalty and respect. But Roosevelt the Democrat politician, the 'renegade aristocrat' and architect of the New Deal, was an object of suspicion, dislike, and even hatred. It was a curious situation, which had no counterpart in the Royal Navy.

After recovering aircraft, TF 57 disengaged to the south-east to replenish. At midday, as the fleet retired, Hellcats intercepted three Zekes forty miles to the north and *Victorious*' Corsairs chased a Dinah escorted by Tojos, but all the enemy aircraft escaped in cloud. TF 57 had completed ICEBERG OOLONG without serious loss – much to Admiral Spruance's relief. He later told Admiral Vian that 'he had kept his fingers crossed the whole time'.[2]

TF 57 met the Logistics Support Group in area Cootie early on 14 April and began fuelling. In the evening *Illustrious* escorted by *Urania* and *Quality* sailed for Leyte and, ultimately, for the United Kingdom. *Formidable*, newly arrived from England, had been brought forward to relieve her. *Illustrious*' two Corsair squadrons had been operational since December 1943, a more than reasonable time. The ship herself had legacies of the underwater damage she had suffered in the Mediterranean and she had increasing difficulty in working up to full speed. *Illustrious* had had a distinguished war. Now, it was time for her to go home.

Formidable (Captain P. Ruck-Keene) was a sister ship of *Illustrious* and had an equally distinguished war record. Her Swordfish had hit *Vittorio Veneto* and crippled the heavy cruiser *Pola* in the action against the Italian fleet off Cape Matapan in March 1941. She was badly damaged by Luftwaffe dive bombers in the battle of Crete and, like

[1] Supplement to *London Gazette*, p. 3298.
[2] *Action This Day*, p. 179.

Illustrious, had been repaired in the United States. After serving with the Eastern Fleet in 1942 she had provided air cover for the 'Torch' convoys and in October 1943, with the Home Fleet, she and the American carrier *Ranger* made successful strikes on enemy shipping off the Norwegian coast. She had also taken part in the landings in Sicily and at Salerno. She was equipped with one squadron of eighteen Avengers (848: Lt. Cdr. T. G. V. Percy) and two squadrons of eighteen Corsairs (1841: Lt. Cdr. R. L. Bigg-Wither, RNVR, and 1842: Lt. Cdr. A. McG. Garland, RNVR).

TF 57 completed refuelling and replenishment on 15 April and at 0600 next day was back on its old pitch off the Sakishimas for a two-day programme of strike and CAP which all by now knew by heart. The Japanese too, were obeying routine: all craters had been filled in and all airfields were serviceable again. Four escorted Avenger and Firefly strikes were launched on 16th against Ishigaki and Miyako airfields, and three more on 17th against Miyako only, where the craters had been filled overnight. All airfields were well cratered and left unserviceable. In the afternoon of the 16th, the fleet fighter direction teams were mystified by a series of fast-moving but erratic bogeys which disappeared while they were being intercepted. They were almost certainly piloted flying bombs, called Okha (cherry blossom) by the Japanese and Baka (foolish) by the Americans, which the enemy were already using off Okinawa. These had been launched from the parent aircraft at long range and run out of fuel short of the fleet. On 16th, *Indomitable* lost a Hellcat pilot, Langdon, who had been so successful four days earlier, shot down over Ishigaki; and Lt. S. C. Barnet, RNVR, and his crew[1] whose Avenger was hit by a 20 mm. shell over Hegina. However, that afternoon Lt. Cdr. Godson and S/Lt. E. J. Hawkins, RNVR, both of 1844 Sq., shot down a Myrt[2] just as it was itself stalking and about to attack an American Privateer aircraft.

As 'new chums', *Formidable*'s air group were eager to show what they could do, but 1842 Sq. made the worst possible start with the loss of their CO Lt Cdr. 'Judy' Garland, shot down by flak while flying CAP over Ishigaki on 16th – his first operational day in the Sakishima Gunto. On 14th, while *Illustrious* and *Formidable* were in company, Lt. Cdr. Tritton, CO of 1830 Sq. had flown over to *Formidable* with 'a child's guide to our operations in the Pacific',[3] intending to warn the

---

[1] Observer: S/Lt. D. W. Baker, RCNVR; Air Gunner: PO L. A. Mellard.
[2] Myrt: Japanese navy Nakajima single-engined reconnaissance aircraft.
[3] A. M. Tritton. Letter of 1.8.68.

newcomers of what to expect. There is the suspicion that Garland may not have taken Tritton's well-meant and hard-won advice sufficiently to heart. *Formidable* also lost an Avenger of 848 Sq. on 16th which crashed in the sea close inshore off Hirara town. The observer, S/Lt. J. B. Gass baled out but the pilot and air gunner[1] were lost. With a fighter CAP overhead, *Victorious'* Walrus landed on the sea and picked up Gass, whilst actually under Japanese small arms fire from shore.

At 0609 Corsairs intercepted a group of bogeys to the north-west and S/Lt. Hemingway of 1836 Sq. shot down a Zeke. Later at 1627, a larger group were detected at 110 miles to the west; Hellcats intercepted at fifty-five miles and two Zekes were splashed. These were the last three enemy aircraft shot down by TF 57 in ICEBERG ONE.

Rawlings had intended the fleet to withdraw after the strikes of 17th, and indeed a withdrawal seemed overdue. No replacement aircraft had been supplied since 9th April, and there was a critical shortage of fighters. The fleet had suffered no dramatic daily loss of aircraft, as in the Palembang strikes, but there had been a steady wastage of aircraft and aircrews. *Victorious*, for example, had left Ulithi with forty-three Corsair pilots and seventeen Avenger crews, and now had only thirty-one Corsair pilots and fourteen Avenger crews fit for flying.

It was reasonable for TF 57 to withdraw now. But in the matter of striking at the Japanese neither Rawlings nor Vian were reasonable men. Admiral Spruance was delighted to accept their offer of yet another strike day, on 20 April. And so, after refuelling in area Mosquito One on 18th and 19th, and receiving reinforcements of destroyers,[2] TF 57 approached the flying off position for the sixth strike period.

The recipe was as before. Four escorted strikes of Avengers were launched with Fireflies carrying rockets. Every airfield on both islands was bombed and strafed and all runways were put out of action except those at Hirara which were 'only partially cratered'. One Avenger of 848 Sq. crashed in the sea off Ishigaki; the crew were picked up twenty-four hours later by an American 'Dumbo' aircraft. In the evening, TF 57 set course for Leyte.

It was a bad time to leave the operational area. On 16th, when the 77th Infantry Division assaulted the off-shore island of Ie Shima, the Japanese mounted a third *kikusui* attack. The destroyer *Pringle* was sunk, the battleship *Missouri* hit twice and the carrier *Intrepid* so

---

[1] Pilot: S/Lt. D. R. Whitehead, RNVR; Air Gunner: PO A. Irvine.
[2] 7th Destroyer Flotilla: HMAS *Napier* (Captain D.7), HMAS *Norman* and HMAS *Nepal*. *Undaunted* also rejoined.

badly damaged she was withdrawn to Pearl Harbour. The American fleet was losing ships to kamikaze attack almost every day. On land the Marines had secured the north of Okinawa. In the south, 24th Corps were poised for an assault on the outer defences of Shuri. The attack began on 19th and after eight days 24th Corps had advanced 1½ miles against bitter resistance. The Japanese fought to the last man and had to be smoked out of their hiding holes and defences with mortars, grenades and flame-throwers. American casualties on Okinawa had reached a daily figure of nearly 1,000 men killed or wounded. It was indeed an unfortunate time for the British fleet to leave. But there was no help for it. There was only one British carrier squadron and temporarily it had shot its bolt.

TF 57 arrived at San Pedro Roads, Leyte, on 23 April with no further incidents except the somewhat bizarre one of an epidemic of mumps in *Gambia* who reached Leyte with forty-five cases on board. Since leaving Ulithi TF 57 had been continuously at sea for thirty-two days, longer than any other British fleet since Nelson's day. It had spent twenty-six days off an enemy coast-line and had completed twelve strike days in which the fleet had lost nineteen of its aircraft to flak and another twenty-eight operationally; sixteen pilots and thirteen aircrew were killed or missing. The air groups had flown 2,444 sorties on strike days, had dropped 412 tons of bombs and fired 325 rocket projectiles. For this expenditure in men, aircraft and ammunition, TF 57 had destroyed thirty-three enemy aircraft in the air and twelve on the ground, not including probables. They had denied the enemy the use of the Sakishima airfields, certainly by day. Best of all, they had proved that a British fleet had been well worth sending to the Pacific. Perhaps the final word on this first phase of ICEBERG may be left to Admiral Rawlings himself, in a wry little poem he wrote on the bridge of *King George V*, one night at sea off the Sakishima Gunto:

Like rooks at eventide the CAP comes in;
Hushed in the carriers is the engines' hum;
Throaty and raucous the loudspeakers call
The Sailor-man to his belated rum.

Ashore, the Habu, from his sun-warmed rock
Creeps to his rest. The town of Ishigaki
Turns from 'Flash Red' to what is left of bed
And, where the Gods are good, a bowl of saki.

Far to the North the evening sky is rent
With gun and bomb flash, tracers red and green;
Let Task Force Fifty-Eight keep at it, we
Shall have, I trust, no bogies on our screen.[1]

[1] Reprinted by permission of Lady Rawlings.

Chapter Five

ICEBERG TWO

Somewhere off the Gunto, Ishigaki way,
BPF patrolling . . . in a desultory way.
Stand by for Kamikaze heroes . . .
Kamikaze . . . K.

King George V Wardroom Song[1]

AT Leyte, the fleet had a more successful repair and replenishment
period than at Manus. The climate was marginally more comfortable,
there was less swell and the fleet did not suffer from its lack of fenders.
The ships were also anchored nearer each other, although distances
were still so great in that large anchorage that boat coxswains caught
out by sunset had difficulty in identifying their own ships amongst the
interminable lines of darkened silhouettes. But in many ways the fleet
was still hampered by familiar deficiencies. There was a shortage of
boats, although all shore leave had been stopped to conserve capacity.
The fleet relied on American help; in terms of the quantities carried,
more than half of the fleet's boats were loaned by the Americans. The
extra strike days off the Sakishima Gunto had delayed the fleet's arrival
at Leyte by a week; much of the perishable food for the fleet went bad
before it could be issued. The British floating docks were still on
passage to Leyte and dockings were carried out in American docks.
As at Manus, there was a shortage of fresh water.

The Fleet Train, of which there were now some sixty ships at Leyte,
headed by the repair ships *Resource* and *Artifex* and the destroyer depot
ship *Tyne*, set about the necessary repairs and maintenance of the fleet.
Their biggest task was the repair of battle damage to *Indefatigable* which
was completed in six working days, so that she sailed fully operational.
In that climate and with the amount of work to be done, there was not

---

[1] To the tune, approximately, of *Lili Marlene*.

much rest or recreation for the men of the fleet. Admiral Rawlings wrote:

'The heat and the lethargic effect of the climate, which being drier was not quite so marked as at Manus, made conditions very trying for personnel employed between and below decks on maintenance, boiler cleaning, etc. Much work of this type had to be done at great speed and personnel concerned did well. Office work, occasioned by the inevitable influx of correspondence after such a long period at sea, was no less trying. There was in fact little time for rest or relaxation for officers or ratings during this period and after a day or two most of us, I feel sure, wished ourselves back at sea again.'[1]

Admiral Rawlings noted that the liberty men could not get ashore to the beer, so he authorised the beer to be brought to them. Beer was issued to the fleet at 1s. 3d. Australian per 1⅓ Imperial pints, on the scale of one can per man per day. The carriers set up 'beer gardens' on their flight decks in the evenings and the Captains of all ships reported that there were no 'scenes' (although 'scenes' were hardly likely on one can of beer for each man).

On arrival at Leyte, Admiral Rawlings called on Admiral Thomas Kinkaid, Commander of the US 7th Fleet, and to his dismay discovered that the BPF's future was once more in the balance. Admiral King wished to invoke the 'seven days' notice' reservation clause and to allocate all or part of the British fleet to the South-west Pacific Area in support of the forthcoming Allied assault on Tarakan in Borneo on 1 May,[2] sailing from Leyte on 15 May. This proposal was resisted by Admiral Nimitz and Admiral Spruance and of course by Fraser and Rawlings. General MacArthur and Admiral Kinkaid were persuaded against it and in a signal on 27 April the proposal was finally cancelled. But it had been an alarming experience which aroused Admiral Fraser's doubts as to who exactly was his operational superior. He was justified in writing that 'this chaotic and nearly calamitous state of affairs arose because there was no supreme commander in the Pacific'.

At 0630 on 1 May Task Force 57 sailed from Leyte ('like giants refreshed', as Rawlings signalled to Fisher) to take part in ICEBERG again. Task Force 57 consisted of:

[1] Supplement to the *London Gazette* of 2 June 1948, p. 3303.
[2] The 26th Australian Brigade Group landed on Tarakan on 1 May, covered by the US 7th Fleet. The town and airfield were captured by 5th, but resistance did not end until 24 June. The 9th Australian Division landed at Brunei on 10 June and secured it by 1 July.

1st Battle Squadron (TU 1)
King George V (Flag of CTF 57 – BS 1), *Howe*

1st Aircraft Carrier Squadron (TU 2)
Indomitable (Flag of 2nd in Command TF 57 and AC 1), *Victorious,*
Formidable, Indefatigable

4th Cruiser Squadron (TU 5)
Swiftsure (Flag of CS 4), HMCS *Uganda,* HMNZS *Gambia, Euryalus,*
Black Prince

Destroyers (TU 8)
25th Destroyer Flotilla, *Grenville* (Captain D.25) *Ursa, Undine,*
Urchin, Urania, Undaunted; 4th Destroyer Flotilla, *Quilliam* (Captain
D.4) *Queenborough, Quiberon, Quickmatch, Quality;* 27th Destroyer
Flotilla, *Kempenfelt* (Captain D.27) *Whirlwind, Wessex.*

Illustrious, Argonaut, Wager and *Whelp* remained at Leyte and sailed
for Sydney for refit on 4 May.

On 3 May an Avenger ranged on *Indefatigable's* flight deck fired 100
rounds from its forward gun which penetrated to a cabin near the
quarterdeck, killing S/Lt. J. A. R. MacIntyre, RNVR, an observer of
1770 Sq., and wounding two pilots, including the Senior Pilot. The
accident demonstrated that the price of survival was eternal vigilance
in an operational carrier, but it was a dismal start for *Indefatigable's*
Firefly squadron.

At 0600 the same day TF 57 kept a rendezvous with the Logistic
Support Group[1] in area Mosquito and cruisers and destroyers topped
up with fuel. *Uganda* fouled a hose round a propeller whilst disengaging
from a tanker, but shallow water divers succeeded in clearing it. By
1530 fuelling had been completed and TF 57 was once :nore on its
way to the operational area, for a second period of strikes against the
Sakishima Gunto airfields.

Whilst refuelling, the fleet heard the news of the deaths of Hitler and
Goebbels. The war in Europe was clearly in its final throes, but news
from 'the other war' had little impact upon the men of the BPF;
Ishigaki and Miyako were once more only just over the horizon.

On 4 May the first CAP was flown off at 0540 from a position seventy-
five miles south of Miyako Shima. There was much enemy air activity
around the Sakishima Gunto and the first bogey of many that day
was detected at 0545. Some replacement pilots had joined the fleet

[1] *Crane, Avon* and *Whimbrel,* with RFAs *San Ambrosio, San Adolpho* and
Cedardale.

at Leyte and two of them, two young Hellcat pilots, S/Lts. W. G. Batham and R. E. Thomas, RNVR, made what sports writers would call a 'dream début' by intercepting and shooting down a Zeke on their first operational flight from *Indomitable*.

The American TF 52 had been covering the Sakishima Gunto in TF 57's absence and although they had left only the previous day, some runways had already been repaired overnight. Two bomber strikes, totalling forty-seven Avengers, with Fireflies and fighter escort were launched against Hirara and Nobara at 0605 and against Ishigaki and Miyara at 0815. Weather and visibility over both targets were excellent but the flak was heavy and accurate; one Avenger of 857 Sq. was hit and crashed into the sea after bombing Ishigaki and Miyara. The pilot, S/Lt. M. G. Dee, RNVR, and his air gunner PO L. B. Denton were both killed.

That morning a single bogey, flying too high for the CAP to reach it, was detected to the west. The fleet opened fire in blind control but the enemy reconnaissance aircraft was not sighted and retired untouched. It had to be assumed that the enemy had now found TF 57.

Admiral Rawlings had been considering the chance of bombarding the airfields on Miyako, to reduce the AA batteries there. The Avengers' bombs had had very little effect on them and the violence of the strike's reception that morning showed that the gunners of Ishigaki and Miyako were as lively and as accurate as ever. It was 'jolly bombarding weather' – wind, sea and visibility were all good. Then there was the question of morale. The ships of TF 57 were hot, uncomfortable and over-crowded. Except for those actually engaged in flying operations, it was proving to be a dull war. The fleet had a minority who had all the excitement, and a great majority who could do nothing except wait, work and keep watch. A bombardment would hearten all hands. The fleet had almost certainly been detected but 'that in itself was nothing strange, and had happened several times before without being followed by any attack'.[1] Admiral Rawlings decided to go ahead. This decision was probably his first, and only, major miscalculation in his handling of the fleet. Admiral Vian concurred with the decision, and afterwards reproached himself.

'I was not sufficiently alive to the effect on our defensive system which would be caused by the temporary absence of the radar sets and anti-aircraft armament of the battleships. The Japanese were.'[2]

---

[1] Supplement to the *London Gazette*, p. 3305.
[2] *Action This Day*, p. 185.

The bombardment force, consisting of *King George V, Howe, Swiftsure, Black Prince, Euryalus, Gambia* and *Uganda,* screened by the 25th Destroyer Flotilla, detached at 1000 and steamed northwards to close Miyako Shima at 24 knots. The carriers provided CAP above the force, and spotting aircraft. At 1155 the bombardment force was on its bombarding course and speed, 070° at 15 knots, steaming some eight miles off the south coast of Miyako Shima, and opened fire at 1205.

The first ships had hardly opened fire when a signal was received from Admiral Vian: the carriers were under attack, *Formidable* had been hit by a suicide bomber and her speed reduced to 18 knots. Mr David Divine was on the admiral's bridge of *King George V.*

'I was with Rawlings that awful morning when the carriers were attacked, when he had left the carriers to go into the Sakishima Gunto for a bombardment, which was really a morale builder and nothing else. It was a misjudgement. He reckoned there was no further possibility of kamikaze attack. So we left the carriers without the artillery umbrella, went in, conducted the bombardment. As we turned on the bombardment run, I was sweeping the horizon on the starboard quarter and I saw a dirty great mushroom of blue smoke and that was the first of the kamikaze hits. I was actually standing next to the Flag Lieutenant when the first hit took place. Rawlings came out from behind the screen almost immediately afterwards and joined us. Rawlings was in a considerable state. There *he* was and there *they* were, being hit, and he wasn't there. He was very sober and very quiet about it, but you could see he was deeply moved by the whole thing. So was I.'[1]

Admiral Rawlings instructed the force to speed up the bombardment and possibly the need for haste may have affected *King George V*'s gunners for Lt. Colonel Hay, flying overhead, reported that of those he could see, 'the salvoes were always just missing'. However, photography showed that at least *Howe*'s salvoes had fallen in the target area. *King George V* and *Howe* bombarded Hirara airfield at a range of 25,000 yards, while inshore of the battleships *Euryalus* and *Black Prince* fired 'air bursts' over the AA defence batteries of Nobara. *Swiftsure* and *Gambia,* in a position some three miles off *King George V*'s port quarter, bombarded Nobara airstrip. *Uganda*'s target was Sukhama airstrip. The bombardment was broken off at 1247,[2] and the force turned southwards to rejoin the carriers at 25 knots.

[1] David Divine. Conversation of 21.3.68.
[2] After 195 rounds of 14-inch, 598 of 6-inch, and 378 of 5·25-inch had been fired.

After the bombardment force had gone, the carriers and the remaining destroyers, feeling somewhat exposed, had huddled together for mutual support. Admiral Vian stationed his eight destroyers so that two destroyers were equally spaced between each carrier and on the line between adjacent carriers, to give the best mutual support and clear arcs of fire.

At 1102 a group of bogies was detected to the west at fifty miles. Two minutes later a second group was detected followed by a third at sixty-six miles, and finally there were four groups of bogies on the radar screens. This was a striking force of some twenty-six aircraft, decoys, suicide bombers and their controlling 'Gestapo' aircraft, of the 8th Air Division flying from Giran in Formosa.

Seafires intercepted the first group and at 1120 S/Lts. R. H. Reynolds and R. C. Kay, RNVR, shot down a Zeke 32; five minutes later, Corsairs from CAP intercepted the third group and shot down a Zeke, but three more slipped past and reached the carriers undetected and unobserved and there were no warning bandit echoes on any radar screen within twenty miles when they made their attack.

At 1131 a Zeke dived from a layer of cloud at 3,000 feet on *Formidable*, and was taken under fire by the ship's guns. The suicider flew down the length of the flight deck pulling over to starboard when just clear of the bow, as though it had missed on its first pass; it then flew down the starboard side and half-rolled, banking steeply to approach from astern. Though hit, the Zeke closed the ship at very high speed from the starboard quarter and appeared to jettison its 500 lb bomb immediately before impact.[1]

The bomb detonated on the flight deck abreast the island. The explosion punched a hole two feet square in the armoured flight deck and caused an indentation in the deck ten feet square and two feet deep at its centre. A large splinter of the armoured deck was driven downwards through the hangar, a ventilation trunking and hatch (which was shut), pierced a steam-pipe in the centre boiler-room and finally came to rest in the ship's inner bottom. The watch below in the boiler-room rapidly shut off steam valves before they were scalded alive. The loss of steam reduced the ship's speed to 18 knots, the maximum on the two outer propulsion units.

On deck, one Corsair and ten Avengers in the deck park were wrecked

---

[1] Eye-witness accounts of the kamikaze attacks on *Formidable* on 4 and 9 May 1945 are given in *A Formidable Commission* (Seeley Service & Co. Ltd., 1956), pp. 76–88.

beyond repair. The pilot of one Avenger, which was taxi-ing forward at the time, actually succeeded in getting out of the aircraft, terribly burned and with his clothes flaming, but died on 16 May in the hospital ship *Oxfordshire*. The petty officer directing that aircraft also died of burns seventy-two hours later. In the Air Intelligence Office in the base of the island, one officer was killed outright and another died a few minutes later. All the other occupants were burned and blasted, even one rating who escaped through a scuttle.

Until a few days before the incident, the Air Intelligence Office had been the flight deck sickbay; if the ship's Senior Medical Officer had not farsightedly changed his action arrangements, the flight deck medical team would have been the first casualties. At the time of the explosion *Formidable* had been about to fly off aircraft and the flight deck was crowded with pilots, observers, and aircraft handlers. The total casualties were eight killed and forty-seven wounded, thirteen of them very seriously burned.

The explosion had put all the ship's radar sets except one out of action. Both flight deck barriers were damaged, the forward irreparably. Fierce fires were raging in parked aircraft, in the remains of the Zeke, in firefighting HQ, in the hangar and torpedo shop below, and in flight deck trucks and machinery parked on the starboard side. All the bridge and island superstructure windows had been blown in and paintwork scorched black. Flaming oil and debris had been scattered over the sea around a wide area. The reports of bullets fired from the burning aircraft, the towering column of smoke and steam visible for many miles, and the sound and smell of the fires contributed to one of the most dramatic scenes in the war at sea.

Whilst his ship's company were extinguishing fires, carrying casualties below, and pushing undamaged aircraft clear and wrecks over the side, Captain Ruck-Keene signalled with feeling to the flagship: 'Little yellow bastard.' Admiral Vian made the memorable reply: 'Are you addressing me?'

Indomitable herself was now under attack. At 1134 a second Zeke was seen flying along *Indomitable*'s starboard side. After being engaged by the flagship's guns, the Zeke disappeared into cloud but it soon emerged, diving towards *Indomitable*'s starboard side. The ship was turning to starboard towards the aircraft and the helm was put hard over. This may have disturbed the pilot's aim, for the Zeke flattened out, made a form of 'deck landing' across the flight deck and bounced over the port side where its bomb exploded in the sea alongside the ship. The pilot's

right hand, some ornamental combs and other sentimental gewgaws
were blown on board, with some documents describing the social life
led by special attack pilots before their final flights. These were later
read with great interest by Captain Eccles, who was himself a qualified
interpreter in Japanese.

Eight minutes later, another Zeke dived on *Indomitable* but was hit
and shot down by gunfire from the flagship and from *Quality*, crashing
in flames some thirty feet off *Indomitable*'s starboard bow. *Indomitable*'s
damage from kamikaze attacks was minor, but very inconvenient. As
flagship she was the only carrier in TF 57 fitted with a superior type
of American air-warning radar set. It was put out of action and because
of spares shortage not repaired for some time.

But with or without *Indomitable*'s master radar sets the carrier fighter
direction teams, led by Captain E. D. G. Lewin in the flagship, kept
their interceptions 'in the groove' all day. Japanese aircraft continued
to approach and continued to be shot down: at 1220 a Jill by *Indomitable*'s Hellcats; at 1252, a Val by two of *Indefatigable*'s Seafires; and
at 1725, in a brisk interception and action which lasted only six minutes,
three Seafires piloted by Lt. A. S. MacIeod, RNZNVR, S/Lt. D. Challik,
R.NETH.N., and CPO Pilot B. Bird shot down three Zeke 52s out of a
group of four, while *Victorious*' Corsairs shot down their controlling
'Gestapo' aircraft, a Judy.

Shortly afterwards, *Formidable* accidentally shot down a Hellcat
which was returning for an emergency landing. The pilot was fortunately rescued unharmed by *Undaunted*.

Admiral Rawlings and the bombardment force returned at 1420, to
find the carriers grimly licking their wounds. *Formidable* had extinguished
her fires, and the work of repairing the hole in the flight deck with steel
plates and quick-hardening cement was progressing. Hand jury blocks
and tackles were rigged to work the one remaining barrier. By 1300 the
ship was capable of 24 knots, and by 1700 Captain Ruck-Keene was
able to signal that *Formidable* could land on her aircraft (which had
been dispersed to other ships). Armoured flight decks made the British
carriers hot to live and work in, and reduced the number of aircraft
they could carry, but there was now no doubt that they were the best
means of survival against a kamikaze hit; without armour there would
now have been no British carrier squadron in the Pacific. Even the
most sceptical Americans were convinced. Shortly after the kamikaze
had crashed Captain Ruck-Keene seized the arm of his US Liaison
Officer, Lt. Cdr. B. van D. ('Ben') Hedges, USNR, in a grip of iron.

'What do you think of our flight decks now?' he roared, in a voice 'like a fog-horn in the mating season'. 'Sir,' answered Ben, 'they're a honey.'[1]

With the day's strike programme completed, and because of the reorganisation that was required with *Formidable*'s flight deck out of action, TF 57 began to retire to the southeastward during the afternoon. At 1820, *Victorious*' Corsairs from the CAP intercepted a bogey to the north and shot down a Zeke. So ended the day.

The enemy had pressed home their attacks with great skill and determination, making intelligent use of cloud cover, decoys, and variations of height. It appeared that the first attacking force of Zekes had flown very low until they were within twenty miles of the fleet and had then climbed steeply before making their attacks.

Four of *Formidable*'s Corsairs remained overnight in *Victorious* as 'non-paying guests'. When the first CAPs were flown off on 5 May, this flight led by Lt. P. Clarke, RNVR, intercepted a high snooper at 0920 after a chase of 300 miles and 108 minutes. S/Lt. I. Stirling, RNZNVR, shot down the intruder, a Zeke, from 30,000 feet – in Admiral Vian's words, 'What a splash!'

After the eventful day before, 5 May was something of an anticlimax. The airstrips of Ishigaki and Miyako were all bombed again and all left unserviceable. Three aircraft were destroyed on the ground. The strikes reported no flak over Miyako, so Admiral Rawlings was consoled that his bombardment at least had had the right result. TF 57 retired towards the replenishment area after flying off two Avengers with fighter escort, to Yontan on Okinawa, with press material and David Divine and Captain Anthony Kimmins, the fleet's Press Liaison Officer. These were the first British aircraft to land on Okinawa in the campaign. They arrived in the midst of an attack on the airfield by Japanese suicide troops but managed to transmit, by US Radio, the first information of the fleet's doings since leaving Leyte.

Compared with the highly polished and organised press facilities of the United States Navy,[2] press arrangements for the British Pacific Fleet were comically amateurish. Since the sending of a British fleet to the Pacific had been primarily a political inspiration, and since much of the gesture's significance would be lost if nobody knew the fleet was there, it might have been thought that especially careful and thorough

---

[1] *A Formidable Commission*, p. 82.

[2] Some Americans actually became self-conscious about their own expertise in press relations. See William Brinkley's amusing book *Don't Go Near The Water* (Cape, 1957).

arrangements would have been made for press coverage of the fleet's activities. In fact, Admiral Rawlings and his staff received no special instructions about press facilities. There was at first no means of transmitting press copy at sea, and the first party of correspondents accredited to the fleet were misdirected and almost missed the fleet on sailing. On arrival in their assigned ships the press were understandably tetchy. Some of them were rude to Admiral Rawlings and he replied very competently in kind. A few correspondents even filed stories making personal attacks on Admiral Rawlings. It was no wonder that when Kimmins reported personally to Rawlings in *King George V* he 'found a man fuming with rage and indignation, and constructive conversation was for the moment out of the question'.[1] Admiral Rawlings took some time to be placated and indeed he was to the end guarded and suspicious of the press. Although he managed some working relationship with the Admiral, David Divine frankly regarded his own assignment to the flagship as being 'fed to the lion'.[2] Rawlings's Flag Lieutenant described his admiral's attitude to the press – 'No brighter red was ever shown to a fiercer bull!'[3]

The press themselves were by no means blameless. Many of the war correspondents were experienced men at the top of their profession,[4] who had a great affection and respect for the Service and who had served with the Navy faithfully through all the disasters and triumphs of the war at sea. These men knew their job and asked only some co-operation and reasonable facilities to be allowed to do it. But there were some others, of whom Admiral Rawlings wrote with unusual bitterness after the war:

'. . . His Majesty's Ships out here (already overcrowded) have had to put up with a considerable number of second class people living in the wardroom for weeks at a time. I can think of but two who were in any way acceptable to their messmates, and I shall remember the bulk as types concerned with nothing but getting in a sensational story ahead of their competitors, who looked on their ships as hotels, and who had little or no conception that they were onlookers at considerable happenings.'

[1] *Half Time*, by Anthony Kimmins (Heinemann, 1947), p. 264.
[2] Divine. 21.3.68.
[3] Geoffrey Cook (ex-Lt. RNVR). Letter of 23.8.67.
[4] Kimmins particularly mentions A. D. Divine of Kemsley Press, A. J. McWhinnie of the *Daily Herald*, Astley Hawkins of Reuters, Stanley Maxted of the BBC, John Loughlin of the *Melbourne Argus*, and Graham Stamford of the *Daily Mail*. *Half Time*, p. 264.

Admiral Fraser was well aware of the vital importance to his fleet of good press relations and he and his Chief of Staff made strenuous efforts to improve facilities. But although matters did improve, slowly and slightly, the problem of transmitting press copy from ships at sea was almost insurmountable and as Evans Lombe admits 'quite honestly, the plain fact is that we never really solved it properly'.[1]

The kamikaze attacks on TF 57 had been the fringe of another massed *kikusui* on Allied shipping off Okinawa. This fifth massed attack,[2] of 125 suicide aircraft had been timed to coincide with the Japanese 32nd Army's counter-attack on 4 May. The counter-attack plan had been opposed by Colonel Hiromichi Yahara, Ushijima's senior staff officer (operations), who had also opposed the earlier attack on 12 April and who generally played the part of a kind of Quintus Fabius Maximus Cunctator of Okinawa throughout the campaign. Yahara advised a policy of attrition, to make the Americans pay for every knob and knoll of Okinawa, but his caution was overruled and the militant arguments of the Chief of Staff, Lt. Gen. Isamu Cho, persuaded Ushijima.

Every Japanese soldier was instructed to 'kill at least one American devil' and the attack was launched after a massive artillery bombardment north of Shuri at dawn on 4 May. By midnight on 5th the main attack in the centre and the two simultaneous sea-borne landings behind the American lines had all ended in utter failure. The Japanese 24th Division suffered 5,000 casualties. Every tank used in the attack was destroyed and the magnificent Japanese artillery, which had been deployed in the open for the first time in the campaign, was badly battered. General Ushijima declared, with tears in his eyes, that henceforth he would be guided by Yahara's opinions.[3]

TF 57 met the Logistic Support Group[4] in Area Cootie at 0630 on 6 May and spent the day and the next refuelling and taking on replacement aircraft. The US Task Group 52.1 covered the Sakishima Gunto.

Bomber strikes on Ishigaki and Miyako and a bombardment of Ishigaki had been planned for 8 May. Admiral Rawlings intended to take extra precautions for this bombardment: the 5·25-inch cruisers

---

[1] Vice Admiral Sir Edward Evans Lombe. Conversation of 8.11.67.
[2] The 2nd, 3rd, and 4th, of 185, 165, and 115 aircraft respectively, had been on 12–13, 15–16 and 27–28 April.
[3] See *Okinawa: The Last Battle*, by Roy E. Appleman, James M. Burns, Russell A. Gugler and John Stevens (Washington, 1948) for an excellent account of the whole campaign.
[4] *Crane, Ruler, Striker, Napier, Norman, Nepal, Avon, Whimbrel, Pheasant,* and RFAs *Wave King, Wave Monarch, San Ambrosio, San Adolpho* and *Cedardale. Napier* joined TF 57 vice *Kempenfelt* with defects.

would stay with the carriers and the whole carrier force would follow closely behind the bombardment force, remaining just out of range of land radar echoes while the bombardment took place. However, the first CAPs of 8th had difficulty in finding the islands in the very bad weather. Meteorological reports showed that Formosa was also closed in by cloud and rain. In these conditions the enemy was not likely to make use of the Sakishima airfields and the day's operations were cancelled, although CAPs were kept up. In the evening visibility shut down completely in heavy continuous rain. The last CAP of the day were guided back to their carriers by searchlight. The fighters landed on in driving rain after an anxious time of searching for the fleet at sea-level.

On 9 May, when victory in Europe had been proclaimed and the United Kingdom given over to celebration, the British Pacific Fleet was engaged in another furious battle against suicide bombers. Four bomber strikes, two on each island, were launched with a total of seventy-three Avengers, with rocket-carrying Fireflies and fighter escort. Lt. D. Cameron, of 1834 Sq., failed to return from one strike. All runways were cratered again, motor vehicles and grounded aircraft were shot up. At 1145 CAP fighters drove off but could not catch a high snooper to the west. TF 57 had been discovered again.

That afternoon, at 1645, a group of five low-flying bogeys was detected to the west, range twenty-eight miles. Six minutes later four Seafires intercepted fifteen miles from the fleet and shot down one Zeke, but in so doing allowed themselves to be drawn away from the remaining four Zekes. As Admiral Vian commented 'their foolishness . . . cost the fleet dear'. The Zekes evaded another flight of intercepting Seafires and at 1650 closed the fleet at high speed.

It was Admiral Vian's normal practice to manoeuvre the carrier squadron continuously under helm while an air attack was in progress. The fleet had just made a large alteration to starboard when a Zeke 52 was sighted from *Victorious*, descending through scattered cloud at 3,000 feet, range three miles. The suicider was taken under fire and hit but dived over the starboard quarter and crashed on the flight forward, abreast 'B' 4·5-inch turrets; the Zeke appeared to release a small white parachute when about 300 yards from the ship. The explosion of the 500-lb bomb holed the flight deck and put the catapult, one 4·5-inch gun and one of the forward lift hoisting motors out of action. The fire was quickly extinguished. A few minutes later a second Zeke approached *Victorious* in a shallow power glide from astern. The Zeke was well hit by *Victorious'* close range weapons and set on fire but carried through its attack and landed on the flight deck aft before skidding over the side. There was no explosion but in its flaming passage across the flight deck the suicider damaged one arrester wire unit, destroyed an anti-aircraft director, and wrecked four Corsairs parked on deck. A minute later *Victorious* was threatened a third time when a Zeke made a pass at the ship and then appeared to shift target to *Howe*, next in line ahead, approaching her over the starboard quarter. The Zeke was taken under fire by *Howe*, *Victorious*, and *Formidable* and, hit some way out, burst into flames, flew over *Howe*'s quarterdeck and crashed in the sea a hundred yards beyond.

The fourth and last kamikaze, probably a Zeke or Jill, with overload fuel tanks under each wing, approached *Formidable* from dead astern, flying along the ship's fore and aft line at a height of about thirty feet above the water. The suicider was hit repeatedly by *Formidable* and by *Indomitable* but dived into the aircraft parked aft on the flight deck. The weapon was a 250-lb bomb or heavy shell which only partially detonated on impact, but once again *Formidable*'s flight deck was swept by flame and explosion. Six Corsairs and an Avenger were destroyed, and two Corsairs damaged. The scene on deck was as it had been five days before, one of burning wreckage, figures of firefighting crews running through a column of fire and smoke, against a background of a blackened and scorched island superstructure (which had just been repainted). The explosion blew out a rivet in the flight deck plating and burning petrol fell in to the hangar below, starting a fire which was extinguished by spraying the hangar. Four more Avengers and eight Corsairs were damaged by flame and water. An aircraft wheel hurled by the bomb blast decapitated one rating on the flight deck and several others were wounded, but casualties were much lighter than on 4 May, possibly because of the ship's company's naturally increased agility about the flight deck after their earlier experiences, but more probably because of an improved 'kamikaze approach' alarm system of klaxons and warnings.

Formidable's ship's company reacted with remarkable resilience. All fires were out within fifteen minutes and at 1755, less than an hour after the attack, Captain Ruck-Keene signalled that his ship could land on aircraft. Furthermore, he claimed that his gunners had shot down one of the enemy. The courage and steadiness of the gunners in exposed positions under kamikaze attack was outstanding, as Admiral Vian noticed: 'With the suicide planes screaming straight down at them and seemingly bound to burst amongst them, the guns' crews remained serving their guns undismayed, but for which fact more kamikazes would have scored direct hits. On board *Indomitable* their coolness filled me with admiration. Reports from the other ships of the squadron told the same tale.'[1]

There was an element of personal threat in the kamikazes which had been absent in naval warfare since the days of boarding and hand-to-hand fighting. Those who had served in the Mediterranean had become expert at judging the flight of bombs, which of course followed a predictable path once they had left the aircraft. But a kamikaze could turn again and become a threat even though it had apparently passed the ship. Most eye-witnesses are agreed that they were sure, at the time, that the suicide pilot intended to immolate himself upon them personally. Since the attacks in April some men in exposed flight deck positions had taken their own measures for self defence; in *Victorious* Captain Denny noted that a number of ratings who normally resided unarmed in flight-deck edge pockets and who had their hair lifted by the close passage of the suicider had provided themselves with Bren guns, suitably mounted. However, some of *Victorious*' ship's company failed to take a more elementary precaution; the two suicide attacks on 9 May caused casualties of three killed and nineteen wounded, four of them seriously, and *Victorious*' Medical Officer afterwards reported that some of the casualties had not been wearing proper anti-flash clothing.

One important part of the fleet's defences against kamikaze attack were the 'Y' Groups: small parties of specially trained officers and men, normally embarked in the flagship, who monitored enemy radio transmissions, particularly those from the 'Gestapo' aircraft controlling and directing groups of kamikazes. In 1942 when the Japanese were carrying all before them, it had been realised in the Admiralty that there was a serious shortage of Japanese linguists. At that time the Japanese themselves looked upon their own language almost as a secret code, not to be vouchsafed to outsiders. A number of university graduates were selected to undertake intensive joint service courses in either spoken or written Japanese (it was considered too great a mental burden, in the time available, to learn both). 'Y' parties were first embarked for the OUTFLANK series and served in the Pacific until the end of the war. Whenever there was enough enemy radio traffic, they were able to give valuable intelligence information. One 'Y' Officer served in *King*

---

[1] *Action This Day*, p. 186.

George V during ICEBERG, and in *Formidable* for the July–August operations off Japan:

'Both of them were fairly strenuous times, *KGV* probably more because it was the longer period. There was an insufficiency of linguists in those days and one did have to do much longer stints of work; three days on and twenty-four hours off, and even that twenty-four hours could sometimes be broken. I had a staff of a sub-lieutenant and six ratings. The heat in our little *hell-hole* almost directly under the Admiral's sea-cabin was intense, with all the ports battened down. We listened out on the Japanese broadcasts. They had particular frequencies, which you had to search for, but that wasn't very difficult because you knew what you were looking for. I don't think they knew they were being monitored. Sometimes you were foxed, but very often they spoke in clear, and particularly that was true of the kamikazes. We used to get their target and full operational orders. The 'Gestapo' aircraft used to give them directions as to what to attack and where to attack, with positions and simple orders, such as aircraft carrier *there*, at such and such a position, number one will attack that. They used to give heights and compass directions, speeds, even the weather. All of which helped enormously. The 'Gestapo' aircraft then went home. Sensible man.'[1]

TF 57 emerged from the attacks of 9 May with four carriers still intact, but the state of their air groups and flight decks caused some reorganisation of the programme. *Victorious* could only operate a few aircraft at a time, because of the damage to her forward lift. *Formidable* had only four Avengers and eleven Corsairs serviceable. Admiral Rawlings and Vian agreed that the fleet must withdraw for the time being, to fuel, 'sort out and make good damage, etc.', and return to the operating area on 12 and 13 May.

While the fleet was refuelling and replenishing in Area Cootie One on 10 May,[2] Admiral Rawlings held a flag officer's conference in *King George V*, Admiral Vian and Admiral Brind (CS 4) both attending. Clearly the enemy had changed their tactics to very low-level attacks which made them difficult to detect and intercept. New counter-measures had to be devised. It was decided to move the flying-off position further to the east, and to station two radar pickets, one to the

---

[1] Rt Hon. John Silkin, PC, MP (ex-Lt. RNVR). Conversation of 30.10.67.
[2] Tanker Group: *Speaker, Ruler, Nepal, Crane, Pheasant, Whyalla, Ballarat, Woodcock* and tug *Weasel*, and tankers *Arndale, Aase Maersk, Dingledale* and *San Amado*.

north-west and the other to the south-west, each twelve miles from the fleet. The pickets would consist of one 6-inch gun cruiser and a destroyer, with an overhead CAP of two fighters which could be augmented at the first threat. The 5·25-inch gun cruisers *Black Prince* and *Euryalus* would be taken from the screen and positioned in the main body of the fleet to reinforce the fleet's close-range AA fire-power. The kamikazes had shown a marked tendency to attack the carriers from astern. One 'counter kamikaze' or 'KK' destroyer was detailed to steam close astern of each carrier. But the most effective surface defence against air attack was for the fleet to close its ranks and bring the maximum concentrated fire-power to bear upon the attacking aircraft. It was decided that when an air attack threatened the fleet would close in until the major units were only a mile apart. Earlier, this might have hampered the carriers' landing and take-off circuits, but the air groups were now considered skilled enough. Finally, all commanding officers were impressed with the vital need for their guns crews to take kamikaze aircraft under fire at the earliest possible moment because once a suicide pilot had committed himself to his final dive there seemed no way of stopping him. So far, several kamikazes had been hit, and hit hard, but not one had failed to complete its dive. TF 57 simply did not have the weight of AA fire-power physically to break up the aircraft in flight.

Replenishment was completed in the afternoon of 11 May. Before dawn on 12th, TF 57 was in its new flying off position, one hundred miles south-east of Miyako Shima. The four 'KK' destroyers and the two radar pickets, *Swiftsure* and *Kempenfelt*, and *Uganda* and *Wessex*, were all in position. The first CAPs and Avenger strike were off at 0540, twelve minutes before sunrise. Despite the efforts of TG 52.1.3 in TF 57's absence, several runways on Miyako and Ishigaki were still serviceable. Four Avenger strikes, one against Ishigaki and three on Miyako, were launched to recrater them. A total of ninety-nine offensive sorties were flown by Avengers, Corsairs, Hellcats and Fireflies during the day; barracks, AA gun positions and grounded aircraft were bombed and strafed. Lt. Cdr. M. S. Godson, CO of 1844 Sq. was shot down by flak while on a bombing and target CAP mission over Hirara airfield. He had been specifically warned against flak but he was a most experienced aviator and no Hellcat pilot in the fleet knew the gun dispositions of Miyako better. It may have been a case of a pitcher going too often to the well. He was the fifth squadron commander to be shot down since the fleet's formation. Two Avengers were forced to ditch during the day but both crews were picked up, one by *Kempenfelt* (in

spite of being given a ditching position one hundred miles in error)
and the other by USS *Bluefish*.

The next day, 13 May, airstrips were again found to be serviceable
and four more Avenger strikes were flown, three to Miyako and the
fourth to Ishigaki. One hundred and two offensive sorties were flown,
runways cratered, barracks, buildings, radio stations, barges and storage
dumps were bombed, strafed and set on fire.

At 0948 on 13th, there was a most unusual occurrence. A possible
submarine contact was reported close to the fleet. Three destroyers
with a CAP of four Corsairs were detached to hunt and at 1203 attacked
a possible contact with depth-charges. Two Avengers were flown off
on anti-submarine patrol and a third, armed with depth-charges,
assisted the destroyers but the contact was not confirmed and it was
improbable that the contact was a submarine, indeed there is no record
of any genuine attack by a Japanese submarine on any unit of the fleet
at any time in the Pacific. It was an amazing omission on the part of
the Japanese Navy, and a lucky escape for the fleet and its train:

'To me the most astonishing part of the whole operation was the complete failure of the enemy submarines to attack our oilers and fleet
train, upon which everything depended. Whilst on passage a collection
of slow but valuable repair and supply ships was wont to steam at ten
knots, screened by half a dozen small minesweepers. What would the
U-boats have done to such a target?'[1]

It is easy to imagine the effect a few competent submarine commanders
would have had on the British Pacific Fleet and its train, committed
to moderate speeds and almost steady courses during replenishment.
The fleet's line of communication, always fragile, would have disintegrated. The resources of personnel and fuel which the Japanese devoted
to kamikaze operations, including *Yamato*'s last sortie, might have been
more profitably invested in submarines.

Also on 13 May, *Indefatigable* suffered a private trial – a wardroom
messman's nightmare: an acute epidemic of gastro-enteritis broke out
amongst the officers. At the peak of the epidemic fifty-five of the ship's
pilots and observers, and twenty-seven other officers including the
majority of the fighter direction team, were all unfit for duty. Nevertheless, *Indefatigable* still succeeded in flying off twenty-three Avenger and
six Firefly sorties, and forty-eight Seafire CAP sorties during the day.

[1] Rear Admiral William Weston (then Captain (E), Staff Engineer Officer to
RA(D)). Letter of 9.1.68.

On land, the battle for Okinawa was now well behind schedule. Colonel Yahara's delaying tactics, and heavy rainfall in the latter half of May, brought the American advance almost to a standstill. Around Shuri the Japanese were making brilliant use of mutually supporting defensive positions with interlocking arcs of fire. One such position, known as Sugar Loaf Hill, west of Shuri, held out for nearly a month. Every assault on it was thrown back by supporting fire from adjacent hills. Those adjacent hills could not themselves be assaulted because of supporting fire from Sugar Loaf. Another position to the east of Shuri, Conical Hill, was taken and retaken several times by the American 96th Division before it was finally secured at the end of May. The bloodiest fighting on Okinawa took place on features with these simple 'nursery rhyme' names, such as Sugar Loaf, Chocolate Drop, Strawberry Hill. The irony evidently struck Tokyo Radio, in a broadcast in English to the American troops on Okinawa:

'Sugar Loaf Hill . . . Chocolate Drop . . . Strawberry Hill. Gee, those places sound wonderful! You can just see the candy houses with the white picket fences around them and the candy canes hanging from the trees, their red and white stripes glistening in the sun. But the only thing red about those places is the blood of Americans.'[1]

The stubborn Japanese defence on land had a direct effect on Allied losses at sea. The Allies still had not enough airfields on Okinawa to base the aircraft needed to give 10th Army complete air protection. The balance of air cover was provided by the 5th Fleet. The Fast Carrier Task Force was thus forced to remain offshore, within effective range of a suicidally inclined shore-based enemy air force for many weeks. The Force had not been designed or intended for this role and the 5th Fleet continued to be battered by suicide bombers, which launched two further *kikusuis* on 11–12 and 24–25 May, besides almost daily attacks by individuals or smaller groups of aircraft. Already, in April, Admiral Mitscher had rearranged the Fast Carrier Task Force in three instead of four task groups, because of losses to the kamikazes. On 11 May his flagship *Bunker Hill* was hit twice and the Admiral transferred his flag to *Enterprise*, but she too was hit two days later and Mitscher was forced to transfer a third time to *Randolph*. The fleet commander's flagship had also been under fire; Spruance's first flagship the cruiser *Indianapolis* was hit by a kamikaze on 31 March, and his new flagship the battleship *New Mexico* was hit on 13 May.

[1] Quoted in *Okinawa: The Last Battle*, p. 343.

However, the kikusuis were inevitably a wasting asset. As one American admiral remarked, there could be no such thing as an experienced suicide pilot and indeed some of the later special attack pilots had received such rudimentary flying training that they could not navigate and could barely land their aircraft. The later raids contained successively fewer aircraft. Their tremendous losses, with bombing of the Kyushu airfields by B-29s from the Marianas and strikes by TF 58, began to have their effect. Admiral Mitscher suggested that land-based air forces were now strong enough to hold their own and the carriers could retire. Admiral Spruance, cautious and shrewd as ever, rejected the proposal and it was as well he did, for the kamikazes returned in force on three more occasions, 27–28 May, 3–7 June and 21–22 June, to inflict still more losses on Allied shipping off Okinawa.

TF 57 met the Logistic Support Group[1] in Area Cootie on 14 May, and during this replenishment Admiral Rawlings exchanged signals with Admiral Spruance concerning TF 57's future. The fleet expected to take part in the operations off Japan beginning in July (the 'seven days' notice' clause had, it seems, been tacitly abandoned) which were the preliminaries to the landing in Kyushu (Operation OLYMPIC) planned for November. The fleet was due for major replenishment, some ships at Manus and the main body in Australia, early in June. Apart from the enormous work-load of storing and preparing the fleet for another extended period in enemy waters, repair of battle damage to the carriers would obviously take some time. Admiral Rawlings therefore proposed that TF 57 complete its strikes on the Sakishima Gunto on 25 May, but, if losses were light, it could undertake two more strike days on 28 and 29 May. Admiral Spruance replied on 15 May, as the fleet was completing replenishment, that it would not be necessary to cover the Sakishima Gunto after 25 May. TF 57 now had a date to look forward to.

The aircrews were by now feeling the strain of battering away at the same targets for day after day, against anti-aircraft gunners who were still unsubdued and in constant shooting practice. Apart from flying time, pilots spent many hours sitting in their cockpits under a hot sun, 'at readiness'; it was not unknown for a pilot to be in his cockpit for a total of ten hours in one day. The standard of flying had noticeably deteriorated. Watchers on the flight decks and islands had their hearts in their mouths as veteran fighter pilots who normally took pride in

---

[1] *Ruler, Crane, Woodcock, Pheasant*, RFAs *Arndale* and *Dingledale, Striker, Nizam*, RFAs *Wave King* and *Wave Monarch*. The Hospital ship *Tjitjalengka* was also in position some eighty miles east of the replenishment area.

their expertise, but who had now 'lost their art', flung their aircraft on
to the deck with no regard for technique or finesse. The Avenger crews
had also lost their edge. Lt. Cdr. Foster, CO of 849 Sq., was concerned
that his Avenger crews were showing definite signs of strain. Their
flying, and especially the accuracy of their bombing, was deteriorating.
Squadrons had had no chance for collective training. Replacement
aircrews had had to fit themselves in and pick up the routine as best
they could, with the result that after a period of continuous operations
without any training period the air groups consisted largely of veterans
who were past their prime and replacement aircrews who had never
properly settled down. In *Indefatigable* the squadrons first embarked
in June and July 1944 were beginning to show signs of strain and
tiredness. Many of the Firefly and Avenger crews had taken part in a
number of operations off Norway in July, August and September and
in all the operations since leaving England; they were reaching the state
when Captain Graham thought they should be rested. Commanding
officers of ships and squadrons, and ship's medical officers, were ever
on the look-out for symptoms of 'twitch': young pilots who had lost
their gaiety, pilots who were beginning to drink too much or, oddly,
writing many more letters home; or pilots who were argumentative
and resentful at briefings, with an aversion to the deadlier of the two
islands – 'It's not my turn to go to Ishigaki again'.

The American carriers had the same problem but solved it by replac-
ing entire air groups after four to six months combat flying. They
preferred to use inexperienced but fresh air groups rather than continue
with aircrew who were battle-hardened but 'over the hill'. The British
fleet did not have the resources for replacements on this scale.

In spite of the heat and tedium of the Sakishima Gunto operations,
the fleet's morale had remained reasonably high. After years of serving
in scratch forces, scraped together from the few ships available and
often with no air cover, the men of the BPF had the comfortable
knowledge that at last they were on the side of the big battalions – and
they were to have this comfortable feeling trebly reinforced in July,
when they met the United States Third Fleet at sea off Japan. Mail
deliveries, so far from home, were regular and swift. Many ships had
their own newspapers or news-sheets and later the BPF had its own
newspaper *Pacific Post*, which was edited by Captain Kimmins, printed
in Australia and distributed to the fleet on the scale of one copy to
every five men. On board, there were film-shows, deck-hockey, and
tug-of-war on the upper deck, and in the evenings many ships ran

their own internal 'radio stations' over the ship's loudspeakers, with brains trusts, quizzes, sketches, record request programmes and other material devised and produced by the ship's company.

Food in the ships was almost all dehydrated or tinned, and tended to be monotonous. A staple of the fleet's diet was dehydrated potato, served in a variety of ways – mashed, cubed, boiled, roast, fried; when *Indefatigable*'s Chief Cook was awarded the DSM, the ship's company were convinced it was for his ingenuity as 'Distinguished Spud Maker'.[1] *Indomitable*'s ship's company were less charitable; in one of the ship's 'Suggestion Boxes' one correspondent wondered whether it was Their Lordships' intention that *Indomitable* should return to the United Kingdom with 'a skeleton crew'.

The only serious threat to morale, and then in only one ship, arose from circumstances outside the fleet's control. In April the Canadian Government, evidently wishing to act democratically, had announced that only officers and men who specifically volunteered to fight against Japan would be sent to the Pacific after the surrender of Germany. This naturally caused uncertainty and unrest in the cruiser *Uganda*, the only Canadian-manned ship in the BPF, and Captain E. R. Mainguy, RCN, remarked that there was 'a tremendous amount of talk on the messdecks and speculation regarding the outcome of the "non-Volunteering act". The latter has been and remains our only major problem'. Despite inducements of increased pay and special leave, 605 ratings (or more than two-thirds of the ship's company) did *not* volunteer to serve in *Uganda*, or elsewhere in the war against Japan. Although *Uganda* had thus voted herself out of the war, Admiral Fraser succeeded in retaining her with the fleet until a relief could arrive.

In the second half of ICEBERG, there was an unlooked-for improvement in the performance of the Seafires. In March and April, the Seafire deck-landing accident rate had been seven out of every hundred. In May, it had dropped to less than two in every hundred. This was due to better flying conditions in May; the fitting of more robust tyres; some changes in the Deck Landing Control Officers; and, most of all, fresh pilots. At Leyte inefficient or fatigued pilots in both Seafire squadrons had been replaced by 899 Sq. pilots, although this replacement had been opposed by 899 Sq. CO, Lt. Cdr. G. Dennison, RNVR, who objected strongly and quite understandably to his squadron being

[1] Chief Petty Officer B. J. Wilcock. Letter of 15.10.68.

dismembered and fed into the battle 'piecemeal'.[1] It was a sign of changing times that no Seafire pilot was lost operationally in the second half of ICEBERG.

When TF 57 returned to the operational area on 16 May, there were signs that the enemy were at last weakening and making much less use of the Sakishima airfields. Enemy air activity was light or non-existent, and grounded aircraft as targets for strafing were very rare (in fact no enemy aircraft destroyed on the ground was officially credited to TF 57 after 9 May).

The Japanese gunners, however, were quite uncowed by the continual attacks on their positions. The Avengers met heavy flak opposition on 16th and several were damaged. One Avenger of 820 Sq., whose single 1600-lb bomb hung up on the first run over Ishigaki, had to run the gauntlet of the AA batteries again:

'We came down, dropped the bomb (I felt it go this time), and I saw some tracer gunfire from a small wooded area at the end of the runway – I was jigging and twisting and kept low to keep up speed. Then I caught the smell of cordite. I thought at first, foolishly, that it was from the ground fire, but suddenly the air gunner, PO Pearce, said: "We've been hit and I think the observer's hurt."

'The air gunner had a job to get out of his turret position but he soon reported that Tanky (S/Lt. D. M. James, RNVR) had been hit at the back of the knee by an explosive bullet. I spoke to Tanky once, almost as soon as I heard he'd been hurt. He said "Never mind, Dickie, we got a direct hit." They were his last words to me.

'The bullet put our radio out of action. The intercom was working. I had no note of the ship's rendezvous and certainly had long forgotten how to do DR navigation. I couldn't pick up the Beacon. So I had to catch up with the squadron quickly.

'They were still in sight, and still completing the complicated job of reforming aircraft from several carriers. I caught up with Denis Bellham in the outside position of our squadron and zogged (sent a morse signal with my clenched fist) to say "Observer wounded". I mimed to tell him I had no radio and he should guide me quickly back to the fleet and *Indefatigable*. He made a couple of calls to the Wing Leader and the ships, then broke away, leading me at top speed back to the ship.

'Meanwhile, I can only imagine the horror that was in the back of the aircraft. PO Pearce injected morphine, his own and Tanky's, from

[1] George Dennison. Letter of 16.7.68.

the emergency packs, and I passed mine back to him. He reported that Tanky was losing blood and I asked if he could possibly apply a tourniquet with a scarf or anything at all at hand.

'I believe that we took about fifty minutes to get back to the fleet. Suddenly it came in sight, a huge fleet which as we got nearer, seemed to stretch from horizon to horizon. I realised that this huge fleet was turning into wind for us. Then from one of the carriers came a green Aldis lamp flash – "land on straight away" – and they were timing it exactly so that I could land on as soon as the turn was complete.'[1]

PO Pearce succeeded in fixing a tourniquet during the flight, which had the professional approval of the ship's Medical Officer, but sadly James died of his wounds later that day.

Five bomber strikes were flown during the day, three of them at Miyako where the flak was heaviest. The airfields, by now strewn with a litter of burned-out wrecks of aircraft and dummies, were recratered, shipping offshore strafed, 'four lorry loads of Japanese troops were exterminated', and there was a large explosion, possibly an ammunition dump, in Ohama town on Miyako.

On the forenoon of the next day a series of deck crashes in *Victorious* succeeded where the kamikazes had failed and put her temporarily out of the battle line. A Corsair piloted by S/Lt. K. W. Hardiman, RNVR, making an emergency landing, tore out two arrester wires, crashed through both barriers and fell in flames over the port side. Hardiman, the Assistant Flight Deck Officer Lt. W. A. L. Banning, RNVR, and Stoker PO E. H. Groves of the flight deck engineer officer's party were killed, and four others wounded. Two Corsairs and an Avenger in the deck park were damaged. Two jury barriers had been rigged by 1145 but the second aircraft to land on after they had been erected bounced in the gap left by the two missing arrester wires and demolished one barrier. The other was destroyed in a deck landing crash early in the afternoon. *Victorious* again had no barriers, and twenty of her aircraft had to be distributed amongst the other carriers, but by the evening *Victorious* had once more rigged two jury barriers and some of her aircraft were able to return.

Meanwhile, two strikes had been flown to Miyako and one to Ishigaki. Besides the routine cratered airfields and strafed shipping, a number of Japanese soldiers were discovered; 'their names', Admiral

[1] Mr Richard Douglas-Boyd (ex-Lt. RNVR). Letter of 15.10.68.

Rawlings commented drily, 'will in due course be recorded in Yasakuni Shrine'.

TF 57 met the Logistic Support Group[1] on 18 May and during the forenoon a Corsair in *Formidable*'s hangar accidentally fired its guns into a neighbouring Avenger, which exploded and started a serious fire. The heavy fire-resistant curtains, which were designed to isolate the hangar into sections for just this emergency, had been damaged during the suicide attack and could not be lowered. The fire was only put out after prolonged spraying of most of the hangar. Flame, water and cannon shells cost the ship seven Avengers and twenty-three Corsairs, left in various states of unserviceability from complete 'write-offs' to 'flyable duds'.

Disasters and defects in the fleet carriers were now beginning to accumulate. *Victorious*' damaged forward lift still hampered her flight deck operating cycle and her makeshift barriers would not bear any more barrier crashes or enemy damage. *Indomitable* had a defective stern tube bush on her centre shaft and could not make full speed except in emergency; several ships in the fleet required urgent repairs to boiler brickwork. *Formidable* had sustained two kamikaze attacks and a serious hangar fire and although emergency lighting circuits were rigged in the hangar and she could once more operate aircraft, there was a case for returning her to Leyte. But Admiral Rawlings rejected the idea. *Victorious*' fragile barriers might be put out of action at any time and *Formidable*'s extra flight deck would then be vital. Having so newly arrived, *Formidable*'s ship's company might feel that they were being prematurely and unjustly retired from the battle. And so, on 20 May, TF 57 shaped up for its next two days' strikes with four carriers, as usual.

Just after dawn, when the 'KK' destroyers were closing their carriers, the fleet ran into dense fog and *Quilliam* (Captain R. G. Onslow) collided with *Indomitable* whilst taking station close astern of her:

'There, dead ahead, loomed a dark cliff, close but indistinct, through what I now realised was dense fog. "Full astern together! Hard a port!" There was the clang of reply gongs and we sensed the revolutions building up. And then we hit. None of us on the bridge that day will ever forget what our eyes told us was happening. For we saw our stem

---

[1] *Crane, Ruler, Grenville, Chaser, Norman, Whimbrel, Bendigo, Parrett, Weasel,* RFAs *San Ambrosia, San Adolpho, Cedardale,* ammunition supply ship *Robert Maersk.* Hospital ship *Tjitjalengka* was also in operating area, and embarked casualties. *Norman* replaced *Nepal* in TF 57.

cleave straight into *Indomitable*'s side and bury itself back to the muzzle of "A" Gun. We felt so stunned by this apparition, for apparition thank God it was, that we hardly noticed the scream of tearing plates that accompanied it; and it was not until much later that I felt the pain of two broken ribs. Then suddenly all was quiet. We lay dead in the water in a lifeless blanket of fog – alone as the Ancient Mariner, no sound, no sight, no feeling, for feeling was numbed. I stopped the engines. I thought of *Indomitable*. "She won't sink? She can't sink, can she? But I must have almost cut her in half. And where are my bows? I can't have left them in her." So ran my thoughts. And then light dawned as I saw that the forecastle deck, where it ended, was curving downwards. We had hit her in the armour and the flare of her side had deflected our stem downwards and to port: and the rest of the wreckage had followed it out of sight.

'When the fog lifted we were alone in the wide Pacific as the sun rose on a glassy sea. I could hardly believe my ears when I heard on the TBS a message from *Indomitable* reporting no damage. I learnt later that the Paymaster Commander's looking-glass was cracked, and that he was considerably annoyed.'[1]

Quilliam was taken in tow, stern first, by HMAS *Norman* but she was an intractable tow for another destroyer, for her damaged bows acted as an efficient rudder hard to starboard. At 1300 *Norman* was relieved by *Black Prince*, and the tow was later taken over by the tug *Weasel*.

The weather did not improve until 0745, when the first strike of Avengers and Fireflies set off for Miyako. They had difficulty in finding the target but bombed and rocketed Hirara town through a lucky clearance in the cloud. The Acting CO of 1836 Sq., Lt. Cdr. J. B. Edmundson, the fighter pilot who had so engagingly justified his colleagues after LENTIL, was lost to flak while escorting this strike. His Corsair was seen to ditch but Edmundson did not get out.

The second and third strikes were cancelled because of the weather and the outlook for the fourth was 'not promising'. However, Admiral Richmond Turner had particularly asked for evening strikes on the Sakishimas, to reduce the weight of dusk and moonlight attacks by the Japanese on Okinawa. The strike took off at 1530 for Ishigaki but could not find the island in the bad weather and were recalled. It had been a

[1] 'Radar Assisted Collision', by Admiral Sir Richard Onslow, *Naval Review*, Vol. LVII, No. 1 (January 1969). There were no other casualties, apart from Captain Onslow's ribs

L

sad and rather frustrating day, with only 6½ tons of bombs dropped and
twenty-four rockets expended (the daily average being about 54 tons
of bombs and about sixty rockets).

Monday, 21 May, was Admiral Rawlings's birthday and he noticed
an ironic coincidence. On his 16th birthday, forty years earlier, he had
also been in the Far East, as a midshipman in the battleship *Goliath*,
which was on passage to strengthen the China Fleet in case the Russian
battle fleet under Admiral Rojdestvensky should defeat Britain's allies,
whose fleet was commanded by Admiral Togo.

The weather at the flying-off position was not much better than on
the previous day, but four Hellcats flown off at 0600 found clearer
weather to the east and west and improving weather in the north. The
first strike took off at 0655, the first of five launched in the day, three
of them at Miyako. Runways at Hirara, Nobara, Ishigaki, and Myara
were hit, Hirara town, a radio weather station, a tented camp and some
barges were strafed and rocketed. The best performance of the day was
put up by the unobtrusive *Indefatigable* who flew twenty-three Avenger,
fifteen Firefly and fifty-six Seafire sorties during the day, a total of
ninety-four and a daily record for any British carrier in ICEBERG.

At 1445 Hellcats were sent to intercept a high snooper to the west.
The bandit, a Myrt, turned to escape with a 40-knot wind behind him,
while the pursuing Hellcats at lower altitude were faced by a 40-knot
head wind. In spite of this handicap, S/Lt. W. M. C. Foster shot down
the Myrt from 26,000 feet thirty-four miles from the fleet. This was an
excellent interception, the first since 9 May, and the last enemy aircraft
shot down by TF 57 in ICEBERG.

TF 57 replenished in Cootie One on 22 and 23 May[1] and received
reinforcements of the destroyers *Termagant* and *Quadrant* and the
cruiser HMNZS *Achilles*. Signals received from Admiral Halsey, giving
details of the part the British fleet was to play in future operations,
showed that the maximum strength of all four fleet carriers would be
required. Admiral Rawlings decided reluctantly to retire *Formidable*.
She sailed on the evening of 22nd for Sydney, to repair her battle damage,
escorted by *Kempenfelt* and *Whirlwind* who were both due for refit.

For TF 57's final strike period Admiral Rawlings toyed with the
idea of a 'Sayonara' bombardment of Miyako. But with only three

[1] In Cootie One were: *Weasel* towing *Quilliam*, escorted by *Black Prince*,
Grenville, *Norman* and *Ruler*, *Crane*, *Chaser*, *Speaker*, *Napier*, *Avon*, *Findhorn*;
and tankers *Wave King*, *Wave Monarch*, *Aase Maersk*, *San Amado;* and *Robert
Maersk*.

carriers in the line, he put such thoughts behind him. Seven strikes were flown during the two days of 24 and 25 May. There was no enemy air activity, and the same airfields were bombed and the same targets strafed and shot up. On the evening of 25 May TF 57 retired southwards leaving Ishigaki Shima and Miyako Shima without a backward glance. *King George V*, with *Troubridge*, *Tenacious* and *Termagant*, sailed for Guam, the remainder for Manus and thence to Sydney.

TF 57 had been at sea for sixty-two days, broken by eight days at Leyte. They had not sighted an enemy surface vessel at sea at any time. They had completed eleven strike days, and a twelfth (8 May) on which target CAPs were flown but strikes were abandoned. All five carriers taking part in ICEBERG had been hit at least once by suicide bombers. Since leaving Leyte the squadrons had flown 2449 sorties on strike days, had dropped 546 tons of bombs and expended 632 rockets. They had destroyed, in the air and on the ground fifty-seven enemy aircraft – excluding probables – during ICEBERG.

Against that, TF 57 had to set the loss of another six pilots and two aircrew since leaving Leyte; another seven aircraft had been lost to flak and forty-four operationally, i.e. by ditching, suicide attacks, deck landing and other reasons. The total loss for ICEBERG was ninety-eight aircraft: twenty-six to flak and seventy-two operationally. But if the figures include all aircraft rendered non-operational and requiring replacement the actual losses were much higher. An analysis of aircraft requiring replacement, tabled by causes, is interesting:

	Suicide Attack	*Formidable's* Hangar Fire	Combat/ Flak	Deck Landing Accidents	Other Causes	Total
Av	15	7	14	11	18	65
Co	17	23	11	15	18	84
He			6	3	5	14
Se				28	5	33
Fi			2	4	1	7
Total	32	30	33	61	47	203

Thus a Task Force with an aircraft complement of 218 required 203, or 93% replacements. These losses, for fifty-seven enemy destroyed, suggest that the Fleet Air Arm won a somewhat Pyrrhic victory over the Sakishima Gunto. Nevertheless TF 57 had steadily ground down the enemy's capacity to use the Sakishima Gunto airfields and had made a small but not to be despised contribution to the conquest of Okinawa. Admiral Spruance sent the fleet a gracefully appreciative signal and – much more important – concluded in his report of proceedings that the British carrier task force was experienced and competent enough to take its place in the line with the Fast Carrier Task Force in future operations.

While the majority of the fleet was replenishing, Admiral Rawlings formed Task Group 111.2 to carry out an attack on Truk (Operation INMATE), the objects being to reduce the chance of air attack on Allied Forces in the Carolines and also to give battle experience to new units in the fleet. However, the training aspect of INMATE was not stressed in the briefings. 'I never told my pilots it was a training expedition; if you say that, you start losing a few people.'[1]

Flagship for INMATE was the new large carrier *Implacable* (Captain C. C. Hughes-Hallett), the latest reinforcement to the fleet, with a complement of eighty-one aircraft: 21 Avengers of 828 Sq. (Lt. Cdr. F. A. Swanton), twelve Fireflies of 1771 Sq. (Lt. Cdr. W. R. J. Mac-Whirter) and two squadrons of forty-eight Seafires (801: Lt. Cdr. S. Jewers, RNVR; and 880: Lt. Cdr. R. M. Crosley, RNVR).

With ingenuity and some bribery, *Implacable* had solved the problem of the Seafire's short range. The Seafire's normal long-range tank, known as a 'slipper' tank, was designed for ferrying duties, and not for combat. It was unpopular with the fleet Seafire pilots; extending along the belly of the aircraft, it was not easily jettisoned, made the aircraft vulnerable to flak and caused a 'peculiar drag' when landing on a flight deck. Ashore in Manus *Implacable*'s Commander (Air) discovered a dump of Kittyhawk drop tanks. One was fitted experimentally to a Seafire for aerobatic and decklanding trials carried out by Lt. Cdr. Campbell Horsfall, the Seafire fighter wing leader. The trials were successful and the tank actually improved the Seafire's deck landing characteristics:

'We were very sold on these tanks. But where to get them from? With a lot of signalling, we discovered there was a base for Kittyhawks in New Guinea. Quite a long way away. An Australian destroyer came in and I called on the captain, who was the same rank as I was. I asked him what he was doing here and he said he was not really quite sure, he had to stay at Manus for a few days. I talked him into going to New Guinea. Having just come out from England, we had some booze on board. So I gave him one case of Scotch and said, Take the other case

[1] Admiral Sir Charles Evans (then *Implacable*'s Commander (Air)). Conversation of 16.7.68.

and give it to the chap you're going to get the tanks from. He went off
and when he came back his ship was full of these goddam drop tanks.
We transferred them to *Implacable* and they were absolutely everywhere, in every passageway. Everywhere there were tanks. I had two
in my after cabin and I think the captain had some in his. They lasted
us throughout the war. We flew Seafires on every strike and they made
superb fighter-bombers.'[1]

Task Group 111.2 was commanded by Rear Admiral E. J. P. Brind,
flying his flag in *Implacable*, and was organised as follows:

Task Unit One: *Implacable* (Flag of CTG 111.2)
Task Unit Two: *Swiftsure, Ruler, Termagant*
Task Unit Five: *Newfoundland*, HMCS *Uganda*, HMNZS *Achilles*
Task Unit Fifteen: *Troubridge, Tenacious, Terpsichore, Teaser*

The great Japanese stronghold of Truk had truly declined, that a
force of only two carriers, four cruisers and five destroyers should
approach it on a training exercise. This force left Manus on 12 June
and on passage were instructed to carry out a bombardment of Truk
as well as the planned air strikes. *Swiftsure* and *Uganda* had bombarded
Miyako on 4 May, but *Newfoundland* and *Achilles* had no gunnery
experience with the fleet, although *Newfoundland* had recently bombarded Wewak in New Guinea, where Japanese forces were still holding
out. The force therefore practised bombardment procedures on
passage.

On the evening of 13th, *Swiftsure, Newfoundland*, and *Uganda*,
escorted by *Troubridge, Tenacious* and *Teaser*, were designated Task
Unit Three and detached to remain within twenty miles of the flying-off
position and to rejoin the main force when ordered. At dawn on 14th,
the force arrived at the flying-off position, which was eighty-five miles
south-west of Truk, on the edge of an intertropical front, with heavy
rain squalls and gusty winds. Better weather was reported over Truk
and the first CAPs, strike and photo-reconnaissance flights took off at
0540. *Implacable* continued to launch combined strikes of Avengers,
Fireflies with rockets and Seafires used as fighter-bombers throughout
the day. One Seafire was shot down over Moen 2 airstrip and the
pilot, S/Lt. M. H. Payne, RNVR, was lost; an Avenger ditched with
engine trouble, the observer and air gunner being picked up but
the pilot, S/Lt. R. S. Scholefield, RNVR, was killed. The escort carrier

[1] Evans. 16.7.68.

Ruler shared CAP duties with *Implacable* and provided an invaluable spare flight deck in emergency; on one occasion on 15th *Ruler* landed on six of *Implacable*'s Seafires at a time when *Implacable* herself was hidden in a violent rain squall and had aircraft ranged on deck for the next strike. On the night of 14–15 June *Implacable* flew night strikes, with Avengers bombing by the light of flares, for the first time by a British carrier in the Pacific.

The bombardments took place on 15th. The main body met Task Unit Three at dawn some eighty miles east of Truk, where the four cruisers and three of the destroyers detached and closed Truk, the carriers following ten miles astern to provide CAPs. The bombarding force was divided into three, *Newfoundland* with *Troubridge*, *Swiftsure* with *Teaser*, and *Achilles* and *Uganda* with *Tenacious*, the destroyers to put up counter-battery fire and smoke screens if needed. *Implacable* provided six spotting Seafires.

Except for *Newfoundland*'s contribution, the bombardments did not go well. *Newfoundland*'s gunners had no reply from their target batteries and shifted fire to their alternative target, Eten airstrip. In the centre, *Uganda*'s and *Achilles*' combined bombardment of Doublon seaplane base was 'a tale of communication disasters'. Both ships fired thirty rounds per gun at a range of 20,000 yards with no apparent effect. At one time a spotting aircraft mistook their fall of shot for *Newfoundland*'s and his subsequent 'corrections' compounded the confusion and chaos. *Achilles*' gunnery department were enfuriated by maddeningly unhelpful comments from one spotting pilot, e.g. 'There's only one bit of water near the target, and all the shots are going there.' The bombarding force withdrew at 1110 to rejoin the carriers. *Implacable* flew strikes at intervals for the rest of the day.

The harm done to Truk by the raid was not great. Shipping was damaged, a floating dock, harbour installations, radio and radar equipment were bombed and strafed. Two enemy aircraft were destroyed on the ground. The truth was that Truk had already received such devastating attention from the Fast Carrier Task Force that it was no longer a major objective and targets were hard to find. Task Group 111.2 reformed at 0600 on 16 June and arrived at Manus the next day.

When TF 57 retired from the Sakishima Gunto, the battle for Okinawa was by no means over. From 31 May, after the fall of Shuri, the Japanese conducted a skilful and successful retreat to the south of the island, although the pursuing 10th Army were still hampered as much by mud and rain as by the enemy. On 4 June, Ushijima's troops prepared to make their last stand behind the great hill escarpment which ran from Yuza Dake to Yaeju Dake. By 11th the enemy had been driven into three main pockets containing the remnants of 24th Division, 62nd Division and 44th Independent Mixed Brigade respectively, while the naval base force was still holding out near Naha, on the Oroku peninsula. The Allies were beginning to take significant numbers of Japanese prisoners, for the first time on Okinawa and indeed for the first time in the Central Pacific campaign. On 11th, General Buckner called on Ushijima to surrender, as his situation was hopeless, but Ushijima and Cho apparently regarded the message as highly hilarious, a welcome comic relief in a grim struggle. On 18 June General Buckner went forward to an 8th Marine Division observation post in the line, when a Japanese shell burst above him. A coral fragment embedded itself in his chest and he died ten minutes later. Major General Geiger took command of 10th Army until relieved by General Stilwell on 23rd. Yaeku Dake was breached on 17 June and organised resistance on Okinawa ended on 21st. That night Ushijima and his Chief of Staff committed sepporo in a cave facing the sea on Hill 89, near Mabuni on the south coast. The wily Yahara survived and became a prisoner of war. The last resistance on Okinawa ended on 2 July 1945. The Japanese 32nd Army had been killed or taken prisoner to the last man. The Japanese extra-metropolitan air force had been annihilated, losing 7,830 aircraft.

Okinawa proved to have a strategic value beyond all expectations. There were good harbours at Naha and the Kerama Retto and scope for many more airfields,[1] including strips for long-range bombers, although the first raid on the Japanese mainland by Okinawa-based B-29s did not take place until the last evening of the war. 10th Army casualties were 7,203 killed and missing, and 31,081 wounded; the United States Navy, 4,907 killed and missing, 4,824 wounded; Royal Navy 85 killed and missing, 83 wounded. The US Navy also lost 539 aircraft, 36 ships sunk and 368 damaged.

---

[1] So many in fact, that a further phase of ICEBERG, an invasion of Miyako, was cancelled on 26 April.

Chapter Six

THIRD ARAKAN

In modern theatrical parlance, South-east Asia Command would be called the Theatre of Anomaly. Anomalies, oddities, peculiarities and inconsistencies abounded in every aspect of the theatre, in its strategic planning, its command structures, even in its geography.

Strategically, South-east Asia was a mass of illogicalities. No other theatre of the war occupied so much strategic planning time, and in no other theatre did strategic decisions bear less resemblance to actual events in the field.

Geographically, the land war in South-east Asia was fought on the 'wrong' frontier of India. Pre-war strategic planning and communications had been directed towards the north-west frontier and the Khyber Pass. The possibility of a campaign on the north-east frontier, guarded by the high mountain ranges, poor communications, malarial jungles and phenomenal annual rainfall of Burma, had been discounted – until the Japanese 15th Army proved its feasibility in the spring of 1942.

In its command structures, the anomalies of South-east Asia Command were perhaps best personified in the Deputy Supreme Allied Commander, General Joseph W. Stilwell, US Army, known as 'Vinegar Joe'. As Deputy he was responsible to the Supreme Commander Admiral Mountbatten and through him to the Combined Chiefs of Staff. But he was also Chief of Staff to Generalissimo Chang Kai Shek, and thus responsible to him. But he was also Lease-Lend Administrator for China and Commanding General of the US forces in the China–Burma–India theatre, and thus directly responsible to the US Joint Chiefs of Staff. Finally, when General Stilwell took over the operational command of forces in the Northern Combat Area Command he was theoretically under the command of Lord Mountbatten's army C-in-C, General Sir George Giffard, but as Deputy Supreme Commander himself he was technically Sir George Giffard's superior. Thus General

Stilwell's personal position could well be summed up in the words of a post-war popular song 'I'm My Own Grand-Pa'.

There were anomalies, too, in the command of the Eastern Fleet. The C-in-C, Admiral Somerville, was responsible not only for the waters included in SEAC but also for the Persian Gulf, Aden and much of the east coast of Africa, which were all outside SEAC. As Admiral Mountbatten has explained:

'In all matters concerning the security and support of the land campaigns and amphibious operations in South East Asia, Admiral Somerville was responsible to me. But in all matters connected with the security of sea communications in the Indian Ocean, both outside and inside the area of SEAC, and with offensive action against the enemy's naval forces, he was directly responsible to the Admiralty.'[1]

In practice this extraordinary (though not unique) arrangement meant that Admiral Somerville could be responsible either to Admiral Mountbatten, or to the Admiralty, for any of his ships depending on where the ships were and what they were doing. The situation was not improved by Admiral Somerville's interpretation of his own and Admiral Mountbatten's position, and this was one matter on which Sir James might have been more accommodating. Significantly, Admiral Mountbatten reported that matters 'improved beyond recognition in August, 1944' – when Admiral Fraser became C-in-C.

During the Japanese advance in Burma, the only naval forces of the Allies in the area were a handful of sloops of the Royal Indian Navy, and five Motor Launches (MLs) built at Rangoon, of the Burma RNVR – a volunteer force formed, after many legal and financial difficulties had been resolved, in 1940. By December 1941 the Burma RNVR had considerable sea-going experience of the Mergui Islands and the Rangoon approaches, but they had, of course, only a 'pin-prick' effect on the enemy. Their headquarters ship, the ex-Danish *Heinrich Jessen* was the last ship to leave Rangoon on 7 March 1942. The flotilla were evacuated to Akyab and thence to Chittagong in May. By that time, the Japanese stood on the borders of India where, having achieved their first objectives and being themselves hampered by poor communications, their offensive paused. The front remained in a state of uneasy suspension through the 1942 monsoon period.

[1] Report To The Combined Chiefs Of Staff by the Supreme Allied Commander South-east Asia, 1943–1945, by Vice Admiral The Earl Mountbatten of Burma (HMSO, 1951), A: Introduction, p. 9.

General Sir Archibald Wavell, the C-in-C India, was already laying plans for the reconquest of Burma. He intended an offensive to begin on 1 October with an advance on the Kalewa–Katha–Myitkina front, accompanied by a separate invasion of Arakan, followed on 1 November by a sea-borne landing in southern Burma to recapture Rangoon (Operation ANAKIM). A number of factors – the worsening situation in other theatres of the war, internal disturbances in India, the requirements of the Madagascar operation, malaria amongst the troops, shortage of assault shipping and aircraft, and the detachment of one infantry division and an armoured brigade to the Middle East, all combined at various times to cause ANAKIM to be postponed. A less ambitious scheme was proposed: a diversionary land advance down the Mayu Peninsula in Arakan, to be followed by a main sea-borne assault on Akyab, to capture the airfields.

The province of Arakan lies on the west coast of Burma,[1] a narrow strip of land cut off from the rest of the country by the mountain range of the Arakan Yomas. The country in the north is barren and hilly, with a rich alluvial plain to the south and west. Most of the province consists of steep hills, jungle, paddy fields, scrub and extensive mangrove swamps. The two main passes into the hinterland of the Irrawaddy valley are at An and at Taungup, with other minor tracks across the mountains. Akyab was the only proper harbour along the whole coast.

The land offensive duly began on 21 September 1942 with an advance down the Mayu Peninsula by the 14th Indian Division. The campaign began hopefully, and ended in near-catastrophe. The Allies had local numerical superiority on the ground, more artillery and a small amount of armour; despite the terrible country, malaria and appalling weather conditions (thirteen inches of rain fell on Guy Fawkes Day) the 14th Division pressed down the peninsula and occupied Maungdaw and Buthidaung by 17 December.

But the campaign was conducted with a disastrous mixture of delaying caution – so as not to prejudice this first British offensive against the Japanese – and (for the same reason) a reckless determination to continue long after all hope had gone. The enemy were allowed time to reinforce positions which could have been captured easily earlier in the campaign. By March 1943 the army were bogged down in a bitter struggle at Donbaik and Rathebaung, which the Japanese had made into formidable defensive positions. When the Japanese launched a series of out-flanking hooks through supposedly impenetrable jungle

[1] See map, p. 171.

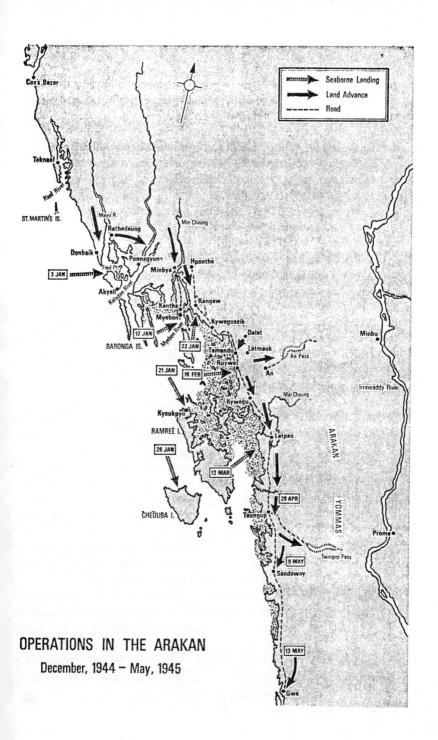

Cox's Bazar

Teknaf

Naaf River

ST. MARTIN'S IS.

Mayu R.
Rathedaung
Min Chaung

Donbaik
Ponnagyun
Hpontha
3 JAN
Foul Pt.
Minbya
Akyab
Kaladan River
Kantha
Kangaw
Myebon
Kyweguseik
12 JAN
Myebon River
Dalet
Minbu
BARONGA IS.
22 JAN
Tamandu
Letmauk
An Pass
Ruywa
An
21 JAN
16 FEB
Kywegu
Mai Chaung
Irrawaddy River
Kyaukpyu
RAMREE I.
Letpan
ARAKAN
26 JAN
13 MAR
YOMMAS
Prome
CHEDUBA I.
28 APR
Taungup
9 MAY
Taungup Pass
Sandoway
13 MAY
Gwa

	Seaborne Landing
	Land Advance
	Road

OPERATIONS IN THE ARAKAN
December, 1944 – May, 1945

and across 'impassable' mountain ranges, the check became a stalemate, the stalemate a withdrawal, which quickly became a full retreat to avert catastrophe. By May the army were back where they had started eight months before, and profoundly depressed; it really did appear that the Japanese were invincible in the jungle. Morale in the Eastern Army sank to the lowest point possibly of any army in British military history.

The naval forces available for the campaign consisted of MLs and a miscellaneous collection of landing craft and river steamers,[1] but the warships, assault shipping and air support for the landing at Akyab could not be provided and the amphibious operation was cancelled. A naval base was established at Teknaaf on the Naaf River and MLs operated in the Mayu River until May.

Considered against the whole panorama of the war, 'First Arakan' was a tiny campaign, but it had colossal world-wide repercussions. Mr Churchill had hoped to take the news of the seizure of the Akyab airfields with him to the Trident Conference in Washington. He was disappointed, and critical of the handling of affairs in Burma. Locally, the divisional and army commanders were dismissed and Wavell's own reputation suffered. It was announced in June that General Wavell would succeed the Marquis of Linlithgow as Viceroy of India in October, and that General Auchinleck would become C-in-C India forthwith. Further, it was proposed to relieve the C-in-C India of responsibility for operations against Japan, and appoint a Supreme Allied Commander in South-east Asia to exercise overall command of all Allied land, sea and air forces prosecuting the war against Japan.

The appointment was the most realistic step yet taken in South-east Asia. The very title 'Supreme Allied Commander South-east Asia' had an heroic ring to it – although, at the time of its inception, all of South-east Asia Command was actually held by the enemy, except Ceylon and a strip of the Burma–Assam frontier. On 25 August 1943, the day after the Quebec Conference, it was announced that the new Supreme Commander would be the then Chief of Combined Operations, Acting Vice Admiral The Lord Louis Mountbatten.

The appointment was well received in South-east Asia. The nomination of such a glamorous figure, who had a place not only on the Chiefs of Staff Committee but also in the Court Circulars, showed the army

---

[1] Six RIN MLs, five Burma RNVR MLs, twenty-four LCAs, six LCS, seven LCPs, nine LCMs, thirty Fleming-type life boats, the river steamers *Torotua, Athitaka, Surmai, Yengua,* paddle steamers *Uzbek, Aimak,* and *Kadari,* two petrol tankers and *Barracuda* (ex *Heinrich Jessen*).

in India that some fashionable metropolitan interest was at last being shown in a theatre of the war which was already beginning to think of itself as 'forgotten'.

Admiral Mountbatten was a notable celebrity, with a flamboyant background of destroyer command and combined operations, who was bound to have his jealous Service critics. For instance, his handling of publicity was sometimes distasteful to officers with old-fashioned views on naval press relations. Yet the proof of the battle is surely in the killing; by the end of the war 150,000 Japanese had been killed in South-east Asia, most of them by an army which nevertheless contrived to remain 'forgotten' – which suggests that Admiral Mountbatten was perhaps a better military strategist and a worse publicist than his critics maintained.

When Admiral Mountbatten took over operational control in November 1943 the strategic situation in South-east Asia was as confused and complicated as ever. After the initial and obvious agreement that the Japanese must be kept out of India, British and American views on future strategy in South-east Asia differed, often sharply. The United States was determined to keep China in the war. At best, she might serve as a future launching point for an assault on the Japanese main islands. At worst, she would serve as a gigantic 'sponge' to soak up a large part of the Japanese war effort. The British were less optimistic about the value of China's contribution and much more concerned about the reoccupation of former British territories in the Far East. The Americans, least of all President Roosevelt himself, had no desire to promote the interests of any 'colonial' power. Thus there was always this basic tendency to disagreement, on the nature and scale of support to China in the north, and on the timing and choice of objectives to be seized in Burma and the Indian Ocean to the south.

Admiral Mountbatten's directive of 23 October 1943 from the Prime Minister, instructed him to engage the enemy closely and continuously, to force them to divert resources from the Pacific. South-east Asia cried out for combined operations and the Supreme Commander's staff began to consider Mr Churchill's long-cherished plan to force the straits of Malacca with an assault on northern Sumatra (Operation CULVERIN). A battle fleet, escort carriers and the necessary assault shipping had been promised. (To old-timers on the naval staff, it must have seemed that the millennium was at hand.)

It was not to be. No more naval forces were allocated to SEAC, and CULVERIN was cancelled. Next, the staff considered a reduced amphibious assault on the Andaman Islands (Operation BUCCANEER). Planning advanced until December when a large part of the amphibious shipping had to be returned to the European theatre for the Anzio landing, and BUCCANEER was then cancelled. A third, and even more modest, amphibious operation was proposed – a landing on the Mayu peninsula (Operation PIGSTICK). Planning advanced for this, too, until 30 December 1943 when all amphibious operations in the Indian Ocean had to be cancelled, and the remainder of the serviceable landing ships and craft dispatched to Europe. PIGSTICK became, in Churchill's phrase, 'pig-stuck' and joined its distinguished predecessors ANAKIM and CULVERIN and BUCCANEER, all in the 'Waiting – Too Difficult' file.

In October 1943 the old Eastern Army was disbanded and a new army, the 14th Army, was created, commanded by Lt. General William Slim, Mountbatten's personal choice and a man who believed that the mere possession of territory in Burma was meaningless; what mattered was the killing of Japanese. To the 14th Army, this was a refreshing thought. Lessons had been learned from the past, new tactics devised, the Allies had growing superiority in the air and greater experience in the use of air power to keep troops supplied. Preparatory moves for a second campaign in Arakan began in December 1943. Maungdaw was taken on 9 January 1944, and 14th Army began to face the coming campaign with uncommon optimism.

Unfortunately, in the words of the old saying, 'the bear blew first'. The Japanese, too, had planned an offensive in Arakan and on 4 February launched Operation HA to drive 15th Corps back to the Indian frontier. For a month the 5th and 7th Indian Divisions were engaged in fierce fighting around the old battlegrounds of Buthidaung and Razabil. Meanwhile the Arakan Coastal Forces,[1] commanded by Captain J. Ryland, RIN (Captain Coastal Forces Arakan), secured 5th Division's seaward flank, transported supplies, carried out bombardments, landed agents and parties of commandos, and in February carried out diversionary attacks on the enemy at Taungup and Ramree Island.

On land, the Japanese made their customary encircling attacks. This time surrounded Allied troops did not retreat but formed themselves into defensive 'boxes' and were supplied by air. A wonder now came to light. The Japanese were not invincible after all. Buthidaung was taken on 11 March, and the fortress of Razabil a day later. The Allies now

---

[1] The 55th and 56th Royal Indian Navy, 49th South African and 59th Burma ML Flotillas.

held the entrance and both sides of the Naaf River. The campaign's limited objectives were achieved, the Japanese had been brought to battle, and had been repulsed. Morale soared in the 14th Army and in South-east Asia Command.

However, 5th and 7th Divisions had no time to savour their success. To the north, on the Central Burma Front, the Japanese had launched Operation U-GO, which was nothing less than an attempted invasion of India. The Japanese attacked on 7 March with three divisions of 15th Army; to succeed, they must capture Imphal, the ancient capital of the state of Manipur, and the village of Kohima. The siege of Imphal and the battle of Kohima were two of the most glorious episodes in the history of the British army and the RAF.[1] Imphal was relieved on 22 June after a siege of sixty-four days. At Kohima British, Indian and Gurkha troops won a smashing victory. In its way, Kohima was as decisive a battle as Midway and Stalingrad. The reconquest of Burma was now possible.

With the Japanese in retreat from the Chindwin River, and General Slim beginning his triumphant and subtle advance to Rangoon, the Arakan assumed importance again. The airfields at Akyab and on Ramree Island would be needed to supply 14th Army's advance. The third and last campaign in Arakan, and the first in which the Navy played a large part, began on 10 December 1944 with an advance down the Mayu peninsula by 74th Brigade. The objects of the campaign were to clear the enemy out of Arakan, to seize the airfields and, ultimately, to cut off the retreating Japanese 54th and 55th Divisions and prevent them rejoining the main Japanese army in the Irrawaddy valley. Of these objects, the last was never wholly achieved.

To support the Army, Force 64 was formed on 17 November 1944 and was commanded by Captain D. C. Hill. By earlier Arakan standards, Force 64 was a considerable collection of shipping: six flotillas of Landing Craft Assault (LCAs), ten flotillas of Landing Craft Mechanised (LCM), two flotillas of Landing Craft Support (LCS), two flotillas of Landing Craft Personnel (LCP), one flotilla of Landing Craft Tank (LCT), one flotilla of Landing Craft Infantry (LCI), five flotillas of MLs, a flotilla of Harbour Defence Motor Launches (HDML), one flotilla of British 'Y' Class Minesweepers (BYM), one flotilla of Motor Minesweepers (MM); also available were the frigates *Jed, Avon, Awe,*

---

[1] The bibliography on Imphal and Kohima is extensive, amongst which *Defeat into Victory*, by Field Marshal Lord Slim (Cassell, 1956) and the works of Mr Arthur Swinson are outstanding.

the sloop *Shoreham* and two RIN sloops, a close support group of *Flamingo* and HMIS *Jumna*, *Narbada* and *Kistna* and, for fighter direction, the cruiser *Phoebe*.

The naval support of 74th Brigade (Operation ROMULUS) was a small classic in applied sea-power, in which the Navy supplied the Army, safeguarded their line of communication and provided offensive fire-power. The bombardment group, the Australian destroyers *Napier* and *Nepal*, with HDMLS 1275 and 1303, arrived off St Martin's Island on 13 December and remained on call for bombardments until 24 December, by which time they had carried out thirteen shoots on targets as requested by the Army. *Napier* and *Nepal* returned, one at a time, to Chittagong for fuel, ammunition, stores and water. The operations were slightly marred by over-zealous publicity, which might have caused a tragedy. Quite justifiably, Captain Buchanan complained that news of *Napier*'s bombardment of Rathedaung on the Mayu River on 19 December had 'been broadcast to the world', at a time when a second bombardment was planned. Surprise was lost and the force might have come under enemy air attack. But the great battles in central Burma had had their effect in Arakan; the Japanese were conspicuous by their absence and there were no reports of any Japanese actually being killed by any of the bombardments.

During their advance to Foul Point, 74th Brigade were supplied entirely by sea, the main bulk of stores, ammunition, guns and tanks being carried by five LCTs and two LCMs, commanded by Lt. Cdr. Langdon, RNVR. The achievement of these craft, particularly the LCTs, was well appreciated by the Supreme Commander:

'The LCTs were in a very precarious state, having been left behind as unfit to be sent to the Mediterranean, and it was with some hesitation that the naval authorities had agreed to let them undertake such tasks which often involved running ashore under surf conditions. It is greatly to the credit of the commanders and crews of these craft that the army's requirements were met and that the craft themselves developed no major defects. No depot or repair ship was available to maintain them and their nearest shore bases, Chittagong and Calcutta, were far out of their reach. For more than three months also, the crews had to live in their craft under conditions for which the accommodation was never designed.'[1]

Like many long-awaited parties, the capture of Akyab was a crashing

[1] Lord Mountbatten's Report, B: Strategy and Operations, p. 110.

anticlimax. On 26 December, a fortnight ahead of schedule, troops of 74th Brigade stood on Foul Point and looked across the waters of the Mayu estuary at the island of Akyab. There was no movement except the flight of sea birds, no sound but the waters of the river, no sign of any Japanese, nor of any activity at all.

The enemy had begun to evacuate Akyab a month before, and there was not a single Japanese on the island. The full-scale amphibious assault on Akyab (Operation TALON), originally fixed for 18 February, was cancelled and after some shuffling of alternative plans the date of the landing, to be carried out without preliminary air or sea bombardment, was hurriedly brought forward to 3 January 1945. In the event, the Akyab landing (Operation LIGHTNING) was planned, mounted and carried out in six days.

Naval forces were under the command of Rear Admiral B. C. S. Martin (Flag Officer, Force 'W') and the Senior Officer of the Assault Group was his Chief of Staff, Captain E. W. Bush.

The 3rd Commando Brigade (Brigadier Campbell Hardy, RM),[1] who were to carry out the assault, embarked at Teknaaf in the early hours of D-Day, 3 January, the majority being lifted in two 5-knot convoys. Convoy 'Able' left at 0430 and consisted of Landing Craft Headquarters (LCH) 261 (Captain Bush), one ML (Cdr. G. G. Mojer, RIN, Senior Officer Convoy), ten MLs towing ten LCSs, twenty LCMs towing twenty LCAs, and two LCIs towing two LCAs each. Convoy 'Baker' left fifteen minutes later and consisted of one ML (Cdr. H. R. M. Nicholl, Deputy Senior Officer Assault Group and Senior Officer Convoy), six BYMs towing two LCAs each, and six LCTs towing nine LCPs. A third 12-knot convoy, 'Charlie', of *Napier* (with Admiral Martin on board), *Nepal* and *Shoreham* for troop-carrying, and bombardment if required, left at 0630.

A naval bombarding force, Force 61, commanded by Rear Admiral A. D. Read and composed of the cruisers *Newcastle*, *Phoebe* and *Nigeria*, the destroyers *Rapid*, *Pathfinder*, and *Raider*, and the escort carrier *Ameer*, had assembled at Chittagong and was available for supporting gun-fire. It was later reported that the Japanese had left and the native population was returning to the assault area. The bombardment was then cancelled to avoid unnecessary loss of life.

The convoys had a passage of some forty-five miles to the landing

---

[1] 3rd Commando Brigade had two Royal Marine and one Army Commandos.

M

position, which was about seven miles off the beach. The haste with which LIGHTNING had been mounted led to a somewhat extempore appearance of equipment on the beach. Limit signs were made of canvas from the officers' wash-place at Teknaaf. Hurricane lamps, borrowed from the Army, were covered with coloured bunting from the base Christmas decorations. But the landing went off almost without a hitch. H-Hour had been fixed at 1230 and the first wave touched down half a minute early. By 1350 the whole Commando and a squadron of medium tanks were ashore. There was no opposition of any kind. The assault craft turned round and went to Bungalow Point where they embarked 74th Indian Infantry Brigade and transferred them to Akyab by 1600 the next day.

Akyab town was occupied on 4 January and the Allies had gained a most valuable island, with an all-weather airfield and command of the Mayu and Kaladan rivers, estuaries and the entrances to the inland water-ways of South Arakan. LIGHTNING had been excellent training and had confirmed the Navy's ability to put the Army ashore where and when they wanted. The RIN crews of the landing craft had both gained and inspired confidence.

Work on Akyab airfield began at once and Spitfires operating from it were able to drive off an enemy air attack on the harbour on 9 January. Akyab harbour had been almost totally destroyed by Allied bombing, and by Japanese demolition and neglect. A Port Construction Company began work on 15th and by 12 February had constructed seven pontoon jetties and made extensive repairs to stone jetties and approaches. In six weeks a new solid timber wharf, 600 feet long and 12 feet wide, had been built, and two ships sunk in the harbour had been removed. The harbour's target was 1200 tons a day; on 4 April a record of 2,406 tons was handled.

Meanwhile, naval forces in the Arakan continued to harry the enemy's lines of communications, sinking his craft and destroying his troops wherever they could be found. One typical operation occurred on 7 January when *Narbada, Jumna* and MLs 381 and 829 went fifteen miles up the Kaladan river to Ponnagyun, where Japanese troops and a headquarters had been reported. That afternoon enemy guns in a village on the east bank opened accurate fire, hitting *Jumna* twice and straddling *Narbada*; the guns were silenced by counter-battery fire from the sloops. Local villagers were taken on board *Narbada,* and it was learned that the enemy had made a general withdrawal but there were still some three to four hundred Japanese troops on the west bank.

One villager was appointed Bombardment Liaison Officer – 'by signs and interpretations the necessary spotting corrections were ascertained and applied, and some well-directed salvoes were then placed in the area. At each salvo the BLO disappeared like a jack-in-the-box below the bridge screen only to be yanked up by the hair in time to see the fall of shot. This delighted him enormously.'

After the capture of Akyab, the Navy's main tasks roughly divided into two: offshore, the support of landings on Ramree Island, to seize the harbour and airfield site at Kyaukpyu, and on the neighbouring island of Cheduba; and inshore, a series of amphibious operations to place troops across the line of communication of the Japanese army retreating southwards down the coast road, and at the same time carrying out innumerable blockading and ambushing operations against enemy craft using the 'chaungs'.

The 'Chaung War', as it became known, was strange, stealthy and secret. It was a war of concealment and camouflage, of lying in wait and listening, of surprise and short, sharp ambush. For a hundred miles south of Akyab as far as Taungup there was not one beach worthy of the name. The only access from the sea to the hinterland was through the chaungs – tidal creeks and inlets which weaved through a vast mazey pattern of mangrove swamps, mud banks and tiny islands. The chaungs were where the sea and the jungle mingled almost indistinguishably, indeed much of that tidal wilderness was marked on Army maps as 'water' and on Admiralty charts as 'land'. The chaungs varied greatly in width and navigability. Some were two hundreds yards wide and could be navigated for certain distances by sloops. Others were only a few feet across and could be penetrated only by canoe. Even in the widest chaungs there were likely to be shoals in mid-channel, rocks, jagged tree stumps and hidden snags. In places the Japanese had planted stakes, covered at high water, and stretched trip-wires between the banks, set to detonate concealed mines, or built booms festooned with grenades. There were crocodiles in the chaungs, and mosquitoes and other poisonous, stinging insects by the millions. At low water, in the perpetual dusk, under the overhanging branches, the mangrove roots assumed fantastically tortured shapes, and every operation was a test of the stoutest nerves. The chaungs made a deep impression on all who saw them:

'The mangrove trees themselves may be anything from ten to forty feet tall. The smell is oppressive, and in hot weather the heat is intolerable.

Crocodiles and water-snakes abound. Mud is plentiful. Ornithologists might like it.'[1]

In this, one of the weirdest battles of the war at sea, the Arakan Coastal Forces evolved new tactics, new methods of camouflage and ambush as they went along. MLs lay with engines stopped up side chaungs, waiting for enemy sampans attempting to slip past on the ebb tide. LCAs, camouflaged with netting and mangrove branches and containing parties of soldiers armed with machine-guns and mortars, patrolled the chaungs. In the winding creeks the enemy was often met at point-blank range, both sides were surprised and, as in the days of the Wild West, survival literally depended upon the fastest draw. On the night of 13 January, in the Daingbon Chaung, MLs 380 and 829 surprised and sank three armed Japanese supply craft. The following night, MLs 391 and 436 sank four enemy supply craft and two large barges. On 15th, two South African manned MLs, 832 and 846, were in action against four Japanese MGBs, armed with one 75-mm. and two 37-mm. guns, sinking two and damaging a third. In the chaung operations of January four Japanese MGBs, twenty supply craft and many sampans were sunk.

The amphibious operations of the Arakan campaign would not have been possible without the Combined Operations Pilotage Parties (COPP) who were specially trained to reconnoitre the chaungs and likely landing places before the operations. Theirs was valuable and extremely dangerous work which involved stealing up the chaungs in canoes during the night or in the mist of early morning to sound for depth, and marking the channel with buoys; it meant climbing ashore at low tide up the slimy banks to reconnoitre beyond them the prospect of assault across the firm or flooded paddy fields. At any bend or confluence the chaung might be mined or ambushed. Indeed the whole distance of this jungle water-maze was a sniper's paradise.

The first of the amphibious operations to exploit the capture of Akyab and to cut off the retreating Japanese was the landing at Myebon (Operation PUNGENT). The 25th Indian Division had been allocated to chaung operations in the Myebon peninsula with the object of seizing Minbya (Operation PASSPORT) whilst the forthcoming assault on Ramree island was assigned to the 26th Division. On 8 January Captain Hill arrived at Akyab with his staff and assumed the duties of NOIC Akyab.

---

[1] *The Watery Maze,* by Brigadier Sir Bernard Fergusson (Collins, 1961), p. 374.

On the same day, all landing craft were allocated to the 25th Division and it was decided that a landing at Myebon (PUNGENT) should be made by 3rd Commando Brigade, as well as the Chaung operations by 74th Brigade, and that PUNGENT should be carried out within seventy-two hours. Captain H. J. Buchanan, RAN, in *Napier*, was put in command of arrangements for the naval support of the chaung operations with 74th Brigade, while Captain M. H. Nott, RIN, in *Narbada* commanded naval support arrangements for 3rd Commando Brigade's assault on Myebon. However, on 10 January the chaung operation was abandoned and 74th Brigade allocated to follow up the Commandos at Myebon.

Earlier, on 5 January, ML 439 had been fired on from the east bank of the Myebon whilst reconnoitring the river; this indicated the enemy's presence, probably in strength, and – possibly – their escape route to the south. On 9 January Brigadier Hardy accompanied Captain Nott in *Narbada* for a personal reconnaissance of the river. *Narbada* could approach within 8,000 yards of the peninsula, by crossing a bar with thirteen feet of water over it; where the water shallowed still further, Brigadier Hardy and Captain Nott transferred to ML 854 to study the beaches. They were fired on by the Japanese but selected three mud-banks, noting that one had been staked, which suggested that it was feasible for a landing.

D-Day was fixed for 12 January, H-Hour 0830, high water. The Commando Brigade embarked at Akyab, *Narbada* and *Jumna* each carrying one Commando, two BYMs and two MMs carrying a third Commando between them, and three LCIs carrying the fourth Commando. DUKWs, vehicles, tanks, guns, bulldozers and stores were carried in five LCTs and twelve LCMs. The assault craft, eighteen LCAs and four LCPs, were towed.

The previous night COPPs and Landing Craft Obstruction Clearance Units (LCOCUs) had fixed delay-action explosives to stakes guarding the beach, which duly blew up on time, at 0630. After a twenty-minute bombardment by *Narbada* and *Jumna* and bombing attacks by 48 B-25s (Mitchells) of US 12th Bombardment Group the first wave of Commandos were ashore under cover of smoke on schedule at 0830, the second three minutes later, against slight enemy opposition. The beach was also defended by about a hundred tree trunks embedded in the mud and by mines, one of which killed the Naval Beach-master.

The assault beach, or mud-bank, had never been an attractive one and as the tide receded it became a quagmire. 44th Commando, the floating reserve, had been transferred from MMs to LCMs which had been ordered to lie off. Later, they were ordered to land, without any reference to the Navy. The Commandos landed neck-deep in mud. Half struggled ashore, but the remainder were rescued by LCMs and taken, somewhat ignominiously, to *Narbada* where they were reclothed and their persons and weapons cleaned.

Two tanks were unloaded at a second beach, but by that afternoon an exit path had been built at a third beach which was much more satisfactory for armoured vehicles and it was on this beach that 74th Brigade, the follow-up troops, landed the next morning. The ships lying offshore were attacked by eight Oscars that day; *Narbada*, *Napier* and BYMS 2204 each shot down one.

Meanwhile, the Commandos pressed northwards up the peninsula against stiffening Japanese resistance. They were relieved by 74th Brigade on 18th, by which time it was plain that the Myebon assault had failed to cut off the Japanese line of communication which ran from Hpontha–Kangaw–Kywegusseik. Another landing would be necessary further down the coast. Kywegusseik was considered impracticable for a landing. Surveys and COPPs set to work to examine the chances at Kangaw.

Kangaw proved to be the nub of the tactical situation. It was the critical concentration point in the disposition of the enemy's forces by Lt. Gen. Miyazaki, the very capable commander of the Japanese 54th Division, to protect both his own withdrawal and the rear of the Japanese 15th Army in the Irrawaddy valley. Akyab had been evacuated, Myebon and Ramree were held only as outposts, but Kangaw was defended by more than 3,000 Japanese troops and in the event, was only taken after one of the bloodiest battles of the whole Burma campaign.

The shortest and most obvious assault route to Kangaw was northward up the Myebon river and then hard-a-starboard for a short reach southward down the Daingbon Chaung. But this way was vulnerable to Japanese artillery on the banks of the Myebon. After several COPP surveys, another route was found, a long and circuitous voyage of nearly twenty-seven miles, south to the Thegyan river estuary and then northwards through almost the whole winding length of the Daingbon Chaung.

D-Day was 22 January, H-Hour 1300. The 3rd Commando Brigade (making their third operational landing in a month) embarked at Myebon on 21st. Captain Hill was once again in command of naval forces, with Cdr. Nicholl in command of the assault. The whole invasion fleet, some fifty miscellaneous vessels,[1] anchored for the night in the Thegyan estuary, sailing up the Daingbon Chaung in three convoys the next morning.

The 'long way round' approach was a happy choice. The exertions of 74th Brigade in the north Myebon peninsula and of *Jumna* and MLs in the Myebon river suggested to the Japanese that an attack on Kangaw would be from the north. The convoys approaching in silence from the south achieved complete tactical surprise. Covered by fire from *Narbada*, *Jumna* and Z Craft,[2] and by a smoke screen laid by B-25s of 224 Group RAF, the first Commandos were ashore at 1303. The landing craft played their parts with tremendous panache – 'it would have interested many experts to see an LCI with masts lowered, proceed into a chaung not more than fifty feet wide–cut its way through overhanging trees, disgorge her troops on a bank of not more than fifteen feet in width and then be towed out stern first by two LCPs'.

No. 1 Commando had actually been landed in a tidal swamp but made some progress and occupied several points including a foot-hold on the dominating feature of the area, Hill 170. The Japanese had been caught 'looking the wrong way' but in the next two days they counter-attacked with infantry and accurate artillery fire. The Commandos' attempts to push inland towards the village of Kangaw were fiercely resisted; on the 26th they were reinforced by 51st Brigade and by a troop of medium tanks. But the Japanese, too, had reinforced and on 31 January made an all-out assault on Hill 170 with infantry and artillery; in the early morning of 1 February ninety screaming Japanese sappers ran down the hill with pole charges and knocked out two tanks. A Commando officer, Lieut. G. A. Knowland of the Royal Norfolk Regiment, remained at his post firing his mortar at the enemy at point-blank range and won a posthumous Victoria Cross. After the action 340 Japanese dead were counted in an area a hundred yards square. The Commandos lost sixty-six killed, fifteen missing and 259 wounded.

The struggle for Hill 170 was the climax of the battle. By now 74th Brigade were approaching from Myebon, the 2nd West African Brigade

---

[1] *Narbada*, *Jumna*, four LCIs, one LCT, one BYMS, three MMSs, twenty-two LCAs, twelve LCMs, two LCSs, two LCPs, and a number of MLs of 36th, 49th and 56th Flotillas.

[2] Z craft were large but manoeuvrable lighters with flat iron decks and end loading ramps carrying a troop of 25-pounder guns and ammunition. The guns were manned by the army, the crews were native and each Z Craft had a naval liaison officer on board – one of whom recommended, after the Kangaw assault, that 'old men should be withdrawn from the crew'.

were advancing down the coast road from the north and the 26th Division had taken most of Ramree. On 8 February Miyazaki ordered his surviving troops to withdraw. 51st Brigade were astride the main coast road but the Japanese had opened a pack-track which ran east of Kangaw, rejoining the road further south, and made good their escape.

The Allies had 600 casualties, most of them Commandos who had suffered particularly severely amongst their officers and NCOs. The Brigade was withdrawn to Myebon on 11th. The Kangaw area was not finally subdued and cleared of the enemy until 18th. Miyazaki had lost 2,000 dead, sixteen guns, fourteen large motor craft and other equipment, but he had gained his main purpose: his force had not been annihilated, and he still held the An Pass.

Clearly, yet another amphibious landing was required and the Army at once began planning another 'hook' to the south. But now, the Navy dug in their heels. For the time being, enough was enough. Force 64 and its supporting craft had been in almost continuous operations since December and needed some time to recoup and replenish. For more than two months the Navy had not only landed the Army and their equipment at the appropriate spot and kept them supplied thereafter with food, water, stores and ammunition, but had patrolled scores of chaungs night and day, evacuated casualties, put parties of raiding Commandos ashore, and carried out several minor amphibious operations.

The Navy had been using the rivers and chaungs of the Arakan as arterial roads – but they were roads which were unlit, unsignposted, of uncertain surface, obstructed by hidden traffic bollards and unexpected road-works, where the motorists were often shelled and mortared by hostile pedestrians. Much of the 'domestic' work of transportation should have been done by the Inland Water Transport – an armada of various craft assembled to supply the Army by water – but the IWT did not arrive until 11 February, and so naval ships and landing craft continued to be used, in Captain Hill's phrase 'for immoral purposes'. When the IWT did arrive their 'turn-round' times for loading and unloading were twice as long as the Navy's, and naval craft shared some of the burden. The naval staff refused a further advance until the Army had taken over its commitments in the Kangaw area and a firm rear base had been established.

In the meantime, plans had been made for the 26th Indian Division (originally intended for the Akyab assault) to assault and capture the

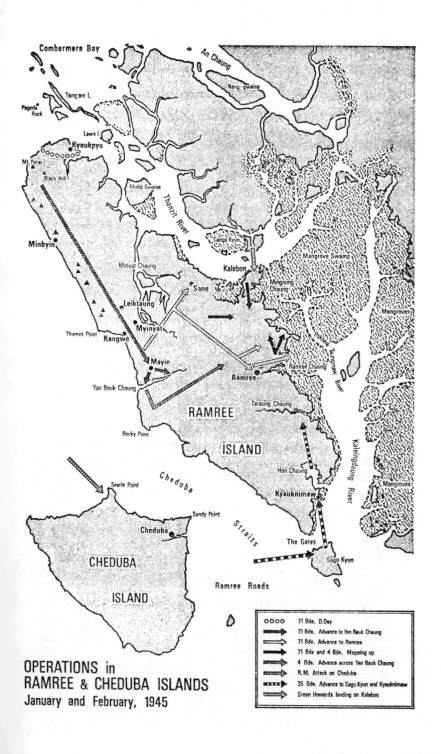

Combermere Bay

An Chaung

Nang-gwaine

Tangaro I.

Pagoda Rock

Laws I.

Kyaukpyu

Mt.Peter

Black Hill

Muddi Gwaine

Thanzit River

Ganga Kyun

Minbyin

Minyat Chaung

Kalebon

Mangrove Swamp

Mingaung Chaung

Sane

Leiktaung

Mangroves

Myinyat

Thames Point

Kangwe

Mayin

Yan Bauk Chaung

Ramree Chaung

Ramree

RAMREE

Taraung Chaung

Rocky Point

ISLAND

Hon Chaung

Searle Point

Cheduba

Kyauknimaw

Sandy Point

Cheduba

Straits

The Gates

Kalengdaung River

Sagu Kyun

CHEDUBA

ISLAND

Ramree Roads

OPERATIONS in
RAMREE & CHEDUBA ISLANDS
January and February, 1945

oooo 71 Bde. D.Day

71 Bde. Advance to Yan Bauk Chaung

71 Bde. Advance to Ramree

71 Bde. and 4 Bde. Mopping up

4 Bde. Advance across Yan Bauk Chaung

R.M. Attack on Cheduba

36 Bde. Advance to Sagu Kyun and Kyauknimaw

Green Howards landing on Kalebon

northern part of Ramree (Operation MATADOR).[1] By Arakan standards of that time, MATADOR was a comparatively leisurely operation – planned, mounted and carried out in fourteen days. The main objective was the harbour at Kyaukpyu and the airfield site there, from which 14th Army could be supplied by air during the monsoon as far south as Rangoon itself. The Assault Force Commander was Maj. Gen. C. E. N. Lomax, commanding the 26th Division and the Naval Assault and Attack Forces commander was Captain E. Tyndale Cooper, with Cdr. E. N. Pumphrey as his deputy.

MATADOR was the largest amphibious operation yet attempted in the Arakan. The 26th Division embarked at Chittagong from 17–19 January in the personnel ships *Egra*, *Ellenga*, *Salween* and *Nevassa* and the infantry landing ships *Barpeta* and *Llanstephan Castle*. The motor transport was carried in *Ikauna* and *Itola*, stores in *Winsang*. The naval assault force also included LCH 261, 24 LCAs, 18 LCMs, two LCI(L)s, three LCTs, 8 LCPs and four LCSs. The attached force was 7 BYMs, 12 MLs, one LCM depot ship, one LCT maintenance ship and two LCIs. *Phoebe*, *Rapid*, *Flamingo* and *Kistna* provided the bombardment force, with *Napier* stand-by (with the Joint Force Commanders embarked).

On 14 January MLs 440 and 474 had embarked Commandos of No. 2 Special Boat Section under Major R. P. Livingstone for a reconnaissance of Kyaukpyu harbour. The Commandos, in canoes, reconnoitred Katharine Bluffs and the harbour and on return to Akyab reported that the enemy were placing guns in caves covering the landing beaches.[2] Heavy bombardment reinforcement was summoned from Trincomalee; the escort carrier *Ameer* with *Raider* sailed on the afternoon of 18th, followed by the battleship *Queen Elizabeth* (Captain G. Norman) flying the flag of Admiral Walker, escorted by *Norman* and *Pathfinder*.[3]

---

[1] See map, p. 185.

[2] An eye-witness account of this reconnaissance, by the officer who led it, is in Purnell's *History of the Second World War*, Vol. 6, p. 2368, *Burma: The War of Stealth*, by Richard Livingstone.

[3] 'I had had a Dakota converted to carry special H/F transmitters and cypher machines by Captain Hodges, RN (my Signal Officer in Chief). She was called *Mercury* and was alongside my own aircraft at Akyab. As soon as Livingstone reported the guns in the Rocky Temple Caves I signalled immediately to Ceylon ordering the C-in-C to send up heavy bombardment units. *Q.E.* got the order to raise steam within less than an hour of my seeing Livingstone. The army could hardly believe it.

'I went on board her later on, in Colombo. I had joined her as my second ship

Convoy 'A', the larger ships, LCIs and sloops, sailed from Chittagong late in the evening of 19 January. Convoy 'B', the landing craft escorted by MLs, left Akyab nearly twenty-four hours later. The beach selected for the assault lay between Georgina Point and Dalhousie Point, Kyaukpyu, in the north of Ramree. D-Day was 21 January, H-Hour 0930, low water. The Japanese garrison on Ramree, later estimated at battalion strength of about 1,000 men, were concentrated in Ramree town and at Thames Point on the west coast, which they imagined was the most likely landing beach. The enemy were therefore surprised by the appearance of the Assault Force in the north, early on the morning of 21 January.

The pre-assault bombardment began when *Queen Elizabeth* opened fire at 0830 (using her main 15-inch armament in action for the first time since the bombardment of the Dardanelles forts thirty years earlier) with 804 Sq. in *Ameer* providing spotting aircraft. She had a most reassuring effect on the assaulting troops of the 71st Indian Infantry Brigade; the sight of the battleship and the explosions of her 15-inch shells on a commanding ridge to the west was most heartening to all concerned. At 0915 *Phoebe* and the other bombarding ships opened fire and again, all troops were delighted by the effect on the hillside. Meanwhile, four squadrons of Liberators bombed enemy positions covering the beaches and twenty-four Thunderbolt fighters bombed and strafed the beaches themselves.

The larger ships had anchored offshore somewhat far apart and the assault craft took some time to make their rounds. In consequence, the first wave reached the beach at 0942, twelve minutes late, against slight enemy opposition on the left, and were followed by the second wave at 1015. Only half the BYMS were available for minesweeping, one being used to tow a radar barge and two others to transport parties of sappers. There was some confusion at 1101 when LCA 2086 exploded a mine and sank, with the loss of twenty-three out of thirty-two troops on board and two of her crew. ML 891 picked up survivors and herself struck a mine, losing three ratings of her ships' company.

By nightfall on 21st Kyaukpyu town had been taken and 7,000 troops (all 71st Brigade and the greater part of 4th Brigade), 121 vehicles and seventy tons of stores had been landed. While 4th Brigade remained in

as a Snotty in 1917 and now, 28 years later, went aboard officially flying my full Admiral's flag, as she was under my command. I wonder if this is a record – one ship to span the entire career of a midshipman?' Admiral of the Fleet the Earl Mountbatten of Burma. Letter of 6.2.69.

defence of Kyaukpyu town, 71st Brigade advanced south down the
west coast of the island, supported from the sea by destroyers and
sloops. After some early skirmishing at Black Hill, the brigade reached
Yan Bauk Chaung on 26th. There, the advance faltered. The Japanese
were firmly established on the south bank of the chaung and resisted
strongly.

The same day, 26 January, the only purely naval assault landing of
the war was carried out on Cheduba Island (Operation SANKEY), twelve
miles south of Ramree. Royal Marines of the East Indies Fleet – Force
Wellington (Colonel P. Picton Phillipps, RM) – and the 707th LCP
Flotilla (Captain M. W. Patterson, RM), embarked at Trincomalee in
the cruisers *Newcastle*, *Kenya* and *Nigeria* which sailed with *Paladin*,
on the evening of 23rd. At noon on 25th they met *Ameer*, *Phoebe*,
Norman, *Raider*, *Spey* and *Teviot* and the force split into two groups;
Group Two, *Phoebe*, *Ameer*, *Teviot* and *Spey* staying at sea to provide
air cover while the remaining ships as Group One anchored off Searle
Point, Cheduba, early on 26th, having been joined by *Rapid* with two
MLs, four BYMS, two LCMs and six LCAs which were made available
by Flag Officer, Force 'W'. The first wave touched down at 0848, three
minutes late, and the rest soon followed, with no opposition from the
enemy. There were still some Japanese on the island who must have
evacuated only a short time before (when the Royal Marines reached
the Japanese HQ in Cheduba village, they found eggs cooking and still
hot on a fire). Force Wellington were relieved by a battalion of the
2/7th Rajputs on 30th (Operation CACTUS) after a ludicrous mis-
understanding: the Army thought the relief was planned for SANKEY
D-Day plus six (1 February), but in fact the relief should have been on
MATADOR D-Day plus six (27 January). The Marines re-embarked on
31 January and that afternoon the detachments of *Newcastle*, *Kenya* and
Nigeria (Rock Force) manned their turrets in the cruisers for a bombardment of the west coast of Ramree. As Colonel Phillipps remarked:
'It is doubtful if ever before in the history of the Royal Marines has so
rapid a change-over from *per terram* to *per mare* been undertaken.'

71st Brigade were relieved by 4th Brigade on the Yan Bauk Chaung
on 31 January and at once headed north-east towards Sane, to outflank
the enemy. Sane was occupied on 1 February. In the south of the island
units of 36th Brigade landed first on Sagu Kyun to secure The Gates of
Ramree, and then on Ramree itself at Kyauknimaw, both operations
being supported by the destroyers and sloops.

The original MATADOR plan had been to seize only the northern part of the island, to safeguard the airfield sites. But on 4 February, General Lomax was ordered to take the whole island and destroy all the Japanese garrison. By this time 71st Brigade were advancing on Ramree town from the north-west and 4th Brigade, who had broken through on the Yan Bauk, from the west. Ramree town was taken on 8 February. The remaining Japanese were now penned in an area east of a line drawn between Sane and Ramree, with odd remnants further south. The Japanese had the choice of surrendering or trying to escape by any means possible through the chaungs and swamps to the mainland. They chose to try to escape. Arrangements were made to stop them (Operation BLOCK).[1]

BLOCK was one of the most ruthlessly executed minor operations of the war. It was a Combined Services man-hunt, in which the Army drove the Japanese survivors off Ramree and into the mangrove swamps, where the Navy and the RAF waited to destroy them and their boats and to prevent more boats being brought to the scene. All forces were briefed to shoot on sight.

Naval forces for BLOCK were the destroyers *Paladin* and *Pathfinder*, six to eight MLs, five BYMS, LCI 279, and four LCSs. From 11 February all blocking operations were under the general command of Captain Tyndale Cooper. By that time two blocks had been established. The larger, which remained throughout the operation, was known as 'North Block', extending from the Thanzit River by way of the confluence of chaungs nick-named 'Piccadilly Circus' to the Kaleindaung River and was controlled by Lt. Cdr. T. F. Hallifax in *Pathfinder*. 'South Block' extended from Ramree Chaung to Taraung Chaung, under Lt. H. Friend, RNVR, in LCI 279.

The plight of the Japanese as they tried to escape was described by Captain Bush, Senior Office Advanced Force 'W', in a memorable passage of his report:

'Dark during the day as well as during the night; acres of thick impenetrable forest; miles of deep black mud; mosquitoes, scorpions, flies and weird insects by the billion and – worst of all – crocodiles. No food, no drinking water to be obtained anywhere. It can hardly be possible that in their decision to quit the island the Japanese could have been fully aware of the appalling conditions which prevailed.'[2]

---

[1] See map, p. 190.
[2] 'Naval Operations in Ramree Island Area 19 January to 22nd February 1945', Despatch of Vice Admiral Sir Arthur John Power, Supplement to *London Gazette*, 26 April 1948, pp. 2583–4.

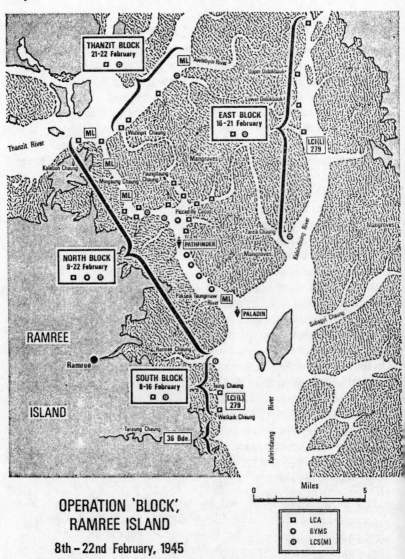

OPERATION 'BLOCK',
RAMREE ISLAND

8th – 22nd February, 1945

▫	LCA
⊙	BYMS
◉	LCS(M)

Some four hundred Japanese were believed to be still on Ramree and it was not long before some were flushed out. On the night of 9th-10th two loaded sampans were sunk by South Block and the following night a motorboat and more sampans were sunk at Piccadilly Circus. The RAF destroyed forty craft near Yan Thitshe and MLs working the

Thanzit river destroyed twenty-three empty boats hidden in the lee of a small island. On 11th the Japanese were stung into retaliation. At tea-time LCI 279 was attacked by four unidentified aircraft as she lay in the Kaleindaung river and half an hour later *Paladin*, anchored off the Pakseik Taungnaw river entrance, was bombed and machine-gunned by four Hamps;[1] at Piccadilly Circus *Pathfinder* was bombed by four more Hamps. One bomb was a near miss and *Pathfinder* was withdrawn to Kyaukpyu for repairs.

But the killing went on; two sampans loaded with Japanese soldiers on the night of 11th–12th, and four more the following night. On 14th two companies of the Green Howards were landed to guard the entrance of Kalebon Chaung, and the same day 71st Brigade reported that there were no more Japanese on Ramree except those in known isolated pockets. Yet some three to four hundred Japanese were still unaccounted for. Tactics were changed; the blocking forces turned from stealth to the full blaze of light. *Paladin* burned all her searchlights, playing them along the rivers, while the MLs and BYMSs illuminated the chaungs with flares, signal projectors and Aldis lamps. South Block was discontinued on 16th and moved further up the Kaleindaung, becoming 'East Block'. Five boats were intercepted and sunk that night and two days later the Japanese made several attempts to cross in daylight; they were hotly engaged and all killed or driven back into the mangroves. On the night of 18th–19th two large formations of Japanese craft made desperate attempts to cross the Mingaung Chaung. Many were sunk and over 100 Japanese killed.[2] The sun rose next morning on a grim sight. The river waters were littered with corpses and crocodiles swarmed on the scene.

That day the first prisoner was captured, as he sat astride a log in mid-stream in the Mingaung Chaung. He was Captain Asahina, of the 54th Medical Unit, attached to the 11/121 Japanese Infantry Regiment HQ. He was unwounded but had spent six days in the swamps. He agreed to help the blocking forces by calling upon other fugitives in the mangroves to surrender. This was a most unusual attitude in a Japanese soldier, but Asahina evidently felt that his privations and his commander's failure to evacuate him released him from his vows to the Emperor. All day long on 20th Asahina cruised up and down the chaungs in an

[1] Hamp–Zeke 32.
[2] *The Guinness Book of Records* (15th edition, 1968), under the 'World's Worst Crocodile Disaster', gives the numbers of Japanese soldiers killed as 'c. 900'.

ML, with an interpreter in Japanese, Captain S. J. Barden, sitting beside him, while behind were LCAs, nets stretched across the holds, ready to contain surrendered Japanese:

'I can hear Asahina's raucous voice as I write. I can see him, in borrowed clothes much too big for him, peering over the bridge screen. "*Atsu-mare*", he shouted all the time as he called on his men to surrender.

'The sun rose high and sank. But not a single Japanese appeared. At sunset I returned to base, telling the chaung blockers to get on with the killing.'[1]

The previous day a map had been recovered from a Japanese body, showing an escape route across the Thanzit river. For the last two days of BLOCK, 21 and 22 February, a 'Thanzit Block' was set up in the river. At the end, some three hundred Japanese had been killed. Not more than a score were ever taken prisoner and they 'were found to be semi-dehydrated and in a very low physical condition'.[2]

The build-up of men and material at Ramree continued. By 12 February, the Navy had landed 23,091 men, 679 vehicles and 9,233 tons of stores. Harbour facilities at Kyaukpyu had been almost non-existent but by April one Port Construction Company had built five pontoon jetties and a timber pier 130 feet long. The cargo handling target was 1,200 tons a day; on 17 March 1,767 tons were handled.

At Ramree, a Division of 23,000 men, a large number of air squadrons, a battleship, cruisers and a host of smaller ships had been employed to take from about 1,000 Japanese an island which would have fallen in any event. Fighters were soon flying from Kyaukpyu, but transport aircraft could not use the airfield until 15 May, by which time Rangoon had fallen. It could be said that the forces which took Ramree might have been better employed, but on the other hand SEAC did not have enough transport aircraft to supply another division in the Central Front advance to Rangoon, and Admiral Power had repeatedly stressed to Admiral Mountbatten that he could find no other active operational employment for the fleet. Without the Ramree assault, all those forces involved would have remained idle.

On the Arakan mainland, Miyazaki had extricated the remnants of his 54th Division from Kangaw and the Allies now faced the problem of trying to encircle them, and to seize the An Pass. The Army proposed a landing either at Kywegu, or at the mouth of the An Chaung, and

[1] *Bless Our Ship*, by Captain Eric Bush (Allen & Unwin, 1958), p. 270.
[2] Supplement to *London Gazette*, p. 2584.

an advance northwards up the An river. The Navy demurred, preferring to avoid a long towing operation, and to stay nearer Myebon, moving in chaungs they had surveyed and now controlled. It was decided to land at Ryuwa, some forty-five miles down the coast from Myebon. The operation was planned to take place in three stages: surveys and COPP reconnaissances; a landing at Ryuwa by 53rd Brigade, to secure and consolidate a bridge-head; a landing by 2nd West African Brigade, to pass through 53rd Brigade and advance the twelve miles inland to An, being supplied by air. D-Day was 16 February.

Though Ryuwa was nearer than Kywegu, its approaches were still long and devious and required extensive surveys in which, as in all the Arakan amphibious operations, the work of the hydrographic ships was unobtrusive but vital. From their own surveys and from a mass of information provided by other ships and by COPPs, the hydrographers (particularly those in *Nguva* (Cdr. J. M. Chaplin) and MLs 1248 and 1368) produced accurate charts of previously unsurveyed areas, often in a matter of days.

Because of the length of the passage, advanced bases, staging and control positions (all whimsically named after English public schools[1]) were set up for the sloops and landing craft in the chaungs approaching Ryuwa. Prior to the main assault, 44 Commando were landed on islands west of Ryuwa to clear them of Japanese and to enable artillery to be placed to cover the assault. Supported by an air strike and by gun-fire from *Narbada*, *Jumna* and *Flamingo*, 53rd Brigade landed unopposed at a chaung near Ryuwa at 1034 on 16th and in twenty-four hours had captured their objectives, and consolidated. However, a serious mistake was made in clearing trees and undergrowth from the landing point. This betrayed the bankhead to the enemy who at once began to shell it. By 19 February Japanese shell and mortar fire was so intense and accurate that the bankhead could only be used at night. The first troops of 2nd West African Brigade were landed on 18th and disembarkation continued after a second, and better concealed, bankhead had been opened.

The sloops fired 9,750 rounds in support of the Army at Ryuwa, at times carrying out bombardments with an accuracy which almost amounted to virtuosity. On one occasion *Narbada* and *Flamingo* successfully bombarded an enemy position on a hill 1,260 feet high, at

---

[1] E.g. 'Winchester': advanced base for sloops and landing craft; 'Eton': staging post for minor landing craft; 'St Paul's': release position; 'Charterhouse': forward base on Setkhaw River, etc.

N

a range of 7,500 yards, although the position was surrounded by the West Africans at a distance of only 1,000 yards. The enemy sometimes retaliated: on 22nd *Narbada* was shelled and straddled while at anchor in the Sekhtaw river. The sloop got under way at once but was hit on the depth-charge rack starboard side aft. Happily, the depth-charges did not explode in sympathy.

Admiral Sir Arthur John Power, the C-in-C East Indies, wrote that 'the Myebon, Kangaw and Ryuwa operations afforded splendid opportunities for enterprise, resource, impromptu operations and close-range fighting. On each occasion the enemy was caught on the wrong foot and defeated.' This was true enough, yet all three operations failed in their main purpose. At Ryuwa, the 2nd Brigade's advance to An was hampered by difficulties in air supply, which affected the West Africans' morale, while 74th Brigade were held up by fierce fighting at Tamandu to the north. It was soon clear that the Japanese 54th Division had escaped once again. Their fighting value must now be very low, but they were safely over the An Pass.

One final amphibious operation remained: a landing at Letpan (Operation TURRET) on 13 March to encircle troops of the Japanese 54th Division retreating from Ryuwa and the Japanese 55th Division at Taungup, and to seize the road to the Taungup Pass. Rear Admiral Martin had been relieved by Commodore A. I. Poland, Naval Force Commander Burma, on 24 February and Captain Hill had withdrawn with his forces on 4 March. The operation was carried out mainly by naval forces, commanded by Captain E. T. Cooper, from Ramree, consisting of the destroyer *Haitan*, LCH 261, *Barpeta*, five LCIs, thirty-five LCMs, forty-two LCAs, nine BYMs, sixteen MLs, three LCTs, eight LCSs, three LCPs, one MMS, two LCIs (Depot), and the store ship *Bandra*. The bombardment group was *Roebuck*, *Eskimo*, *Jumna*, and *Cauvery*. The assault troops, 4th Brigade and a battalion of 71st Brigade, embarked at Kyaukpyu from 9th to 13th. Two hill positions commanding the Ma-i Chaung were captured on the night of 12th–13th and the main body landed at 0934 the next day. 4th Brigade advanced south down the coast road until they were held up at Tanlwe. Taungup was occupied by the West Africans on 29 April. The enemy had vanished. The Japanese 55th Division's fighting qualities must also have been low, but they too had escaped, over the Taungup Pass. Sandoway was taken on 9th, Gwa on 13 May. There, the Third Arakan Campaign petered out.

After TURRET, almost all naval forces were withdrawn, to prepare for the assault on Rangoon. Only a few LCSs, LCPs and HDMLs remained. Probably the very last naval action off the coast occurred on 14 April, when HDML 1374 and LCS 144 destroyed two Japanese craft in the Kaleindaung river off Ramree.

In the third Arakan campaign, an Allied army corps of more than four divisions, hundreds of RAF and USAAF aircraft, and a hetero-geneous but large fleet of ships had all been used to seize territory which the enemy had already decided to give up. On their side, the Japanese 54th and 55th Divisions fought desperately to prevent 15th Corps crossing the An and Taungup passes, which they had no intention of doing. Thus, in one of the greatest anomalies of the whole Burma campaign, each side had sought fiercely to frustrate a non-existent purpose in the other.

It could be asked, in the words of little Peterkin, 'What good came of it at last?' It could be argued that the whole of the Allied forces in Arakan after the capture of Akyab would have been better employed elsewhere – in, for instance, an assault on Rangoon in March, with additional air cover from the carriers of the British Pacific Fleet who also might have been better employed at that time in helping to recover former British territory than in swinging to their anchors at Manus. The Americans were seen to recover their former possessions in the Far East by force of arms. The British, French and Dutch were not. An earlier capture of Rangoon might have allowed the reconquest of all, or at least part of Malaya before the atomic bomb at Hiroshima brought the war to an end. The reconquest of Malaya by British forces in the field would have done much to mitigate what might still be the most lasting effect of the war: the loss of European 'face' in Asia. The end of the third Arakan campaign, like the end of the first, cast a long shadow.

The capture of Rangoon by an assault from sea and air (Operation DRACULA) had everything to recommend it, except the whole-hearted support of the Americans. It was in the old British military tradition of the indirect approach, and was the kind of bold *coup* which appealed to Mr Churchill (though not as much as his old love, CULVERIN). If successful, it would cut the lines of communications of the Japanese armies in Burma and undermine their whole position. Wavell had planned for it in ANAKIM. Mountbatten had planned for it in VANGUARD (DRACULA's predecessor). The British Chiefs of Staff favoured it, the men of SEAC longed for it. Yet, by the spring of 1945, the capture of Rangoon had come to resemble the search for the Holy Grail – long sought after, always disappointed, always just over the next horizon.

In June 1944 Admiral Mountbatten received a directive from the Combined Chiefs of Staff which virtually committed SEAC forces to a long drawn-out struggle in the swamps and jungles of northern Burma against an enemy who had better lines of communications. The priority stressed in the directive was the supply of war materials by air, and eventually by land, to China. However, there seemed to be two ways of carrying out the directive: the direct approach, with an advance by 14th Army to Mandalay and exploitation southwards towards Rangoon (Operation CAPITAL); or the indirect approach, DRACULA. The Americans, particularly General Stilwell, opposed DRACULA; it might divert resources, and would certainly divert attention, from the main objective of supplying China. The defeated Japanese in northern Burma should be pressed as hard as possible. Furthermore, DRACULA would require extra forces from outside SEAC. But by this time, it was just possible that extra forces could be supplied to SEAC. If the war in Europe ended, as expected, before the winter of 1944 then it should be possible to mount DRACULA before the 1945 monsoon. In September, after the Quebec conference, Admiral Mountbatten received a new directive; the recapture of the whole of Burma, but without prejudicing supplies to China. CAPITAL was approved, as far as was necessary to secure the supply line to China, and DRACULA was approved, with a target date of 15 March 1945.

The new directive had hardly been transmitted when the failure at Arnhem removed any possibility of extra resources being sent to SEAC. Only three weeks after it had been approved for March, DRACULA was postponed until November 1945 at the earliest.

SEAC's planning staffs began all over again. In October, Admiral Mountbatten proposed to carry on with CAPITAL; to clear Arakan down to Akyab (ROMULUS) and assault Akyab (TALON); amphibious operations to establish a forward base on the Kra Isthmus; and, like the end of the rainbow, DRACULA after the 1945 monsoon.

The campaigns in Arakan and in central and northern Burma went so well for the Allies in the last months of 1944 and in January 1945 that a new directive was sent to Admiral Mountbatten; the liberation of Burma, followed by the reconquest of Malaya and the forcing of the Malacca Straits. But the directive had important provisos on the United States' strategic policy in South-east Asia; the Americans made it clear that aid to China was still more important to them than 14th Army's operations in central Burma. After much discussion and some wrangling with the Americans, particularly over the question of allocations of transport aircraft, two possible courses of action for SEAC emerged: either to abandon DRACULA and rely upon a rapid advance by 14th Army to take Rangoon from the land side before the monsoon, followed by an assault on Phuket Island, on the Kra Isthmus (Operation ROGER) to prepare the way for the recapture of Singapore; or, to carry out a sea and airborne assault on Rangoon with reduced forces (a modified DRACULA) with a slower advance by 14th Army, and abandon ROGER.

At a meeting with his commanders on 23 February, Admiral Mountbatten was reassured that the first alternative was feasible, provided that the air transport bases in Arakan were developed in time, and this plan was adopted, to be followed by ROGER in June, and, in the future, an assault on the Port Swettenham–Port Dickson area (Operation ZIPPER) in October and Singapore (Operation MAILFIST) in December 1945.

But once again, plans for SEAC were hardly formulated before they were thrown into flux. The overland advance towards Rangoon fell behind schedule. Worse still, the Chinese demanded the return of their troops to China and as a result the Americans announced that 40% of the transport aircraft supplying 14th Army would be withdrawn on 1 June. The monsoon was expected on or about 5 May. If 14th Army had not reached Rangoon and developed some of its port facilities by 1 June then the army would have to retreat to some point where it could be supplied by land, possibly even back to the Chindwin river. The effect on the progress of the war in South-east Asia and on morale in SEAC would be catastrophic. On 2 April, Admiral Mountbatten decided to postpone ROGER and risk the modified DRACULA operation, with one seaborne division and one airborne battalion, early in May.

Planning began, under canvas, at Minbyin, Ramree Island on 8 April. The planning staff used boxes for chairs, boards for tables and oil hand lamps for lighting; by compensation, there was an excellent bathing beach – warmly remembered by all who served on Ramree. The headquarters ship *Largs* lay anchored offshore to provide naval communications.

The assault troops were the 26th Indian Infantry Division, with the 2nd Gurkha Parachute Battalion. The Assault Force Commanders for DRACULA were Rear Admiral Martin, Flag Officer Force 'W', Major General H. M. Chambers, commanding the 26th Indian Division, and Group Captain H. Pleasance. The Assault Group Commanders were Captain E. Tyndale Cooper, Senior Officer Assault Group W1, with

Brigadier L. V. Hutcheson commanding the 71st Indian Infantry Brigade and Captain T. I. S. Bell, SO AG W2, with Brigadier I. Lauder, commanding the 36th Indian Infantry Brigade.

Planning was completed on 23 April (the day the Japanese began to evacuate Rangoon) and the force commanders embarked in *Largs* and sailed for Kyaukpyu to mount the operation.

A sea-borne assault on Rangoon presented special problems. The weather was not likely to be good and after the monsoon would certainly become much worse. The Rangoon river had not been surveyed since 1942, the Japanese had taken away many navigational aids in the river and its approaches, and Allied aircraft had dropped many mines in the river. Tides were so strong that LCMs, LCTs and LCAs movements would probably have to be restricted to certain times. Because of the river depth and the mines, the assault craft would have to be lowered well to seaward of the river entrance (in the event they were lowered thirty miles from the assault beaches), and supporting gun-fire during the assault stage would have to be provided by LCGs and LCSs. The state of the tides on D-Day (2 May) meant that the assault convoys would have to arrive off the Rangoon river in darkness. Wisely, Admiral Sir Arthur John Power ordered that no more shipping was to be concentrated in the assault area than could be discharged in forty-eight hours; Flag Officer Force 'W' was to be prepared to withdraw troops who had been landed if it became impossible to maintain them. He was empowered to postpone D-Day if necessary.

The 7th and 37th Minesweeping Flotillas, under Captain A. Day, Naval Commander Force 65, in *Pickle* sailed from Akyab in two convoys, 'Able' and 'Fox' on 29 and 30 April, beginning their sweeps on the afternoon of 1 May.

The main assault force sailed in four convoys from Kyaukpyu, the slowest, 'Dog' of 4½ knots, on 27th followed by 'Easy' on 28th and 'Charlie' and 'Baker' at roughly twenty-four hour intervals thereafter. Despite some breakdowns and leaking craft, the convoys arrived off the Rangoon river in good order but bad weather on the night of 1–2 May. It was a time of full moon but the sky was almost completely overcast and there were heavy and frequent rain and thunder storms (the whole operation was conducted under the gloom of a meteorological pheno-menon known as the 'Dracula Depression').

Fighter protection for the DRACULA convoys was provided by the 21st Aircraft Carrier Squadron, Cdr. G. N. Oliver, flying his broad pennant in *Royalist* with the escort carriers *Hunter, Stalker, Khedive* and *Emperor*, the cruiser *Phoebe*, and the destroyers *Venus*, *Virago*, *Vigilant* and *Saumarez*. On 2 May, D-Day, the force provided air cover for the assault ships off the Rangoon river estuary.

Meanwhile, unknown to (or at least unreported by) Allied intelligence, the Japanese had completed their evacuation of the city on 29 April. Two days later the pilot of an aircraft flying over Rangoon noted the words 'Japs Gone! Exdigitate!' painted on the roof of Rangoon gaol. That day the Gurkhas were parachuted on to Elephant Point and occupied it after one skirmish with a small party of Japanese.

The first man in Rangoon was a Mosquito pilot, Wing Cdr. A. E. Saunders (CO of 110 Sq. RAF) who landed at Mingaladon on the afternoon of 2nd. His aircraft had been damaged by the state of the runway, so he made his way into the town to the gaol, which he discovered was free of Japanese and thence to the dockside and down river in a commandeered sampan. But his news, that the Japanese had gone, was too late to affect the assault. W1 and W2 assault group landing craft had moved off at 0240 that morning, and, preceded by a bombardment of the assault areas from air and sea, landed shortly after 7 o'clock, 71st Brigade to the east of the Rangoon river, 36th Brigade to the west, both against no enemy opposition. The next day two battalions of 36th Brigade re-embarked and landed on Rangoon water-front.

Rangoon had proved to be a paper fortress and was recaptured, just as it had been lost more than three years earlier, without a shot being fired. The streets of the city were littered with Japanese currency notes. The shops were empty and there was no electric power, water supply nor sanitation. Soon a few cars appeared, assembled from parts hidden from the Japanese during the occupation. There had been some looting in the city since the Japanese evacuation.

Minesweeping continued in the rivers, and berths cleared on the water-front. On 6 May, the large infantry landing ship *Glenroy*, drawing 29 feet, was able to berth alongside in Rangoon. The same day troops from Rangoon on the Pegu road met the advance parties of 14th Army – whose successes in the north had forced the Japanese to evacuate Rangoon.

The only naval casualties were LCT 1238, mined and sunk with some twenty casualties off Elephant Point on 3 May, and the infantry landing ship *Silvio* damaged by a mine in the Rangoon river on 8 May. That day all landing craft, except *Silvio* and one unserviceable LCT, were sailed for India.

General Slim had asked for a naval patrol in the Sittang river, and this was carried out by four MLs, under Lt. Cdr. H. Leslie, RNVR. Two of them, MLs 591 and 905, were swamped and lost in a tidal bore on 9 May.

From 12 May, the 13th, 14th and 59th ML Flotillas and the 146th HDML Flotilla began operations in the Delta, cutting the Japanese escape routes east of the Irrawaddy river, rounding up small parties of Japanese, patrolling the Kokawa, Hlaing, Bawle and China Bakir rivers, and the Irrawaddy as far as Henzada, to impress the Burma National Army and local inhabitants, and to assist in re-establishing some form of local administration and civil government. Eleven Japanese small craft were destroyed, about 100 Japanese killed and ten captured. Some thirty Japanese surrendered. Bassein was reoccupied by two LCPs, who were relieved by a battalion of troops two days later.

The operations were discontinued on 17 June, when the rivers were rising in the monsoon, the main banks disappeared and the channels were lost. Many water-ways began to be overgrown with a variety of water hyacinth. It was perhaps the final irony of the Burma campaign, that the last naval operations were frustrated by hyacinths.

Chapter Seven

OPERATIONS IN THE
INDIAN OCEAN

WHEN the British Pacific Fleet was formed in November 1944, the 'rump' of the remaining ships of the Eastern Fleet became the East Indies Fleet, with Admiral Sir Arthur John Power as Commander in Chief. The BPF departed to carry the flag in the Pacific while those who were left behind must have felt that they had, in a sense, missed the boat, to become a 'Second Eight' operating in an area which was increasingly a back-water. In the latter months of the war, the East Indies Fleet was hard-pressed to find itself some offensive employment. Commodore Evans Lombe had been able virtually to pick and choose the staff officers he wanted for the BPF; this might have caused friction, but Admiral Fraser and Admiral Power were old friends, fellow gunnery officers who had served together at Whale Island, and there were no hard feelings.

At its formation, the East Indies Fleet consisted of the Third Battle Squadron (Vice Admiral H. T. C. Walker), the battleship *Queen Elizabeth* and the battle cruiser *Renown*; nine cruisers including the Dutch *Tromp*, forming the 5th Cruiser Squadron (Rear Admiral A. D. Read); three escort and two ferry carriers; and, eventually, twenty-four destroyers. The fleet, with escort vessels, numbered about seventy ships. Rear Admiral Clement Moody, who had been Rear Admiral (Air) Eastern Fleet, since December 1943, became Flag Officer (Air) East Indies Station, responsible for all naval air shore establishments on the Station and in command of all East Indies Fleet aircraft carriers and escort carriers, although the C-in-C had operational control of carriers when employed on escort duties. The command structure of the East Indies Station was reorganised, as follows:

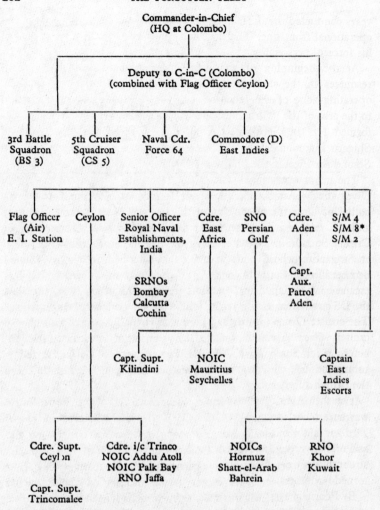

* The 8th Submarine Flotilla was detached to Fremantle under the operational control of the US C-in-C S.W. Pac. Area.

On 8 January, 1945, Admiral Sir Geoffrey Layton was relieved as C-in-C Ceylon by Lieut. General Sir Edward Wetherall. Admiral Layton had been C-in-C China Station in 1941 and had been on his way home, actually on board a trooper within half an hour of sailing, when he heard the news of the destruction of Force Z. He had come ashore to take command of the remnants of the fleet and for the next three years conducted the defence of Ceylon which for some time was in the operational front line. The fleet and the Service owed a great deal to his forceful personality.

At the beginning of 1945 the Japanese reorganised their naval resources in the south-west Pacific and in the Indian Ocean. The operating zone of the Japanese South-west Area Fleet was restricted to the area of the Philippines, and a new fleet, the 10th Area Fleet, was formed for the South-west Pacific; its C-in-C was Vice Admiral Shigeru Fukudome, who had been commander of the now disbanded Second Air Fleet in the Philippines, with his headquarters at Singapore.

The major operational unit of the 10th Area Fleet was the Second Diversionary Attack Force. This consisted of the two converted battleship/aircraft carriers *Ise* and *Hyuga*, forming the carrier squadron, and the two heavy cruisers *Ashigara* and *Haguro*, forming the 5th Cruiser Squadron. Two more heavy cruisers, *Takao* and *Miyoko*, were at Singapore where both had reached sanctuary after being badly damaged in the Battle of Leyte Gulf. *Miyoko* had made one attempt to escape back to Japan in December 1944, but had been torpedoed by the US submarine *Bergol* on 13th, and had then returned to Singapore. The cruiser *Oyodo* joined the fleet from 5 to 20 February and a fourth cruiser, *Isudzu*, joined on 25 March but lasted barely a fortnight before being sunk, on 7 April, in a co-ordinated attack by the US submarines *Charr*, *Gabilan* and *Besugo*, with peripheral assistance from the British submarine *Spark*.

The 10th Area Fleet also included the 13th Air Fleet which, in fact, was an air fleet only in name. Nominally, it had two air flotillas, the 23rd and 28th, but by January 1945 these were only a few airfield units and one air group, the 381st, with four air groups attached. The total strength was only about fifty fighters, five night-fighters and seventeen torpedo-bombers.

By February 1945 the Japanese had begun to withdraw their garrisons in outlying islands in the Moluccas, in Timor, the Lesser Sunda Islands and in the scattered islands of the Panda and Arafura Seas, intending to hold Java, Borneo and Sumatra as long as possible, but to mount their main defence in Malaya and Indochina. On 7 February the 10th Area Fleet was placed under the operational command of Field Marshal Count Terauchi, C-in-C Southern Army Area, with his headquarters at Saigon. Count Terauchi laid plans to reduce his outlying forces drastically and concentrate them in Malaya and Indo-china, in four principal evacuation operations: SHO (Akiraka), the evacuation of troops from the Andaman and Nicobar Islands to Singapore; CHI, movement of troops from Singapore to Indochina, via Saigon; Transportation No. 10, evacuation of about 15,000 men of the 48th Division; and HO, evacuation of troops from Borneo to Sourabaya. (No details are known of HO and it was probably never carried out.)

In February *Ise* and *Hyuga* were recalled and sailed on 10th from Singapore, bound for Japan, carrying aviation spirit and other war materials. With such valuable cargoes the Japanese took great care to safeguard their passage and, by a combination of good luck and bad weather, both evaded numerous attacks by air and by submarine and reached Moji on 19th. *Haguro* and *Ashigara*, and one old destroyer, *Kamikaze*, were now the only sizable warships left in the 10th Area Fleet to protect the troop evacuations.

In 1945, the tasks of the East Indies Fleet were to deny the enemy the use of the Indian Ocean, cutting the supply lines to the Japanese Army in Burma and to the Japanese garrisons in the Andaman and Nicobar Islands; to attack the enemy's shipping, oil and harbour installations; and to give close support to the 14th Army in Burma during the third campaign in Arakan which had opened in December 1944. Since the summer of 1944, the Japanese had practically abandoned the Indian Ocean, at least for the passage of large ships. The Allied submarines and aircraft had forced the enemy to use small ships in coastal convoys which crept close inshore, following the coast-line as near to the land as possible. However, the evacuation or relief of Japanese garrisons might bring large enemy vessels once more into the Indian Ocean and in February 1945 destroyers of the East Indies began a series of anti-shipping sweeps in the Andaman Sea.

The first of these (Operation SUFFICE) was undertaken by Force 68[1] which left Trincomalee on 21 February. The force sank no shipping; *Roebuck* and *Rapid* carried out a short bombardment of Great Coco Island just after midday on 24th, but broke off after an air alarm. An hour later the whole force returned and bombarded for forty-five minutes. The bombardment was carried out with more enthusiasm than effect; 991 rounds of HE and seventeen of star-shell were expended, to achieve severe damage to one hut and slight damage to another. A radar station was possibly destroyed.

Force 68 returned to Akyab to fuel on 25 Febuary, sailing again on

[1] Force 68: The destroyers *Rotherham* (Captain H. Biggs, Captain D.11), *Roebuck*, *Rapid* and *Rocket*.

27th for a second sweep (Operation TRAINING). Three enemy coasters were destroyed between Tavoy Island and Heanzay Basin on the night of 1–2 March and on 3rd the force bombarded the dockyard area at Port Blair, sinking two sailing ships and damaging three more. A number of shore batteries were engaged, and there was one gratifyingly large explosion, which was possibly a magazine detonating.

Neither operation had achieved much but, as their code-names suggested, they were good enough for training and morale. The Japanese lookout and reporting organisation was apparently poor; they did not have enough aircraft to keep air control of the area, and their shore-based radar systems were almost ineffective. Captain Biggs (D.11) reported that the area was 'ripe for development'.

The first 'developers' were Force 70[1] who sailed from Trincomalee on Operation TRANSPORT on 14 March. Sweeping towards Penang, without result, the force abandoned a projected reconnaissance of Langkawi Sound because of reported enemy air activity but, on the evening of 17th, bombarded the railway works at Sigli, in Sumatra. There was no sign of life there 'except smoke from a train and an enormous flock of white birds which withdrew in an orderly manner to the southward'.

Next day, Force 70 arrived off Great Nicobar and spent much of it in an entertaining 'follow-my-leader' in and out of the islands. The weather was fine and the Nicobar Islands, with their palm trees and dazzlingly white sandy beaches, looked most inviting. But no targets were found.

At first light on 19 March the force closed the harbour of Port Blair, but again there were no targets. At midday the force was off Stewart Sound, on the south-east coast, between the North and Middle Andaman Islands. This was known to be held by the enemy and possibly defended by a battery of guns, although the latest intelligence suggested that the gun emplacements were now derelict. *Volage* at this time had had main condenser trouble and was steaming on one shaft only.

Early in the afternoon, *Saumarez* entered the Sound cautiously and alone, leaving *Volage* to fire air bursts over the suspected positions of the shore batteries, and *Rapid* to engage with direct counter-battery fire if required. Some figures were seen in a clearing on the north hillside, around a possible gun emplacement, and *Saumarez'* bofors

---

[1] Force 70: the destroyers *Saumarez* (Captain M. L. Power, Captain D.26), *Volage* and *Rapid*.

crews indicated the target in the best and quickest way, by hosing it down with tracer shells. But the figures were considered to be natives and the gun-site – if it were a gun-site – appeared to be deserted and derelict.

Further into the Sound, *Saumarez* sighted a junk alongside a quay and at 1350, just as the junk was being dispatched, gun-fire was heard to the eastward. The somewhat plaintive signal was received from *Volage*: 'Somebody is firing at us.' Manoeuvring now in confined waters, *Saumarez* went rapidly astern to clear a projecting point of land, swung round and returned the way she had come, at high speed. Rounding an island in the middle of the Sound, *Saumarez* came upon an unpleasant sight.

Rapid was stopped, broadside on in the Sound, about two hundred yards offshore. Large shell splashes were growing around her, clouds of steam were roaring from her funnels, and there was a serious fire burning amidships. Beyond her, *Volage* was steaming protectively to and fro, yapping away at the hillside with every available gun.

While *Volage* made covering smoke, *Saumarez* closed *Rapid* and came alongside her. *Saumarez*' close range weapons could not bear on the enemy and *Rapid*'s guns crews had sustained casualties. Some of *Saumarez*' guns crews were ordered to board *Rapid* and man her guns:

'I had hardly looked at *Rapid* until that moment – I had been fully occupied in trying to get my tracers on the enemy battery – and I was unprepared for the bloody shambles I stumbled into.

'The pompom's crew were dead or dying. Eight bodies were hung around the mounting, and the wounded lay in a bloody heap on the iron deck. There was a human lung draped over the gunsight, and half a man sitting in the trainer's seat. My orders were to get the gun into action again, so we bundled the dead men over the side as best we could. The whole corpses were easy enough to manhandle, but my heart failed me when I took a body by the shoulders – and the upper half of the torso came away in my hands. But worst of all was the removal of the hunks of raw meat from the jagged steel around the gun – bare hands for this job, just like the local butcher in the village shop.

'Our green uniforms soaked and sticky with black blood, we then turned to the gun; but it was useless, solid, and two barrels split by splinters. Meanwhile the wounded were being taken care of by the first-aid parties, so back we clambered to our own ship, bloody, sweaty and shaken.

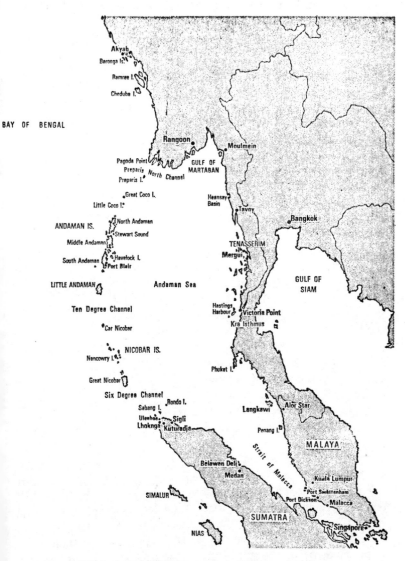

NAVAL OPERATIONS in the INDIAN OCEAN
January – July, 1945

'*Saumarez* and *Rapid* – still under fire – were by now making slow progress towards the exit. *Rapid*'s screws were turning again, and our combined speed was about 6 knots.'[1]

Saumarez had *Rapid* in tow on her starboard side, secured bow to stern, and both ships were heading towards the open sea when *Volage* who was still making smoke and engaging the shore batteries, reported that she was hit, and stopped. 'This', as Captain Power, in *Saumarez*, later commented, 'was an unpleasant moment giving an unattractive prospect of having two ships unable to steam and within the enemy range.' However, *Volage* was able to get under way again and all three ships reached the open sea where at 1600 *Rapid* was slipped and proceeded unaided.

Casualties during the action had been heavy: in *Rapid*, one officer and ten ratings killed, two officers and twenty-one men wounded; in *Volage*, three ratings killed and eight wounded. Force 70 reached Akyab on 20 March where *Rapid*'s battle damage was patched up, with the help of *Suffolk*'s engine room department working day and night, and the ship later sailed to Simonstown for permanent repairs.

The Japanese immediately broadcast accurate details of the action in Stewart Sound, including the names of *Rapid* and *Volage*. This alarmed and puzzled Allied intelligence officers, and the solution was not found until the end of April, when Japanese troops equipped with radio were found hiding on Baronga Island, south of Akyab. They had been there since Akyab was captured in January and had been intercepting signals between ships at Akyab.

Virago and *Vigilant*, two more destroyers of the 26th Flotilla, had left Trincomalee to reinforce Captain Power when the news of the action in Stewart Sound had been received and they were part of a reconstituted and vengeful Force 70[2] which sailed from Akyab on 25 March for the second half of the anti-shipping sweep, Operation ONBOARD.

Force 70 entered the Andaman Sea through Preparis North Channel on the morning of 26th and detected a radar contact almost at once, range 21,000 yards. Force 70 formed line ahead and increased speed to close the target which was sighted at 1047 and immediately turned away to the south-west.

The target was a convoy of four enemy ships, bound from Singapore to Port Blair. They were the 1,500-ton *Rishio* Maru, with a cargo of

[1] 'Action in the Andamans', by Commander Denis Calnan, in manuscript, 2.6.68.
[2] Force 70: *Saumarez* (D.26), *Volage*, *Virago* and *Vigilant*.

rice, 130 men of a naval battalion and eighteen women; the 400-ton *Teshio* Maru, carrying food-stuffs, general supplies and *sekkyu* oil; and an escort of two submarine chasers, Numbers 34 and 63.

Remembering that a British destroyer had once been hit and stopped by a lucky shot from a smaller opponent, Captain Power decided to attack out of range of the submarine chasers' guns. At 1100 *Saumarez* opened fire, range 14,000 yards, whilst the other three destroyers following their flotilla leader opened fire as they came within range.

The submarine chasers were small and elusive targets, highly manoeuvrable and handled with great dash and gallantry. They laid smoke screens to protect their charges, returning again and again within range, to tempt the destroyers away from the convoy. After half an hour's furious firing, Force 70 had expended a vast amount of ammunition, and *Volage* had also fired four torpedoes at *Rishio* Maru at a range of 2,000 yards, and all without success.

Meanwhile, radio contact had been made with two groups of patrolling Liberators, whose pilots seemed at first suspicious of the quality of Force 70's English. One group reported that they were armed only with depth-charges and nothing more was heard from them. The second group were evidently impressed by Captain Power's command of the language and flew down to sea-level to carry out an attack.

The leading Liberator approached *Rishio* Maru at masthead height and dropped a stick of eight bombs. The enemy ship blew up and sank within a few minutes but, before the horrified eyes of the men in the destroyers, the Liberator's port wing tip appeared to strike the ship's mainmast and the bomber cartwheeled over and crashed into the sea.

Force 70 were now very low in ammunition, except *Virago* who had been late into action. Cdr. Durlacher, in *Volage,* was 'appalled by the speed with which the ammunition disappeared. I had not realised how easy it was to get rid of some 900 rounds in a short space of time.' It was therefore a relief when *Teshio* Maru eventually succumbed to *Volage*'s gunfire. *Vigilant* hit one submarine chaser with a torpedo from a salvo of eight and sank her. The other escort was sunk by gunfire from *Vigilant* and *Virago*. And so, at last, after the expenditure of 18 torpedoes, 3,160 rounds of 4.7 inch and a considerable amount of bofors ammunition, all four enemy ships were sunk. It was, in Captain Power's phrase 'an exasperatingly unsatisfactory action'. Later, the Admiralty fully concurred with this opinion.

It only remained to pick up survivors. *Saumarez* had already recovered two RAF sergeants, R. G. Radford and P. Roberts, from the crashed Liberator, both injured, but both glad to be alive and rescued.

The Japanese survivors were another matter. Captain Power signalled: 'Pick up those who are willing. I really only want a few specimens.' The officers and men of the flotilla were extremely reluctant to pick up any Japanese survivors at all. The Japanese for their part, were as loth to be rescued. A few grudgingly allowed themselves to be picked up but most swam away from the approaching ships. One at least preserved the offensive Samurai spirit to the end:

'I was standing abreast the torpedo tubes directing the rescue when I heard and felt a clang on the ship's side. There directly beneath me was a Japanese, heavily built and with a bald head. Half out of the water with one hand gripping the rescue net, with the other he was hammering at the thin plate of our ship's side with the nose of what looked like an oerlikon shell. Instinctively I drew my pistol, and leaning far over the beading with one arm round a guard rail stanchion jammed the barrel hard down on top of his skull. I could not think of anything else to do – I spoke no Japanese. Blood streaming down his face he looked up at me, the pistol six inches from his eyes, the shell in his hand. I suppose I should have shot him – but I knew my gun was unloaded, which was more than he did. I do not know how long I hung in this ridiculous position, eyeball to eyeball with a fanatical enemy, but it seemed too long at the time. At last he dropped the shell into the sea, brought up his feet, pushed off from the ship's side like an Olympic swimmer, turned on his face and swam away.'[1]

Five officers, forty-one men and seven women were rescued. One of the women, 'Mary', was pregnant and another, a half-caste girl 'Chatya', knew scraps of English, including 'kiss me quick' and snatches of popular songs. Other survivors told their interrogators that Chatya was 'Joro', i.e. intended for the entertainment of the Andaman garrison. Shortly before Force 70 entered Trincomalee on 28 March, one of Volage's prisoners was found to have hanged himself with his own loincloth in the Chief and Petty Officers' bathroom.

The destruction of the relief convoy deprived the Andaman garrison not only of the services of their 'Joros' but also of desperately needed food. By the end of the war, the situation in the islands was serious and the Japanese committed several atrocities on the civilian population, including the transportation of three hundred 'useless mouths' to the

---

[1] 'Action in the Andamans'.

uninhabited Havelock Island, off South Andaman, where all but eleven of them died.[1]

During April anti-shipping sweeps were carried out by 11th Destroyer Flotilla, beginning with a sweep of the Tenasserim Coast between Mergui and Amherst (Operation PENZANCE) by Force 62[2] on the night of 1–2 April. During the day the force had reconnoitred Narcondam Island to judge its suitability as a fuel and ammunition dump for coastal forces and that night sighted and sank their first targets, a small auxiliary coaster and a junk. On 4th the unfortunate radar station on Great Coco was again bombarded and Force 62 returned to Akyab on 5th, sailing again on 7th for Operation PASSBOOK, a sweep of the Burma coast between Mergui and the Moulmein River which was carried out between 9th and 11th. Several junks and assorted sailing craft were sunk. Early on 11th, Liberators of 222 Group RAF had a notable success in the sinking of the net-tender *Agata* Maru and her escort Submarine Chaser No 7 north-east of the Nicobars. That afternoon Force 62 closed the scene and picked up sixty-two Japanese survivors and six young Sumatran boys wearing Japanese uniform.

On 27 April, when the Japanese were already evacuating troops from Rangoon Force 62[3] sailed from Trincomalee for Operation GABLE and by 29th were on patrol in the Gulf of Martaban. At 0015 on 30 April an enemy convoy was detected, consisting of four small vessels, seven larger vessels, accompanied by one small escort vessel, which were evacuating some 750 Japanese troops from Rangoon to Moulmein. The whole convoy was destroyed by gunfire. No survivors allowed themselves to be picked up at the time but when Force 62 returned to the scene at dawn, *Redoubt* recovered five. *Roebuck* attempted to rescue a party of six Japanese clinging to some wreckage. They were apparently crouched around a grenade and when they saw the destroyer approaching, one of them pulled out the pin. 'It was', Commodore Poland recalled later, 'an astonishing and rather unpleasant sight so soon after breakfast.' This convoy, and that so laboriously sunk by the 26th Destroyer Flotilla a month earlier, had both been destroyed before transmitting a distress message, and, as far as the Japanese knew, had been sunk without trace. The Japanese therefore ordered all ships to exercise the sending of distress messages when attacked.

---

[1] See also *The Knights of Bushido*, by Lord Russell of Liverpool (Cassell, 1958), Ch. XIII.

[2] Force 62: *Rotherham* (D.11), *Racehorse*, *Redoubt* and *Rocket*.

[3] Force 62: *Roebuck* (broad pennant of Commodore A. L. Poland, Cdre. (D)), *Racehorse* and *Redoubt*.

Meanwhile on the broader strategic front in South-east Asia, the Burma Road land route to China had been reopened on 27 January 1945, and on 3 February the Supreme Allied Commander, Admiral Mountbatten, received a fresh directive from the Combined Chiefs of Staff: subject to the successful liberation of Burma, his next main task would be the liberation of Malaya and the opening of the Malacca Straits. Planning for the reconquest of Malaya (Operation ZIPPER) and the assault on Singapore (Operation MAILFIST) required detailed and recent photographic information on the enemy's dispositions, harbours, airfields and defences on the Malayan peninsula and the neighbouring coast of Sumatra, and particularly at Phuket Island, at the northern entrance to the Malacca Strait, which would be an excellent forward naval, air and general supply base for MAILFIST.

The areas to be photographed were beyond the range of shore-based photo-reconnaissance aircraft and although B-29s of the US 20th Bomber Command carried out a certain amount of photo-reconnaissance the main task was done by the East Indies Fleet in a series of photo-reconnaissance sorties beginning on 22 February 1945 when Force 62[1] sailed from Trincomalee on Operation STACEY. The Tanker Group, Force 61, for the operation consisted of RFA *Echodale* escorted by the frigate *Trent*.

Twenty photographic reconnaissances were planned for STACEY: on the three days from 26 to 28 February, from a flying-off position inside the Andaman Sea, flights over the Kra Isthmus from 7°N to 9°40'N, over Phuket Island, Penang, Langkani and Butong Islands, Victoria Point, Hastings Harbour, and adjacent islands; and on 4 March, from a position off Simalur Island, flights over coastal areas in northern Sumatra around Sabang, part of Simalur Island and Nias Island and Penang.[2]

Vigilant returned to Trincomalee almost immediately after sailing, but rejoined on the evening of 23rd. *Spey* also had engine defects and changed places with *Trent* in Force 61 on 26th. The destroyers and frigates refuelled from the carriers and from *Kenya* on passage on 24th and Force 62 was in position for the first photographic reconnaissance at 0715 on 26th.

[1] Force 62: carriers *Empress* (flag of Vice Admiral Walker) and *Ameer*, the cruiser *Kenya*, destroyers *Volage* (Senior Officer), *Virago*, *Vigilant*, and frigates *Spey*, *Swale* and *Plym*.

[2] Times and positions of flying off were: 26th, 0715, 7°45'N 96°22'E; 27th, 0800, 9°11'N 95°58'E; 28th, 0755, 8°34'N 96°43'E; 4 March, 0740, 3°51'N 95°24'E.

The weather was good for photography, with clear visibility and almost no wind. However, light winds and temperamental catapults forced the carriers to steam at maximum speeds to fly off aircraft. The small escort carriers did not even pretend to be part of the 'fully-tropicalised' fleet and in hot weather living conditions on board them were extremely trying. In the air direction rooms, for instance, a team of twenty-two men were crammed into a small space, with no scuttles leading to the open air, no exhaust ventilation, and no air-conditioning. Habitability in the machinery spaces of these carriers in the tropics was, of course, even worse.

After a poor start on 26 April, when half of the photographs were lost because of camera failures, successful photo-reconnaissances were carried out on the remaining days. On 28th one Avenger dropped 40,000 propaganda leaflets in the Kra Isthmus area but otherwise it was a frustrating time for the bombers; two strikes were cancelled because of the lack of targets, and a third had to be abandoned for lack of maps and briefing material. In spite of the clear weather and a bright full moon, the force remained undetected until 1 March when Japanese aircraft attacked for the first time. 804 Sq. Hellcats had a most successful day: *Ameer*'s shot down a Dinah and an Oscar, and *Empress*'s flight of four another Oscar. These were the first Japanese aircraft to be shot down by fighters from British escort carriers. Force 62 returned to Trincomalee on 7 March.

The work begun in STACEY was taken a stage further with photo-reconnaissance of the Port Swettenham and Port Dickson areas in Operation SUNFISH a month later. Force 63,[1] commanded by Vice Admiral H. T. C. Walker in the battleship *Queen Elizabeth*, sailed from Trincomalee in two groups on 8 April for a mixed programme of photo-reconnaissances, air strikes, anti-shipping sweeps and bombardments.

While embarking their aircraft from shore on 8th, *Khedive*'s air group made a bad start when a Hellcat of 808 Sq. crashed into the ship's stern and burst into flames. The pilot was killed. Two days later, another Hellcat of 808 missed the arrester wires and crashed on deck, taking a Hellcat from the deck-park over the side and killing the pilot, a petty officer and two air mechanics on the flight deck. It was a dispiriting debut for a squadron new on the Station.

[1] Force 63: Group 1, *Queen Elizabeth* (flag of Vice Admiral Walker), the French battleship *Richelieu* (relieved *Renown* on 28 March), cruiser *London*, destroyers *Saumarez* (D.26), *Verulam* and *Vigilant*; Group 2, carriers *Emperor* (flag of Rear Admiral Patterson, who relieved Read as CS 5 on 11 March), and *Khedive*, cruiser *Cumberland*, destroyers *Venus* and *Virago*.

The first photo-reconnaissances were planned for 12th but were postponed for two days because of defects in *Emperor*'s catapult. Instead the bombardments were brought forward to 11th: *Queen Elizabeth, Richelieu* and *London* bombarded Sabang, *Saumarez, Vigilant* and *Verulam* bombarded Oleelhoe. There were no shipping targets at Sabang and the bombarding ships were themselves attacked by a group of about ten Oscars as they were retiring. 808 Sq. Hellcats shot down an Oscar and later, in the afternoon, a Dinah. During the day one unidentified enemy aircraft slipped out of cloud and dropped two bombs amongst the force, without causing any damage.

After fuelling from Force 70 (RFA *Echodale,* escorted by *Lossie*) on 12 April, Force 63 closed the west coast of Sumatra and photo-reconnaissance flights were flown as planned, from a position west of Padang, on 14th and 15th. The weather on 14th was bad over Malaya, the photographs were of poor quality and one experienced P.R. Pilot, S/Lt. J. W. Tomlinson, RNVR, was lost when his Hellcat ditched in the sea ten miles from Port Swettenham.

Enemy aircraft were approaching the force at heights above 30,000 feet, where the Hellcats had to expend quantities of fuel and oxygen to reach them. The Hellcats were not carrying long range tanks, and at least one Hellcat on 15th had to break off action because of lack of oxygen. The aircraft were in one pilot's words, 'becoming distinctly jaded'. One Oscar was shot down on 15th, and another the next day, during a strike on Emmahaven. However, an Oscar penetrated to the fleet on 15th and dropped its bombs. Although they did no damage, Admiral Walker signalled a sharp reminder to the Force, pointing out that the enemy had escaped without being fired on by a single ship.

By this stage of the war, there was a quite unusual tide of personal hatred running against the Japanese. The terrible treatment of prisoners of war and interned civilians in Japanese hands was by now common knowledge. Anything which might have any use for the Japanese, or any connection with them, was mercilessly attacked. At 0530 on 16th *Venus* and *Virago* were detached to carry out an anti-shipping sweep close to the Sumatran shore.

The only targets found were a handful of junks and small fishing craft, of very dubious value to the enemy, hidden behind islands in Ayerbangis Bay, Temang Roads, and Natal Roads:

'We had no wish to slaughter the crews of these junks, believed to be Sumatran fishermen, and generally fired a warning shot before opening fire. In one case the next round brought down the mast on a man's head as he was abandoning ship. We set fire to the junks as we passed or sank them. Admiral Walker called it Butchery.'[1]

This admittedly unedifying episode perhaps illustrates the difficulty of distinguishing, in action, between neutral and enemy. The prevailing mood in the fleet at that time was to destroy anything suspected of being Japanese first, and inquire later.

The third and last sequence of photo-reconnaissance flights, over southern Malaya, was successfully carried out on 18, 19 and 20 June by Force 63[2] in Operation BALSAM. By the third day of photo-reconnaissance, the fighter pilots of the force were growing restless on a diet of undiluted CAPS but Commodore Oliver reassured them they would have an opportunity to 'leave their cards'. Their chance came on 20th, when Hellcats of 804 and 808 Sqs. and Seafires of 809 Sq. (on their first offensive sorties over Sumatra) made strikes on airfields at Lhokseumawe, Medan and Bindjai. Runways were put out of action, buildings, installations, hangars, locomotives, rolling stock and grounded aircraft strafed. There was no enemy air opposition but one Hellcat was lost to flak over Medan – a particular tragedy for 808 Sq., since the pilot was their CO, Lt. Cdr. O. F. Wheatley, RNVR. His Hellcat was last seen in flames, with its tail shot away. It was his first flight after taking over command of the squadron.

At the end of April all available units of the East Indies Fleet not involved in DRACULA took part in a covering operation (BISHOP) to confuse the enemy and to prevent sea or air interference with the landings. On a minor scale the East Indies Fleet was to do for DRACULA what the Fast Carrier Task Force had done for the assault troops so many times in the Pacific. *Haguro* and *Ashigara* were still at Singapore and *Takao* was, just possibly, seaworthy again. It was also possible that the Japanese might stage replacement aircraft through the airfields in the Andaman and Nicobar Islands. (It was, of course, not realised at that time that the successes of the 14th Army had already forced the Japanese to begin evacuating Rangoon.)

Force 63,[3] under the command of Vice Admiral Walker, sailed for

---

[1] Commander Graham de Chair. Letter of 18.1.69.

[2] Force 63: the 21st Aircraft Carrier, consisting of the cruiser *Royalist* (broad pennant of Commodore G. N. Oliver) and carriers *Stalker*, *Khedive*, and *Ameer*, cruiser *Suffolk*, destroyers *Rotherham* (D.11), *Relentless*, *Redoubt*, *Roebuck* and *Racehorse*.

[3] Force 63: *Queen Elizabeth* (Flag of Vice Admiral Walker), *Richelieu*,

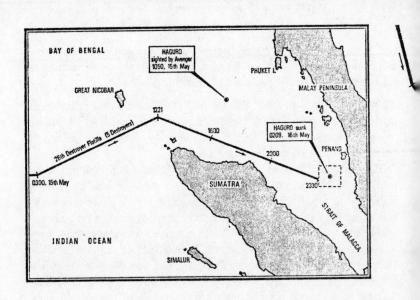

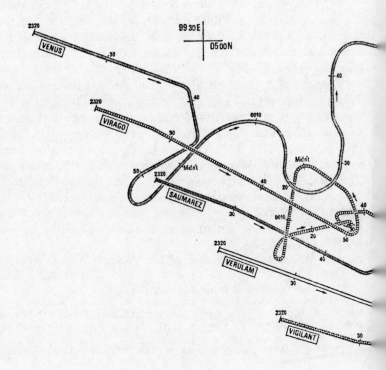

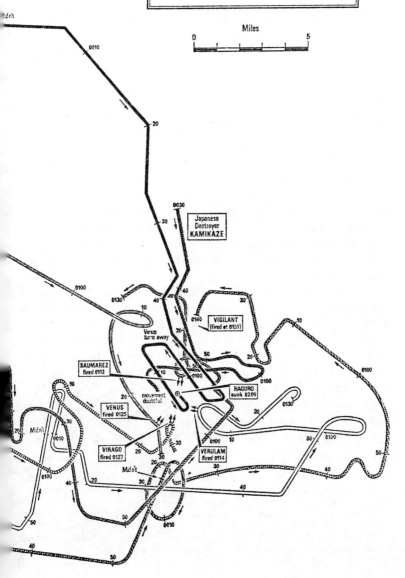

THE SINKING OF HAGURO

by the 26th Destroyer Flotilla
Malacca Strait, 15th / 16th May, 1945

Miles
0   5

Midn't

0010

20

0030

30

Japanese
Destroyer
KAMIKAZE

40

30

0100

0130

10

40

0140

VIGILANT
(fired at 0151)

10

Venus
turns away

20

50

SAUMAREZ
fired 0113

0100

10

50

20

0100

HAGURO
sunk 0209

0130

movement
doubtful

VENUS
fired 0125

20

0100

10

50

0100

10

Midn't

0010

30

VIRAGO
fired 0127

20

30

VERULAM
fired 0114

50

40

50

Midn't

20

0010

30

40

40

40

0100

40

20

50

50

0010

40

50

their part in BISHOP from Trincomalee on 27 April. The submarines *Scythian, Statesman* and *Subtle* established a patrol line across the southern reaches of the Malacca Strait, with *Strongbow* in the eastern Bay of Bengal and *Seadog* off the Tenasserim Coast. RAF Sunderlands and Liberators based in the Arakan patrolled the Andaman Sea, from the Tenasserim Coast across to South Andaman Island.

The destroyers fuelled from Force 69 (RFA *Olwen,* and *Paladin*) on 29 April and next day the main force carried out a dawn bombardment and Hellcat strike on both airfields at Car Nicobar. Both were cratered, installations destroyed, two 150-ton ships strafed and set on fire at Malacca, and a pier collapsed. That evening Port Blair was bombarded, airfield runways cratered, anti-aircraft and coastal batteries strafed and two hits were scored on Government House.

For the next two days the force shuttled between the Andaman and Nicobar Islands, bombarding Car Nicobar and Malacca again on 1 May, and Port Blair again on 2nd (D-Day).

Meanwhile the 21st Aircraft Carrier Squadron, of four escort carriers, commanded by Commodore G. N. Oliver in the cruiser *Royalist,* with *Phoebe* as fighter direction ship and four escorting destroyers,[1] had sailed from Trincomalee on 23 April. After calling at Akyab, they provided air cover for the assault convoys from 30 April to 4 May, in spite of bad weather due to what became known as the 'Dracula Depression'.

On 3 May Force 63 carried out armed air reconnaissances for coastal shipping along the Burma coast between Heanzay Basin and the Tavoy River. Two 80-ton coasters were found and bombed at Cap Point, Tavoy. At 1500 the fleet separated, Force 64[2] fuelling on 4 May, while Force 68 made armed air reconnaissances of coastal shipping between Mergui and Victoria Point: airfields at Victoria Point were strafed, and grounded aircraft destroyed.

The two forces made a rendezvous on 5 May and again separated, Force 68 this time going to fuel, while Force 64 took up the strikes against shipping at Port Blair and in Phoenix Bay and against the radar

---

Cumberland (flag of CS 5), *Suffolk, Ceylon,* H.M.Neth.S. *Tromp, Empress* (with 20 Hellcats of 804 Sq.), *Shah* (10 Avengers of 851 Sq., 4 Hellcats of 804 Sq.), *Rotherham* (D.11), *Tartar* (D.10), *Verulam, Nubian* and *Penn.*

[1] Escort carriers: *Hunter, Stalker, Khedive, Emperor.* Destroyers: *Saumarez, Venus, Virago* and *Vigilant.*

[2] Force 64: *Queen Elizabeth, Suffolk, Tromp, Tarter, Penn.* Force 68: *Cumberland, Richelieu, Ceylon, Rotherham, Roebuck* and *Redoubt.*

and D/F station on Mount Harrier. On 6 May *Queen Elizabeth* lay off Stewart Sound and with four 15-inch shell hits cleaned out the gun positions which had caused the 26th Destroyer Flotilla so much anguish on 19 March. The following day, the operations concluded with a final Hellcat strike on Car Nicobar airfield. During the twelve days of BISHOP, one Hellcat had been lost to flak, over Port Blair on 6th; there had been no enemy air opposition, only one bogey being reported, early on 1 May.

Victory in Europe was announced on 8th. All ships spliced the main brace and held services of thanksgiving, and the force returned to Trincomalee on 9 May.

The fleet had little chance to celebrate VE Day properly. On the evening of 9 May, ratings from the destroyer flotillas had barely had time to burn down some basha huts and start a fight with ratings from *Richelieu*, when a signal was flashed around the fleet ordering all ships to raise steam and prepare to leave harbour at 0600 the following morning.

Allied intelligence had reported that the heavy cruiser *Ashigara* and the destroyer *Kamikaze* were due to sail from Singapore on 10 May, bound for the relief of the Andaman and Nicobar garrisons. The Japanese were about to try and put into effect their evacuation plan SHO (Akiraka). In the event, *Ashigara* did not take part in Operation SHO but sailed instead for Lingga Roads, to carry out exercises with Army Air Force torpedo aircraft, starting on 21 May. In the meantime the evacuations were to be undertaken by two forces: Force One, the heavy cruiser *Haguro* and the destroyer *Kamikaze*, were to take food to the Andamans and return with troops to Singapore; Force Two, the auxiliary supply vessel *Kuroshiyo* Maru No 2, escorted by Submarine Chaser No 57, was to do the same for the Nicobars.

At Trincomalee, Force 61 was constituted at once, commanded by Admiral Walker and including every available ship in harbour.[1] The force sailed early on 10th and steamed eastward towards the Ten Degree Channel, to find and destroy the Japanese evacuation forces (Operation DUKEDOM). In the evening, a signal was received from *Subtle* (Lt. B. J. B. Andrew), on patrol in the Malacca Strait, reporting

---

[1] Force 61: *Queen Elizabeth* (Flag of Vice Admiral Walker BS 3), FS *Richelieu*, *Royalist* (broad pennant of Cdr. Oliver AC 21), *Hunter*, *Khedive*, *Shah*, *Emperor*, *Cumberland* (flag of Rear Admiral W. R. Patterson, CS 5), H.M.Neth.S. *Tromp*, *Saumarez* (Captain M. L. Power, D.26), *Venus* (Cdr. H. de Chair), *Verulam* (Lt. Cdr. D. H. R. Bromley), *Virago* (Lt. Cdr. A. J. R. White), *Vigilant* (Lt. Cdr. L. W. L. Argles), *Rotherham* (D.11), *Tartar* (D.10) and *Nubian*.

a Japanese cruiser, painted pink and escorted by a destroyer steering north-west at 17 knots.

'Pink cruiser' sighting reports from submariners so soon after VE Day might have been treated with some reserve, but in fact Andrew had already attempted an attack. The target was sighted at 1640 and identified as a 'Nachi' Class cruiser, escorted by two submarine chasers ahead of her, and a destroyer. By 1704 *Subtle* had closed to a range of 1,200 yards, in a good attacking position, and Andrew was just about to shoot when the target made a large alteration of course away (towards *Statesman*, who sighted her upper-works, but was unable to attack). Disappointed, Andrew broke off the attack and ordered a depth of ninety feet; to his astonishment, *Subtle* hit the bottom at thirty-five feet. Had torpedoes been fired, they would probably have hit the mud.

Force 61 hoped to intercept the enemy on 12 May. On 11th, Group 3[1] were detached to steam fifty miles ahead of the main body, to be in position in the Six Degree Channel, between the Nicobars and Sumatra, by dawn on 12th. However, an unidentified aircraft was detected to the north-east and the whole force altered course to the south. The 'bogey' was a Japanese army reconnaissance aircraft which had sighted part of Force 61. It was also suspected that Force 70, the tanker group,[2] had been sighted and it was ordered to steam south-west at full speed, and to expect suicide attacks.

Warned of Force 61's approach, *Haguro* and *Kamikaze* turned back into the Malacca Strait where they were sighted once again at 0640 on 12th by *Subtle*. *Haguro* now had an air escort of three Jake[3] seaplanes overhead. She was steering south-east, zig-zagging twenty degrees either side of her course, at 25 knots. *Subtle* closed the target's track and fired a salvo of six torpedoes at a range of 2,500 yards. The sea was glassy calm, the torpedo tracks were sighted, and *Haguro* turned right away – again towards *Statesman* who tried to attack but was foiled by *Haguro*'s frequent and violent alterations of course. Meanwhile, *Subtle* was hunted for three hours, enduring careful, deliberate and accurate depth-charge attacks which did considerable internal damage, before escaping. Andrew and his ship's company were bitterly disappointed; to be given two bites at such a large cherry – the target of a submariner's lifetime – and to fail both times was hard to bear.

After surfacing that evening, *Subtle* attempted to send an enemy

---

[1] Group 3: *Cumberland*, *Richelieu* and the 26th Destroyer Flotilla.
[2] Force 70: RFA *Echodale*, with *Paladin*.
[3] Jake: Japanese Watanabe twin-engined reconnaissance/bomber sea-plane.

sighting report but her W/T equipment had been wrecked by depth-charging. Luckily, *Statesman* had already transmitted a report, which was received by Force 61: *Haguro* now steaming due south, speed 18 knots.

Although their quarry had been alarmed, Admiral Walker hoped that if Force 61 remained unobtrusively to the southward, the enemy might gather confidence for another sortie. In the meantime, he asked for all available reinforcements. The cruiser *Nigeria*, lately arrived from Durban, sailed from Trincomalee on 13 May, with *Roebuck, Racehorse* and *Redoubt*, forming Force 62. A second tanker group, Force 67 of RFA *Olwen* and *Penn*, also sailed on 13th. *Rocket*, escorting a south-bound troopship, was ordered to leave her and join Force 62 on 14th.

Force 61 destroyers fuelled from the escort carriers on 13th, during which *Virago* was in collision with *Emperor*.[1] The whole force then steered eastward, reaching the Six Degree Channel at 0400 on 14th. There had been no fresh news of the enemy now for many hours – although, in fact, *Haguro* was just about to leave One Fathom Bank in the Malacca Strait for a second attempt and *Kuroshiyo* Maru No 2 was only a few miles off the Nicobars. At 0530 Force 61 turned round and steamed towards a position two hundred miles south-west of Achin Head – the north-western point of Sumatra – to wait, and to make contact with Force 70, the tanker group.

Kuroshiyo Maru No 2 and her escort reached Nancowry in the Nicobars unmolested on 14th, embarked 450 troops, and sailed again for Penang. They were sighted that evening in the Andaman Sea by a patrolling Liberator of 222 Group RAF.

Admiral Walker at once detached *Cumberland*, the 21st Aircraft Carrier Squadron and the 26th Destroyer Flotilla to carry out an air and sea sweep off Diamond Point to intercept and destroy the enemy force (Operation MITRE). From midnight on 14th, the search which was eventually to lead to *Haguro* began to gather momentum. At 0217 on 15 May, the 26th Destroyer Flotilla were ordered to raise steam

---

[1] Captain (later Admiral Sir Charles) Madden, BT., in *Emperor*, later drew a cartoon showing an emperor in knee breeches and buckled shoes, dancing on one toe, crown flat aback and coat tails flying, being bitten in the backside by a three-stripe Wren officer. The caption was – 'You really must be more careful how you approach these great men!' *Emperor* also fuelled *Venus*, resulting in a somewhat Delphic exchange of signals. *Emperor* to *Venus*: 'When purple emperors toil by day and night providing bread and oil for Venus, how should the lady pay?' *Venus* to *Emperor*: 'The lady always pays, but virtue has its own reward.' And from *Saumarez*, overhearing this TBS exchange from some distance away: 'Can't take you in her arms because she hasn't got any.'

for full speed and twenty minutes later were detached to 'search for an enemy auxiliary vessel'. At 0325 Rear Admiral Patterson was ordered to take command of the operation, Admiral Walker himself in *Queen Elizabeth* remaining to the westward to refuel, and at 0525 *Cumberland* and *Richelieu* proceeded in support of the 26th Destroyer Flotilla.

At dawn on 15th the 26th Destroyer Flotilla were alone, steaming ENE at 27 knots. Members of the flotilla remember it as a beautiful morning, with hot sunshine, a slight following wind, and the blue hills of Sumatra in sight on the starboard bow. At 0750 four Avengers were sighted to the north, flying eastward. This was an armed reconnaissance of 851 Sq. which had been flown off at 0730 (from *Emperor*, because *Shah*'s catapult was defective) to search for the enemy convoy.

The flight had been briefed that the first Avenger to sight the convoy was to shadow and report, whilst the other three closed up. All four were then to attack with bombs (851 Sq. were not equipped with torpedoes.)

Avenger 'B', piloted by S/Lt. J. Burns, RNVR, was the first to sight the enemy ships but Burns disobeyed his orders and attacked at once. At 1029 the 26th Destroyer Flotilla heard him signal that he was attacking two small merchant vessels. The bombs did no damage and the Avenger was shot down. The ditching position was wrongly reported, the aircraft's dinghy was not sighted, and Burns and his crew drifted ashore to the Burma coast where they were taken prisoner by the Japanese.

At 1041 Captain Power (Captain (D) in *Saumarez*) received the dismaying signal from the C-in-C East Indies: 'Cancel MITRE. Repeat cancel MITRE.' According to a signal received in the early hours of that morning, the flotilla should now have given up the hunt, and returned to Force 61. With a Japanese cruiser the main objective of the search, Admiral Walker had arranged for the C-in-C East Indies to signal the 26th DF direct, cancelling MITRE if that operation appeared to interfere with the major issue of finding the cruiser. Yet Avenger B's signal showed that there were worth-while targets still ahead, and probably not far away. The C-in-C's signal had almost certainly been made without the latest knowledge of the situation. A paragraph in the Fighting Instructions cautions any Captain against prematurely relinquishing contact with the enemy: Captain Power believed that this paragraph had always been better interpreted as giving freedom to a Captain to disregard an order he believes to have been initiated in ignorance of the presence of the enemy. Captain Power therefore decided on a compromise:

he signalled Rear Admiral Patterson for confirmation and, in the mean-time, slowed to 15 knots – but continued to steer ENE. This was the crucial decision of the operation; had the 26th Destroyer Flotilla turned back as ordered, *Haguro* would have escaped.

Meanwhile *Emperor* had launched four more Avengers. The first returned early with engine trouble. Two met the 26th Destroyer Flotilla and wasted thirty-five minutes in establishing whether they were friend or foe after which, short of fuel, they also returned.

The fourth Avenger, searching for Burns's dinghy, sighted a cruiser and a destroyer in a position about fifteen miles south-east of the earlier attack on *Kuroshiyo* Maru. At 1150 the pilot, Lt. Cdr. M. T. Fuller, RNVR, CO of 851 Sq. transmitted the electrifying signal to the fleet: 'One cruiser, one destroyer, sighted. Course 140. Speed 10 knots.' Thus, with a slice of luck, and as Admiral Walker himself later admitted 'my own illogical decision to allow the Avenger search to go forward after I had realised that the aircraft would be flown off before the latest time when a signal cancelling MITRE would be received from C-in-C', *Haguro* and *Kamikaze* had been found.

Haguro had abandoned her second attempt to relieve the Andamans and turned back. Her position was just inside the northern entrance to the Malacca Strait, about 100 miles south-west of Phuket Island. Singapore was less than a day's steaming away. Her ship's company must have believed themselves almost home and dry.

Captain Power received the aircraft's signal shortly after noon. He was now in no doubt what to do. The flotilla increased speed to 27 knots and, rounding the northern tip of Sumatra, turned to a course of ESE, going 'like a rugby full-back for the corner flag'. In the destroyers the atmosphere was one of anticipation mixed with apprehension:

'The prospect of action was greeted with a cheer and the usual ribald sailor's comment on most things Japanese. At first I felt the familiar eager excitement taking hold of me, but as the hours passed the full appreciation of our prospects began to sink in.

'We were all well-blooded and expert in action against aircraft, shore batteries and ships of our own size, but a heavy cruiser was something beyond our experience. We knew that if we met her in daylight our chances would be slim indeed: with her great speed and overwhelming gun power she could destroy the flotilla piecemeal long before we could get close enough to retaliate. My excitement, mounting all the time, became more strongly tinged with apprehension.'[1]

Later in the afternoon Captain Power received a signal from Rear Admiral Patterson reassuring him that he was not to break off, and adding: 'You should sink enemy ships before returning.' *Haguro* was big, fast, and well armed; she was a heavy cruiser of 13,380 tons, with a top speed of 33 knots, armed with ten 8-inch guns which had a range of 32,600 yards, a secondary armament of eight 5-inch guns, and eight torpedo tubes. In the circumstances, Admiral Patterson's signal was like reassuring David that he should kill Goliath before returning from the valley of Elah.

Haguro was now about 130 miles to the ENE, keeping a course of south-east. At 1355 *Shah* flew off a strike of three Avengers which, at 1530, found and attacked *Haguro* with bombs. One Avenger pilot, Lt. K. Crompton, RNVR, claimed a hit on the cruiser's forecastle and a near miss on the port side by the bridge. They were probably both near misses but the attack caused *Haguro* to alter to the eastward. This small diversion may have been vital, giving the 26th Destroyer Flotilla a critical few minutes more to intercept.

After receiving the report of the Avenger attack, the flotilla spread out on a line of bearing 290° through 110°, with the two Divisions[2] five miles apart. *Verulam* and *Vigilant* had a long way to open out ahead of *Saumarez* and Captain Power, anxious they should not overstress their machinery at this stage, signalled: 'Don't bust yourselves.'

There was still some doubt whether the enemy would be encountered by day or by night. The timing was vitally important for the destroyers. If contact were made by day, the flotilla would attempt to lure the enemy westwards, towards *Cumberland* and *Richelieu*, whilst keeping out of range themselves. If by night, then 'it was quite simple, we were to sink her'.[3]

At 1900 Diamond Point was abeam to starboard twenty miles and the destroyers spread out four miles apart on a line of bearing 215° through 115°, course 110°, in the order from west to east: *Venus, Virago, Saumarez, Verulam* and *Vigilant*.

----

[1] 'It Was Quite Simple: We Were to Sink Her', by Cdr. Denis Calnan from 'Freedom's Battle', Volume I, *The War At Sea, 1939–45, An Anthology of Personal Experience* (Hutchinson, 1967), p. 374.

[2] 51st Division: *Saumarez, Verulam* and *Vigilant.* 52nd Division: *Venus* and *Virago.*

[3] 'Freedom's Battle', p. 375.

At dusk the weather turned appropriately Wagnerian, with heavy rain squalls, thunder storms, and lightning. But with the darkness Captain Power's confidence grew. 'Once darkness fell, it only remained to find him; I had no doubts as to the result. It was a flotilla party, and I felt that we all knew each other's form and that no confusion or lack of understanding could arise.'

Haguro was now some seventy-five miles north-east of the destroyers, estimated course 140°, speed 20 knots. Failing further reports, Captain Power's intention was to sweep across the Malacca Strait at his present course and speed until midnight, and then reverse course and reduce to 20 knots. At that point the flotilla would be about forty miles south-west of Penang, where the Malacca Strait was roughly 130 miles wide. It was still possible that *Haguro* would slip past in the night.

Venus was nearest to the enemy and at 2245 her radar operator reported an echo, bearing 045°, range 68,000 yards. The bearing was feasible, but for that set the range was unbelievable and was duly disbelieved. The radar operator Ordinary Seaman N. T. Poole 'had the courage of his convictions to the point of insubordination' and insisted the echo was genuine.[1] Though still having private reservations, Cdr. de Chair, commanding *Venus*, ordered the echo to be plotted.

The echo faded at 2304 but reappeared at 2310, bearing 039°, range 53,000 yards. *Venus'* radar officer himself examined the echo and thereafter it was plotted every minute from 2315 to 2330. By 2322 the plot had shown enough to confirm the contact as a genuine ship echo and *Venus* signalled to *Saumarez*: 'Contact, bearing 040 degrees, 23 miles, course 135, speed 25 knots.'

Captain Power was as sceptical as de Chair had been and acknowledged with *Popeye*, i.e. meaning 'Cloud?' *Venus* indignantly responded with a fresh report: 'contact now bearing 034, range 20 miles, course 130, speed unchanged at 25 knots.' *Venus'* plot now suggested that the contact was altering to starboard, closer to due south, and at 2338 *Venus* also altered to the southward, to 170°. The destroyers were now flying along in an extended line, twenty miles ahead of *Haguro* and on her starboard bow.

By 2345 Captain Power had been convinced by the stream of reports from *Venus* and signalled to Rear Admiral Patterson 'Vessel size unknown detected by RDF' and at the same time allocated his flotilla their sectors for a 'star' attack. In this form of attack the destr

---

[1] The unusual detection range was attributed to a phenomenon known as 'anomalous propagation'.

would converge upon the target each from their own appointed sectors; 'it had not actually been exercised in the flotilla for some six months, but it was known by all to be favoured and was never far from our thoughts.'[1]

Three minutes later *Venus*' echo faded from the screen and at 2355 she was ordered to close and shadow her target. The flotilla followed, turning north at 20 knots. At three minutes after midnight, *Saumarez* also detected a radar echo: bearing 010°, range fourteen miles. The plot showed that this was *Venus*' contact. The flotilla turned south and slowed to 12 knots, running before the enemy and allowing him to catch up, as though quietly stretching a net. *Haguro* at twenty knots was still driving southwards into it.

At 0015 on 16 May, when *Haguro* was thirteen miles off, the flotilla altered back to north and increased to twenty knots. One by one, the rest of the destroyers picked up the radar contact. The radar scans 'at this time presented a picture that would have been approved by Medina Sidonia – the flotilla bearing down on the enemy in a deep crescent with the tips of the horns about to complete his encirclement'.

The enemy was now very near, and the flotilla made their final preparations. Captain Power allocated new attack sectors and at 0039 ordered the flotilla to get into their attack sectors. Three minutes later he signalled that he intended to attack with torpedoes at 0100, thus giving his flotilla a datum time at which to try and synchronise their attacks. *Haguro* might appear at any moment.

'It was like a net closing in and we were expecting the quarry to begin snapping at any moment. In spite of the very close ranges, not a shot had been fired, and it seemed uncanny to be chasing this silent and so far invisible monster around his own backyard without once being bitten.'[2]

The radar echo had now split and a second, smaller contact, the destroyer *Kamikaze*, had appeared astern of the first. *Venus* was still some distance to the west and Captain Power signalled to her: 'Close the enemy.' *Venus*' engine telegraphs were put to 'Full Ahead', although she was already steaming at full power. The whole flotilla were closing on *Haguro* at top speed, ready for the encounter.

But at this point, the attack began to go temporarily awry. By now

[1] *Venus* and three of the flotilla had actually practised a 'star' attack a few nights previously. De Chair. Letter of 18.1.69.

[2] 'Nocturne in V Minor': Broadcast by *Saumarez*' Navigating Officer, Lt. C. H. H. Knollys, over South African Broadcasting Company, Capetown, 18 June 1945.

thoroughly alarmed, *Haguro* was manoeuvring freely, first to the west and then back to south-east. The attacking destroyers were approaching her from what should have been a direction of safety and *Haguro* was puzzled enough to challenge them by light. Finally, *Haguro* turned through nearly 180 degrees and fled at full speed to the north, ruining Captain Power's carefully laid ambush; instead of a planned, deliberate bow shot, *Saumarez* now had to chase from astern at 30 knots. Captain Power signalled that he was 'unable to attack now' (which he later described as a 'stupid signal', as it caused uncertainty in the minds of the other destroyer captains).

Soon *Haguro* altered to port, directly in the path of *Venus* closing at full speed from the west. *Venus* was in a perfect attacking position. Her moment had come:

'I ordered the Sub Lieutenant (who was Torpedo Control Officer) to come up on the bridge and prepare to fire torpedoes, and reported "Attacking". We could see the cruiser ahead with night glasses and were obviously going to be in a perfect position to fire torpedoes on the beam at very close range. When nearing the firing position I said to the TCO "Are you ready, Sub?" but received no answer. By this time the enemy was very close, about 45 degrees on our bow, her two funnels filled my glasses and I repeated "Are you *ready*, Sub?" He said, in a quiet voice: "We've missed it, sir." He had angled the torpedoes ahead, in spite of my orders for straight running on the beam, and it was too late to alter the settings. Short of ramming the cruiser or possibly fouling *Saumarez* or *Verulam* somewhere astern of her, I had no alternative but to turn to port, which I did under full helm, to try and prevent the Jap from breaking out of our circle. Evidently he saw us turn, and assuming we had fired torpedoes turned away to comb the tracks. This threw him back into the arms of Captain (D) and *Verulam*. . . .'[1]

Haguro's violent turn away changed the situation dramatically. *Saumarez* now found the enemy racing down towards her port side at a relative speed of nearly 60 MPH. *Kamikaze*, following astern of *Haguro*, passed so close in front of *Saumarez* from starboard to port that Captain Power had to swing his ship hard to starboard and back to port again to avoid her. *Kamikaze* passed very close down *Saumarez'* port side and was taken under fire by both main and close range armament.

[1] 'Notes from Memory', H.M.S. *Venus* – East Indies Fleet, 1945, by Commander H. G. D. de Chair, RN, in manuscript. 4.9.67.

Opening with star-shell, *Saumarez* shifted fire to *Haguro* herself at
0108, the enemy replying with main and secondary armament. The two
enemy ships could now be clearly identified from *Saumarez'* bridge,
Haguro at about 5,000 yards and *Kamikaze* about 2,200 yards range.
'We had a glimpse of the cruiser by starshell, but now it was dark.
She looked pretty big and her direction easy to see by her bow-wave
and wash. Inclination vague but obviously broad. I thought she was
going very fast. Her side was shining like a wet wall, with the reflection
of her own starshell from behind us, I think.' To Lt. Reay Parkinson,
also in *Saumarez*, *Haguro* 'seemed to tower above us like a sky-scraper
and her guns were depressed to their lowest angle'.[1]

Haguro's fire was accurate and splashes from near misses drenched
the bridge personnel, binoculars and sound-powered telephones. But,
as Captain Power philosophically remarked, 'if you are only getting
wet there is nothing to worry about'.

However, *Saumarez* was unfortunately not merely getting wet. At
about 0111, when Captain Power was just considering turning to fire,
'one boiler got hit. There was a lot of steam and smoke amidships and
a sort of queer silence. The ship was obviously slowing down and I
thought she was going to stop.'

Saumarez' torpedo tubes had been trained to starboard, ready for
the bow attack, with torpedoes angled to run 70° left. There was no
time to train the tubes to port. Captain Power swung his ship to port
'like a shotgun' and at 0113, as *Saumarez* was slowing down but still
swinging hard to port, a salvo of eight torpedoes was fired at *Haguro*'s
beam, at a range of 2,000 yards. Still under heavy fire, *Saumarez*
continued her turn to port to open the range, telegraphs being put to 'Full
Ahead' to get the utmost speed from whatever engine power remained.
A minute after *Saumarez'* attack, *Verulam* made an unmolested attack
from 2,000 yards on *Haguro*'s port bow, firing eight torpedoes. *Saumarez*
and *Verulam* were rewarded by three hits, shared between them – 'very
distinct, three gold-coloured splashes like a Prince of Wales' feathers,
more than twice as high as her bridge'.

Meanwhile, *Saumarez* had been hit on the fo'c'sle and on the top
of her funnel. A 5-inch shell had penetrated No 1 Boiler Room, severed
a main steam pipe and lodged inside the boiler. Fortunately, it did not
explode. The compartment immediately filled with scalding steam. The
watch below were all killed except Stoker Petty Officer Enoch Davies

[1] *Times of Ceylon*, Sunday Illustrated, 27 May 1945.

who, though burned, shut steam and oil spray valves and shut down the boiler before evacuating the boiler room.

On deck, the screech of escaping steam, the roar of gunfire, the sound of rushing water from near misses and clouds of smoke and steam naturally caused a certain amount of confusion. Communications between bridge and steering and engine room had been cut. On the bridge, they believed that the after part of the ship had been destroyed or at least badly damaged, while the men aft were under the impression that the bridge had been hit and everyone on it killed. *Saumarez* was still swinging to port, apparently out of control. The Captain's Secretary, who was captain of a bofors guns' crew, made his way to his emergency station, which was the emergency steering position abaft the funnel, with Petty Officer Writer R. Pollitt, also of the bofors crew. Together, the pair put the ship's steering in local emergency control. The Secretary was experimentally swinging the wheel hard a port and back amidships, while Pollitt was clamouring for him to ram the Japanese cruiser. The Secretary was considering the matter when a figure appeared out of the smoke, yelling 'Put it back! Revert to main steering!' The Captain's Secretary did so, having been in a sense for some three minutes the first officer of his branch to take command of one of HM Ships in the presence of the enemy since Stanning in *Hardy* at First Narvik.

Vigilant now fired star-shell to illuminate what she thought was the Japanese destroyer, and signalled *Saumarez* that she had done so. Captain Power replied, dampingly: 'Think that is me.' At this time there was a very large explosion, which Captain Power believed was *Kamikaze* blowing up. *Virago* and *Vigilant* also saw it, and believed it was *Saumarez*; as Captain Power later commented, they 'apparently eagerly assumed that this marked the end of yet another dictator. Such was happily not the case'. The explosion was probably two torpedoes colliding.

Now *Haguro* was under fire from the destroyers and everywhere she turned there was another destroyer waiting. At 0125 *Venus* fired six torpedoes and scored one hit. Two minutes later *Virago*, ordered by Captain (D) to 'Finish her off', fired a salvo of eight torpedoes and obtained two hits. She reported that the cruiser's upper deck was now awash. Missed torpedoes were racing all over the battle scene; in *Venus*, at the height of the action, the Engineer Officer and the Chief ERA in the engine-room actually heard the whirring sound of two torpedoes passing very close along the ship's side.

Saumarez had retired some five miles to the north-west to collect herself and examine damage. The engine telegraphs were still at 'Full Ahead', and *Saumarez* withdrew further than Captain Power had intended. One boiler was still serviceable and the ship was still able to steam.[1] Down below the Engineer Officer, Commander (E) Geoffrey Robins, with three men, re-entered the steam-filled boiler room and saw the unexploded shell 'cooking' in the boiler, and presumably about to detonate at any moment. Ordering the fire and repair party to withdraw to safety, Commander Robins and Petty Officer Davies together manhandled the shell from inside the boiler, carried it up to the upper deck, and threw it over the side. Robins evidently had a somewhat diabolical sense of humour: he telephoned the bridge to report an unexploded shell in the boiler, waited until his sensational news had caused the maximum furore of consternation on the bridge, and then added: 'But not to worry, I've thrown it over the side.'

Vigilant had been rather 'left in the cold' and squeezed out by the other destroyers and was not able to attack until 0151 when she fired eight torpedoes, with one probable hit. *Haguro* was lying motionless in the water, in her last throes. 'The rest of the flotilla were snarling round the carcass like a lot of starving wolves round a dying bull. I was too far away to make out what was going on and told them all except *Vigilant* (who I knew had torpedoes) to come away and join me, with a view to getting formed up and the situation in hand. Of course they did nothing of the sort. I should not have done myself.'

Venus was ordered to 'Close and make a job of it' and at 0202 administered the *coup de grace* with her two remaining torpedoes:

'We closed to within 500 yards, ensured two more hits and watched the Japanese cruiser sink, at the same time lowering the asdic dome which gave the operator the satisfaction of hearing her break up under water.'[2]

At 0206 *Venus* signalled that the cruiser had sunk. *Haguro* had gone, in a position about forty-five miles south-west of Penang.[3] Fifty miles away, *Cumberland* and *Richelieu* had had tantalising glimpses of star-shell and lights but were too late to take part. *Saumarez* transmitted Vs for Victory and Captain Power signalled: 'Pick up survivors. Stay no more than ten minutes.'

---

[1] In action, the main propulsion machinery was in 'units', i.e. one 'unit' (boiler, main turbine, etc.) to one shaft. The units were isolated, so that damage to one still left the other unaffected.

[2] de Chair. 4.9.67.

[3] In position 5°0′N 99°30′E.

Only 'a few specimens' were wanted but in the event no survivors were picked up:

'She sank quickly and when we steamed through the bubbles we could see hardly anything, no survivors, perhaps a boat and just one winking light like a calcium flare. Miraculously 'Lanchester' carbines appeared on 'B' gun deck all ready to discourage any saboteurs among the survivors. We had both our 20″ search-lights on and we felt most insecure. But *Vigilant* saw an aircraft with lights switched on, circling us (or so she said) and we got to hell out of it.'[1]

The aircraft was almost certainly imaginary (as even *Vigilant* later admitted) but the flotilla were well within range of enemy airfields and Captain Power was 'not taking any chances and took the whole party away at once'. In any case, the task of picking up Japanese survivors had a very low priority in the fleet at that time (although intelligence dearly wanted some for interrogation). *Kamikaze* had only been slightly damaged by *Saumarez*' fire and returned later to pick up *Haguro*'s survivors. So ended 'a very satisfying and enjoyable party. E & OE' – although in his account Captain Power was almost embarrassingly self-critical of his own handling of the action. *Saumarez*' casualties were comparatively light: two men killed and three burned.

The flotilla formed up and steamed westwards at 25 knots (full power on *Saumarez*' remaining boiler) to rejoin the fleet who greeted them next morning with a rapturous chorus of signalled 'bouquets and bunches of flowers'.[2] The sinking of *Haguro* was the last major surface gun and torpedo action against the Imperial Japanese Navy in World War Two. In Lord Mountbatten's words, 'an outstanding example of a night attack by destroyers'.[3] Captain Power received a bar to his DSO, an award which, in the circumstances, was not over-generous.

Enemy aircraft made a belated appearance that day. Scattered groups of Oscars made sporadic attacks on Force 61. Had the Japanese Navy and Army resolved their differences over the responsibility for air escort and used these Oscars the day before, *Haguro* might still have been afloat. In the last attack of the day, just after dark, an Oscar

[1] Midshipman (now Captain) John Robathan, RN, then serving in *Venus*. Diary for 16 May 1945.
[2] There was, however, one unpleasant sequel. An Able Seaman in *Saumarez* was later court-martialled for deserting his post as bridge look-out in the presence of the enemy. This was a capital charge, but the offender was dismissed the Service and sentenced to six months' imprisonment.
[3] Report to the Combined Chiefs of Staff, B, p. 175.

dropped a bomb on *Virago*. White avoided a direct hit by ordering
hard a port but the bomb exploded only a few feet from *Virago*'s
quarter, setting off a bofors ready-use ammunition locker. Four of the
guns' crew were killed and eight of the ship's company seriously
wounded.

Kuroshiyo Maru No 2 and Submarine Chaser No 57 reached Penang
safely, but the submarine chaser was slightly damaged by a mine on
18 May while on passage to Singapore. However, their fate was not far
off. On 5 June Force 65[1] sailed from Trincomalee on an anti-shipping
sweep between the Nicobars and Sabang (Operation IRREGULAR). Force
64 (RFA *Olwen* escorted by *Test*) sailed from Rangoon. On 7th *Paladin*
was detached to evacuate a clandestine party from the Batu Islands, off
the west coast of Sumatra and remained on patrol until relieved by *Penn*.
On 12th, *Penn* sank a camouflaged Japanese Type A landing craft with
20 men on board. The submarine *Trident* took over the patrol on 15 June.

Previously, on 11 June, the same submarine on patrol off Diamond
Point had reported a large Japanese LST with escort heading northwards.
This was *Kuroshiyo* Maru No 2, and SC 57. 222 Group RAF Liberators
were to have begun searches at dawn but Force 65 forestalled them.
At 0526 on 12 June, Force 65 which was then about fourteen miles
north-west of Rondo Island (twenty miles NE of Sabang) detected two
small radar echoes. The masts of the enemy convoy were soon sighted
and *Eskimo* and *Nubian* opened fire at 0552. *Nubian*'s gun-fire sank
SC 57 at 0619 and a minute later *Kuroshiyo* blew up after two torpedo
hits from *Eskimo*.

The Japanese survivors continued to fascinate and repel the men of
the fleet. Passing the spot where *Kuroshiyo* had sunk, *Nubian*'s officers
saw thirty or forty Japanese in the water close to starboard. 'They were
all wearing red and white skull caps and looked like a large water polo
team.' None of the team wished to be picked up. The enemy retaliated
with air attacks as Force 65 was retiring to the north-west and one
bomb exploded only fifteen yards from *Nubian*'s port side but did no
damage. The patrol ended on 15 June. Afterwards, *Test* and RIN
sloops maintained a patrol of the Tenasserim Coast from 10°N to
14°39'N until 27 July.

Patrols were also maintained between the Andamans and the coast
of Burma (Operation ADOPTION) by Force 69.[2] The force was replaced

[1] Force 65: *Tartar* (D.10), *Eskimo*, *Nubian*, *Penn* and *Paladin*.
[2] Force 69: Cruiser *Phoebe* (relieved by *Ceylon*, 1 June), HMIS *Sutlej* and
Cauvery.

on 15 June by a single frigate or sloop, the frigate *Lossie* and the RIN sloops *Kodri*, *Kodabari*, *Kistna* and *Narbada* sharing the patrols between them. None of them saw any enemy activity.

In June the Japanese began to accelerate their evacuation operations. All of them met disaster. On 8th June the one remaining heavy warship of the 10th Area Fleet, the cruiser *Ashigara*, was torpedoed and sunk by the submarine *Trenchant*[1] while carrying out Transportation Nos 10 and 11 (transport of troops from the Lesser Sunda Islands to Singapore via Batavia). Her escort, *Kamikaze*, escaped. Of three convoys attempting Operation CHI (movement of troops from Singapore to Indochina) the first was wiped out. The second, of three small tankers, reached Rean in Cambodia. The third convoy consisted of the 10,238 ton tanker *Toho* Maru, escorted by a minesweeper and by *Kamikaze* (who was fast becoming the Jonah of the Japanese Navy; she had accompanied *Haguro* and *Ashigara* on their last voyages and her very presence as escort was a certain omen of disaster). The convoy left Singapore on 12 June, bound for Rean, but were attacked by USAAF aircraft off the south-east coast of Malaya on 15th. *Toho* Maru was sunk. The indestructible *Kamikaze* escaped with minor damage and picked up two hundred of *Toho* Maru's survivors.

In July the East Indies Fleet turned its attention to the minesweeping of areas which might shortly be invaded. By this time most of the fleet were short of match practice and so, on 2 July, Force 62 (6th Minesweeping Flotilla)[2] supported by Force 61,[3] commanded by Rear Admiral Patterson in *Nigeria* sailed from Trincomalee for Operation COLLIE; it was a 'coat-trailing' expedition, to provoke the enemy's remaining air power, and a combined minesweeping and air and surface bombardment operation off Car Nicobar.

Mines had not been much of a problem in the sea war against the Japanese, although the minesweepers had been kept occupied off the Arakan coast. Mining was a passive form of warfare which did not appeal to the Samurai spirit. The 6th Flotilla had been employed almost entirely on escort duties and their technique and equipment were both a little rusty. Nevertheless they swept 167 mines from 5 to 10 July off Car Nicobar. It was a fair score, close to an enemy coast-line, and a

---

[1] See p. 258.

[2] 6th Minesweeping Flotilla (Senior Officer, Cdr. D. L. Johnson), *Melita*, *Gozo*, *Lennox*, *Persian*, *Postillion*, *Lightfoot*, *Immersay*, *Lingay* with *Pelorus* joining operation 4 July.

[3] Force 61: *Nigeria*, *Ameer* (896 Sq. Hellcats), *Emperor* (800 Sq. Hellcats), *Roebuck*, *Eskimo* and *Vigilant*.

reasonable achievement, but Commander Johnson rather surprisingly described the operation as 'good working up practice'.

Meanwhile, *Nigeria* carried out eight bombardments between 5 and 9 July and Hellcats from *Ameer* and *Emperor* flew strikes against Car Nicobar and Nancowry. The Japanese flak was still very accurate and four Hellcats were shot down. Another squadron CO was lost: Lt. Cdr. R. M. Norris, of 896 Sq., being shot down in flames on 7 July. The Japanese obviously thought the Allies were about to make a landing and planted stakes on the airfield runways. On 11th a strike of twenty-four Hellcats strafed airfields at Kota Radju and Lho Nga in northern Sumatra. No enemy aircraft were seen at either airfield and one Hellcat was lost. The same day the only enemy air opposition, one solitary Dinah, approached the fleet and was shot down by Lt. W. Saltykoff, Royal Netherlands Navy.

The next area chosen for minesweeping was off Phuket Island (Operation LIVERY). The assault on the island, Operation ROGER, had actually been postponed, and LIVERY was intended to mislead the enemy. Force 63,[1] including the 7th Minesweeping Flotilla and commanded by Admiral Walker in *Nelson*, sailed from Trincomalee on 19 July.

On the evening of 24th, the first day's sweeping, a mine exploded *Plucky*'s starboard sweep. The next in line to starboard, *Squirrel*, did not turn to port into swept water quickly enough and struck a mine. She was badly damaged and seven ratings were killed. Two and half hours later the ship took a serious list, the rest of her ship's company were taken off and she was sunk by Force 63. Minesweeping continued on 25 and 26 July, and twenty-four mines were swept.

On the morning of 26th, a group of Japanese suicide bombers attacked the force. They were first detected by *Nelson*. *Ameer* and *Emperor* both had Hellcats airborne at the time but *Nelson* did not direct them and the enemy were not intercepted. They were seen from *Nelson*, disappearing into cloud at about 4,000 feet. Soon afterwards, two Val dive-bombers dived out of the sun and were taken under fire by *Nelson* and *Ameer*. *Ameer* shot down one which dropped its bomb five hundred yards off the ship's bow and followed it into the sea. *Sussex* shot down the other which hit the water fifty yards from the ship's starboard side, the pilot being seen 'to throw up his hands' immediately before the impact. The bomb did not explode but the

---

[1] Force 63: *Nelson* (flag of Vice Admiral Walker), cruiser *Sussex*; *Empress* (896 Sq. Hellcats), *Ameer* (804 Sq. Hellcats); *Rotherham* (D.11), *Racehorse*, *Raider* and *Paladin*.

aircraft bounced off the sea and stove in an eight-foot length of plating above the ship's waterline. Later, *Sussex* shot down a second aircraft, but in the evening a suicide bomber crashed on the minesweeper *Vestal*, killing fifteen men and setting the vessel on fire. She had to be sunk by Force 63.

The carriers' Hellcats had been striking at airfields in the Kra Isthmus. One Hellcat of 896 Sq. failed to pull out of its strafing dive and crashed into a locomotive at Dhung Song railway station.

Force 63 returned to Trincomalee. Operation LIVERY was the last offensive action of the East Indies Fleet in World War Two.

Chapter Eight

SUBMARINE OPERATIONS

'Press home all attacks. Pursue relentlessly, remembering that the mission is to destroy every possible enemy ship. Do not let cripples escape or leave them to sink – make sure that they do sink.' *Admiral James Fife*, USN

WHEN Japan attacked Pearl Harbour, there was one British submarine in the Far East. She was the ten-year-old *Rover*, damaged in the Battle of Crete and being refitted at Singapore, with all her propulsion machinery removed.[1] There had been submarines on the China station before the war, a fine flotilla specially trained and prepared to wage defensive submarine warfare in the Far East, but they had all long since been dispersed to other theatres and indeed by December 1941 seven of the original fifteen submarines of the pre-war China Fleet had already been sunk. The only submarines under British control in the Far East were seven Dutch submarines. By Christmas 1941 only three of these were still operational.

One of Admiral Sir Geoffrey Layton's first acts on taking over the Eastern Fleet was therefore to request, as a matter of the utmost urgency, that some submarines be sent to the Far East from the Mediterranean. The year 1941 had been a grim one for the submarine flotillas in the Mediterranean: eight boats had been lost, and there was worse to come. Nevertheless, *Trusty* sailed from the Mediterranean on 26 December 1941 and arrived at Singapore on 31 January 1942; *Truant* followed on 3 January, but Singapore fell before she could reach it, and both submarines went to Sourabaya where they operated for a time with the remaining Dutch and American submarines. *Trusty*, *Truant* and four Dutch submarines arrived in Colombo in March 1942 (where the

---

[1] *Rover* was towed to Batavia at the end of the year and thence via Trincomalee to Bombay where she was refitted but never used operationally again.

submarine depot ship *Lucia* had been since 10 January).[1] The passenger ship *Colombia*, former flagship of the Royal Dutch Line, acted as depot ship for the Dutch submarines.

When Admiral Somerville became C-in-C in March he repeated the urgent request for more submarines. But this time there were none to spare and submarine strength in the Indian Ocean followed the same pattern as the surface fleet: a long period of weakness in 1942 and the greater part of 1943, a resurgence after the Italian Armistice, followed by massive reinforcement in 1944. The submarines that were available in the Indian Ocean carried out sporadic patrols from June 1942 until March 1943. *Trident* arrived in August but had to return to United Kingdom with engine defects after only one patrol. At the beginning of September 1943 the submarine strength of the Eastern Fleet sank to its absolute nadir: only one operational submarine, the Dutch O.24.

However, reinforcements were on the way. *Severn, Templar, Trespasser, Tally Ho, Tactician, Taurus* and *Surf* all arrived in late September or October and *Taurus* quickly opened her account by sinking the Japanese U-boat I-34 off Penang on 13 November. The depot ship *Adamant* had sailed from United Kingdom on 23 March 1942 but did not reach Colombo until 2 April 1943 having spent the intervening time at Kilindini, in East Africa. She left Colombo again on 6 June but finally set up residence in Ceylon on 8 October. The submarine base was moved to Trincomalee, with Captain H. M. C. Ionides in command of the 4th Flotilla.

All new and refitted 'S' and 'T' Class submarines were now being sent to the Eastern Fleet and the newly designed 'A' Class – larger, faster and with a longer range than the 'T' Class – were also intended for the Far East, although none of them was completed in time to take part in the war. British submarines never had the range, speed or amenities of the American submarines, but special efforts were made to convert them for service in the tropics: stowage for extra fuel, lubricating oil and water was provided, and a second air-conditioning plant and increased refrigerating capacity were fitted. At the beginning of 1944, Flag Officer Submarines forecast that the Eastern Fleet submarine force could be built up to forty by 1945. To keep this number operational a total of eighty submarines would be required, because the only dockyards capable of undertaking major submarine refits were

[1] *Lucia* was hit but only slightly damaged in the Japanese air raid on Colombo on 5 April 1942.

in the United Kingdom – several weeks' passage-time away from the operating area.

In 1944, submarine strength of the Eastern Fleet built up rapidly. In January the 4th Flotilla had six 'T' Class and one 'S' Class. Four more 'S' Class and one 'T' Class joined in February. A second depot ship *Maidstone* (Captain L. M. Shadwell) arrived on 3 March. The 8th Submarine Flotilla was formed from the 'S' Class submarines.

From January to September 1944 Eastern Fleet submarines carried out 88 war patrols, mostly in the area of the Malacca Strait, looking for enemy shipping, minelaying, and landing special clandestine parties. Ship targets became increasingly difficult to find: between January and May only eight enemy merchant vessels of over 500 tons were sunk, for a total tonnage sunk of 15,920 tons. Occasionally, submarines had opportunities against enemy warships: *Tally Ho* sank the Japanese cruiser *Kuma* on 11 January and the ex-Italian U-boat U-It.23 on 23 February, while *Telemachus* sank the Japanese U-boat I.166 off One Fathom Bank on 17 July and *Trenchant* U-859 off Penang on 23 September. To set against these successes, *Stonehenge* was overdue on patrol in the Malacca Strait, on 20 March, and was presumed lost.

A third depot ship *Wolfe* (Captain J. E. Slaughter), formerly depot ship for the 3rd Flotilla in the Clyde, arrived in Trincomalee on 19 August 1944 and by 1 September the Eastern Fleet had twenty-six submarines. The flotillas were reorganised: the 2nd Flotilla (*Wolfe*) had six 'S' Class[1] with *Porpoise*, *Severn* and *Clyde*; the 4th Flotilla (*Adamant*), seven 'T' Class;[2] and the 8th (*Maidstone*) four 'T' Class including D.S. *Zwaardfisch*, six 'S' Class,[3] and D.S. O.19.

By now the Eastern Fleet had more submarines than could be usefully employed in the Malacca Strait area. The proposal was put to Admiral King that British submarines should operate in the South China and Java Seas, running from a base in Western Australia. Admiral King agreed, with two conditions: first, a familiar one, that the British must provide their own base support, including a depot ship capable of carrying out major submarine repairs; and second, that the British submarines must operate under the control of the US Commander, South-western Pacific Area. Both these points were agreed. Escorted by *Nigeria*, *Maidstone* sailed on 25 August 1944 and reached Fremantle

---

[1] *Statesman, Strongbow, Subtle, Stygian, Shalimar* and *Spirit*.

[2] *Terrapin, Trenchant, Tradewind, Tally Ho, Tudor, Thorough* and *Thule*.

[3] *Telemachus, Tantivy* and *Tantalus. Spiteful, Sea Rover, Sturdy, Stoic, Sirdar* and *Storm*.

on 4 September, berthing at North Wharf next to the US submarine tenders *Euryalus* and *Griffin*. Her submarines joined her in Fremantle at the end of their next patrols.

At Fremantle, the British submarines became part of one of the most successful Allied weapons of the war. By September 1944 US submarines had already torn the heart and bottom out of the Japanese Merchant Navy. From the summer of 1943, when defects in US torpedoes had been rectified, the rate of sinkings by submarines soared, and reached further peaks in 1944 with the introduction of wolfpack tactics. The quarterly totals of sinkings dropped sharply in 1945, for sheer lack of targets, but by the end of the war American submarines had sunk nearly $5\frac{1}{2}$ million tons of Japanese shipping. The British submarines, slower, smaller and the majority without radar, had a glamorous history behind them in the Mediterranean but were at a disadvantage compared with the Americans in the Far East. British submarines of the 8th Flotilla were conscious that they were joining a most successful team and had yet to prove themselves. For their part, American submariners were not entirely convinced of the British submarines' battle-worthiness until the arrival of the 4th Flotilla in April 1945.

The first patrol from *Maidstone* at Fremantle was carried out by *Porpoise* who sailed on 11 September for a special operation (RIMAU) to land Lt. Col. Lyon, Gordon Highlanders, and twenty-four men, with $8\frac{1}{2}$ tons of stores and thirteen 'sleeping beauties' (one-man submersible canoes). Their purpose was to penetrate Singapore roads and attack Japanese shipping, repeating on a larger scale a similar exploit of a year before. Colonel Lyon and his men were transferred from *Porpoise* to a captured junk at the end of September and set off on their adventure, but were later captured by the Japanese and executed.[1]

The 8th Flotilla's first major success was achieved in the Java Sea by D.S. *Zwaardfisch* (Lt. Cdr. H. A. W. Goossens, R.NETH.N.) who sank U-168 on 6 October and the minelayer *Itsukushima* on 17th.

Meanwhile, from Trincomalee, the 2nd and 4th Flotillas extended their patrol coverage to include not only the Malacca Strait but the west coast of Burma and both coasts of Sumatra, carrying out air-sea rescue duties, minelaying, and taking a steady toll of enemy coasters, junks, small tankers, schooners and landing craft.

The Japanese had succeeded in salvaging two ex-Italian ships in the

[1] See also *Winning Hazard*, by Noel Wynyard (Sampson, Low, Marston & Co., 1949) and *Return of the Tiger*, by Brian Connell (Evans, 1960).

harbour at Phuket Island. On 20 October *Trenchant* (Lt. Cdr. A. R. Hezlet) sailed from Trincomalee with two 'chariots', which were launched off the harbour on 27th and sank the 4,859-ton *Sumatra* and badly damaged the 5,292-ton *Volpi*. The 'charioteers' were successfully recovered and their chariots dropped overboard. *Trenchant* returned to Trincomalee on 16 November, after a brush with an escorted convoy and a mild counter-attack on 10th.

Although nobody equalled Goossens' feat of sinking a U-boat, it was not for want of trying. In October and November several submarines in the Malacca Strait had shots at U-boats, including *Strongbow* (Lt. J. A. R. Troup) who fired six torpedoes in two daylight snap attacks on 12 October, *Stygian* (Lt. G. S. Clarabut) on 18 October and, on 16 November, *Tally Ho* (Cdr. L. W. A. Bennington) in an 'all singing, all dancing' final patrol before returning to the United Kingdom. In this patrol *Tally Ho* carried out air–sea rescue duties and a search for aircrew survivors from 5–7 November, a special operation to land agents on 9th, and sank Minelayer No 4 (600 tons) with three torpedo hits on 20th. After which, Bennington rounded off his patrol by sinking ten junks by gun-fire and arrived at Trincomalee on passage home on 23rd, he and his ship's company very well satisfied after a most successful operational tour in the Far East.

On 10 November, *Stratagem* (Lt. C. R. Pelly) sailed for her fourth patrol in Far Eastern waters, in an area south of One Fathom Bank in the Malacca Strait. At 1500 on 19th, when *Stratagem* was at periscope depth off the port of Malacca, smoke was sighted to the southward. It was a convoy of five enemy ships, escorted by three torpedo boats. The merchant ships were all in ballast, steaming in line ahead on a steady course. At 1530 *Stratagem* fired three torpedoes at the second ship in the line, range 2,500 yards, and scored one hit. The submarine then went deep whilst the escorts conducted a wild and ineffective attack, dropping about twenty depth-charges. When *Stratagem* returned to periscope depth, the damaged ship could be seen still afloat. One torpedo was fired from the external stern tube at 1,000 yards and the ship, the 1945-ton cargo ship *Nichinan* Maru, sank at once.

Stratagem returned to Malacca on the night of 21 November and at dawn on 22nd was at periscope depth about four miles offshore. A Japanese destroyer could be seen patrolling closer inshore, and a Japanese float-plane was very active overhead. It is possible that *Stratagem* was sighted by the aircraft, in the shallow water, for at about midday a destroyer detected the submarine and severely damaged and flooded her with an accurate depth-charge attack. *Stratagem* was overdue on 3 December, having failed to answer signals, and was presumed lost. The story of her last moments is most movingly told by a survivor, the Torpedo Officer, Lieutenant D. C. Douglas:

'At approximately 1210 I was awakened by the order "Diving Stations". As soon as I arrived in the tube space the order "Shut off for depth-charging" was passed. This was carried out and a report sent to the control room. After four minutes had elapsed without any further orders coming through – nobody in the fore ends knowing what was taking place – then the thrash of the Japanese destroyer could be heard very loud as he passed overhead. Almost immediately a depth-charge exploded somewhere extremely close under us, lifting the stern and causing us to bottom hard. This charge extinguished the greater part of the lighting, although one or two of the emergency lights held. About five seconds later a second charge exploded, as far as I could calculate right amidships, extinguishing the remaining lights.

'By this time I had a torch in operation and could see water flooding through the door at the after end of the torpedo stowage compartment. Immediately I gave the order "Shut watertight doors" and turned to make sure that the three ratings in the tube space were brought out of that compartment, before the door was shut. By the time the door was shut the water was flooding very much faster and had risen above the deck boards in the torpedo stowage compartment. It was now above our knees. It was flooding through the after door so fast that the ratings were unable to shut this door. The position of the stop, retaining the door in the open position on this watertight door, was such that to remove it one had to stand in the doorway, as the port-side of the door was blocked by stores. Hence, due to the furious rate of flooding, this stop could not be removed.

'According to Able Seaman Westwood, who came forward from the control room, the Captain gave the order for main ballast to be blown as soon as he found that the ship was being flooded. The valves on the panel were opened, without effect. In what appeared to be an incredibly short time, I was keeping above water by clinging on to a hammock, which was slung from the deckhead. The crew in my compartment began to sing, but I ordered this to stop and told the crew to get out and put on DSEA[1] sets. The first I managed to reach had a defective valve on the oxygen bottle and I could not move it.

[1] Davis Submarine Escape Apparatus.

Q

The second was in working order and I put this over the head of one of the older ratings, who was panicking and in tears, due to the pressure effect on his eyes. The pressure in the boat at that time was immense and the chlorine content in the air considerable. The water all around us must have been full of oil fuel as we were all drenched with it although I did not notice it at the time. The air could be heard to be escaping through the hull forward and the water was still rising fast.

'At this time, Leading Seaman Gibbs was in the escape hatch, trying to slack back the clips. He shouted to me that he could not move the third clip. Speaking was nearly impossible due to the pressure. I swung up into the trunk alongside Gibbs and tried to remove the clip. After what seemed like an hour and what I suppose was really a minute I managed to move the clip by hammering it with my fist. By this time there was no hope of using the escape trunk as the water was already up to the metal coaming which houses the twill trunking. I took off the last clip and as I did so the hatch commenced to open. Immediately this clip was free the hatch was blown open and Leading Seaman Gibbs was shot out so suddenly that I cannot remember him going. The hatch slammed shut again and hit me on the top of my head but immediately blew open again and I was shot out in a bubble of air.

'Ten of the men in the compartment which contained fourteen at the time are known to have left the submarine alive, though only eight were picked up. The ship's cook was later seen to be floating face downwards on the surface but was obviously drowned. Another rating was seen while in the submarine to have on a DSEA set and apparently working it correctly. Although he was observed to leave the boat he was not seen on the surface.

'The Japanese destroyer had dropped two more charges after we were hit but these were not so close and did not seem to harm us, although they probably accelerated the flooding. Throughout the above experiences the behaviour of the crew in my compartment was magnificent. I should especially like to mention the ship's cook, Leading Cook Weatherhead, who kept up a cheerful narrative about the wonderful fruit cake which he had recently cooked and who showed great bravery and coolness throughout the dreadful experiences in the flooded submarine. This rating was responsible for the singing and by his behaviour greatly assisted in preventing panic. It is with the deepest regret that I have to report that this extremely brave rating failed to survive the ascent to the surface.

'The destroyer circled us for about three-quarters of an hour, dropping a life-belt and some baulks of timber. All of us were suffering from 'bends' and I do not know about the ratings but I myself was scared "pea-green" at the sight of the Japanese ensign flying from their masthead. This was more or less justified, as we later found out. However, I managed to overcome this somewhat by swimming round and seeing to the ratings. Able Seamen Westwood was just on the verge of sinking. His eyes were full of oil and he could hardly keep himself afloat. I fixed him into the lifebelt and then went to the assistance of Able Seaman Phillips. He was in a similar plight but a puff of air into his DSEA set kept his head above water and he was all right although he was almost delirious with shock.

'The Japanese eventually lowered a cutter and picked us up, clubbing us as they hauled us into the boat. Then we were each compelled to pull an oar. This was practically impossible, due to the bends, but we reached the destroyer assisted by their clouts and unpleasantness.

'By this time another destroyer of a similar type had arrived on the scene. The Japanese were certain there was another submarine in the vicinity and got furious with us when we denied this. On being hauled on board we were bound, blind-folded and beaten. We were not given food at any time whilst on board the destroyer and spent the night on the top of the hatch which was about three feet square all bound together. We were not clothed and the night was extremely cold. The pain from the bends was now at its worst and every time someone murmured the guards would come and hit us over the head with their clubs. We were being taken to Singapore, where we arrived at about 2100 on 23 November. No food was given us and we were locked in separate cells, still bound and blind-folded. We remained in this condition for twenty-eight days, although I was allowed to remove my bonds after about ten days.'[1]

Another tragedy was only narrowly avoided in the New Year when *Shakespeare* (Lt. D. Swanston) sailed for her first patrol in Far East waters, on 20 December. The patrol, in the Andaman Sea, was uneventful until the morning of 31 December when a convoy of two merchant vessels, with air and three surface escorts, was sighted leaving the

---

[1] Lt. Douglas and seven ratings were taken to Singapore. On 19 December Douglas, Ldg. Sea. Gibbs and AB Robinson were flown to Japan and taken to Ofuna, an unregistered PoW camp unknown to the Red Cross, where they endured terrible hardships before being released, suffering from beri-beri and malnutrition, by the US Navy in August 1945. These three were the only survivors of *Stratagem*. The others died or were executed in captivity.

Nancowry Strait. *Shakespeare* closed to 1,500 yards and fired a salvo of six torpedoes, sinking the larger of the two merchantmen, the 2,515-ton *Unryu* Maru. The escorts counter-attacked but appeared to be happily depth-charging the hundred fathom line and *Shakespeare* was untouched.

On 2 January 1945 *Shakespeare* was at periscope depth off Port Blair when an A/S vessel was sighted, apparently carrying out anti-submarine sweeps in the Nancowry Strait. This suggested that a convoy might be on its way and *Shakespeare* dived at dawn the next day ten miles east of the Strait. At 0715 Swanston was rewarded by the sight of the mast and funnel of a small unescorted merchant ship, heading south. He was unable to get closer than 3,500 yards for his attack and at 0750 fired four torpedoes, all individually aimed. All missed and so, at 0758, *Shakespeare* surfaced to attack with gun-fire. As there was no air or surface escort at the time, Captain Slaughter later stressed 'in view of subsequent happenings, I wish to make it clear that this was an entirely legitimate submarine operation with no undue risk attached to it'.

Shakespeare approached the enemy vessel on the surface at full speed and at a range of 5,000 yards opened fire with 3-inch and oerlikon. The enemy also turned towards and opened fire with a 12-pounder gun on her fore-deck. *Shakespeare*'s oerlikon jammed, but the 3-inch scored one direct hit on the enemy's waterline, and two probable hits.

After about five minutes' action, a vessel like a submarine chaser was seen some 9,000 yards away, approaching from the Nancowry Strait. *Shakespeare* turned away, and Swanston cleared the bridge and gun positions, before diving. The enemy merchant ship was now less than a mile away, and before *Shakespeare* could dive, scored a hit on the submarine's pressure hull, starboard side amidships, just on the waterline. Water poured into the control room and engine room, flooding the wireless office, and the auxiliary machinery space below the control room.

Shakespeare's guns were manned again and although the oerlikon was still jammed the 3-inch and Vickers machine-gun opened fire on the enemy, now only half a mile away. The 3-inch gun layer AB F. Foster and trainer AB R. F. Whitelam had both been wounded and their places were taken by the First Lieutenant and Telegraphist Britton. Acting on their own initiative, PO Telegraphist V. G. Harmer and Ldg. Tel. K. Wace climbed down on to the submarine's ballast tanks, to try and plug the hole with blankets. The enemy scored four more hits, one of them so close that the blast blew off Harmer's boots and burned his feet. However, he and Wace continued to plug the hole.

At about 0820 *Shakespeare*'s fire put the merchant vessel's gun out of action and the enemy turned away listing noticeably to port. The submarine chaser had opened fire from 6,000 yards but now broke off the action and went to the assistance of the merchant vessel. For some extraordinary reason, but most fortunately for *Shakespeare*, both enemy ships headed for Port Blair and took no further part.

Nevertheless, Swanston and his ship's company were now in a perilous position. *Shakespeare* had a hole some nine inches by four ripped in her pressure hull and was unable to dive. Her wireless and gyro compass were both out of action; the submarine was steered by the portable magnetic compass (traditionally nicknamed 'Faithful Freddie') perched on the helmsman's knee. The motor of the main ballast pump (the chief means of pumping water out of the submarine) was flooded down in the auxiliary machinery space, and the ship's company formed a chain to pass buckets up the conning tower. With his wireless out of action, Swanston could not summon help and there was nothing to do but set course for the Ten Degree Channel, with land twenty miles away to starboard, and wait for the air attack which he considered inevitable as they were close to enemy airfields. Ironically, the British Pacific Fleet was at sea, to the southward, steaming towards its second strike on the Pangkalan Brandan refinery, and had it known could have provided all the CAPs *Shakespeare* so urgently needed.

At about 0900 the port main engine seized and *Shakespeare* continued on the starboard engine, maximum speed now only about seven knots. Shortly afterwards Harmer fell over the side. Swanston stopped and picked him up.

The first of the expected air attacks came at 0930, when a Japanese seaplane made a low level bombing run from astern, dropping his bomb about twenty yards from *Shakespeare*'s port side. The Second Coxswain on the Vickers gave the enemy a short sharp accurate burst. The seaplane caught fire and crashed in the sea half a mile on the starboard bow, with a most heartening effect on the ship's company.

Half an hour later, two Jakes made passes at the submarine and then dived on their bombing runs, each dropping two small bombs, one of which exploded so close that it fractured a high-pressure air line in the flooded auxiliary machinery space bilge; the escaping air causing the water to boil up like a fountain and for several heart-stopping moments the control room crew thought the submarine's hull had been holed again.

Shakespeare endured five more attacks by Jakes in the forenoon and early afternoon. The Jakes each carried two 50-lb bombs, making their bombing runs from dead ahead or right astern, raking the submarine's upper deck with their stern gun as they passed overhead. All the attacks were beaten off.

At 1420 an escort vessel was sighted, overhauling *Shakespeare* from the starboard quarter. This seemed to be the end. Swanston ordered all deciphered signals, patrol orders, and Admiralty publications to be burnt. Confidential books and signal publications were put in weighted sacks, ready to be thrown over the side. The remaining two torpedoes were brought to the action state.

But, incredibly, the escort vessel did not close the range and apparently had no offensive intention. Swanston considered that it was probably leaving them to the tender mercies of the Japanese air force but later thought it possible that it may have been carrying out air–sea rescue duties. It must be assumed that the Japanese did not sight *Shakespeare*; their mission may have been air–sea rescue, but it was unlike the Imperial Japanese Navy to pause and recover a ditched pilot while there was a surfaced enemy submarine in sight.

The 'tender mercies' of the Japanese air force continued until sunset, when *Shakespeare* had survived a total of twenty-five air attacks, by seaplanes, by bombers, fighters, fighter-bombers, attacking in groups or in pairs or singly and dropping fifty bombs varying in size from 50 lb to 1000 lb. The men on *Shakespeare*'s bridge and gun platform had been repeatedly drenched by splashes from near misses, and raked by machine gun and cannon fire and by bomb splinters. Seventeen members of the ship's company had been wounded, two of them mortally. However, when the sun went down on 3 January, *Shakespeare* was still afloat, with the bucket chain in operation, and still making good seven knots to the westward.

At dawn on 4th the Vickers had been stripped and cleaned, and it was hoped that the oerlikon, which had jammed frequently the day before, would function properly. *Shakespeare* awaited another day of air attacks. To the surprise and intense relief of everyone on board, there was no attack throughout the day. The Second Coxswain took the chance to go over the side and improve the blanket plugging, to reduce the flow of water. A hammock was rigged as a chute, to lead the water from the hole in the hull to the engine room bilges where the port main engine circulating water pump could take a suction.

The Vickers gunner AB T. A. Motterham, whose left thigh had been shattered by a cannon shell, had died of his wounds during the night and was buried at sea on 4th.

Shakespeare had no means of calling for help but Swanston happened to remember that *Stygian* was due soon in that area, outward bound on her next patrol. Fortunately the signal with her patrol details had not been burned. It was deciphered again and *Shakespeare* set course to intercept her.

On 5 January, speed was reduced to five knots and the submarine was listed seven degrees to port, to bring the hole in the pressure hull clear of the sea. A patch was applied, using part of the bridge steel chart table, soap, rubber jointing, and clips and bolts from reload torpedo safety bands. This splendidly improvised repair took five hours, entirely stopped the flow of water, and the bucket chain was disbanded. The ship's company had their first hot meal for three days.

Swanston expected that they would meet *Stygian* at about midnight. From 2100 onwards *Shakespeare* fired recognition grenades and Very lights every half hour.

At 0100 on 6th lights were sighted to the west. It was *Stygian*. *Shakespeare*'s grenades had been the correct colours but Clarabut in *Stygian* was cautious. He was a personal friend of Swanston and demanded the christian name of Swanston's wife as extra corroboration. The name Stella was given and for good measure Swanston added that Clarabut's wife was also called Stella.

Reassured, Clarabut closed *Shakespeare*, and *Stygian* and *Shakespeare* proceeded in company towards Trincomalee, whilst *Stygian* transmitted details of the action and names of casualties by wireless.

At 0730 on 6th both submarines reduced speed and half-masted colours while AB G. Taylor, who had died the previous evening of splinter wounds he had received when working in the gun-tower bucket chain, was buried at sea.

Shortly afterwards, *Stygian* sent over a working part of six men by folboat, with torches, medical supplies and bread.

At 1530 the same day the two submarines were met by the destroyer *Raider* who took over *Shakespeare*'s escort, while *Stygian* resumed her patrol. Water was still being pumped from *Shakespeare*'s engine room, with too much success for, on the morning of the 7th, the water level dropped below the propeller shafts and the starboard shaft, which had actually been cooled by the bilge water, at once overheated at the bulkhead gland. The engine had to be stopped and the submarine taken in tow by *Raider*.

After one false start *Shakespeare* was comfortably in tow by 1300, making good 10 knots, when to *Shakespeare*'s extreme annoyance *Raider* was relieved by *Whelp* and the tow had to be slipped. Doubtless the relief was ordered by some officer at Trincomalee who had no personal experience of the difficulties of taking up and slipping tows from a submarine's casing.

Towed by *Whelp*, *Shakespeare* secured alongside *Wolfe* in Trincomalee on 8 January. She was unfit for further operational service, but her last patrol had been, in Captain Slaughter's words, an epic in the history of the submarine service.[1]

Any elation at Trincomalee over *Shakespeare*'s escape was quickly overcast by tragedy. On 3 January, the veteran minelayer–submarine *Porpoise* (Lt. Cdr. H. B. Turner) sailed for her fourth Far Eastern war patrol, to lay mines in the Malacca Strait. She laid two minefields off Penang on 9th, and signalled that she had done so. Nothing more was ever heard from her. Having failed to answer signals she was reported overdue on 16 January, when it was believed she was sunk by Japanese aircraft. The enemy made no claims at the time and showed no interest in her until the official Admiralty announcement of her loss on 17 February (when Douglas and the other survivors of *Stratagem* were at once interrogated about her). *Porpoise* was the 75th and last British submarine to be lost in World War Two.

Japanese escorts' counter-attacks were often of no more than nuisance value, but occasionally an unlucky submarine encountered a member of the 'First Eleven' and was very severely handled. *Strongbow* (Lt. J. A. R. Troup) left Trincomalee on 30 December, for her fourth Far Eastern patrol, in the Malacca Strait. After one depth-charge attack by a destroyer on 10 January which caused no damage, *Strongbow* was detected on 13th by a group of A/S vessels and subjected to a series of damaging attacks which lasted most of the day. Troup was forced to abandon his patrol and *Strongbow* was not fit for any more operational patrols.

When Admiral Fraser hoisted his flag as C-in-C the submarine strength of the British Pacific Fleet had not been decided. An Admiralty signal of 25 November 1944 proposed that *Adamant*, with six 'T' and three 'S' Class submarines, should transfer to the Pacific theatre in

---

[1] A fuller account of *Shakespeare*'s patrol and of the design history of her main battery, which performed magnificently, is given in *Devices of War* by Norman Kemp (Werner Laurie, 1956), Ch. 5 'HMS *Shakespeare* The Unsinkable Submarine'.

January 1945. Another depot ship, *Aorangi*, with a further eight 'T' and two 'S' Class was to leave United Kingdom for the Pacific in February; the depot ship *Bonaventure*, with six XE-craft midget submarines of the 14th Flotilla, was also to leave United Kingdom, in January. The intention was that *Adamant* and *Maidstone* should move to a forward base, probably in the Philippines, as soon as possible.

Admiral Fraser opposed *Adamant*'s move. If her submarines reached the Pacific before a proper base had been prepared, they would be in a kind of operational limbo and their high state of training would be impaired. In any case, they were still doing very useful work in the East Indies Fleet. After discussions with Admiral Kinkaid, and Admiral Christison, it was clear that there was no room for *Adamant* until a base was established in the Philippines, and her move was deferred for three months. *Bonaventure*, with the 14th Flotilla embarked, left the Clyde for the Far East, via the Panama Canal, on 21 February.

On New Year's Day 1945 Rear Admiral R. W. Christison, USN, was relieved by Rear Admiral James Fife, USN, as Commander Submarines, Seventh Fleet. Admiral Fife was a splendid submarine officer and leader of men, and a good friend to British submariners. He had been attached to Flag Officer Submarines' staff as an observer in 1940 and 1941 and he had carried out several war patrols in British submarines in the Mediterranean and the Bay of Biscay. He was on deck to meet every British submarine returning from patrol, and he visited each one to chat with her officers and ship's company before she sailed. He had, too, an astonishing gift of memory for faces, names, incidents and places; on one occasion, while he was visiting a British submarine in Fremantle, he recognised a signalman from one of his patrols in *Cachalot* in the Mediterranean. He not only remembered the man's name, but that he came from Birmingham, and enquired after his family who, at the time of their previous meeting, had been enduring the Luftwaffe's raids on the city. From the British submariners' point of view, there could have been no happier choice of commander, as one submarine CO who served under Admiral Fife recalls:

'Admiral Fife was a remarkable man and the chief architect of Allied cooperation. He was a delightful personality, utterly and absolutely dedicated to the Submarine branch. At the end, his command (Task Force 71) consisted of some forty US, thirty British and five Dutch submarines. In my view he was one of the outstanding submarine leaders of the war on either side and was regarded with great respect and affection by all nationalities serving under him. We were furious when at the end of the war he was only awarded a CBE by the British. We reckoned he was worth far more than that.'[1]

At Fremantle, *Maidstone* had her own alarms and excitements. On 17 January fuel oil lying on the surface of the harbour caught fire between *Maidstone* and a 15,000-ton liner berthed just ahead of her. The flames were fierce enough to scorch paintwork on *Maidstone*'s upper deck, and ready-use ammunition on the fo'c'sle had to be moved. *Maidstone* was towed away by two tugs shortly before she would have caught fire herself.

The 8th Flotilla 'S' Class submarines patrolled in the Java and Flores Seas and in the Macassar Strait, while the larger and longer-ranged 'T' Class patrolled the South China Sea (although *Spiteful*, on her last patrol before returning home, from 12 January to 17 February, patrolled in the South China Sea – the first 'S' boat to do so). To reach their patrol areas the 8th Flotilla had to overcome obstacles of distance and geography. From Fremantle they had first to make the long passage up the west coast of Australia, generally refuelling at the intermediate fuelling base established at Exmouth Bay, before penetrating the barrier of the Indonesian island chain. The shortest route to the Java Sea was through the Lombok Strait, between the islands of Lombok and Bali. The strait was guarded by enemy shore batteries and anti-submarine patrols, and was swept by a fierce south-running current. The British submarines did not have the high surface speed and excellent surface warning radar sets of the large American patrol submarines. For them the Lombok Strait hung like a shadow over the start of every patrol. The Japanese strengthened their shore batteries and increased the frequency of their patrols at the end of 1944; in December, two submarines, *Tantivy* and DS *Zwaardfisch*, were depth-charged hard and had to abandon their patrols. Thereafter a few British submarines made longer passages into the Java Sea via the Ombai Strait, between Ambeno and Alor, or even via the Timor Sea and Darwin. However, in spite of its difficulties the Lombok Strait remained the favourite for most British submarine COs; it was wider than its alternatives and too deep for mining. Returning from patrol, of course, a submarine merely had to dive at the northern end and be sucked southwards by the current and shot into the Indian Ocean 'like a cork from a bottle'.

From Fremantle, British submarines began to make longer patrols

[1] Commander (now Vice Admiral Sir Arthur) Hezlet. Letter of 19.9.68.

than ever before. The normal length of patrol was twenty-eight days for 'S' Class and thirty-five for 'T' Class, giving fourteen and twenty-one days respectively on patrol in areas north of the Malay barrier. 'S' Class were normally provisioned and stored for forty days, 'T' Class for forty-five days, and all submarines carried emergency provisions for a further fourteen days. Every bit of space was utilised for stores and provisions; additional ammunition was stowed behind the main engines, and a 'false deck' of provision boxes 18 inches thick was laid along the passageways.

Tantalus (Lt. Cdr. H. S. Mackenzie) sailed from Fremantle on 3 January 1945. Between 22 and 24 January she was on air–sea rescue duties for the BPF strike at Palembang and from 30 January to 1 February sank a variety of small targets – coasters, luggers, lighters, tugs – in the South China Sea. Target prospects appeared so good that Mackenzie asked for a ten-day patrol extension, which was granted. Shortly after noon on 11 February, east of the Anamba Islands, Mackenzie sighted the fighting tops of two capital ships and the super-structure of a third ship: *Ise* and *Hyuga* and one of their escorts, making their escape back to Japan.[1] It was a sight to make a submarine captain smile in his dreams. Mackenzie tried desperately to get ahead of his targets. But he was hampered by the air escort, detected, bombed, forced to go deep, and was unable to intercept. *Tantalus* returned to Fremantle on 26 February after a patrol of fifty-five days (39 in the patrol area) and 11,692 miles – the longest patrol of any British sub-marine.

Targets were not always so easy to find, and some submarine captains lived dangerously in searching for them. *Tantivy* (Lt. P. H. May) sailed from Fremantle on 14 January for a patrol in the Sunda Strait, her eighth in the Far East and her last before going home. On 3 February, a tug and two coasters were sunk by gun-fire. Later, when *Tantivy* went into the harbour of Panjang in Java to look for targets her bows ran hard aground. Manoeuvring full astern on both shafts and pumping out the forward trim tanks and forward fuel groups, failed to dislodge her. May and his ship's company began to face the possibility of becoming prisoners of the Japanese. Destruction charges were placed about the submarine. Confidential books and signal publications were collected for burning. Luckily, the tide was still flooding. By firing four torpedoes from the bow tubes (with tail guards still on, to prevent them running) and simultaneously going full astern together, *Tantivy* came

[1] See p. 204.

off the mud – only to take the ground aft at once. Eventually, after some two hours of furious manoeuvring, *Tantivy* wriggled clear and reached the open sea. She arrived, all hands mightily relieved, at Trincomalee on 14 February, on passage to United Kingdom.

While fresh submarines were arriving in the Far East every month, veterans who had finished their operational tours were returning home. On 20 February *Storm* (Lt. Cdr. E. P. Young, RNVR) completed her ninth and last patrol, in the Sunda Strait and on the west coast of Sumatra. Young was the first RNVR officer to command a submarine; he and his successors had shown beyond question that the 'amateurs' could compete equally with the 'professionals'.[1] Another submarine to go home at about this time was *Telemachus* (Cdr. W. D. A. King). Her last patrol in the Java and South China Seas was a bitter anticlimax. No targets were found, and the Engineer Officer, Lt. Cdr. (E) H. T. Meadows, was badly injured on 23 February while working on the port main engine. His right hand was nearly severed at the wrist. In an impromptu combined air and sea rescue operation an RAAF Catalina landed alongside *Telemachus* and took Meadows off to Australia. Bill King was the only pre-war submarine CO in the flotilla; his advice and experience were much appreciated by the other COs. He was one of the very few men, on either side, to survive the whole war as a submarine captain.[2]

In April, on patrol in the Flores Sea, *Spark* (Lt. D. G. Kent) assisted in the last rites of the 5,700-ton Japanese cruiser *Isudzu*. *Spark* had missed a coaster with four torpedoes on 31 March but surfaced and sank it by gun-fire. On 4 April she fired her remaining four torpedoes at *Isudzu* at very long range in a flat calm sea. The torpedoes missed but *Spark* was able to pass an enemy sighting report to the US submarine *Gabilan*. On 7th, *Isudzu* was sighted again, crawling along after *Gabilan*'s attack; she was seen to blow up and sink after five minutes, as a result of *Charr*'s attack.

Meanwhile, in the opening months of 1945 the 2nd and 4th Flotillas at Trincomalee continued to wage submarine warfare along the west coast of Burma, off the Andamans and Nicobars, along the coasts of Sumatra, and down the length of the Malacca Strait. Their work was mostly routine and unspectacular; acting as air–sea rescue pickets for

---

[1] Edward Young has written an excellent account of his war experience in *One Of Our Submarines* (Hart Davis, 1952).

[2] Commander King has also written most movingly of his war experience in *The Stick and The Stars* (Hutchinson, 1958).

RAF and USAAF bombers attacking targets on the mainland, landing and retrieving clandestine parties at remote beaches,[1] maintaining a blockade of all enemy traffic by sea, sinking ships by torpedo or gun-fire, or by boarding and placing demolition charges. In the restricted waters of South-east Asia, with its mazes of tiny offshore islands and shoals, the small handy 'S' boats in particular did excellent work. Conditions were against them. They seldom had either the sea-room or the depth of water to take evasive action if they were surprised and attacked. Patches of sea mist or sharp tropical squalls could conceal an enemy air or surface escort. The Japanese were experts in camouflage and several targets skilfully covered with foliage and palms were only discovered through their unnatural rate of change of bearing. The sea was often glassy calm, so that submarines had to attack with the periscope sticking out as prominently as a finger-post, shouting attention to the submarine below (sometimes, too, native fishermen jeopardised a submarine by gaping and pointing at the periscope as it passed). By Atlantic or Mediterranean standards, targets were minute.[2] A ship of 500 tons was an event. One of 2,000 tons was a leviathan. More usual targets would be a junk carrying twenty tons of rice, a schooner with coal, a landing craft carrying 100 troops, a lighter with a few thousand gallons of petrol, or a tiny coaster with a cargo of foodstuffs. Yet each in its small way was contributing to the Japanese war effort. The Chinese and Malay junk masters and their crews, many of whom had been pressed into the enemy's service, were always philosophical and sometimes even co-operative – but they did prefer their junks to be sunk by gun-fire and not by demolition charge, so that they could gamble on the number of rounds required.

Sometimes a junk's cargo was not only denied the enemy but used for the Allied war effort. On patrol in the Malacca Strait during February and March, *Trenchant* (Cdr. A. R. Hezlet) and *Terrapin* (Lt. R. H. H. Brunner) sank several junks, coasters and lighters whilst operating independently. Then, on 4 March, the two submarines co-operated in a combined gun action which sank the 290-ton Special Submarine Chaser No. 5. The action exhausted *Terrapin*'s ammunition, except star-shell, and that night she replenished with sixty rounds transferred from *Trenchant* by rubber boat – exchanging ammunition for twelve hundred eggs taken from a captured junk. They were duck

---

[1] Submarine clandestine operations in the Far East are well described by Lt. Cdr. Alastair Mars in *HMS Thule Intercepts* (Elek, 1956).

[2] See Appendix D.

eggs, quite fresh and very welcome. *Trenchant* and *Terrapin* were among the pioneers of joint patrols by British submarines, having already operated together in the Malacca Strait from 22 December to 4 January. The joint patrols were not in any sense 'wolf-pack tactics', with only two submarines and both lacking good TBS communications, but they enabled submarines to give mutual support to each other during patrols.

Some submarines were particularly lucky in finding targets, and particularly aggressive in dispatching them. On her fifth Far Eastern patrol, in the Malacca Strait from 31 January to 25 February, *Statesman* (Lt. R. G. P. Bulkeley) sank or drove ashore two junks, an armed trawler, seven coasters, a small tanker, two lighters and a tug and deservedly received a signal of congratulation from the Admiralty. In what Admiral Sir Arthur John Power called 'an outstanding patrol', again in her favourite killing ground of the Malacca Strait from 31 March to 19 April, *Statesman* sank an entire convoy of seven armed landing craft, six by gun-fire and the last by demolition charge. Between 6 and 15 April she also sank a schooner, eight junks, and three motor lighters. Four hundred and ninety-three rounds of 3-inch ammunition were expended in that patrol.

Thorough (Lt. A. G. Chandler, RNR) also lived up to her name. In her fifth Far Eastern patrol off the west coast of Burma from 6 February to 5 March she destroyed nineteen junks and a coaster by gun-fire, ramming or demolition charges. A landing craft, cleverly camouflaged with palm leaves and foliage to 'look remarkably like an island', was also sunk by gun-fire; it had been carrying petrol and 100 Japanese troops, six of whom were taken prisoner.

British torpedoes had periodic bouts of unreliability, although failures never approached the crisis pitch of the American torpedoes earlier in the war. After some alarming experiences in an early 1944 patrol, Bennington in *Tally Ho* complained: 'One cannot help feeling sore about the torpedoes. To be chased three times in one patrol by one's own maddened torpedoes is surely an aspect of war which would lead one's mother to write a stiffish note to the Prime Minister.' After *Tantivy*'s eventful first patrol out of Fremantle (in which she sank eight out of twenty-one 'sail of the line' – schooners loaded with nickel ore – appropriately on Trafalgar Day 1944) May reported that he had lost confidence in his torpedoes. On 26 October he had fired two at a large coaster. Both circled and one exploded prematurely. However, four days earlier, he had accidentally sunk a Japanese A/S corvette, when it hit one of *Tantivy*'s torpedoes which had expended its fuel, come to the surface, and acted as a mine. On 21 January, in the southern Malacca Strait, *Shalimar* (Lt. W. G. Meeke) fired a salvo of six at a surfaced Japanese U-boat. One torpedo exploded prematurely, almost certainly alarming the target, and the rest missed. There were other occasions when targets were missed, or surprise lost, by torpedo failures.

In April 1945 the disposition of British submarines in the Far East was reorganised. *Adamant* left Trincomalee on 1st and arrived at Fremantle on 11 April. Her submarines joined her after completing their current patrols. At Fremantle the 4th and 8th Flotillas were adjusted, to give each depot ship one homogeneous class of submarine. An anomaly in *Maidstone*'s administrative position was also adjusted. She and her submarines had been operating for some months in the South-west Pacific area but for administrative purposes were still part of the East Indies Fleet. From 1 April *Maidstone* and the 8th Flotilla became officially part of the British Pacific Fleet.

Maidstone left Fremantle on 19 April and after calling at Sydney, Manus and Leyte arrived on 20 May at Subic Bay in the Philippines, where two flotillas of US submarines and their depot ships were already based. *Maidstone*'s submarines joined her at Subic after they had completed their patrols in the Java Sea.

The disposition of British submarines in the Far East for the last four months of the war was therefore: at Subic Bay, *Maidstone* and the 8th Flotilla of seven 'S' Class, to operate in the China Sea[1]; at Fremantle, *Adamant* and the 4th Flotilla, of nine 'T' Class[2] and *Rorqual*, to operate in the Java Sea; and at Trincomalee, *Wolfe* and the 2nd Flotilla, of six 'S' Class and three unconverted 'short-range' 'T' Class,[3] to operate west of the Malay barrier.

Clyde (Lt. R. H. Bull) sailed from Trincomalee on her final war patrol on 9 May. She carried out one successful clandestine operation on the west coast of Siam, but a second had to be cancelled because of defects in *Clyde*'s hydroplanes. She was the oldest operational submarine in the Royal Navy, having been completed in April 1935. The patrol was her thirty-sixth of the war. Afterwards, she sailed for Kilindini and the breaker's yard.

---

[1] *Solent, Sleuth, Spark, Supreme, Stygian, Sturdy* and *Seascout; Selene, Spearhead, Stubborn* and *Sidon* all joined later and carried out war patrols.

[2] *Thorough, Taciturn, Trump, Tiptoe, Tudor, Thule, Trenchant, Terrapin* and *Tradewind.*

[3] *Statesman, Spur, Subtle, Seadog, Shalimar* and *Sibyl; Torbay, Thrasher* and *Trident.*

The 'S' and 'T' Class submarines at Trincomalee patrolled areas west of the Malay barrier until the end of the war. The only submarines of the 2nd Flotilla to sight major warships during this period were *Subtle* and *Statesman* in Operation DUKEDOM.[1] *Statesman*, possibly the most successful submarine of the flotilla, arrived at Trincomalee from her last patrol on 25 August 1945. She had carried out nine operational patrols in the Far East and destroyed or damaged forty-nine enemy vessels totalling about 10,000 tons, expending over 1,200 rounds of 3-inch ammunition. The last submarine to return was *Trident*, who arrived at Trincomalee from a weather reporting patrol in the Andaman Sea on 3 September. It was her thirty-fourth patrol of the war. She had sailed on her first on 24 October 1939.

The minelayer *Rorqual* (Lt. J. P. H. Oakley) had been included in the 4th Flotilla at Fremantle, but there was no further requirement for minelaying after May 1945. In her final patrol, in the West Java Sea from 30 April to 20 May, *Rorqual* laid mines between the Sunda Strait and Batavia on 10 May; the next day, *Rorqual* showed that she also had a talent for gunnery. Off the coast of Java she surfaced, sank a coaster with 15 crisp hits from 21 rounds, and dived again – having been surfaced for a bare five minutes. *Rorqual* then returned to the United Kingdom. She had laid 1,350 mines, in 38 lays, during the war, and she was the only one of a class of six minelaying submarines to survive the war.

Admiral Fife forecast that there would still be targets in the Java and Flores Seas until September 1945, when submarine warfare in the Pacific would be virtually at an end. Although the tide was running so strongly in favour of the Allied submarines, a submarine captain still needed a little luck and a nice judgment. *Terrapin* sailed on her first patrol from Fremantle in the West Java Sea on 3 May. In the early hours of 15th she ran hard aground on Arnemuiden Bank, in the Thousand Islands west of Batavia; all internal trim tanks and 15,700 gallons of external oil fuel were pumped out, and two torpedoes fired from the bow tubes, before *Terrapin* came off, after being stuck for nearly two hours. Four days later, Brunner attacked a small tanker, escorted by a frigate and one other vessel, in very shallow water. After the attack Brunner ordered a depth of sixty feet, but *Terrapin* struck bottom at fifty-seven feet on the depth-gauge, and stayed there. After five minutes, propeller noises and asdic transmissions were heard to seaward and five depth-charges exploded 'fairly near'. After another

[1] See p. 220.

ten minutes, five more charges exploded. This pattern was very much closer and drove in *Terrapin*'s pressure hull to a depth of 18 inches in the tube space and did considerable damage inside the submarine.

Brunner was faced with a nice decision. The frigate certainly knew where *Terrapin* was, and could now depth charge and destroy her at his leisure. Yet if she attempted to move off the bottom *Terrapin* would certainly break surface. The frigate had six 4-inch guns, and the submarine would be a sitting target. Brunner decided to stay where he was, balancing a faint chance of survival on the sea-bottom against almost certain destruction on the surface; his decision was later backed up by Captain Ionides. The frigate depth-charged for another five hours, but *Terrapin* survived and surfaced at 1900, after dark. The frigate was 5,000 yards away but did not sight the submarine. *Terrapin*'s wireless was out of action, but on 21 May she met the US submarine *Cavalla* who escorted her to Fremantle. She was unfit for further operational service without a major structural refit.

The enemy's desperate shortage of shipping at this stage of the war was well demonstrated on 16 June, off Sourabaya, when *Thorough* and *Taciturn* (Lt. Cdr. E. T. Stanley) met one of the oddest-looking convoys of the war. It consisted of an armed trawler, an old and rusty ex-Dutch submarine with its forward gun removed, and a submarine chaser towing a large hulk which had 'several promenade decks and a roof overall'. *Taciturn* closed the convoy in water too shallow for diving and destroyed them all by gun-fire, except the trawler, which turned away 'into *Thorough*'s arms'.

However, there was still one chance left of a shot at a major target and, most appropriately, it came to one of the most resourceful and successful British submarine commanders of the war.

Trenchant (Cdr. A. R. Hezlet) sailed from Fremantle for her first patrol in the South-west Pacific area (but her sixth in Far Eastern waters) on 13 May. From 19 to 22 May, *Trenchant* examined anchorages along the south coast of Sumbawa, without finding any targets, but on 25th, west of Sourabaya, an escorted coaster was sighted. Hezlet missed with one torpedo, which ran beneath the target, so surfaced and sank the escort, the 215-ton Special Minesweeper No. 105, with gun-fire, while the coaster beached itself in despair. On 29th, off the north entrance to the Sunda Strait, Hezlet witnessed a torpedo from the US submarine *Boarfish* hit the rear ship of a convoy of three. There was a counter-attack, but *Trenchant* was too far away to create a diversion.

Two days later *Trenchant* was ordered to a patrol line off the Malayan

R

coast at Pulo Tengol, to cover the Allied assault on Brunei, but on passage heard the US submarines *Blueback* and *Chubb* report a Japanese cruiser and a destroyer entering Batavia. Hezlet guessed that the cruiser would be returning to Singapore and on 5 June reported that he would be late in his patrol position and asked permission to patrol the northern entrance to the Banka Strait. Admiral Fife agreed, with reluctance. The strait was confined water, with shoals, strong tidal currents, and a minefield laid by DS O.19 in April. He would certainly never have *ordered* a submarine to patrol there.

In the early hours of 7th *Trenchant* sighted and challenged *Stygian*, and the two submarines came alongside for a commanding officers' conference. Hezlet and Clarabut agreed that *Trenchant* should patrol inside the strait, while *Stygian* patrolled a few miles to the north, outside the minefield:

'I was prepared to toss a coin for who went in the inner berth, which was the most promising. But Clarabut demurred and didn't like the look of it, so I didn't give him a second chance and snapped it up!'[1]

Trenchant took up her patrol position in the narrows off Tanjong Bessajap with *Stygian* five miles north of Hendrik Klippen Shoal.[2] *Trenchant* surfaced at 2115, and kept sonar watch. With luck, the enemy could be expected any time in the next twelve hours.

At 0400 on 8 June, Hezlet received *Blueback*'s signal that the enemy cruiser and destroyer had left Batavia, northbound, on 7th.

The cruiser was the Nachi Class *Ashigara*, a sister ship of *Haguro*, and now the only major operational warship left in the 10th Area Fleet. The destroyer was the ubiquitous *Kamikaze*. They had both left Singapore on 3 June for Batavia, and were now returning with 1,200 troops of the Japanese 48th Division as part of Transportation No. 10.

At 0423 a ship (which proved to be *Kamikaze*) was sighted to the south, steering NNW at 15 knots up the Banka Strait. Hezlet refrained from diving, not wishing to lose the initiative, but kept *Trenchant* bows on to the destroyer as it approached. At 0435 *Kamikaze* passed close ahead of *Trenchant*, less than five hundred yards away, with *Trenchant* still keeping bows on to her, wheel hard a-port. When *Kamikaze* had passed, Hezlet ordered hard a-starboard and revolutions for 14 knots, intending to disengage on a reciprocal course. At that moment *Kamikaze* sighted *Trenchant* and turned sharply to port, opening fire with close

[1] Vice Admiral Hezlet. Letter of 22.10.68.
[2] See map, opposite.

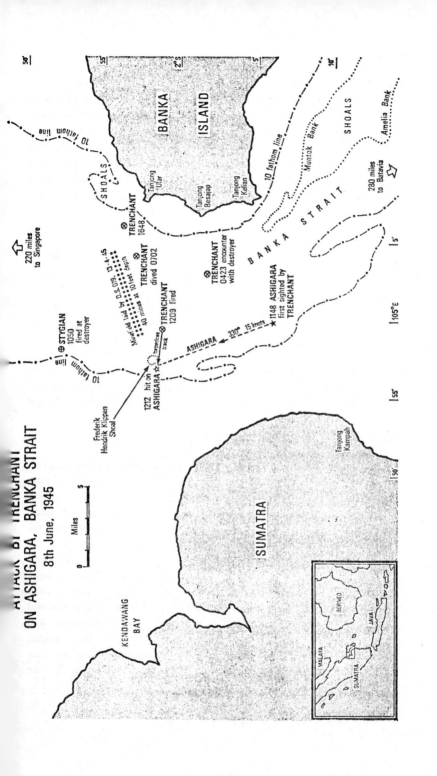

ATTACK BY TRENCHANT
ON ASHIGARA, BANKA STRAIT
8th June, 1945

220 miles to Singapore

280 miles to Batavia

STYGIAN 1050 fired at destroyer

Minefield laid by O.S. 019, 13-4-45
40 mines at 10 feet depth

TRENCHANT dived 0702

TRENCHANT 1209 fired

torpedoes track

1212 hit on ASHIGARA

Frederik Hendrik Klippen Shoal

10 fathom line

TRENCHANT 1648

Tanjong Ular

Tanjong Besajap

Tanjong Kelian

TRENCHANT 0423 encounter with destroyer

1148 ASHIGARA first sighted by TRENCHANT

ASHIGARA 330° 15 knots

BANKA ISLAND

10 fathom line

Muntok Bank

BANKA STRAIT

SHOALS

Amelia Bank

KENDAWANG BAY

SUMATRA

Tanjong Kampah

Miles
0   5

MALAYA

SUMATRA

BORNEO

JAVA

range weapons, which straddled the submarine, and one round from her main armament. But *Trenchant* was inside the enemy's turning circle and, swinging hard to starboard and increasing speed, fired a torpedo from No. 9 tube as *Kamikaze* passed the stern; the torpedo was set to run at a depth of six feet but at a range of less than four hundred yards it had not time to take up its correct depth and ran underneath. *Kamikaze* sighted the track and swung away. The range opened rapidly and although *Kamikaze* soon turned back again, *Trenchant* still kept stern on to her at 14 knots and was able steadily to draw away and work round to seaward. *Kamikaze* was apparently not using radar and probably only sighted *Trenchant* once, after crossing her bows. At 0450 *Kamikaze* made off to the southward, baffled, and Hezlet signalled to Clarabut that he had a destroyer in sight and the enemy had sighted him.

Stygian was then some ten miles to the north. Clarabut had seen star-shell to the south at 0439 and had closed Hendrik Klippen Shoal to see if he could help but he heard and saw nothing more and so returned to patrol the ten-fathom line north of the Shoal.

Trenchant reached the edge of the minefield at 0615 and stopped, waiting for daybreak, and at 0702 dived one and a half miles south of the minefield, and six miles east of the Shoal. *Ashigara* must surely pass that way, if she were coming at all.

Kamikaze was sighted again at 0955, following the ten-fathom line on the Sumatran side of the strait. *Trenchant* merely turned stern on and plotted her track. *Kamikaze* passed out of sight to the north at 1030 and twenty-five minutes later explosions were heard from that direction.

Stygian had picked up the enemy at 1015. By this time *Kamikaze* was zig-zagging widely, and obviously carrying out an anti-submarine sweep. There were also reconnaissance aircraft overhead. Clarabut, too, was hoping for a shot at the cruiser but the minutes passed and no other target appeared and so, at 1050, *Stygian* attacked with two torpedoes, range eight hundred yards. *Kamikaze* sighted the water turbulence of the torpedoes leaving the tubes, turned towards *Stygian* and increased speed. The destroyer evaded the torpedoes and delivered a sharp counter-attack of twenty-seven depth-charges which did *Stygian* minor damage. After that Clarabut cautiously 'kept an eye on her', and at 1247 heard heavy explosions to the south. *Kamikaze* was then 4,000 yards to the north-west, and heading south. Clarabut did not see her again. Clarabut later referred to the 'ignominious' part he had played, but in fact he had been the perfect 'catspaw' for *Trenchant*, keeping the enemy destroyer preoccupied whilst Hezlet dealt with the cruiser.

At 1148 *Trenchant*'s officer of the watch on the periscope sighted the masts and upperworks of a cruiser, almost due south, range 12,000 yards. It was *Ashigara* at last, steering NNW at a moderate speed of about 15 knots. Before leaving Fremantle, Hezlet had 'got his eye in' against Nachi Class cruisers on the Attack Teacher. Now was the time to turn rehearsal into performance.

Hezlet made no attempt to close the enemy's track, assuming that *Ashigara* would leave Hendrik Klippen Shoal to port, putting *Trenchant* in an ideal position for an attack. Astonishingly the Japanese navigating officer had chosen to leave the Shoal to starboard, presenting Hezlet with a difficult shot from abaft the enemy's beam, at a torpedo running range of 4,700 yards. At 1209 *Trenchant* fired a full salvo of eight (including the two bow external tubes). The periscope dipped after firing but when trim was regained Hezlet could see the torpedo tracks stretching towards the target 'like an arterial road'.

The tracks were also sighted by the troops packed on *Ashigara*'s quarterdeck and boatdeck and by *Ashigara*'s captain who, ironically, could do nothing to save his ship. In spite of his unfavourable attacking position, Hezlet actually had *Ashigara*'s captain by what submariners term 'the short and curlies'. *Ashigara* could not turn away to port, to comb the tracks, or she would have run aground. But neither could she alter towards – a turn of a full 120° which would have taken too long. *Ashigara* could do nothing except increase speed, which she did (although she also made a navigational alteration of some 20° to starboard at this time).

The first torpedo hit abreast 'Y' turret at 1212 followed two seconds later by simultaneous hits amidships and right forward. Four seconds later two more hits 'filled in the gaps'. *Ashigara* was completely enveloped in a great cloud of smoke. When it cleared *Ashigara* appeared to be stopped and already listing to starboard, with her bows blown off and a large fire raging on her fo'c'sle. However, at 1220 *Ashigara* opened fire on *Trenchant*'s periscope which 'was not surprising as about the 30th member of the ship's company was goofing with about eight feet of the large periscope up and we were still turning at 5 knots'. When Hezlet regained his periscope (by queueing up for it) *Trenchant* fired two more torpedoes from the stern tubes at 1224, allowing *Ashigara* 5 knots. But *Ashigara* evidently still had considerable way on and may also have altered further to starboard possibly to beach on

Hendrik Klippen Shoal, and the torpedoes missed. The fire forward was now clearly out of control and *Ashigara*'s list had increased to 25 degrees. *Kamikaze* was observed again, approaching at high speed from the north, and 'zig-zagging like a snipe'. At 1239 *Ashigara* capsized to starboard and sank[1] in clouds of smoke and foam, while *Kamikaze* dropped three 'face-saving' charges, three miles away from *Trenchant*.

Trenchant headed north, worked her way between Banka Island and the minefield, and surfaced some six miles north of it that evening. Meanwhile, a passing junk and an Examination Vessel from Muntok picked up *Ashigara*'s survivors.

It seems incredible that *Ashigara* should have continued to approach a position where a submarine had been definitely sighted, at a steady speed, without air cover and with her destroyer escort detached, through a narrow and shallow strait where for navigational reasons very little evasive action would be possible. In this sense, it could be said that *Ashigara* hurried on her own fate. However, it is probable that both *Ashigara* and *Kamikaze* were misled by *Stygian*'s activities.

'When *Stygian* attacked *Kamikaze*, I think *Kamikaze* assumed it was *Trenchant* again. *Kamikaze* then sat on the contact and told *Ashigara* to hurry by while he held the submarine down. This was, in my view, *Stygian*'s part in the affair, which was a vital one.'[2]

Trenchant's patrol was by no means over. On 11 June she met the US submarine *Puffer* and patrolled off Pulo Tengol. Two days later, at 1130 in the morning, masts and aircraft were seen to the southward. It was a large tanker in ballast,[3] with a destroyer and a minesweeper, all hugging the five-fathom line, and two aircraft overhead. *Trenchant* closed to attack but the water was very shallow; Hezlet realised that it would be foolhardy to carry on in such conditions and wisely broke off the attack.

Trenchant arrived at Subic Bay on 20 June, after one of the outstanding submarine patrols of the war, in which valour had been brilliantly tempered with discretion.

Commander Hezlet received the DSO, a signal of commendation from the War Cabinet, and the Order of Commander of the US Legion of

[1] In position 1°59·1′S 104°57′E.
[2] Vice Admiral Hezlet. Letter of 21.10.68.
[3] Possibly *Toho* Maru. See p. 233.

Merit which was presented to him by Admiral Fife on board *Trenchant*, alongside *Maidstone*, at Subic Bay.

Although the Allies were waging unrestricted submarine warfare, submarine COs were not given complete *carte blanche*. Admiral Fife made his policy quite clear: 'Gunning of small craft in the Netherlands East Indies or Philippines does the enemy little or no harm and is forbidden. We are not at war with the natives of the Netherlands East Indies. Small Japanese craft shall be destroyed when identified.' Submarine captains were thus constantly faced with the problem of deciding whether or not a small craft was in the service of the enemy. In practice, this meant boarding, and the risks attached were illustrated in *Trenchant*'s next patrol, which began on 26 June. On 13 July a small schooner was intercepted at the head of the Gulf of Bone. When the boarding party arrived on the schooner's deck they were met by an armed Japanese soldier at the top of the hatch and there were four more Japanese soldiers below, firing up through the deck planking. The boarding party retreated, and the schooner was sunk 'soldiers and all' by gun-fire. *Trenchant* arrived at Fremantle on 24 July, having spent eighty-two of the previous ninety-four days at sea, and run 15,000 miles.

The last two patrols of the 4th Flotilla were carried out jointly in the west Java Sea by *Thorough* and *Taciturn*, and by *Tiptoe* (Lt. R. L. Jay) and *Trump* (Lt. A. A. Catlow), in July and August. Oddly, for that late hour in the war, there were targets in plenty and on 3 August off Batavia *Trump* hit and sank a cargo ship of 6,000 tons; Japanese records were in disorder by then and the success was not officially recorded. All four submarines returned to Fremantle on 21 August – after *Thorough* had been bombed by two aircraft in the Lombok Strait the day after the war ended.

Subic Bay was some thirty miles north of Manila, on the west coast of Luzon. The sailors called it 'Superheated Scapa'. Certainly, life in *Maidstone* was hot and seriously overcrowded; there was a lack of messdeck and living space, and particularly of wash-places and bathrooms. To set against this, there was the magnificent co-operation of the Americans. Of all the 'special relationships' established between British and American fighting men during the war, one of the closest was that between the two nations' submariners in the Far East, at Fremantle and Subic Bay. (Only one small sartorial point jeopardised this relationship, both in the submarine flotillas and in the main Pacific Fleet. This was the curious British habit of wearing uniform shorts in the tropics. Some Americans, the more charitable, ascribed the custom to typical Limey quaintness, on a par with cricket, afternoon tea, and the Barracuda aircraft. But others frankly regarded shorts as 'pansy' or 'cissy' and just one more symptom of the decline of a once-great Imperial power).

However, British submariners, like their colleagues in the fleet, benefited from the incomparable (and quite unofficial) 'can do' spirit of the US logistics and repair forces. On Friday, 13 July, a serious fire broke out in *Seanymph*, lately arrived from the United Kingdom, while she was lying alongside *Maidstone* at Subic. Main battery charging leads had been wrongly disconnected, causing a flash. When the submarine was shut down her hull was so hot that pieces of wood in her casing caught fire. When the fire was out and the hatches opened it was found that the submarine's accommodation space had been gutted. The American repair ship *Anthedon* at once put a hundred men on board *Seanymph* and they worked twenty-four hours a day to refit, rewire and repaint. They finished in less than a week and *Seanymph* sailed for Darwin and the United Kingdom only eighteen days after the fire.

The 'S' Class submarines of the 8th Flotilla patrolled the South China Sea and the Gulf of Siam until the end of the war, carrying out air–sea rescue duties and attacking surface targets. On the evening of 28 July in the South China Sea *Sidon* (Lt. H. C. Gowan) picked up 2nd Lt. Stanley Reed, USAAF, who had been adrift for five days, with little food and no water, and was 287 miles from his reported position. The frustrations and rewards of ASR work were well summed up by Gowan: 'The joy on his face when he saw *Sidon* amply repaid all the fruitless searching and false hopes we had experienced.'

Surface targets were mostly small, but *Stubborn* (Lt. Cdr. A. G. Davies) on her first Far Eastern patrol, torpedoed and sank an old Japanese destroyer, the 750-ton Patrol Boat No 2, at dusk on 25 July north of Bali. The brothers Martin (Lt. Cdr. J. D. in *Solent* and Lt. K. H. in *Sleuth*) carried out joint patrols with particular success, sinking the 215-ton special Minesweeper No 3 with combined gun-fire in the East Java Sea on 26 April, and narrowly missing a Japanese U-boat in the approaches to Singapore on the night of 6 July.

While the large 'orthodox' submarines were performing east and west of Malaya, the 14th Flotilla in *Bonaventure* (Captain W. R. Fell) had been steaming across the Pacific, looking forward to bringing their unorthodox talents to bear upon the war. *Bonaventure* reached Pearl Harbour on 7 April, where the flotilla were told there was no employment for XE-craft in the Pacific. After much uncertainty, and with flotilla morale dropping lower every day, *Bonaventure* reached Brisbane on 27 April. Captain Fell set out with evangelical fervour to preach the gospel of XE-craft to anyone who would listen.[1] He obtained Admiral Fraser's permission to move *Bonaventure* nearer to the operational zone, and to approach the Americans directly. *Bonaventure* arrived at Townsville in Queensland in May and Captain Fell went on to Subic Bay to call on Admiral Fife. He was received very civilly, but sent empty away. *Bonaventure* would probably be converted for Fleet Train duties, and the midget submarines scrapped.

Actually, there were suitable targets for X-craft in the Far East at that time: Japanese shipping at Singapore, at Hong Kong, Camranh Bay, and Saigon, and, as the war moved nearer Japan, there might be opportunities in harbours in the Japanese home islands. Nor was Captain Fell advancing unsubstantiated claims for an untried weapon; the 14th Flotilla need only point to the great *Tirpitz* adventure.

The real reason for American reluctance to employ the flotilla probably lay in the difference in British and American national temperaments. The British were used to 'messing about in small boats'. They had a long history of cutting-out expeditions in fortified enemy harbours, and of daring night raids by specially trained parties. As the Official Historian has remarked, midget submarines were in the Elizabethan tradition.[2]

The Americans, on the other hand, were either indifferent or even actively hostile to such methods. Also, it may be ungenerous but it is probably true to say that some startling exploit by British midget submarines in an almost exclusively American war theatre would not have been kindly received by the American publicity machine.[3]

The Japanese codes had been broken and the only messages which were still secure were those sent by the submarine telegraph cables which ran from South-east Asia to Japan. On 31 May, when Captain Fell was attending a staff conference in Sydney, he was asked whether his midget submarines could cut such cables.

[1] Captain Fell has described his peregrinations, and the ultimate triumphant success of the flotilla, in *The Sea Our Shield* (Cassell, 1966).

[2] Roskill, *The War At Sea 1939–45* (HMSO, 1960). Vol. III, Part 1, p. 64.

[3] The Americans were as reluctant to use another unorthodox British weapon – Highball, which was a smaller version of the 'Dambuster' bomb, designed for use against shipping. No. 618 Squadron RAF, flying Mosquitos, began trials in April 1943 but did not reach the Far East until January 1945. Highball was never used and 618 disbanded on 14 July 1945. See also 'The Dambusters who never flew', by G. R. Lane, *Liverpool Daily Post*, 18 June 1968.

It was like asking a duck if he could swim. In June *Bonaventure* moved to Hervey Bay, on the east coast of Queensland, some 250 miles north of Brisbane, to carry out experiments and intensive training, practising on a disused Australia-New Caledonia telegraph cable in the bay.

Despite the loss during training of two experienced divers through oxygen poisoning, the flotilla were ready in July. When Captain Fell presented his plans to Admiral Fife he was delighted to hear that further targets were suggested: the two Japanese heavy cruisers, *Miyoko* and *Takao*, at Singapore. Thus when *Bonaventure* arrived at Victoria Harbour, Labuan – with Admiral Fife on board – three separate expeditions were planned. They were: Operation STRUGGLE, an attack on *Miyoko* and *Takao*; Operation FOIL, to cut the submarine telegraph cables in the Lamma Channel, off Hong Kong; and Operation SABRE, to do the same at Cap St Jacques, Saigon.

The three operations took place at about the same time. *Stygian* and *Spark* with XE-3 (Lt. I. E. Fraser, RNR) and XE-1 (Lt. J. E. Smart, RNVR) respectively in tow,[1] sailed from Labuan on 26 July for STRUGGLE. *Spearhead* (Lt. Cdr. R. E. Youngman, RNR) sailed for SABRE with XE-4 (Lt. M. H. Shean, RANVR) a day later. *Selene* (Lt. H. B. Newton) sailed with XE-5 (Lt. H. P. Westmacott) in tow for FOIL also on 27th, from *Maidstone* at Subic.

Of the three, SABRE was the neatest and quickest, a thoroughly professional job. Shean was an experienced X-craft commander; he had taken part in the penetration of Altenfjord with Cameron and Place in 1943, and had commanded one of the marker X-craft off Sword Beach for the Normandy landings.

XE-4 was slipped forty miles off Saigon on the evening of 30 July. Next morning Shean carried out a reconnaissance of the shore line, and began a sweep with the grapnel. After an hour's sweeping, the grapnel snagged and the diver, S/Lt. A. K. Bergius, RNVR, left the submarine and found two cables. He returned on board with two pieces cut out from each which were taken back to *Bonaventure* tied with pink ribbon. XE-4 was taken in tow by *Spearhead* that night and both returned to Labuan in good order and perfect harmony on 3 August.

Westmacott, in XE-5 had a far more harrowing time. The tow parted

---

[1] X-craft were normally towed, dived, by 'orthodox' submarines to some position near the scene of their operation, with a 'passage crew' on board. The crews were then changed, an 'operational crew' taking over for the actual operation.

near *Selene*'s end in the early hours of 30th. XE-5, over 300 feet of wire hanging from her bows, began to plunge towards the bottom of the sea, with Westmacott furiously blowing all main ballast tanks and XE-5 going full ahead with hydroplanes hard to rise. XE-5 had sunk nearly to 300 feet before the towing wire could be slipped, whereupon the submarine bobbed up to the surface like a cork. Westmacott decided to go on alone, and reached the Lamma Channel on 31 July.

Although XE-5 was hampered by poor visibility and by dozens of fishing junks, sampans and small craft, grappling began on the morning of 1 August. When an obstruction was found, the first diver, S/Lt B. G. Clark, RNVR, not only had difficulty in the deep mud on the bottom but injured his hand with the wire-cutter and had to return. The second diver, S/Lt. D. M. Jarvis, RNVR, took over. XE-5 grappled to and fro in the mud all that day and on 2 and 3 August, retiring to charge her battery at night. Eventually, Westmacott gave up and was taken in tow by *Selene* on 4th, both returning to Subic Bay on 6th. When the Allies reoccupied Hong Kong, it was found that XE-5's activities had put the cable out of action after all.

Operation STRUGGLE, and especially Fraser's attack on *Takao*, was one of the epic exploits of the war.[1] XE-3 was slipped off Singapore on the night of 30 July and penetrated the Johore Strait boom the next morning. In the early afternoon, Fraser made his first approach, but decided that he had attacked from too fine an angle on *Takao*'s bow. He withdrew for a second attack, which was successful; limpet mines were fixed to *Takao*'s hull by Ldg. Seaman J. J. Magennis and two explosive charges jettisoned under the ship. After some very anxious moments, when the port explosive charge failed to disengage, and when it appeared that *Takao* had settled on XE-3 with the falling tide, XE-3 cleared the harbour, was taken in tow by *Stygian* and arrived in Labuan on 4th August. XE-3's charges blew up on the evening of 31st, badly damaging but not sinking *Takao*. Fraser and Magennis were both awarded the Victoria Cross.

Meanwhile, Smart's target was the other cruiser *Miyoko*, further in the Strait. XE-1 was delayed by patrol craft and was approaching *Takao* only shortly before XE-3's charges were timed to detonate. Smart added his burden to Fraser's under *Takao* and withdrew. XE-1 and *Spark* returned to Labuan on 5 August.

At 1915 on 15 August, 1945, when *Solent*'s wireless aerial broke

[1] See Ian Fraser's own vivid account of the operation in *Frogman VC* (Angus & Robertson, 1957).

surface in the Gulf of Siam, the PO Telegraphist heard the words from Subic Bay '. . . the war is over'. Within minutes, a notice appeared on the board in the control room: 'To all "Hostilities Only" ratings. The price of cigarettes to you is now 2/4d for twenty.' Later, the Coxswain was heard inviting the hands to fill in the request forms on his table to complete their twelve years' service. 'Only derision greeted the honest fellow.'

Vice Admiral Sir Bernard Rawlings, KCB, KBE. Second-in-Command, British Pacific Fleet. From a painting by Sir Oswald Birley

Vice Admiral Sir Philip Vian, KCB, KBE, DSO. Flag Officer commanding the First Aircraft Carrier Squadron, British Pacific Fleet

The Battleship *King George V*, flagship of the British Pacific Fleet

The aircraft carrier *Formidable* with *Indomitable* and other ships of the British Pacific Fleet (in the background), at Manus

Fireflies strafing Japanese shipping at Hirara, Sakishima Gunto, April 1945. From a painting by S/Lt. V. M. G. Bennett, RNVR, of 1770 squadron.

A brilliant little encounter: two Fireflies of 1770 squadron shoot down four Sonias and damage a fifth, off the Sakishima Gunto, 12 April 1945. From a painting by S/Lt. Bennett.

Two British combat aircraft of the British Pacific Fleet. (Top) the Seafire and (bottom) the Firefly. From paintings by John Batchelor

The first British Pacific Fleet strike at the Palembang oil refineries, at Pladjoe,
24 January 1945

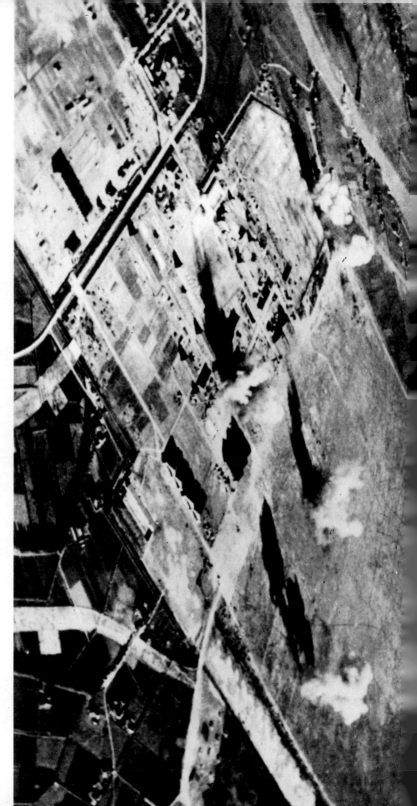

An attack by aircraft of the British Pacific Fleet on the airfield of Tokushima, Shikoku, July 1945

A Japanese Kobe Class escort carrier, after bombing attacks by aircraft of the British Pacific Fleet, Inland Sea, 24 July 1945

The Japanese heavy cruiser, *Haguro*, sinking after gun and torpedo attacks by the 26th Destroyer Flotilla, off Penang, 15–16 May 1945. From a painting by Cdr. H. G. de Chair, DSC, commanding the destroyer *Venus* during the action

A direct hit by a kamikaze suicide bomber on *Formidable*, off the Sakishima Gunto, 4 May 1945

Chaung Warfare in the Arakan. A Motor Launch and Landing Craft (Assault)
(in the background) waiting for the Japs to break. From a drawing by Lt. H. D
Rowe, RNVR.

Admiral Raymond Spruance, Commander US Fifth Fleet (left), Admiral Sir
Bruce Fraser, GCB, KBE, Commander-in-Chief British Pacific Fleet (centre), and
Admiral Chester Nimitz, Commander-in-Chief Pacific Ocean Area (right), at
Honolulu, 1944

The Surrender of Japan. Admiral Fraser signing on behalf of Great Britain. Standing (left to right), General MacArthur, Admiral Rawlings and Admiral Brind

Chapter Nine

THE FLEET TRAIN

'. . . The distances involved are similar to those of a fleet based in Alexandria, with advanced anchorages at Gibraltar and the Azores, attacking the North American coast between Labrador and Nova Scotia.' *Admiral Sir Bruce Fraser.*

THE Fleet Train in the Pacific was one of the most remarkable examples of the national British genius for what is known as 'muddling through'. The formation of the Fleet Train was a masterpiece of improvisation, its operations triumphs of endeavour over circumstances.[1]

The purpose of a fleet train was to supply a fleet at sea with whatever it needed, whenever and wherever it needed it. The ability to keep a large fleet supplied at sea for long periods was the lynch-pin of the naval war in the Pacific. The United States Navy had had years to plan, prepare, practise and perfect their Fleet Train; the very name was American. Not so with the Royal Navy. The question of whether or not a British Fleet should serve in the Pacific was not decided until the Quebec Conference of September 1944. The way in which the fleet should be employed, that it should emulate the American tactics of staying at sea almost indefinitely, was not decided until December. The first elements of the Fleet Train arrived in Australia in January 1945. And yet the fleet, supported by its still embryonic train, was in action off the Sakishima Gunto by March. Thus the Fleet Train sprang from what was virtually a standing start to operation off an enemy coast in six months. It was an almost incredible achievement.

The British Fleet Train was formed from what ships were available, manned with such personnel as were available, and sent out to the Pacific as they became available, in varying states of capability, efficiency and morale. At its peak, on VJ Day, 1945, Task Force 112 (the Fleet

[1] See map, p. 271.

Train and escorting force) consisted of 125 ships, totalling 712,000 tons, manned by 26,200 officers and men.[1]

Task Force 112 was the most extraordinarily motley collection of shipping ever assembled in British maritime history. It was an international fleet, including Norwegian masters and Chinese deck-hands, Dutch mates and Lascar firemen, Captains RN and Papuan winchmen. It was a Commonwealth fleet, with officers and men from Australia, New Zealand, South Africa, India and Canada. There were warships flying the White Ensign, Royal Fleet Auxiliaries flying the Blue and merchantmen under charter flying the Red. There was a Panamanian collier, and a Dutch hospital ship, and a Danish tanker, and Norwegian and Belgian ammunition ships. Some ships were brand new, others were thirty years old. There were floating repair shops, floating docks, and, latterly, a floating brewery. There were accommodation ships, and netlayers, and salvage tugs and deperming ships, and water-distilling ships, and aircraft-ferry ships, and aircraft-maintenance ships, and armament, air naval and victualling store issuing ships. With personnel of different nationalities, different charter parties, articles of agreement,[2] racial customs, even different diets, the problems of administration were enormous. It was no wonder that the Americans with their modern homogeneously manned train of ships, each commissioned as a warship under naval discipline, looked upon the British fleet train with frank amazement. In the event, the Fleet Train was arguably the Navy's most important innovation of the Second World War and almost the only one which still survives into the modern Navy of today.

Ironically, a fleet train on the American pattern was forced upon the Admiralty by the speed of American successes in the Pacific. Since the advent of steam the Royal Navy had grown used to 'short-haul' operations, where the fleet returned to its base after a few days. The blockades of Nelson's and Collingwood's ships were no more than a remote race-memory, deeply embedded in the Navy's history; the twentieth-century Navy relied on a string of shore bases stretched across the world from Sheerness to Singapore. For years, the planning for the support of a Far Eastern Fleet centred on the concept of an 'intermediate

---

[1] Had the war continued, the scheduled figures for Task Force 112 for 1 January 1946 were: 309 ships, of 1,335,000 total tonnage, and 53,800 officers and men. See Appendix A.

[2] Serving in the Fleet Train were men of the RN, RM, RNR, RNVR, RANVR, RCNVR, RNZVR, RNPS, DEMS, and MRA, SRR(D), men who had signed forms T.124X and T.124T, and civilians borne for time.

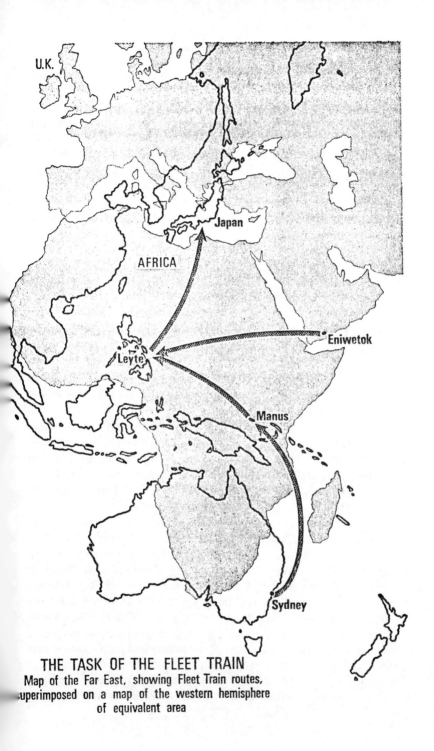

U.K.

Japan

AFRICA

Eniwetok

Leyte

Manus

Sydney

THE TASK OF THE FLEET TRAIN
Map of the Far East, showing Fleet Train routes,
superimposed on a map of the western hemisphere
of equivalent area

base' (a base for bulk supplies and stores) which was nothing more than an attempt to reproduce in the Pacific the 'short-haul' conditions the Navy were accustomed to in the Mediterranean and the North Sea. Although the Admiralty, with their own inimitable determination to put first things first, actually approved a name for it – HMS *Pepys* – the intermediate base was overtaken by events and was never built. However, the idea had its effect on planning so that, for instance, two vital fleet train requirements, tankers capable of fuelling the fleet at sea and carriers to ferry replacement aircraft, were not provided for.

The Admiralty have been criticised for their short-sightedness in failing to realise the need for a fleet train. For example, it has often been said that the 'cliff-hanging' fuel situation in Admiral Tovey's capital ships and destroyers while searching for *Bismarck* would have been avoided if the Admiralty had had the wit to provide an accompanying oiler group. In fact, Admiralty planning for the logistic support of a fleet afloat began as long ago as 1936, when a committee was set up to 'consider the numbers and types of auxiliary vessels (except oilers, colliers and hospital ships) required for maintaining supplies to the fleet in certain emergencies and the arrangements for manning and fitting out the vessels required, taking into consideration the possibility of certain bases not being available and others having to be improvised, and to make recommendations'.

The committee was formed on 5 November 1936, and included representatives of the Directors of Stores, Victualling, Plans, Armament Supply and the Military Branch. One of the hypothetical 'certain emergencies' considered by the committee was the loss of Singapore and Hong Kong, but they were reassured by the Admiralty that they could assume Singapore would always be available.

The committee reported in the spring of 1938. Bearing in mind that Singapore would be available, the recommended scale of support for a fleet in a Far Eastern war was: thirteen store issuing ships/carriers, twenty or thirty armament store issuing ships(ASIS), an armament maintenance ship, a mine depot ship, a torpedo repair ship, fourteen mine carriers, a naval store issuing ship (NSIS), which would have spare water distilling capacity, two victualling store issuing ships (VSIS), a large frozen meat carrying ship, and four store carriers of the 'China Coaster' type (remembering that oilers, colliers and hospital ships were not in the committee's brief). All ships were to have a minimum range of 4,000 miles. The committee recommended that half the ships required should be taken up for conversion and Admiralty use before a war broke out, and the remainder as soon as possible afterwards.

The Admiralty accepted the recommendations and some ships were taken up for conversion in 1939 and 1940. A few ships taken up at that date, including the NSIS/VSIS *City of Dieppe* and the hospital ship *Oxfordshire*, actually survived the war and eventually served in the Fleet Train in 1945.

No more ships could be taken up after the outbreak of the war with Germany. By the time Japan entered the war the United Kingdom's losses in warships and merchantmen were already so great that the Admiralty's main preoccupation was the country's survival at sea rather than fleet trains. It should be made clear, therefore, that the Admiralty's failure to provide a fleet train was not due to lack of intent, but to lack of ships.

After the loss of Hong Kong and Singapore, the Navy had no resources either afloat or ashore east of Ceylon. In January 1942, before the fall of Singapore, the Director of Dockyards had already become alarmed about the lack of fleet repair facilities in the Far East and had pressed the Admiralty for more repair ships. At that time the Navy had one specially designed fleet repair ship, *Resource*, which had been built in 1930 to provide repair facilities and personnel for ships in the Singapore floating dock. A second similar ship was proposed in January 1939 but not approved, although permission was given for two merchant ships to be converted. However, no ships were available after the outbreak of war. The old cadet training cruiser *Vindictive* was converted to carry out emergency hull repairs and did good service at Freetown. The ex-Cunard White Star liner *Antonia* was also converted into a fleet repair ship and was completed under her new name of *Wayland*.

In the spring of 1942 the United States Navy assumed responsibility for the West Indies and South Atlantic areas, and five armed merchant cruisers, *Aurania*, *Montclare*, *Ausonia*, *Alaunia* and *Ranpura* were released for conversion to either repair or depot ships; one of these, *Montclare*, was to play a considerable part in the Pacific fleet train.

Meanwhile, the Eastern Fleet, deprived of Singapore, retreated to Ceylon and, after Nagato's raid in April 1942, to Kilindini in East Africa – more than 2,500 miles from Ceylon and 4,000 from Singapore. There matters rested until 8 March 1943 when Admiral Somerville, already looking forward to the time when the offensive could be taken against the Japanese, submitted his proposals for establishing Eastern Fleet bases in territory recaptured from the enemy. The proposals were considered at a meeting in the Admiralty on 6 May, and rejected

S

because of the resources of men and building materials they would require.

However, it was at this meeting in May 1943 that there first emerged the concept of 'the rapid provision of the facilities necessary for the sustained operation of the fleet in an area removed from established bases', i.e. the shape of the fleet train as it was to become. Two 'Mobile Fleet Base Organisations' were suggested, one for the Indian Ocean and one for the Pacific; they would provide all the services and facilities of the normal shore-base, with everything afloat except airstrips, temporary accommodation and piers. Each MFBO would service a fleet of four capital ships, two fleet aircraft carriers, four light fleet carriers, fifteen escort carriers, fifteen cruisers, fifty destroyers, fifty escorts, twenty submarines, fifty combined operations ships, and a number of minesweepers, landing craft and harbour auxiliaries.

But, like many seemingly promising ideas in the Admiralty, the MFBOS soon began to leave the bounds of reality. When all departments had contributed their requirements and suggestions it was seen that the country did not have the men and ships for what was proposed, and even if by some miracle the men and ships were provided, there were very few anchorages in the world large enough to contain an MFBO.

Planning for a fleet train (if not precisely MFBOS) progressed through the summer of 1943 – with the underlying assumption at that time, and indeed for a long time afterwards, that the British could rely on a good deal of assistance from American sources. Meanwhile, the first serious rumblings of opposition grew from the Ministry of War Transport and the War Office. The subject of the fleet train was tabled at the first Quebec Conference in August 1943. The Admiralty's case received support and sympathy from the Americans who were themselves expanding their logistic arm for the forthcoming drive across the Central Pacific which was to start at Tarawa in November. The Americans knew just what was involved in setting up a fleet train.

The Admiralty, too, were coming to know just what was involved. By September 1943 their estimate of the ships required for the fleet train had risen to a total of seventy-four and included repair and depot ships; accommodation ships, maintenance ships for escorts, minesweepers and motor torpedo boats, and for armament, torpedoes and radar equipment; boom defence vessels; air, armament, naval and victualling store issuing ships and carriers; distilling ships; hospital ships; tankers; and tugs, lighters and miscellaneous small harbour craft – nineteen different types of ship in all (although no mention was made of ferry aircraft carriers). After a meeting held on 21 September, the Joint Chiefs of Staff put in a bid to the Ministry of War Transport for the necessary ships. It was the first of a series of bids, and the first move in a long and uncomfortable wrangle between the Admiralty and the Ministry.

To build a fleet train meant depriving the present in order to invest in the future, because the conversion and fitting out of fleet train ships used large amounts of scarce skilled labour, while the ships themselves were making no direct contribution to the war effort. As many ships as possible were converted while building, and orders for ship conversion were placed in Canada. Where a particular type of ship was only required in small numbers, e.g. hospital ships, conversions were carried out as far as possible in the United Kingdom.

The bulk of the large ships for the fleet train had to come from America. To make the best use of British and American shipbuilding resources it had been agreed earlier in the war that British shipyards should build warships and certain types of specialised shipping, while the American shipyards built merchantmen and any types not included in the British programme. This arrangement was certainly achieving its object but it had caused an imbalance in the types of ships built in British yards. Any merchant ships for the fleet train would have to come out of the American shipbuilding programme, because there was no surplus in the British programme, and no provision had been made in that programme for fleet train ships.

It was these decisions, taken in the autumn of 1943 which enabled the fleet train to reach the Pacific at all. Nevertheless, planning was bedevilled by the uncertainty of future British strategy in the Far East. It was now high time matters were settled. The Admiralty decided to press for a decision on the employment of a British fleet in the Pacific at the joint Anglo-US-Russian talks in the winter of 1943–44. The British Pacific Ocean Force was planned and proposed. For this force it was assumed that a small rear base in Australia would be used, and that the United States would allow the use of their advanced bases and docks, and would supply all 'common-user' stores. The fleet train, such as it was, would be provided from South-east Asia Command, except for some additional store carriers and a few coal-burning ships which would be replaced by oil-burners.

The First Sea Lord, Admiral Cunningham, raised the matter at the British Chiefs of Staff Committee in Cairo on 23 November 1943. He pointed out that no plan for the employment of a British fleet in the

Pacific had yet been presented either to the British or the US Chiefs of Staff, and there was no time to be lost. On 7 December the British and US Chiefs of Staff agreed on a tentative deployment of a British naval force in the Pacific and produced a joint memorandum: the Joint Chiefs of Staff were requested to approve that the Ministry of War Transport and the War Shipping Administration consider the need for fleet auxiliaries for a British fleet in operations against Japan, and take steps to provide the requisite ships, after agreement in detail between Admiral King and Admiral Cunningham.

And so, in December, the Admiralty set to work again to examine the revised requirements of the fleet train, in the light of the tentative decisions reached at Cairo. Some progress on the future of a British fleet in the Pacific was made in Cairo and later at Teheran, but the planning still went forward against a background of vagueness and inspired guesswork. In January 1944 the Admiralty sent a mission headed by Rear Admiral Charles Daniel to Washington to discuss with the Americans the implications of forming a fleet train and the support the Americans would be able to give. The two sides reached agreement that the United States Navy would share its excess facilities afloat and ashore in forward areas; maintain harbour defences and minimum port facilities and personnel; carry out emergency and temporary battle damage repairs to British units; and make available airfields under its control near the British fleet anchorage (but would not carry out aircraft maintenance).

The phrase 'excess facilities' conjured up exciting visions in London, for by British standards the Americans always supported their forces in lavish style. However, in a memorandum of 10 January 1944, the American naval staff representatives made it clear that the British must maintain their own services of naval, victualling, armament and aircraft stores.

On 8 February 1944 the First Lord of the Admiralty, the Rt Hon. A. V. Alexander, fired the first heavy broadside in a running engagement between the Admiralty and the Ministry of War Transport which was to last for the rest of the war and after. In a memorandum addressed to the Defence Committee he stated in unambiguous terms that there would never be the men nor the resources to build advanced bases and that therefore a floating fleet train was essential. The memorandum included the schedule of required shipping agreed by Admiral King and Admiral Cunningham (in what was known as the 'Cunningham–King agreement'). By now the estimates for the fleet train had soared to 134 ships of 1½ million gross tonnage. Of these, thirty-nine ships were required for the Indian Ocean, nine before the defeat of Germany and the rest afterwards; the requirement for the Pacific was ninety-five ships, four before German's defeat.

Alarmed by the effect of these requirements on the overall Allied shipping situation, the Ministry of War Transport replied somewhat obliquely ten days later commenting on the implications of the 'Cunningham–King Agreement' and suggesting that the Canadian government be invited to prepare a planned programme of materials and equipment, in case it was finally decided to meet the whole of the fleet train requirements, and that the final decision should be deferred. On 16 March the First Lord returned to the charge a second time with a memorandum entitled 'The Provision of a Fleet Train'. Once again the First Lord set out the imperative reasons for a fleet train, and pointed out that the Ministry's reply meant that the fleet train for the initial strength of the fleet would be available, but only after a delay, while the train for fleet reinforcements and build-up would never arrive. Combined operations in the Indian Ocean, and possibly later in the Pacific, would also be affected. The First Lord asked the Defence Committee if they would at least authorise the shipping requirements for the maintenance of the fleet itself if not for the combined operations 'circus'. (The decision to send a British fleet to the Pacific was still some six months in the future; it says a great deal for the Admiralty's faith and pertinacity that there appears to have been no doubt at any time that a British fleet would, sooner or later, serve in the Pacific.)

Here the Prime Minister himself entered the fray, with a personal minute dated 9 April 1944:

'The Fleet Train is limited by the need of getting an absolute irreducible minimum of 24 million tons of imports this year and next. All Naval and Military requirements must be subordinated to this decisive rule, without which the life and war effort of Britain cannot be maintained. In working out your Fleet Train you must observe these requirements.

'2. The Fleet which you could operate in the Indian Ocean or in the South-west Pacific, whether north or south of Australia, must be limited by the Fleet Train. It is not a question of making the Fleet Train up to your ideas of the Fleet. However, a searching and austere examination of naval requirements will probably give you a good deal of margin. For instance, why should sailors have a great quantity of accommodation ships as well as hospital ships when soldiers might be content with only the latter?

'3. The priorities are as follows:

(a) 24 million tons of imports this year and next.

(b) The Fleet Train permissible on this basis.

(c) The fighting Fleet that can be carried by the said Fleet Train.

'4. It follows from the above that the great concession made to the Navy, by allowing them to have 230,000 tons of brand-new merchant shipping available in about a year, must be made good by ton for ton replacements in ocean-going tonnage to the Ministry of War Transport, which in principle must be simultaneous. In practice, a little latitude may be given for individual ships, and any tonnage turned over by the Navy beforehand will give them something to veer and haul on. Please take this as a decision; but ask me if there are any points about it which are not clear.'[1]

The Prime Minister's meaning was clear enough: the Fleet Train was the horse, and the fighting Fleet the cart. They must be kept in their proper order. As the size of the horse was fixed, it was pointless to plan an ambitious cart.

Two days later, the First Lord sent a copy of the Prime Minister's minute to the Minister of War Transport and urged him to take action with the Canadian merchant shipping authorities to select eighteen ships from the building programme for completion as Maintenance Ships as soon as possible. Meanwhile, the Admiralty would order five fleet repair ships (which Admiral King in an uncharacteristic fit of generosity had already promised Admiral Cunningham) to be converted in the United Kingdom. The Minister replied on 14 April that he would take action about the eighteen ships and that the five repair ships promised would be released. 'Let us', wrote Lord Leathers, 'agree to carry out the Prime Minister's decision faithfully but reasonably.' The point was taken in the Admiralty, but it was to be shown that those two adverbs were capable of different interpretations.

The principle of 'ton for ton replacement' was easier to state than to carry out, indeed the Fourth Sea Lord had already reported on 8 April that he had considered the implications of returning (a) 250,000 tons or (b) 500,000, and both were impracticable. The Admiralty were then employing 560 merchant ships, of about 2½ millions total tonnage,

---

[1] Personal Minute M.393/4: see *Grand Strategy*, by John Ehrman, Vol. V, pp. 477-8 (HMSO, 1956).

including about 1 million tons of tankers and colliers on single-voyage charter, and 573,960 tons in service in direct support of the fleet all over the world. After examining their tonnage the Admiralty found that in fact only about 111 ships, of 450,000 tons, were suitable for service in the Far East. The Admiralty continued through April and May to search for tonnage which could be released, but very few of the ships in Admiralty service were suitable for trade and most of those would not be available until Germany's defeat. Meanwhile, of course, a fleet train would almost certainly have to be provided for the war against Japan before the war with Germany was over. On 12 May the Admiralty issued a stern edict: 'Demands for allocation of further merchant tonnage to permanent or semi-permanent naval service will not be entertained by the Board unless it can be clearly shown that they are vitally necessary to the furtherance of the war effort.' ('This', commented the fleet train historian,[1] 'surprised many departments who already made bids for shipping only on such grounds.')

The state of conversions and buildings for the Fleet Train in the spring of 1944 was as follows:

1. Fleet Repair Ships: two ex-armed merchant cruisers to be converted in Royal dockyards, and five to be converted by the United States.
2. Two hull repair ships, two dockyard workmen's accommodation ships and two submarine crew accommodation ships to be converted in the United Kingdom.
3. Five escort maintenance ships, two armament maintenance ships, and one local craft maintenance ship, to be converted in Canada.
4. Two aircraft maintenance ships, three engine repair ships and two aircraft component repair ships were being converted from escort carriers.

This was satisfactory so far as 'floating workshops' were concerned, but still left the Fleet Train short of twenty-seven supply ships of various kinds, eight hospital ships, two fast tankers and two base accommodation ships.

Through the summer of 1944 estimates of the numbers of British warships, landing craft and aircraft which could eventually be deployed in the Far East were still increasing. Each increase brought a corresponding increase in the Fleet Train requirement. On 17 August, after a further recalculation, the Admiralty gave a list of added vessels which

[1] 'The History of the Fleet Train', by Captain R. F. Leonard, RN, in MS.

would be required in the Far East by January 1945; these included three NSIS, one ASIS, two naval store carriers and one VSIS – all to start conversion that autumn. With some mutterings that the Admiralty were acting 'reasonably but not faithfully', the Ministry of War Transport agreed to provide the ships, except the store carriers, and arranged for them to be built in Canada. At this time, a slight movement of shipping began from the European to the Pacific theatre; for example, in August the Minesweeper Maintenance Ship *Kelantan* was withdrawn from duties in the invasion of Europe to prepare for service in the Far East.

Nevertheless, the Admiralty were disturbed by a mood of creeping inertia which seemed to have overcome planning for the Fleet Train. For instance, there was still no plan for the conversion of supply ships for the later phases of the Far Eastern war; in March the Defence Committee had recommended that the procurement of ships for the Fleet Train should be left as late as possible, because of the lack of a firm strategic policy. From the Admiralty's point of view there were great dangers in this line of thought. Once a decision had been made, a fleet could reach the Pacific very quickly. But the Fleet Train, which was just as important, would take much longer and might never reach the Pacific at all at the present rate of progress. Planning, if it could be so called, continued in a strategic vacuum. There was still no indication even of where the fleet would serve; planning support for an Indian Ocean fleet covering landings in Burma, and returning to Trincomalee, and planning support for a fleet taking part in the operations in the Central Pacific, were two very different propositions.

At last, at Quebec in September, the situation was partly resolved. A balanced and *self-supporting* British fleet to take part in the main operations against Japan was offered and accepted. The fleet's method of operation was to be decided from time to time according to prevailing circumstances. Mr Churchill stated, with more enthusiasm than accuracy, that a Fleet Train of ample proportions had been built up, which would render the fleet independent for a considerable time of shore base resources. At the word 'ample' a great hollow laugh must have echoed through the corridors of the Admiralty. However, the host of imponderables had now been reduced to three: the date of the end of the European war (and hence the rate at which the Far Eastern fleet and train could be built up); the form of operations which the fleet would undertake; and the amount of shore-based assistance which could be given.

Now that the situation was clearer the Admiralty worked out the

Fleet Train requirements again and in October 1944 put in another massive bid for shipping in what was known as the 'October Bid'. This was for ten ASIS, with a further three after July 1945; six armament store carriers; twelve NSIS; eight naval store carriers; three Air SIS; twenty-two VSIS; two SRR(D) accommodation ships; one submarine accommodation ship; five hospital ships; four distilling ships were also added to the bid, a coal-burning ship being accepted in the meantime. The Americans were now operating in the Philippines and it was clear that by the time the British fleet reached the Pacific and operated at full strength the distance from Australia to the operating area would have increased from the planned 2,000 miles to 3,500. In November the bid was raised by an extra four VSIS, one NSIS, four naval store carriers, one ASIS and two armament store carriers, all required by July 1945. On 18 November the total bids were sent to the Ministry of War Transport, where they were coolly received; the Minister did not reply until 20 January 1945, and then to say that he could not make shipping allocations of this sort.

When Admiral Fraser became C-in-C he quickly discovered that the logistic support which he knew had been already planned for the fleet would be inadequate. Ships would be required to operate in the forward areas for much longer than had been expected; they would need logistic support in those forward areas (i.e. from the Logistic Support Groups, as they were to be known). The Americans had found from experience that it was uneconomical in time and shipping to operate a fleet more than 2,000 miles from its base; the BPF would be operating at least 3,500 miles from Sydney and therefore would need a base somewhere between Sydney and the operating area.

From Admiral Fraser's signals, though they as yet gave no facts and figures, the Admiralty could see at once that a larger fleet train would be needed, but it was decided that it would be a waste of effort to ask for more ships at that time. This was wise, for at the 'Argonaut' Conference at Yalta in February, Lord Leathers stated firmly that he could only proceed on the assumption that no more ships beyond those specified in the 'October Bid' would be allocated to the Fleet Train. On 26 January the War Cabinet had discussed Admiralty shipping requirements and had decided that no more shipping could be allocated to the Navy; the First Lord was invited to raise the matter again in two months time, or earlier if he thought fit.

This decision might have caused a shortage of shipping later in the year, but fortunately an inquiry set up to arbitrate in the dispute between the Admiralty and the Ministry, headed by Sir John Anderson, the Chancellor of the Exchequer, reported in February 1945 and its findings were agreed by both sides. The shipping situation improved and the Fleet Train's needs were almost all met eventually. On 5 February Admiral Fraser reported that the BPF would have a strength of 100,000 men by July 1945, with between 80,000 and 90,000 of them in the forward area. The Admiralty were able to plan for a fleet train on this basis.

The Americans had insisted from the beginning that the British fleet should be self-supporting, except for bulk fuel supplies and certain W/T and radar spares, which they would supply. They agreed to pool resources, but the British must contribute their proper share to the pool. In fact, the Americans were much better than their word and Admiral Fraser commented: 'I have found the American logistic authorities in the Pacific have interpreted self-sufficiency in a very liberal way. American authorities are most open-handed in allowing the BPF to draw surplus items.' It was certainly true that many of the British fleet's difficulties at Manus, and elsewhere, were lessened by the splendid 'can do' attitude of the United States Navy. The experience of all who served in the BPF was that 'the further you got from Washington, the more helpful the Americans became'. Admiral Fraser had experience himself of the remarkable contrast between Admiral King's jealous eye in Washington, and the helpfulness of American officers on the spot:

'When the fleet left Sydney, they were short of three Avengers. So I made a signal to Nimitz asking, could he possibly supply three Avengers when the fleet got to Manus? They had hundreds of them there. Nimitz replied that he was very sorry, he couldn't do it. So I sent for my American liaison officer – he was a first class chap – and I said to him, This is an extraordinary thing, this signal? He puzzled his head over it and went away and presently he came back and said, I know what it is. This signal has gone through Washington, so Admiral Nimitz was bound to reply as he did. He said, I think it will be all right when you get there. I went up at about that time to have a look at Manus and I said to the American admiral in charge of the place, Look, do you think we could possibly borrow three Avengers from you? And he said, Well, actually we don't issue them in less than six at a time. If you've got a bottle of whisky you can have a dozen! And he made me out a signal for them on the spot.'[1]

[1] Lord Fraser. Conversation of 12.10.67. Hard liquor was hard currency in

There was never any doubt that the BPF's main base, at least until some other base was constructed, would be in Australia. The nearest Australian harbour to the operating area was at Darwin, in the Northern Territory. Provided the approach channels of the Clarence and Dundas Straits to the west and north-east were dredged for capital ships, Darwin was a harbour big enough to hold a large fleet and its auxiliaries. But the northern territories of Australia were remote and undeveloped, and Darwin did not have the urban and technological resources for a fleet base.

The obvious choice was Sydney, where there was a large (and very enthusiastic) population, a temperate climate and a world famous harbour, with docks for heavy cruisers and below; the Captain Cook graving dock, for capital ships, was due for completion early in 1945. The BPF's main base was established in Sydney, with smaller bases at Brisbane and Cairns to the north, Adelaide and Melbourne in the south, and Fremantle on the west coast.

Australia had been a military base, in a sense, since the early days of the war against Japan. An American convoy of troop reinforcements, ammunition and aircraft intended for the Philippines was diverted to Brisbane after the fall of Manila in December 1941, and the Americans had remained in Australia ever since. In March 1942 Brigadier General Dwight D. Eisenhower, the future Supreme Allied Commander in Europe, reported on the suitability of Australia as an advanced air base. General MacArthur arrived in Australia from the Philippines on 17 March and was appointed Commander in Chief, South-west Pacific in April. Although Roosevelt and Churchill had decided to give the war against Germany priority, the success of the Japanese advances made it necessary to strengthen the defences of Australia and by the summer of 1942 over 30,000 American troops were stationed there. With the Japanese at Wake and Guam, the route through the islands of the South Pacific from Hawaii to Australia was the United States' only way back into the Far Eastern war.

The people and government of Australia were genuinely delighted to welcome the British Pacific Fleet, but, as Admiral Fraser later wrote, 'they did not realise the implications of having a fleet based there'.

---

the Pacific. Off Japan, *King George V* ran short of certain radar spares. It was decided to ask the next US destroyer to come alongside whether they would exchange the spares for a bottle of whisky. Back over the loud-hailer in a rich Ohio accent came the reply: 'Man, for a bottle of whisky you can have this whole goddamned ship.'

For instance, the fleet required a vast amount of construction work, in the building of airfields, barracks, offices and training facilities ashore. These used Australian labour and materials which the Australian Government were reluctant to allocate; by the end of 1944, the war had moved a long way from Australia and the Australian Government were understandably looking forward to peacetime building, houses, schools, etc. There were more difficulties caused by labour troubles on Australian waterfronts, where dockers' strikes were almost endemic.

The difficulties eventually yielded to negotiation, but the situation was further complicated by the continuing presence of the Americans who were supposed to move on, as the war moved northwards, but who stayed in Australia, using it as a base for the rehabilitation of territories recaptured from the Japanese. There were some serious disputes between the Allies; for example, the British Pacific Fleet and the USAAF both wanted the use of Eagle Farm airfield, near Brisbane – a dispute, Admiral Fraser wrote, 'which would never have arisen if there had been a Supreme Commander for the Pacific'.

For her size, New Zealand made an equal contribution. She provided much of the British Pacific Fleet's food, docking facilities for ships, and of course, her own incomparable seamen – 'every New Zealander is potential officer material, every single one'.[1] In general, the shore-based support of the British Pacific Fleet was a remarkable example of Commonwealth co-operation:

'I have always felt that the Australians and New Zealanders did magnificently. We were in the curious situation of not being in a position to give an order. The *whole* thing was done, from beginning to end, by good will. It was a curious situation which had never happened before and has not happened since. We had a very large Imperial fleet, with ships and men of every member of the Commonwealth, all based on two members of the Commonwealth – and those two doing everything for us by good will.'[2]

The officer who was most closely involved in all the negotiations with both Governments and who was responsible for the logistical organisation of the BPF was Rear Admiral Charles Daniel. He had headed the British Naval Mission which had visited the United States at the beginning of 1944 and, on arrival in Australia in the spring, became Vice Admiral, Administration, British Pacific Fleet (short title: VA(Q)).

---

[1] Admiral Sir Charles Evans. Conversation of 16.7.68.
[2] Vice Admiral Sir Edward Evans Lombe. Conversation of 8.11.67.

From his visit to America Admiral Daniel concluded that the functions of the directing organisation of a British fleet in the Pacific, based on Australia, were: firstly, strategical and operational planning, in co-operation with the United States Navy, and the direction of the fleet's own operational and administrative policies; secondly, the supply, logistic support and air support of the fleet and the detailed administration of its personnel; and, thirdly, co-operation with the Australian Government in the establishment and manning of fleet bases in Australia.

Normally the C-in-C BPF and his staff would have carried out all these functions, but it was intended that Admiral Fraser would fly his flag at a headquarters, afloat or ashore, forward of Australia and would undertake only the strategical and operational planning, and the direction of the fleet's administrative and operational policies. Another flag officer was therefore required to organise the logistic support of all kinds and to co-operate closely with the Australian Government. This officer was the Vice Admiral, Administration, and his appointment in the words of Official Historian, 'if unspectacular compared with command of a fighting squadron, was certainly one of the most arduous allocated to a British flag officer during the entire war'.[1]

Admiral Daniel set up his own headquarters at Melbourne, which was more than four hundred miles from Sydney but enabled him to keep in close touch with the Australian Commonwealth Naval Board and, through the Board, with other Australian Government departments. In the event, the fleet never had a main forward base and returned to Sydney for major replenishments; Admiral Fraser decided to remain at Sydney, at the main fleet base, where all ships and flag officers returned from time to time. So, with the benefit of hindsight, it seems that it would have been more convenient for all if VA(Q) had also been at Sydney. However, such a move by VA(Q) – well established in Melbourne – would have caused great delay and disruption at the time.

In October 1944 another very able officer, Rear Admiral D. B. Fisher, was appointed Rear Admiral Fleet Train (RAFT). Charles Daniel and Douglas Fisher were together the main architects of the fleet's logistic support, without which the BPF would have remained impotently at Sydney. Admiral Fisher's appointment was unprecedented in the Royal Navy and his duties are worth defining in detail.

Rear Admiral Fleet Train was responsible for the operation of the

[1] *The War at Sea 1939–1945*, Vol. II Part 2, by Captain S. W. Roskill (HMSO, 1961), p. 331.

Fleet Train as a whole, transferring to the operational task force commanders detailed operational control of Fleet Train groups whilst employed on servicing their Task Forces at sea. He was responsible to the C-in-C for the administration of the ships of the Fleet Train and to Vice Admiral Rawlings for keeping the fleet directly supplied, including detailed logistic planning for each specific operation and the transport of supplies from the supply bases to the Fleet, in ships of the Fleet Train. He was also responsible to Admiral Rawlings for the maintenance and repair of ships, auxiliaries and aircraft of the fleet, within the capacity of the Fleet Train; arrangements for the evacuation of sick and wounded by sea; mails, distributing authorities, and chart offices afloat; fleet amenities; and salvage and tugs. It could be said that Admiral Fisher's appointment was also one of the most arduous allocated to a British flag officer in the entire war.

With his embryo staff, Admiral Fisher spent the first weeks of his new appointment 'in trying to find out from Plans Division (Q) what provision had been made for the formation of the Fleet Train, in deciding on the composition of a staff for the Rear Admiral Fleet Train, in getting a general picture of the functions of the Fleet Train, and in endeavouring to have the essential requirements installed in HMS *Montclare*' (fitting out at Harland and Wolff as the Fleet Train flagship). Only those who have themselves tried to get information on a new and unprecedented project from the multitudinous departments of the Admiralty will appreciate Admiral Fisher's task.

On 1 December 1944 Admiral Fisher with his Secretary and his Staff Officer (Intelligence) left United Kingdom for the Far East via the United States. En route they visited the British Admiralty Delegation in Washington, two auxiliary repair ships *Assistance* and *Diligence* completing for the Fleet Train at Baltimore, the Admiralty Technical Mission in Ottawa and the Commander Service Force, Pacific Fleet, at Honolulu.

Meanwhile those officers of the Fleet Train who had taken up their appointments began, in temporary accommodation in Sydney, to build up and organise the Fleet Train. Almost at once, on 3 January, Admiral Fisher's Chief of Staff, Captain Barraclough and Cdr. Rowell, his Staff Officer (Operations) were called to a meeting in *Howe* and bluntly asked by Admiral Fraser whether or not the Fleet Train could support the fleet for its part in ICEBERG in March. The Fleet Train Engineer Officer, Captain J. G. C. Given, whom Barraclough immediately consulted: 'Time did not permit of intricate statistical calculation. Even slide-rules were too slow and the limited available crystals of instinct cum experience were heavily over-worked. The answer to the Commander in Chief's question was "Yes", with certain provisos, but not without considerable doubts and fears on my part as to how our contract was to be kept.'

'Yes' was a very brave answer. At that time very few Fleet Train officers, not even Fisher himself, had arrived in Sydney. Almost nothing was known of the number or the capacities of the ships or of the state of their machinery. Indeed, very little was known of fleet trains in general and how to operate them. Captain Given's doubts and fears were amply justified in the event, but the Fleet Train did support the fleet in ICEBERG and therefore the answer given after that meeting does the Fleet Train the greatest credit.

Admiral Fisher arrived in Sydney on 7 January and set about the solution of problems which were again succinctly put by Captain Given: 'the customers, vide the Fleet, gave no detailed order of what they required except that they, the Fleet, must be supported for a certain time and in places sometimes uncertain. Hence there were two problems, namely, What do they require? And, how is it to be provided and delivered?'

Ships and men for the Fleet Train continued to arrive in Sydney throughout January and February 1945. Admiral Fisher took command and responsibility for the Fleet Train on 29 January (and was officially presented by Admiral Rawlings with a large green flag and a guard's whistle), hoisting his flag in *Lothian*, as *Montclare* had not yet arrived. On 24 February Admiral Fisher and his staff sailed in *Lothian* for Manus, arriving on 2 March.

Lothian had been flagship of Flag Officer Force X and had been fitted out as a headquarters ship for combined operations in northern latitudes. Her W/T installations and lay-out were excellent, but her living and working spaces were quite unsuitable for the tropics. Admiral Fisher later recalled the period spent in *Lothian* at Manus: 'It is amazing what was achieved by the Fleet Train staff in those three months under conditions which were nothing less than awful.' None of *Lothian*'s offices had any daylight, all were stiflingly hot, and the ventilation was bad. The messdecks were grossly overcrowded, while the officers' cabin flats aft were known as the 'Arab Quarter'. Washing and sanitary arrangements were inadequate for the numbers on board. 'In these conditions, which can only be described as appalling, 110 officers and 650 men lived and worked in a space suitable for two-thirds their number, and it is not surprising that the great majority suffered in varying degrees from skin trouble. This varied between prickly heat at the best to a multitude of boils and consequent invaliding at the worst.'

Manus[1], a hilly, heavily wooded island some fifty miles long and four wide, is the largest of the Admiralty Islands, which lie two degrees south of the Equator, about two hundred miles north of the New Guinea coast and more than 2,000 miles from Sydney. First discovered by the Dutch in 1616 and named by Captain Carteret in 1767, the Admiralties were annexed by Germany in 1880 and mandated to Australia in 1920. The climate is hot, with a very high humidity and an annual rainfall of over 150 inches – at Manus 'boots, shoes and blue clothing turned green with mildew within forty-eight hours'.[2] In 1939 the islands were inhabited by a native population of about 13,000 – much studied by anthropologists – and forty-four white men, mostly cocoa plantation managers. The Japanese occupied the Admiralty Islands almost casually in 1942 and although they built airstrips at Lorengau, on Manus, and at Momote, on the neighbouring island of Los Negros, they did not develop the islands, tolerated the mosquitoes and the poor communications, made little strategic use of the airstrips, and had no serious plans nor positions for their defence.

The capture of the Admiralty Islands was first proposed by the US Joint Chiefs of Staff in July 1943. The islands lay beyond the 'Bismarck Barrier' and across the axis of New Guinea–Mindanao, dominating a huge area of the South Pacific, from Bougainville to Truk, to the Palaus, to Biak; their seizure would not only by-pass, but substitute for, the base at Rabaul. Seeadler Harbour, fifteen miles long and four miles wide, with a depth of water from twelve to fifteen fathoms, would shelter a large task force, and there was ample level ground for airstrips on Manus and particularly on Los Negros.

The original date set for the assault was 1 January 1944, but there were delays due to the assault on Cape Gloucester and to planning and command difficulties; the assault troops, the warships of the 7th Fleet and the aircraft of 5th Air Force would be provided from General MacArthur's South-west Pacific Area, but the 'Seabee'[3] battalions and service personnel for developing the air and sea base could only be

---

[1] See map, p. 289.

[2] 'The Manus Story', by Captain H. F. Waight, *Navy News*.

[3] USN construction battalions (CBs), composed of men who usually had construction knowledge and skills in civilian life, who cleared damage on captured islands and built harbours, airfields and support facilities during the advance across the Pacific. The RN had no counterpart.

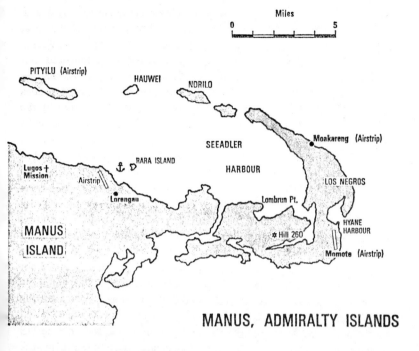

MANUS, ADMIRALTY ISLANDS

provided by Admiral Halsey's South Pacific Area. A simultaneous assault on Manus and on Kavieng in New Ireland was then planned for 1 April. But the plan for capturing Kavieng was dropped. The date for Manus was brought forward to 1 March 1945.

Manus and Los Negros were defended by about 4,600 Japanese troops. They were commanded by Colonel Yoshio Ezaki and on his orders deliberately made themselves inconspicuous from the air – so successfully that air reconnaissance in early February seemed to show that the Japanese had evacuated the Admiralty Islands. General MacArthur decided on a reconnaissance in force, to begin on 29 February. There was no point in delay, if the Japanese had gone.

Watched by MacArthur himself from the cruiser *Phoenix*, troops of the US 1st Cavalry Division landed at Hyane Harbour, on the east coast of Los Negros, on 29 February and captured Momote airstrip the same day. In spite of the unexpected strength of the Japanese, actually outnumbering the assault troops, General MacArthur took a calculated risk and decided to turn the reconnaissance in force into a proper invasion. Very ably abetted by fire-power from the American and

T

Australian ships of the 7th Fleet, the gamble succeeded. While troops
of 7th and 12th Cavalry Divisions advanced north up Los Negros,
other units of 7th and 8th Cavalry Divisions landed on Manus at Lugos
Mission on 15 March. The last organised Japanese resistance in the
Admiralties ended at Hill 260 on Los Negros, on 24 March, and the
islands were virtually secured by 3 April. Small parties of Japanese
remained in the wild interior of Manus (known as 'The Reservation')
until the end of the war, being used occasionally for combat practise
by troops fresh to the operational area.

The Seabees set to work at once; some of them, in the early days at
Momote, alternately driving their bulldozers and beating off enemy
counter-attacks. The derelict, overgrown airstrip at Momote became a
busy airport, with other airstrips at Lorengau, Mokerang and Pityilu.
The mosquito was eliminated. Wharves, piers, bridges and accommodation huts were built, buoys were laid, and 150 miles of roads metalled
with coral and rock blasted from the sea bed; there were two floating
docks large enough to take battleships, and three smaller docks for
destroyers and submarines. There were saw-mills, water pumping
stations delivering 3,300,000 gallons of filtered water a day, a church
with seating for 1,000, and a hospital with 1,500 beds, a recreation
centre on Pityilu with facilities for 10,000 men a day, and an open-air
cinema for an audience of 7,000 at Lorengau, where the main communications and administrative centres were situated. In a few months
Manus was astonishingly transformed from a remote undeveloped
tropical island into a major military base with a peak complement, later
in the war, of some 37,000 US personnel. Work went on at Manus
night and day. The base was never blacked out 'and the lights compared
well with Blackpool of peaceful days'.[1] This probably assisted the two
Japanese bombers from Truk which attacked Manus on 29 April,
scoring direct hits on the ships in both large floating docks.

To the British fleet, Manus appeared in a somewhat different light.
Although the Admiralties were technically a colony of the Crown, the
'Brits' were there only by permission of the Americans and for many
months depended almost entirely on American good will and assistance
for equipment and facilities of all kinds. Captain H. F. Waight was
appointed Senior British Naval Officer at Manus (the Americans having
objected to the title 'Naval Officer In Charge') and arrived at Momote
from Sydney on 16 February. The advance party of base personnel,
with stores and boats, arrived ten days later in the chartered vessel

[1] 'The Manus Story'.

City of Paris. In setting up the British camp, on a high ridge overlooking Lorengau harbour, three miles from the main base, a great deal depended upon the relationships Captain Waight established with the American base commander, Commodore J. F. Boak, USN, and his Chief of Staff Captain A. C. Day, USN. 'These two officers', Waight noted, 'were great supporters of the Royal Navy.'[1]

Captain Waight eventually had a staff of some thirty officers and five hundred ratings, to organise port duties, sailing and berthing of ships, and mail and recreational facilities, and the communications centre. At first, these were shared with the Americans, but in time separate British communications centre, mail office and messing accommodation and galleys were established. Similarly, a British naval air liaison office was set up at Momote, and runways, lay-bys, and huts for stores and mail allocated to the British. Later a Mobile Naval Air Base (MONAB) was set up on the island of Ponam, some nineteen miles NNW of Manus, where the Americans had resettled the native population on other islands and built an airstrip as an 'overflow' for Pityilu. Ponam was only one and a half miles wide and completely surrounded by a coral reef. There was one jetty and the ferry carriers had to lie a long way offshore. Nevertheless, there were workshops, a hospital, cinema, church, officers and ratings messes, a cookhouse and several hundred thousand pounds worth of equipment which the Americans generously turned over to the British, lock, stock and barrel.

The men of the BPF had mixed feelings towards Manus. Some liked it. Others found it intolerable. One submarine officer called it 'the island of lost souls'.[2]

The main fleet arrived at Manus on 7 March and the Fleet Train set about fuelling and provisioning ships prior to ICEBERG, and adjusting outfits of ammunition in the battleships and cruisers. The Fleet Train (Task Force 112) now consisted of *Lothian*; the repair ships *Resource* and *Artifex*; the netlayer *Guardian*; the aircraft repair ship *Unicorn*; accommodation ships LS(I)s *Empire Spearhead* and *Lamont*; the hospital ship *Oxfordshire*; tankers *Arndale, Brown Ranger, Dingledale, Cedardale, San Adolfo, San Amado, San Ambrosio, Wave Monarch, Wave King, Aase Maersk*; NSIS and distilling ship *Bacchus*; Air SIS *Fort Colville*; VSIS *Denbighshire* and *Fort Edmonton*; ASIS *Gudrun Maersk, Hermelin, Heron, Kheti, Robert Maersk* and *Thyra S.*; escort carriers *Speaker, Slinger*, and *Striker*; and escort vessels.

---

[1] 'The Manus Story'.
[2] *Dark Seas Above*, by John Frederic Gibson (Blackwoods, 1947), p. 262.

The fleet left Manus for ICEBERG on 18 March, the first tanker group to refuel the fleet on passage having sailed the day before. Close logistic support during ICEBERG was to be mounted from Leyte, 780 miles from the operating area. Originally, Admiral Fisher had intended the CO of *Resource* to be Senior Officer Fleet Train at Leyte, whilst he himself remained at Manus, where the Commander-in-Chief was shortly expected to come and fly his flag. However, this was not to be, and as Leyte would clearly be the centre of Fleet Train operations Admiral Fisher himself sailed for Leyte in *Lothian* on 19th with a convoy of Fleet Train ships.[1] Captain Given commented: 'Though our convoy to Leyte may not have looked very war-like it was an inspiration to see the Fleet Train both in being and under way for the first time.'

The convoy arrived at Leyte on 26 March and anchored in widely scattered berths on the western side of San Pedro Bay. By the US Commander Philippine Sea Frontier's safety regulations, the armament ships were even more widely dispersed, and were anchored some six miles from the rest of the fleet.

For ICEBERG, Admiral Fisher organised his ships into Task Units, to ply back and forward between Leyte and the fleet's replenishment area. A typical Task Unit consisted of three tankers, an escort carrier, and escort vessels. A second escort carrier remained in the replenishment area to provide CAPs. At this stage there was still a shortage of store issuing ships and none could be sent forward of Leyte. So the tankers each carried extra stores; about five tons of fresh vegetables for the destroyers, survivor's kits, aircraft de-icing fluid, lubricating oil, depth charges, 20- and 40-mm. ammunition, and one tanker in each group also carried a medical officer and two sick berth ratings to look after casualties sent to the rear. On the first sorties the tankers also carried passengers (e.g. relief officers and men), mails, and urgently required naval and air stores. Latterly these were carried in the escort vessels, to save double handling in the replenishment area and to relieve the overworked and undermanned tankers. The risk of depleting the anti-submarine screen was accepted. The CAP carrier and escorts, and any ships and Task Units joining in the replenishment area, came under the tactical command of the Commander Logistic Support Group

---

[1] *Lothian; Empire Spearhead, Artifex; Bacchus, Wave King, Wave Monarch, Arndale, Dingledale, Fort Colville, Aase Maersk, Denbighshire, Robert Maersk, Thyra S.,* and *Hermelin,* also *Tyne* and *Slinger.*

(CLSG) who was, in effect, RAFT's representative at sea. CLSG for ICEBERG ONE was Captain P. Frend, RN (Captain Escort Forces, BPF) embarked in the sloop *Pheasant*.

The tankers made seven replenishment sorties in ICEBERG ONE and, in spite of defects in the gear and the inexperience of both fleet and train, supplied the fleet with 93,000 tons of oil fuel, 1,300 tons of aviation spirit, exchanged 1,064 bags of mail, and quantities of fresh vegetables and other stores. Twenty casualties for *Oxfordshire* were brought back in *Striker*.

Replacement aircraft were carried by the 30th Aircraft Carrier Squadron (Cdre. R. P. Carne, flying his broad pennant in *Striker*). The problems of transporting replacement aircraft from Australia to the advanced anchorage and thence to the fleet at sea had not been foreseen nor, as yet, properly appreciated. Four escort carriers had been allocated to the fleet, to join in March 1945, but in January they had still not been nominated. The first of them, *Slinger*, joined in February. While the future of the BPF itself was still in doubt no forward planning for aircraft replenishment could be done; the 30th Aircraft Carrier Squadron, in Commodore Carne's words, left Sydney 'with only the broadest conception of its duties'. There were no shore facilities at Leyte, nor any opportunities for flight testing, and the reliability of replacement aircraft was always an unknown quantity. However, the 30th Aircraft Carrier Squadron, like the rest of the Fleet Train, responded magnificently, improvising and perfecting their techniques as they went along. In ICEBERG ONE *Slinger* and *Striker* ferried fifty-six aircraft to the replenishment area, supplying forty-three of them to the fleet carriers, in three aircraft replenishments. They returned to Leyte with nineteen 'flyable duds'; 'non-flyable duds' had their engines removed and were ditched over the side. Meanwhile, *Speaker*'s sixteen Hellcat pilots flew 446 hours CAP duties in thirty-three days. The 30th Squadron were 'Woolworth' type American carriers which already had a distinguished record in the war at sea. Admiral Fraser conceded that it was a pity to reduce fine fighting ships to the role of mere ferries, but there was no help for it.

The Fleet Train's first fortnight at Leyte was spent filling the tankers from the American freighting tankers and dispatching them in their groups to the replenishment area. Meanwhile, repair staffs maintained ships of the Fleet Train. Soon, ships of the fleet began to return with defects, and the main fleet arrived for replenishment on 23 April *Indefatigable* and *Ulster* both had damage from the kamikaze attacks of 1 April. *Indefatigable*'s island structure was repaired in six working days. There was no British floating dock, and the docking and repairs to *Ulster*'s hull were willingly undertaken by the US Service Squadron 10, while machinery repairs were carried out by *Tyne*. *Ulster* was eventually able to sail for Australia, on one shaft, but capable of 24 knots.

The repair staff in most of the repair ships were 'Special Repair Ratings (Dockyard)', a category of service introduced in 1942. They were men drawn from all categories of ship-repairing trades, but they were not all recruited from shipyards. About 10% came from Royal Dockyards. Before entry the men underwent a trade test and were then rated according to qualifications; there were in all seventy-one trades and rates of SRR(D), varying from Engine Room Artificer (4th Class) for tradesmen, to Stoker 1st Class for skilled labourers.

The hardest worked men of the Fleet Train were the tanker crews. Some of them did not arrive at Leyte until after the fleet, and others had to leave early, to be in position for the first fuelling. All were fully occupied at Leyte in fuelling the fleet and topping up before sailing. Admiral Fisher was unable to give the tanker crews the rest and recreation they needed; this was another price to be paid for the bare margin on which the Fleet Train was working.

Curiously, in an area of high annual rainfall, one of the fleet's most serious shortages, both at Leyte and Manus, was fresh water. 'As for water, vital for both personnel and material,' Captain Given discovered, 'the previous appreciation of the situation was governed either by a child-like faith or ostrich-like escapism.' HM ships had distilling plants, which normally produced enough water for usual purposes, but they had to be shut down some time for maintenance; most merchantmen had no distilling plants and needed water at frequent intervals. The Americans at Leyte lent a water barge, *Bacchus* had surplus distilling capacity, and *Brown Ranger* was converted to carry water. The only shore supply at Leyte was from a water-hole at Balusao, which was virtually uncharted and could only be approached, at some risk, by *Brown Ranger*.

The fleet existed in an almost permanent state of crisis over fresh water and the arrival of the distilling ship *Stagpool* was eagerly awaited. But *Stagpool* was a coal-burner and a collier, the Panamanian *Atlas*, had to be found to supply her. Unhappily, the collier's numerous feed-water leaks and open feed system meant that she herself required most of *Stagpool's* output. The result was that 'the two ships spent most of their time furiously maintaining each other. The incident was not amusing at the time'.[1]

Coaling in *Stagpool* (who had no coaling gear on board) was done by a body of men known as the 'Fleet Train Porters' (a name specially chosen to avoid the term 'working parties'). In February the Commodore Royal Naval Barracks at Sydney provided fifteen petty officers and leading hands, and 150 ratings, to maintain the airstrip at Manus, to work cargoes on store issuing ships, to act as relief boats' crews and signal messengers. None of them had the slightest previous experience of working cargoes but, in the true spirit of the Fleet Train, they learned the job as they progressed and became skilful winchmen, stevedores, lightermen and hatchway hands. The Fleet Train Porters were reinforced at Leyte by a drafting pool of two hundred ratings who arrived in *Glenearn* on 13 April, to replace casualties and provide reliefs, and who were used as porters until the fleet returned.

The fleet sailed, 'like giants refreshed', for ICEBERG TWO on 1 May, the first Tanker Group having left a day earlier. In spite of a serious shortage of boats and catamarans, the period at Leyte had been a success. The weather had been good and replenishment had been completed in time. In Admiral Fisher's words, 'we were extremely lucky'.

The arrangements for ICEBERG TWO were broadly as before, with some improvements. Each tanker now had on board a rigging party of one petty officer and six naval ratings, and an extra officer to assist in watchkeeping. The hospital ship *Tjitjalengka* (an ex-Dutch liner of the Java–China–Japan Line which had escaped from Sumatra in 1942 and had been converted in Liverpool) had arrived at Leyte to join *Oxfordshire* and *Maunganui* on 19 April. She had by far the largest fresh water capacity of any of the hospital ships, and sailed for the replenishment area on 10 May. A salvage tug, *Weasel*, was also available in the replenishment area for the first time.

In ICEBERG TWO nine tankers made eighteen sorties and fuelled the fleet on five occasions, supplying 87,000 tons of fuel and 756 tons of aviation spirit and exchanging 1,473 bags of mail. *Robert Maersk* supplied a total of 470 500-lb bombs to *Victorious* and *Indomitable* on 19 May. *Striker*, *Speaker* and *Chaser* ferried 117 replacement aircraft, transferring seventy-eight to the fleet and bringing back ten 'flyable

---

[1] Vice Admiral Sir Douglas B. Fisher, 'The Fleet Train in the Pacific War', *Quarterly Transactions of the Institute of Naval Architects*, Vol. 95, No. 2, April 1953, p. 224.

duds'. *Ruler*'s twenty-three pilots flew 654 hours on CAP and A/SP duties, with sixteen Hellcats and four Avengers, in twenty-four days; her CAP and A/SP aircraft were also used for fleet practices. *Tjitjalengka* met the fleet on 13 and 25 May to take off casualties from destroyers alongside.

After ICI BERG the main part of the fleet was to carry out major replenishment in Australia and after withdrawing from the operating area on 25 May most of the fleet sailed for Australia while some ships, for whom there was no room at Australian ports or who were to take part in the strike at Truk (INMATE), sailed for Manus. The Fleet Train withdrew from Leyte, sailing in two convoys, one slow and one fast, leaving on 20 and 25 May respectively. Admiral Fisher sailed for Manus in *Lothian*, escorted by *Whimbrel*, on 24th. The hospital ships *Maunganui* and *Oxfordshire* sailed independently on 21 and 24 May.

Waiting at Manus was *Montclare*, the new Fleet Train headquarters ship. She was an ex-Canadian Pacific liner, designed for the North Atlantic run, and her after funnel passed through Admiral Fisher's quarters, so that he could not use them in the tropics. She was also the base W/T ship and flew Admiral Edelsten's flag as a destroyer depot ship – two functions which conflicted with her role as Fleet Train flagship. But still, she was a great improvement on *Lothian* and on 29 May Admiral Fisher and his staff transferred to her with alacrity. Urged by the keenest desire to get away from *Lothian*, forty-three officers, seventy ratings and several tons of apparatus including office furniture and the baggage of the individuals concerned, were transferred in two or three hours, the ships being berthed alongside each other for the purpose.

After ICEBERG, the fleet had much to discuss – not only lessons learned from the past, but future planning for the forthcoming July–August operations off the Japanese home islands and, looming beyond, the problem of logistic support for the fleet in the assault on Kyushu (OLYMPIC). Admiral Fisher decided that the hub of Fleet Train affairs in the coming weeks would be in Australia, and on 31 May he sailed in *Montclare* for Brisbane where on arrival he and members of his staff went by air or train to Sydney for conferences. In the meantime Captain D. B. O'Connell, of *Resource*, and Cdr. J. M. Rayner, RNR, Deputy Maintenance Captain, in *Lothian* remained in charge at Manus.

In Australia the Fleet Train had a badly needed time of recuperation. In general the Fleet Train's morale and efficiency were astonishingly high but there were men of so many nationalities, with so many different terms of service, that dissatisfaction and friction were bound to occur.

In the escort carriers, for example, there was much resentment because general service naval ratings and men who were basically civilians (but had signed form of service T.124X) were carrying out the same duties – but with different rates of pay and terms of service. In some ships there were 'trade unions': merchant seamen abiding strictly by their articles, 'Defensively Equipped Merchant Ships' (DEMS) ratings who would only do ship's work in an emergency, and naval working parties. The naval ratings were quite understandably annoyed when DEMS ratings or native crews stood by, looking on, whilst they were working. Different articles and terms of service created a jungle of regulations: at Leyte the bos'n and six crew members of *Green Ranger* refused to work their derrick. They were removed under armed guard, but a naval court found them not guilty under the terms of their articles.

Some of the crews had not seen their homes and families for many years and to the European nationals, except the Dutch, a war against Japan meant very little. There was indiscipline at Sydney amongst the Belgian crews of the ammunition ships *Prince de Liege* and *Princess Maria Pia*; some of the crew of the latter ship were replaced by naval ratings. In the Danish tanker *Aase Maersk* the seamen, engine-room and catering departments all refused to take the ship to sea after their articles had expired and these, too, were replaced by naval ratings. By the end of the war so many places were filled by naval ratings, with other rigging and working parties on board, that as Admiral Fisher pointed out, with the addition of a few officers and another few hundred ratings the Fleet Train could have become fully White Ensign, which would have been most desirable from the start.

The state of the machinery and the general upkeep of Fleet Train ships varied from good to appalling. *Tjitjalengka* was an asset to the fleet, but another hospital ship, the ex-Italian liner *Gerusalemme*, not only had a serious fire on board but earlier arrived in Australia in such a condition that Admiral Fisher begged the Admiralty 'never again to allow a ship to join the BPF in such a shocking state of efficiency'. Defects could be expected in a ship such as *Rapidol*, a small tanker twenty years old with six years of war already behind her, but some of the new *Wave* Class tankers arrived in Australia with serious defects, of design or manufacture. Of the twelve ammunition ships which had joined the Fleet Train by mid-March, five needed docking and two, *Kistna* and *Kola*, arrived late, with a speed of only seven knots and even that of 'doubtful reliability'. Amongst the other tankers, *Cedardale* had leaking tanks, *Darst Creek* had defective steering gear and had to be towed round Manus, and *Aase Maersk* broke down completely during the July–August operations. Considering the troubles which beset them, the performance of Admiral Fisher's men was not so much a fine achievement as a miracle.

In its early days the Fleet Train was absurdly under-staffed. There were the usual difficulties of getting personnel out to the Pacific in wartime, and the original establishment had been ludicrously under-estimated. The Fleet Train staff were to have assembled in Australia by 1 January 1945, but in fact only four officers had joined by that date and staff continued to arrive until the end of the war; the Fleet Train Electrical Officer did not take up his appointment until June and his first assistant, a warrant electrician, not until the day before the war ended. Few of the officers had served on an admiral's staff before, and many of the typists could not type. Furthermore, four valuable staff officers were killed on the evening of 19 July in a Liberator which crashed shortly after taking off from Sydney. But, under the pressure of actual operating conditions the Fleet Train grew at a remarkable rate, dividing and subdividing, multiplying and throwing out shoots like some vast luxurious tropical plant.

The greatest expansion was in the Air Train. At the outset the huge and complex problems of air logistics were supposed to be handled by a single staff officer (one Lieutenant Commander (E)) later reinforced by one Lieutenant Commander (A). On arrival at Manus responsibility for air logistics was delegated to Captain C. M. Merewether, in the aircraft maintenance ship *Unicorn*. Finally, on 10 June, Commodore H. S. Murray-Smith, flying his broad pennant in *Pioneer*, was appointed Commodore Air Train (COMAT) responsible to Admiral Fisher for the air logistic support of the fleet.

By this time Admiral Fisher's empire had grown so large that a major reorganisation of the staff structure was carried out, with certain of Admiral Fisher's functions being delegated to subordinate commanders. The new shape of this unique organisation is best shown in a diagram: (*See opposite page.*)

This reorganisation relieved the situation, but the Fleet Train staff were still so hard-pressed by immediate events that they had little time for forward planning. If an intermediate base had been constructed a new authority would have been created (Rear Admiral (Q)) responsible for forward logistic planning. As it was, Admiral Fisher's staff had to make do as best they could.

In Australia, responsibility for air logistics was delegated by Admiral

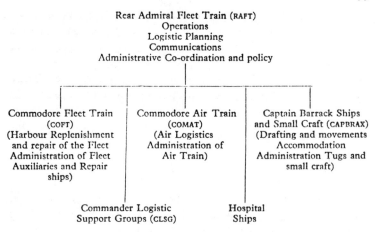

Rear Admiral Fleet Train (RAFT)
Operations
Logistic Planning
Communications
Administrative Co-ordination and policy

Commodore Fleet Train (COFT) (Harbour Replenishment and repair of the Fleet Administration of Fleet Auxiliaries and Repair ships)	Commodore Air Train (COMAT) (Air Logistics Administration of Air Train)	Captain Barrack Ships and Small Craft (CAPBRAX) (Drafting and movements Accommodation Administration Tugs and small craft)

Commander Logistic
Support Groups (CLSG)

Hospital
Ships

Daniel to the equivalent of the 'Fifth Sea Lord' in Admiral Fraser's miniature Admiralty, Rear Admiral R. H. Portal, who was Flag Officer, Naval Air, Pacific (FONAP), with his headquarters at Sydney. Admiral Portal was responsible for the supply of aircrews, aircraft and air stores to the fleet.

Aircrew training in Australia and the assembly and flight testing of replacement aircraft (which normally arrived in crates) were carried out at Mobile Naval Air Bases (MONABS). MONABs, which all had the prefix 'Nab-' in their names, were constructed at Nowra (MONAB I: *Nabbington*), Bankstown (MONAB III: *Nabberley*), Schofields (MONAB III: *Nabthorpe*), Jervis Bay (MONAB V: *Nabswick*), Maryborough, (MONAB VI: *Nabstock*), and Brisbane (MONAB VII: *Nabsford*). The airstrip at Manus, on Ponam Island, was MONAB IV, *Nabaron*, and after the war MONAB VIII *Nabcatcher* was constructed at Hong Kong.

Towards the end of the war the supply of pilots from the United Kingdom almost dried up and those that did arrive 'were nearer the bottom of the barrel than the top'. After negotiations with the Australian Government, twenty-four RAAF Spitfire pilots turned over to the RANVR(A) for training as naval fighter pilots. A replacement British Seafire pilot at that time probably had no more than 150 flying hours – a novice. The Australians were veteran Spitfire pilots who had flown over the Middle East, Italy and Europe; some had more than 2,000 flying hours, and had commanded their own squadrons. Their war was now over and they were only too glad to volunteer for active service. After five weeks' conversion training ashore at Schofields ('a keener and better disciplined lot than those twenty-four Aussies I have never met anywhere'),[1] they successfully carried out their deck landing qualifications at sea in *Indomitable*. They were at Manus, waiting to join the fleet, when the war ended and to their great disappointment saw no operational service with the BPF. However, they made their mark when they eventually joined the Seafire fighter wings in *Indefatigable* and *Implacable* after the war:

'About twenty-five per cent of my Seafire pilots were Australian. They were a different class of pilot. You'd get a relief pilot of our own and you'd be lucky to get someone with 150 hours flying in. These chaps had 2,000. They were the typical 'Digger'. The best type. They started this game of getting a very fast take-off, because they had discovered it was rather fun. Before going to be a trooper after the war, we had to fly off our whole air group. They got the whole Seafire wing, about thirty aircraft, off at seven second intervals. Quite frightening.'[2]

Traditionally in the Royal Navy an air group joined and worked up in their parent aircraft carrier and would expect to stay with that carrier at least for the larger part of the commission; an air group was considered an integral part of the carrier, rather than an interchangeable attachment. But in the Pacific theatre it was recognised that an air group's efficiency deteriorated after six months' operations and the American doctrine of '100% air group replacement' was accepted; it would have been implemented in the light fleet carrier squadron of *Colossus*, *Glory*, *Venerable* and *Vengeance* which was to have formed the BPF's Second Task Group had the war continued. However, the BPF was using six different types of aircraft of which only the Avenger was operated from every carrier. Air groups would probably have been trained for one specific carrier, or class of carrier, in any event.

Admiral Fraser – and indeed every man in the fleet – attached the greatest importance to mail. Regular and quick mail services were one of the most important factors in morale. In December 1944 Commander C. A. Jenkins arrived in Australia to examine and report on the facilities available and the organisation necessary for a mail service for the fleet and train. He was subsequently appointed to the C-in-C's operational staff as Chief Mail Officer responsible in liaison with VA(Q) and RAFT for the general planning and direction of mail services. The appointment of a mail officer to the operational staff, with immediate access to top-

[1] G. D. Dennison (ex-Lt. Cdr. RNVR). Letter of 3.8.68.
[2] Vice Admiral Sir Charles Hughes Hallett. Conversation of 23.5.68.

secret information, was perhaps a breach of security, but it was noticeable that wherever mail officers were denied such information, e.g. latest ship movements, the mail service deteriorated.

In addition to offices at San Francisco and Colombo, fleet mail offices were set up at Sydney, Fremantle and Brisbane, Manus and Leyte and, after the defeat of Japan, at Hong Kong and Shanghai. The experienced nucleus of the mail office staff were ex-GPO employees who after a short period of naval training were given RNVR commissions or rated Writers (Postal). The majority of the mail office personnel were Wrens (the Brisbane office was staffed entirely by Wrens throughout its existence). Like the Fleet Train itself, the mail service grew at a remarkable rate; the Sydney office had one officer and fourteen ratings in January 1945, and ten officers and eighty-four ratings by August.

The route for first-class mail from the United Kingdom to the fleet at sea was long and precarious; by air, via Colombo or San Francisco, to Australia; by RAF Dakota to Manus and Leyte; by escorts of the Logistic Support Groups to the fleet, where bags of mail were transferred at sea. Some mail was lost in aircraft accidents, or jettisoned by aircraft in difficulties, and mail was always liable to be off-loaded at any stage on the route, without warning or authorisation. Nevertheless, the Dakota services by 300 Wing RAF which began to Manus on 26 February and to Leyte on 21 March had carried 100,000 lb of mail for the fleet by mid-April. In the same period 60,000 lb of mail were carried by sea.

A card index system assisted mail officers to identify the '946 Smiths and 630 Jones' in the BPF. The task was complicated by letters addressed to 'HMS Same as Before' or 'HMS Same Old Gashbarge', written by wives or girl friends who had assumed that their naval correspondent's normal letter heading was the official name of his ship.

Possibly no mail service, however quick, could satisfy the sailor's natural impatience for mail, but on 27 June Captain F. J. Butler, commanding Achilles, took the trouble to write to the Chief Mail Officer from Manus to congratulate him: Captain Butler had just received from his wife in Hampshire an answer to a letter he had posted at Manus on 2 June. Twenty-five days, from the Admiralty Islands to the United Kingdom and return, would not be a wholly unreasonable transit time even today.

Another important factor in morale was the ship's canteen. It appears that NAAFI had a grasp of military strategy at least as good as that of the Combined Chiefs of Staff. They were apparently never in any doubt that a British fleet would operate in the Pacific, for as early as October 1943 their agents in Fremantle were instructed to rent a warehouse and the following February a Naval Canteen Service representative, Commander G. H. Rogers, RNVR, was despatched from the Middle East to Australia as NAAFI representative. By the end of the war there were NAAFI warehouses at Fremantle, Sydney, Melbourne and Brisbane and at thirty-one shore establishments. There were four NAAFI canteens in the Admiralty Islands. The BPF was perhaps NAAFI's biggest challenge of the war; never had NAAFI been asked to provide for such numbers of NAAFI stores as they were asked to do, through the medium of the Fleet Train, to the ships of the British Pacific Fleet. NAAFI stores were issued from the VSIS such as *Glenartney* and the *Fort* Class and NAAFI succeeded in keeping the fleet supplied (even with such items as beer in quantity) in the face of dock strikes, loading difficulties, shortages of boats, winches, and refrigerated space, the climate and, of course, the great distances involved. Members of the Naval Canteen Service took a full part in the operational life of their ships, sharing the same hardships and discomforts and, at action stations, serving in stretcher parties, ammunition handling parties and as navigational plotters; at least one Canteen Manager, Mr T. Chapman of *Formidable*, was mentioned in despatches.

The task set the Fleet Train for the July–August operations off Japan was far more difficult than anything they had faced in ICEBERG. Admiral Halsey's operational plan was so flexible and the distances to be covered so enormous that both Admiral Fraser and Admiral Fisher resorted to geographical similes in an effort to illustrate to those at home the true size of the problem. 'With the fleet operating off the coast of Japan itself,' wrote Admiral Fisher, 'the length of the supply line between Manus and the fuelling area was at times as much as 2,500 miles, which is roughly the same as the distance between Montreal and the Clyde, or between Portsmouth and Tobruk.' To shorten this supply line, the Americans began to deliver bulk fuel for the British fleet to Eniwetok, in the Marshall Islands, which reduced the tankers' passages by a thousand miles. Even so, Admiral Fraser compared the position of the British Pacific Fleet, operating between Hokkaido and Kyushu, with a main base at Sydney and advanced anchorages at Manus and Eniwetok, to 'a fleet based in Alexandria, with advanced anchorages at Gibraltar and the Azores, attacking the North American coast between Labrador and Nova Scotia'.

But in spite of these vivid comparisons, it is still very doubtful whether everyone in the Admiralty ever appreciated the vast size of the Pacific theatre. In 1950, when Admiral Sir Denis Boyd returned to England after three years as C-in-C Far Eastern Fleet, he remarked sadly: 'One was tempted at times to believe that the operations rooms at home had a map of the Far East hanging alongside one of the coast of Palestine, and that the charts were of the same size.'[1]

Admiral Fisher left Brisbane in *Montclare* on 24 June and reached Manus on 30th. The main fleet sailed from Sydney on 28th, arriving at Manus on 4 July to top up with fuel and stores before sailing to join the US 3rd Fleet at sea off Japan. Allowance had been made to replenish the destroyers with fresh provisions but the VSIS's *Fort Dunvegan* and *Fort Wrangell* were disconcerted to receive unexpectedly heavy demands for fresh fruit, vegetables and eggs from larger ships such as *Formidable*, *King George V* and *Victorious* so soon after leaving Sydney. Bad weather in Sydney had apparently prevented them replenishing completely. The fleet also sailed with many demands for air stores unfilled.

At Manus, repairs were carried out on *Formidable*'s centre shaft stern bush and to *Indefatigable*'s four high-pressure air compressors – but not, however, in time for her to sail with the rest of the fleet on 6 July.

Admiral Fisher's main problem was, as before, the tankers. There were twelve available, which he split into four groups of three. The tanker groups sailed initially from Manus to rendezvous with the fleet at sea, and then went to Eniwetok to refill, returning again to rendezvous with the fleet. The tankers' operating cycle, from port to port, was anything from a fortnight to a month. *San Adolfo* and *San Ambrosio*, for example, who could make about 8 knots, left Manus on 1 July, and reached Eniwetok to refill on 31st. Even *Wave Emperor*, who could make 14 knots, took 14 days from Eniwetok to rendezvous with the fleet, and return to Eniwetok.

There were not enough tankers and they were all too slow, both in speed and in pumping rates. After the fleet fuelling of 13–15 July (which, in spite of the absence of *Indefatigable* and three destroyers, was only completed in time thanks to Admiral Halsey's twenty-four hour strike postponement) Admiral Rawlings signalled that with the fleet well down in oil, three tankers with many of the usual old troubles were not enough, and took all daylight for $2\frac{1}{2}$ days to complete the job, if moderate weather. In ICEBERG TWO, nine tankers making eighteen sorties had kept the fleet supplied, with a 40% margin, over a period of thirty days whilst operating 700–800 miles from Manus.

[1] Admiral Sir Denis Boyd. Lecture to the RUSI.

But in July and August the fleet operated for forty-three days more than 2,000 miles from Manus and twelve tankers, making eighteen sorties, could not supply the fleet with all the fuel it required; the balance was provided by American tankers. In ICEBERG the fleet had fuelled in approximately the same position each time. In July and August the fuelling position was often changed, on two occasions 700 miles from the original, and tanker movements were controlled from the forward area. This threw Admiral Fisher's careful arrangements into confusion. The tanker situation got quite out of hand, drastic diversions of route had to be ordered while they were on passage, the composition of escorts and groups was completely mixed and disorganised, there were insufficient opportunities for repairing tankers and escorts, and a very serious situation was developing when the end of the war brought an end to the problem. Unless there was a surplus of tankers (a state, in the circumstances, which was difficult to visualise) drastical terations to the fuelling plan could not long be continued without a fiasco. However, the tanker groups fuelled the fleet on six occasions during the operations and pumped 160,000 tons of oil fuel.

The replacement aircraft situation was also saved by strike postponements. At the average escort carrier speed of about 14 knots, the operating cycle from Manus, to the fleet, and return to Manus, was about three weeks. There were four ferry carriers, which made five sorties: *Arbiter* making two sorties, *Striker*, *Speaker*, and *Chaser* one each. The 30th Aircraft Carrier Squadron ferried 116 aircraft to the operating area; the fleet needed ninety-nine replacement aircraft, and 102 were provided – but they were not all provided as soon as they were needed, and had there been a strike period between 2 and 6 August the fleet might have been short of aircraft, especially for *Formidable*'s Corsair squadrons, whose losses were three times as high as *Victorious*' squadrons. As in ICEBERG, *Ruler* with eight Hellcats, eight Corsairs and six Avengers remained in the forward area with the Logistic Support Group to provide a ready-use supply of aircraft and to keep replacement pilots in flying training. Her CAP duties were secondary.

The Logistic Support Group included two types of ship, a Victualling Store Issuing Ship and a Radio/Radar Maintenance Ship, which had not been seen in the forward area before. The VSIS *Glenartney* supplied the fleet with fresh provisions such as fruit and potatoes and was one of the great successes of the Fleet Train: all classes of ships were to be seen queueing up to draw provisions from her, and destroyers were never without fresh provisions, although *Glenartney* herself, with an efficient and highly co-operative ship's company, reported when she returned to Manus that she could have done much more and was often disappointed through lack of customers. When *Glenartney* was relieved by *Fort Wrangell* and left the forward area on 6 August she signalled that she had provisioned a total of seventy-seven ships and discharged 422 tons of stores at an average rate of $7\frac{1}{2}$ tons an hour. In Admiral Rawlings's opinion, *Glenartney* had made a very satisfactory contribution to the well-being of the fleet. Fifty tons of the stores transferred were NAAFI items; the Fleet Train NAAFI Officer noted that the only casualties were seven cases of apples and one case of lambs' tongues.

The Radio/Radar Maintenance Ship was a converted corvette, HMNZS *Arbutus*. She was fitted for minor radio and radar repairs and carried small quantities of spare parts in her magazines and shell-rooms, leaving barely enough ammunition for her own protection. Her staff were able to give advice on radar and radio repairs and supply such spares as she carried but she had neither the space nor the personnel to provide much more than a 'First Aid' advisory service. *Arbutus* had retained her asdic and was useful as an extra escort on passage to and from the service area.

The ASIS *Robert Maersk* sailed from Manus on 7 July, followed by *Corinda* on 15th. *Robert Maersk*, one of the gamest ships of the Fleet Train, issued two hundred 500-lb bombs to *Victorious* and 150 14-inch shells to *King George V*; *Corinda* forty 500-lb bombs to *Formidable*. This was a total of only 300 tons issued and both ships returned to Manus on 17 August somewhat disappointed that they were not called on more heavily.

The hospital ship *Tjitjalengka* sailed from Leyte on 12 July for the forward area, where she remained at a distance from the Logistic Support Group, casualties being transferred to her by destroyer from time to time. (She arrived at Sagami Bay, Japan, after the war was over, on 28 August, having been at sea for forty-seven days.)

To service the British tankers at Eniwetok, Task Group 112.3 consisting of *Tyne* (Captain S. Boucher, CTG 112.3), *Kelantan*, *Bacchus*, *Brown Ranger*, *Fort Wrangell* and escorts, sailed from Manus on 12 July, and remained at Eniwetok from 18 July to 6 August. Captain Boucher was also to report on Eniwetok's suitability as a base for the British Fleet Train in OLYMPIC. The British were a novelty at Eniwetok and TG 112.3 was very cordially received by the Americans. US officers enjoyed *Tyne*'s hospitality 'on occasion with almost embarrassing gusto' and reciprocated with entertainments which 'normally took the

U

form of a "barbecue" (a sort of beef-steak picnic) conducted, not unwisely, under cover of night'.

The most originally conceived and imaginatively designed ship of the Fleet Train, and the one which aroused most speculation amongst the sailors, unfortunately arrived in the Far East too late to take part in the war. This was the 'Amenities Ship', better known as the 'floating brewery'. In April 1945, in answer to a question from Lt. The Hon. W. W. Astor, RNVR, MP, the First Lord said: 'The fleet is to have an amenities ship which will contain a combined theatre and cinema, a canteen, a NAAFI shop and restaurant, lending library, reading and writing rooms, as well as tailors', barbers' and boot repair shops. It is intended to install brewery plants in the amenities ship and the supply of ice cream plant and soda fountains are also receiving special attention in view of the climatic conditions.'[1]

Two amenities ships were authorised, one each for SEAC and the Pacific. Two ex-Blue Funnel Line ships *Agamemnon* and *Menestheus*, which had earlier in the war been requisitioned and converted as mine-layers, were taken up for the Fleet Train with the highest priority in September 1944 and in November sailed for Vancouver, where they were to be fitted out as amenities ships. Five brewery experts and 120 men of the Naval Canteen Service went to Vancouver to assist and advise in their construction and to man their facilities when they were commissioned. A most unusual feature of these ships was the brewery, the revolutionary design of Mr Stephen Clarke, which operated under a completely enclosed process and was capable of brewing 1,800 gallons of excellent beer a day.[2]

The conversion of *Agamemnon* was stopped at the end of the war but *Menestheus* was completed and sailed for the Far East in January 1946, arriving in Japan on 26 February.

Menestheus was undoubtedly a huge success. She had a 400-seat theatre running a professional revue 'Pacific Show Boat', library, bars, shops, swimming bath, ice cream and soda fountains. Admiral Fraser tried to retain her in the Pacific, for the entertainment of the Occupation Forces and the Pacific Fleet. The Americans were charmed, and offered to buy her. But her owners were agitating for her return and after a cruise of five days at Yokohama, ten at Kure, six at Shanghai and three weeks at Hong Kong during which she entertained 40,000

---

[1] *Hansard*, 11 April 1945.
[2] See also *The Devices of War*, by Norman Kemp (Werner Laurie, 1956). Ch. 7 'The Davy Jones Brewery'.

officers and men, *Menestheus* sailed for the United Kingdom on 18 May, 1946, via Singapore, Trincomalee, Aden and Malta.

The 'intermediate base', which had influenced so much planning for the Fleet Train and for which so many preparations were actually made, was intended to be a 'storage reservoir' of bulk supplies and personnel, placed between Australia and the operating area. In February 1945 Admiral Fisher and some of his staff flew up to Manus hoping, indeed expecting, to be offered some of the US installations ashore and to begin establishing what was to be a form of intermediate base. It was soon made clear to them that they could expect only anchorages, bulk fuel supplies and 'anything else that could be given without Admiral King's knowledge'. In the event, a great deal was given without Admiral King's knowledge; Captain Waight and his officers had a close liaison with their American colleagues and counterparts and by the end of the war British shore facilities at Manus were quite extensive. But a full British intermediate base required much more than could be supplied by American goodwill and although some facilities would have been ready by October 1945, the base would not have been properly completed and established until February 1946, by which time Manus would be too far from the operating area. When Admiral Fraser told the Admiralty that he would ask Admiral Nimitz whether some harbour in the Philippines such as Subic Bay could be allocated to the British, the Admiralty postponed a decision on the intermediate base until Admiral Fraser could report. As might almost have been expected, the reply was that for political reasons the Americans were very unlikely to make any base or shore facilities in the Philippines available to the British on anything but a very small scale – certainly not the full intermediate base. It was now clear that there might be an early end to the war and the intermediate base would not be built in time to be of any use. The project was abandoned. By the time the base would have been in use, the war was already long over and the ships of the Fleet Train dispersed, to take their part in the reoccupation and rehabilitation of British territories.

Chapter Ten

THE JULY–AUGUST OPERATIONS

'With easy grace he [Halsey] is striking here one day and there the next, replenishing at sea or returning to harbour as the situation demands. With dogged persistence the British Pacific Fleet is keeping up, and if anything is going to stretch its muscles, these operations will. But it is tied by a string to Australia and much handicapped by its few, small, slow tankers.' *Admiral Sir Bruce Fraser.*

FOR all the Fleet Air Arm's exploits at Taranto and off Matapan, against *Bismarck* and *Tirpitz*, in the Atlantic and the Western Desert, the operations against the Japanese home islands in July and August 1945 were still their most finished professional performance of the war. Operating in close company with the US Fast Carrier Task Force, the British carrier squadron achieved a higher rate of intensity of flying effort than ever before. Through the courage, dedication and endurance of the aircrews, the British fleet was able to overcome its many handicaps and relatively strike blow for blow with the Americans almost until the final surrender of Japan.

The fleet sailed from Sydney on 28 June 1945, replenished, repaired and refreshed after three weeks in harbour. There were new faces in the ships and in the briefing rooms – the battle-fatigued aircrews who had flown in ICEBERG had been relieved by fresh squadrons. Many of the 20-mm. oerlikons had been replaced by heavier calibre 40-mm. bofors. New anti-aircraft tactics had been devised; new self-defence routines for the aircraft carriers, new V/T fuse procedures and new anti-aircraft co-ordinator systems.

Indomitable was undergoing refit and Admiral Vian transferred his flag to *Formidable*. At full strength the 1st Aircraft Carrier Squadron had a total complement of 255 aircraft:

	He	Co	Se	Fi	Av	Wa	Total
Formidable	6	36			12		54
Victorious		37			14	2	53
Implacable			48	12	18		78
Indefatigable			40	12	18		70
Total	6	73	88	24	62	2	255

Indefatigable was unable to sail with the fleet. All four of her high-pressure air compressors were defective. These seemingly domestic items of machinery were actually vital; without high-pressure air supplies a carrier could not operate aircraft. The fleet arrived at Manus on 4 July, after intensive fleet exercises on passage, to fuel and collect the ships which had undergone their major replenishment there. The fleet, now designated Task Force 37, sailed from Manus on 6 July and consisted of:

King George V (Flag of VABPF)
Formidable (Flag of AC 1), *Victorious* and *Implacable*
Newfoundland (Flag of CS 4), *Black Prince, Euryalus, Achilles, Uganda* and *Gambia*
Grenville (D 4) *Undine, Urania, Urchin, Ulysses, Undaunted, Quiberon, Quickmatch, Quality, Quadrant*
Troubridge (D 24), *Tenacious, Termagant, Terpsichore* and *Teazer*

On the afternoon of 6 July, shortly after TF 37 left harbour, *Implacable* signalled that she had had to stop her port outer shaft. A fragment of metal had broken off the port outer main turbine thrust and adjusting block, and had obstructed the lubricating oil supply to the bearing.[1] The metal on the bearing pads had wiped.

This was a major defect in the ship's main propulsion machinery. In normal circumstances repairs would have been carried out by a dockyard. But circumstances were not normal. TF 37 was already one carrier short, and was due to rendezvous with the Americans on 16 July. Working in shifts round the clock *Implacable*'s engineering department, led by the Engineer Officer Cdr. D. S. Holt Wilson, began the repair; in spite of the heat, the difficulties of working *in situ* in a ship under way, and the dilution of skilled engineering personnel at that stage of the war, repairs were completed by the afternoon of 15

[1] 'This was a metallurgical failure. The designers would have used other material if it had been available when the engines were built.' Cdr. D. S. Holt Wilson. Letter of 13.5.68.

July. It was a splendid performance, showing the spirit of the fleet at that time.

Meanwhile, TF 37 had met the fuelling group on 13 July. Although *Indefatigable* and three destroyers were still missing, the fleet took three days to fuel, because of the inadequacies in the tankers and breakages of hoses and gear. After repeated partings of messenger lines and burstings of hoses *King George V* went alongside a tanker to fuel, the first occasion on which a British battleship had fuelled abeam; thereafter, fuelling abeam became accepted and normal practice. Luckily, the Third Fleet's operations were postponed for twenty-four hours because of bad weather and the fuelling delays did not cost TF 37 a day's strikes. But it was an uneasy portent for the future.

Early on 16 July some 300 miles east of Japan, the American fleet was sighted. Its three Task Groups were then fuelling, the whole fleet, in Admiral Rawlings's words, 'forming a striking and unforgettable picture'. The US Third Fleet at that time consisted of nine fleet carriers, six light carriers, seven battleships, fifteen cruisers, and sixty destroyers. An Able Seaman in *Implacable* recalled that scene, with the British matelot's typical concern for the underdog: 'Everywhere you looked there were ships. You felt we couldn't lose the war now. In fact, we almost felt we were being big bullies.'[1] In the battleship *Missouri*, the Third Fleet flagship, the British Liaison Officer Cdr. Le Fanu[2] was delighted to see the British Fleet – it was 'the high spot of one man's Pacific war – the end and the beginning'. (Cdr. Le Fanu was British Liaison Officer to Admiral Spruance and Admiral Halsey and earned the complete trust and confidence of them both.)

The operations in which the British fleet was now to take part were the preliminaries intended to exert unremitting pressure on the enemy, before the landings in the Japanese home islands already planned for later in the year. On 25 May 1945 the US Chiefs of Staff had decided that Japan could not be defeated quickly enough by air and sea blockade alone and instructed MacArthur and Nimitz to carry out a landing in southern Kyushu on 1 November (Operation OLYMPIC), followed by an invasion of Honshu and an assault on the Tokyo plain (Operation CORONET) in March 1946.

Even now, no Supreme Commander was appointed for the Pacific theatre, although MacArthur was to command OLYMPIC. A compromise arranged on 5 April 1945, giving MacArthur command of all army

---

[1] Mr D. Cartin. Letter of 18.9.67.
[2] Now Admiral Sir Michael Le Fanu.

forces and resources in the Pacific, and Nimitz command of all naval forces and resources, was continued. Only in the direction of the strategic air offensive against Japan was a fresh command structure achieved and that not until July when General Carl Spaatz (who had commanded the US Strategic Air Force in Europe) arrived in the Far East to take command of the US Strategic Air Force in the Pacific. His air forces consisted of 20th Air Force and 21st Bomber Command, in the Marianas, 20th Bomber Command in Okinawa, and 7th Fighter Command, on Iwo Jima. The Far Eastern Air Force in direct support of MacArthur's armies was still commanded by Gen. G. C. Kenney, in Okinawa. Naval carrier-borne and shore-based aircraft in Okinawa were still commanded by Admiral Nimitz at Guam. Thus, success in the final assault on Japan would depend more than ever before on close co-operation between MacArthur, Nimitz and, latterly, Spaatz.

The Third Fleet's tasks in July and August were: to reduce the enemy's tactical naval and army air forces; to attack strategic targets on the Japanese mainland; and to probe the strength of the enemy defences in northern Honshu and Hokkaido, which were both beyond the reasonable range of long-range aircraft based in the Marianas. In the event, the tasks were amended during the operations to include the destruction of the remnants of the Imperial Japanese Navy and Japanese merchant shipping wherever they could be found. To carry out these tasks, the Third Fleet intended to use all the modes of warfare available to a modern fleet – air strike, bombardment, surface sweep, radio deception, submarine operations, and mining, all played their part.

The Third Fleet had been released from ICEBERG on 10 June and had replenished at Leyte. Early in July the fleet approached the coast of Japan, having first taken all seaman-like precautions. Hundreds of aircraft reconnaissance sorties had been flown to examine the numbers and dispositions of Japanese warning picket vessels. Submarines fitted with active sonar mine-detecting equipment had plotted the positions of mine-fields. The fleet's advance was preceded by a massive air barrier and by anti-picket sweeps of seven submarines. The Japanese had withdrawn small craft from their home waters, and the Third Fleet achieved complete tactical surprise. The first exploratory strikes, against airfields on the Tokyo plain on 10 July,[1] met only slight opposition. Some 340 enemy aircraft were claimed destroyed or damaged on the ground, and the significantly small number of two in the air. Clearly, the Japanese were not committing their metropolitan air forces to an

[1] See map, p. 312.

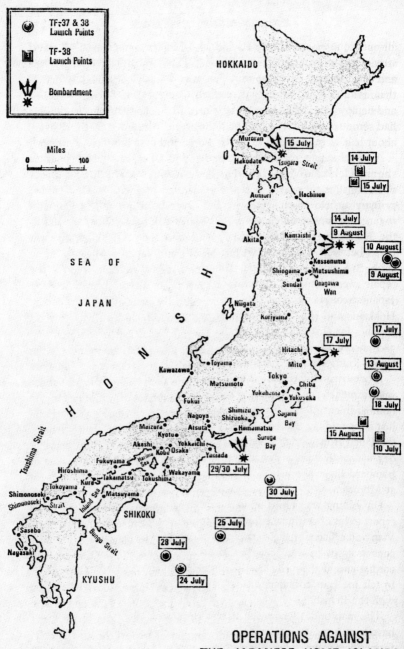

**OPERATIONS AGAINST
THE JAPANESE HOME ISLANDS**
July and August, 1945

all-out counter-attack, as at Okinawa, but were husbanding their strength, dispersing their aircraft and making cunning use of camouflage and concealment. After the war, the Japanese air commander confessed that his aircraft had been so successfully dispersed he could not assemble and deploy them when they were most needed. At that time, the enemy had some 10,500 aircraft for the defence of the home islands, of which about half were intended as kamikaze suicide bombers.

After refuelling, the Third Fleet moved north to attack northern Honshu and Hokkaido on 13, 14 and 15 July. Fog and low visibility hampered operations (as they were to do so often in the coming weeks) and the primary airfield targets were weathered in. The strike aircraft turned to targets of opportunity and scored an important success by disrupting the Hokkaido–Honshu railway ferry which ran across the Tsugaru Strait between Hakodate and Aomori. Eight out of twelve ferries were sunk, two more beached and flooded, and the remaining two, under repair, were damaged. Several colliers were sunk in the Strait. The Japanese could not replace the ferry vessels, and coal shipments between Hokkaido and Honshu dropped to almost a third of their normal. Food supplies for Hokkaido were also affected. In the two days' strikes, some 380 enemy ships of 159,000 tons total were sunk or damaged, and eighty-four railway locomotives destroyed.

A bombarding force of battleships and cruisers, designated TU 34.8.1, was formed from TF 38 on 14 July and carried out the first surface bombardment of the Japanese mainland. The heavy guns opened fire just after midday and continued for two hours, doing great damage to the Japan Iron Works, in the coastal city of Kamaishi. At dawn the next day a second bombardment group, TU 34.8.2, closed the coast and bombarded the Wanishi Iron Works and Japan Steel Company works at Muroran.

On joining the Third Fleet, Admiral Rawlings's first duty was to report to his operational commander. In the forenoon of 16th, Rawlings, Vian and officers of their staffs repaired on board *Missouri*. 'The day's conversations in the Third Fleet flagship could not have been more cordial and at their end the Fleet Commander sent for me [Le Fanu] to tell me how confident he felt about the prospects of co-operating with the British.'

The man under whom the British fleet were now to serve could not have been a greater contrast, in personality or in temperament, to their former fleet commander Admiral Spruance. Admiral William F. Halsey, Jnr., sometimes known (though not to his face) as 'Bull' Halsey, was

probably the most colourful and best known personality of the naval
war in the Pacific. He was, in a sense, the United States Navy's answer
to General George Patton. Whilst Spruance abhorred personal publicity
and shrank from any statement which could be attributed to him, Halsey
could be relied upon to make war correspondents' hearts glad within
them with some striking phrase – such as, for instance, his famous
boast that when victory came he would 'ride the Emperor's white horse
through the streets of Tokyo.'[1] In British eyes Halsey's flamboyance,
his flair for publicity, and his astonishing informality of speech and
manner, have all tended to obscure his merit as a commander. He was
a fine sea commander, and a lovable man, much loved by those who
served under him. He was a simple man, in some ways almost naïve,
who relied a great deal on his instructions from Washington and on his
own brilliant personal staff, who served him faithfully. Admiral Halsey's
leadership could be described as inspirational rather than intellectual.
His approach to tactical operations, as reported by the British officer
who attended many of his conferences, could be paraphrased as: 'We'll
clobber those yellow bastards! What's the best way of clobbering
those yellow bastards? We'll get after them!'[2]

When Rawlings and Vian arrived in *Missouri* their fleet's future was
still not clear. As always with the BPF, tactics had to be disentangled
from politics. At Pearl Harbour in December 1944, Nimitz and Fraser
had agreed that the British task force would be a separate task force
as far as possible, with no more tactical co-ordination with the US Task
Force than the immediate situation required, although Admiral Fraser
certainly had no objection to a British force coming under American
command, having never intended to exclude the possibility of a British
task force operating in an American force. However Admiral Nimitz
(possibly under duress from Washington) countermanded Hasley's
expressed intention to operate the British fleet as part of his own.
Halsey, understandably, chafed at this restriction and in a well-
known passage in his memoirs described his reactions. In short, he
offered Rawlings three alternatives: TF 37 could operate in all respects
except name as another task group of the Third Fleet; or, operate
semi-independently some sixty miles away (Halsey made it clear

---

[1] One Texas city sent Halsey a beautiful saddle with silver bridle and fittings,
ostensibly for him to ride through Tokyo. When it arrived in *Missouri*, Halsey
placed the saddle across the backs of two chairs, mounted it and pretended to
ride. When, inevitably, he caught himself in the crutch he bellowed: 'Why
cain't I remember I'm just a pore old clapped out old bastard!'

[2] Admiral Sir Michael Le Fanu. Conversation of 26.3.68.

he would agree to this course only if it were put in writing); or, operate entirely separately, against 'soft' targets which Halsey's staff would recommend if so required. Without hesitation Admiral Rawlings accepted the first alternative and Halsey wrote: 'My admiration for him began at that moment.'[1] It was agreed that TF 37 should act in practice as part of the Third Fleet and take part in battleship and cruiser bombardments and surface sweeps. Thus – 'Commander 3rd Fleet, while accepting this restriction in its nominal sense, in fact completely disregarded it and continued to operate the British Task Group as part of his own Task Force'.

Consciences were absolved with a somewhat transparent subterfuge. It was intimated that the British fleet would operate 'sixty miles apart', which sounded splendidly aloof. In fact, the task groups of TF 38 were stationed fifteen miles apart. Sixty miles was the distance across the van of the fleet, and would place the British fleet neatly on the right of the line. This was done.

The whole episode demonstrated an unexpected duplicity in the American nature. Admiral Fraser, though privately satisfied with the outcome, commented: 'Provided he obeys the letter of the law, even if he completely disregards its spirit, every American is quite happy that the right and sensible action has been taken.'

At 1600 on 16 July the combined fleets moved off towards the first flying-off position, course 250, speed 15½ knots, in the order from north to south: TF 37 (Rawlings), TG 38.1 (Rear Admiral T. L. Sprague), TG 38.4 (Rear Admiral A. W. Radford), TG 38.3 (Rear Admiral G. F. Bogan), with the Task Force Commander, Vice Admiral J. S. McCain, flying his flag in the carrier *Shangri La*. The two Allied fleets were at last in close company, under the same fleet commander. Admiral Rawlings, with his infallible sense of occasion, noted: 'It may well be that 4 pm on 16 July 1945, will prove a not unimportant milestone on the long road of the world's history.'

Targets for 17 July were airfields and shipping north of Tokyo. At 0210 the Fighter Direction Picket Groups were detached to take up their stations. These pickets with their attendant CAPs (code-named TOMCATS and WATCHDOGS) were the lynch-pin of the fleet's air defences. Each picket (four destroyers with four CAP fighters overhead at 30,000 feet) was stationed from forty to sixty miles from the fleet guide, to cover an arc of 180° in the most likely direction of attack. The two flank pickets were also used as rendezvous and examination stations

[1] *Admiral Halsey's Story* (McGraw-Hill, 1947), p. 261.

for returning aircraft, to prevent enemy aircraft slipping in behind a
returning strike. The pickets were specially fitted and manned for
directing aircraft and, with their radar scans free of echo saturation and
their crews in constant action practice, they performed excellently;
more than half of the successful interceptions during the July–August
operations were directed by the radar pickets.

At 0350[1] on 17 July the first British aircraft to strike at the Japanese
mainland were launched from a position some 250 miles ENE of Tokyo.
Ramrods of sixteen Corsairs from *Formidable* and seven Fireflies from
Implacable flew north-west to bomb, rocket and strafe airfields at
Sendai, Masuda and Matsushima, destroying five enemy aircraft on the
ground and damaging two, besides buildings, hangars, locomotives and
a junk. Three Corsairs were lost to flak but the pilots were recovered,
one by the US destroyer *John Rodgers* and two by British destroyers.
The next two Ramrods, of sixteen Corsairs from *Victorious* and twelve
Seafires from *Implacable*, were aborted because of bad weather but two
more (ten Corsairs from *Formidable*, twelve from *Victorious*) took off
at 0850. This Ramrod was led by Lt. Cdr. J. G. Baldwin, CO of 1834
Sq., and was the first British sortie across to the west coast of Japan.
Whilst strafing Niigata airfield, a flight of Corsairs detached to strafe
a 4,000-ton tanker in the Sea of Japan – the first visit of British aircraft
to this enemy waterway. It was, altogether, a day of 'firsts'.

Meanwhile, farther south, Task Force 38 had flown off two strikes
which had been thwarted by bad weather and Admiral McCain had
cancelled further strikes for the day. Task Force 37 had flown seventy-
three offensive Ramrod sorties, and 153 CAP and A/S patrol sorties. Nine
enemy aircraft had been destroyed and nine damaged.

That afternoon *King George V*, with *Quality* and *Quiberon*, detached
from TF 37 to form TU 37.1.6 and join an American bombarding
group TU 34.8.2[2] under Rear Admiral Oscar Badger, USN, for a
bombardment of the heavily industrialised areas around Hitachi and
Mito on the east coast of Honshu. This was the first combined British
and American bombardment of Japan.

While Task Force 37 provided a night CAP (also for the first time)
the bombarding force closed the Japanese coast after dark, in rain,
fog and very poor visibility. No spotting aircraft could be flown because
of the weather and the shoot was guided entirely by radar and loran

---

[1] For some reason, the Third Fleet off Japan kept Honolulu, not local, time.
[2] The battleships *Missouri*, *Iowa*, *Wisconsin*, *North Caroline* and *Alabama*,
the cruisers *Atlanta* and *Dayton*, and six destroyers.

navigation. The bombardment opened at 2310 and lasted for about an hour. Nearly 2,000 tons of shells were fired, at ranges between thirteen and fourteen miles. *King George V* was allocated independent targets: an unidentified industrial works (ninety-seven rounds of 14-inch); Hitachi (Densen) Engineering Works (ninety-one rounds); and Hitachi (Taga) Engineering Works (seventy-nine rounds). The American battleships bombarded a copper refinery, an armament factory and other targets along the coast. The bombardment ended at 0010 and the force retired to the east at high speed. A few enemy aircraft were detected, but the force was not attacked.

Admiral Halsey was present in *Missouri* and as the bombardment force disengaged signalled: 'Well done, which I pass on with the hope that the results are what your performance deserves.'

Photo-reconnaissance showed that in fact the results were not quite what the performance deserved. Only three out of nine industrial areas had been hit and damage done was slight. However, the bombardment had an indirect success; many people evacuated the area during the shelling and twenty-four hours later, when B-29 bombers from the Marianas carried out an incendiary raid, firefighting and other essential services were under-manned; nearly 80% of the built-up area was devastated by fire.

When *King George V* and escorting destroyers rejoined Task Force 37 the next day the weather was too bad for flying and the whole fleet turned south to search for clearer weather. A CAP was flown off at 0930 and two hours later Admiral McCain ordered strikes to be launched.

The main objective for the American task groups was the Japanese naval base at Yokosuka and the main target the 38,000 ton battleship *Nagato*. She was moored alongside in a position where she could not be attacked with torpedoes and Task Force 38's aircraft had to make bombing runs through very heavy anti-aircraft fire. Twelve aircraft and sixteen aircrew were lost. *Nagato* was badly damaged, but stayed afloat.

The British fleet was not allowed to take part in these attacks. The reason, as reported by Cdr. C. E. A. Owen, Admiral McCain's British liaison officer, was the short range of British aircraft. This, as the Americans later admitted, was a specious pretext. The truth was that the United States Navy believed that the Japanese fleet was their 'pigeon'; revenge for Pearl Harbour was not the business of outsiders.

TF 37's targets for 18 July were airfields and installations in the Tokyo area. Airfields at Nobara, Naruto, Chosi, Konoike, Katori, Miyakawa and the seaplane base at Kitaura were attacked; twelve enemy aircraft were destroyed, and eighteen damaged. Aircraft strafed by *Implacable*'s Seafires at Miyakawa were almost certainly dummies. The Japanese had skilfully constructed mock aircraft of bamboo slats resting on trestles and covered with camouflage netting. *Implacable*'s pilots noticed that some of the 'aircraft' actually had grass growing from them. The burden of the day's Ramrods was borne by *Formidable*'s Corsairs and *Implacable*'s Fireflies and Seafires, because *Victorious*' petrol system had become contaminated with sea-water. She was able to launch only one Ramrod of six Corsairs late in the afternoon.

Formidable's Corsair squadrons were already making a name for themselves with their aggressive low-level strafing tactics. But they were bound to invite losses, and on 18th the inevitable occurred. S/Lt. W. Stradwick, RNVR, of 1842 Sq. failed to return from the first Ramrod of the day, and S/Lt. W. H. Asbridge, RCNVR, of 1841 Sq. was lost from the afternoon Ramrod; they were the first TF 37 aircrew to be lost over Japan. Several other Ramrod aircraft returned with flak damage that day.

The weather worsened again in the afternoon and strikes were cancelled. The last Ramrod landed on at 1700, after Admiral Vian had had an anxious time manoeuvering the carriers so as to keep in touch with the neighbouring TG 38.1 and still find clear patches to land on the returning strikes some of which, especially the Seafires, were very short of fuel. A bogey was reported over one of the WATCH-DOGS, but escaped in the bad weather.

That evening a small force of four US light cruisers and a squadron of destroyers carried out a short bombardment of the radar installations near Nojima Saki.

A CAP was flown off at 0415 on 19 July and further strikes were planned. But the weather was still bad, the CAP landed on at 0528 and the strikes were cancelled. The weather was to bedevil the combined fleets' operations throughout July and August off Japan. It was rare for the weather to be good at sea, and inland, at the same time; frequently strikes would be launched in the clear only to find their targets weathered in, or the fleet would be shrouded in fog and rain whilst targets inland were clear and open to attack.

The fleets were due to have refuelled by noon on 21 July – a tight schedule for the British fleet. On 19th Admiral Rawlings asked permission for TF 37 to proceed independently to the rendezvous. This was approved. A typhoon was threatening the fuelling area, and the rendezvous was moved farther north, to a position near the next launching point. Admiral Halsey extended the fuelling period by twenty-four hours, until noon on 22 July. This allowed the American ships to reammunition, and was also very acceptable to the British units.

On passage eastwards to the rendezvous Admiral Rawlings received Admiral Halsey's full 'Operational Plan' and saw, with consternation, that on two future occasions the fuelling was to be completed in one day, with long passages to be accomplished on the same day. The programme held no terrors for the Americans, equipped with fleets of large, fast tankers with high rates of pumping. But for the British, with their few slow small tankers, it was quite another matter. Admiral Rawlings foresaw that fuelling difficulties might even cause his fleet to miss a day's strikes. In the event Task Force 37 did not miss a single day's operations but this, as Admiral Rawlings freely admitted, was to the credit of a typhoon which forced Admiral Halsey to alter his plans and gave the British fleet invaluable time. Throughout the July–August operations, keeping his fleet supplied with fuel was far more of a problem to Admiral Rawlings than were the enemy.

The British tankers filled from American sources at Manus and latterly at Eniwetok, 2,000 and 1,700 miles respectively from the operating area. The passage distances were so great and the average speeds of many of the twelve tankers which took part were so low (between 8 and 10 knots), that Rear Admiral Fisher could guarantee only three tankers at each fuelling rendezvous. There was no surplus margin, either in time or in capacity, and even this basic schedule could only be met on some occasions by sailing tankers for Eniwetok at once after the fuelling, without pausing to 'consolidate cargoes', i.e. pumping part cargoes from one tanker to another to ensure that tankers returned to Eniwetok empty.

The British Logistics Group[1] was met early on 20 July. It included *Indefatigable* and the destroyers *Wakeful*, *Wrangler* and *Barfleur* (Flag of RAD). *Indefatigable* had come up from Manus at high speed to take her place in the line and required more fuel than had been expected. Furthermore, the tankers were 2,500 tons of oil short of that necessary to fuel the whole fleet completely. Admiral Rawlings was forced to ask Admiral Halsey if three of the British cruisers could refuel from American tankers, referring in his signal to the five logistically unpre-

---

[1] Tankers *San Ambrosio*, *Wave Monarch* and *San Adolpho*; Victualling Stores Issuing Ship (VSIS) *Glenartney*; CVEs *Ruler*, *Arbiter* and *Striker*; destroyers *Napier* and *Nizam*; sloops *Pheasant*, *Whimbrel*, *Redpole*; frigate *Findhorn*; fleet minesweeper *Gawler*.

pared virgins in the parable.[1] Admiral Halsey agreed at once. *Uganda*, *Gambia* and *Achilles* fuelled from TG 30.8, the US Logistics Group.

Past experience had shown that given good weather, good luck and a minimum of hose breakages and delays, the British fleet still took two whole days of fourteen hours daylight to refuel completely. A simple calculation from Admiral Halsey's Operational Plan of times, distances and pumping capacities showed that the fleet would not be able to complete in time. *Wave King*, one of a faster class of tanker, was brought forward from refit in Sydney and the new fast Royal Fleet Auxiliary tanker *Olna*, with a higher designed rate of pumping, had also arrived on the station. But these reinforcements would not be enough. Rear Admiral Fisher was instructed to convert two escort carriers, *Arbiter* and *Ruler*, as 'auxiliary oilers' (able to fuel through one buoyant hose streamed astern) when they next arrived at Manus, and to despatch them with their replacement aircraft back to the operating area as soon as possible. Admiral Rawlings had now done all he could, but the 'one-day' fuellings, looming ever nearer, continued to weigh on his mind.

On 20 July the steering gear in the rescue tug *Weazel* broke down and she herself required rescue, being taken in tow by *King George V* whilst the defective parts were repaired in the flagship's workshops. The tow parted that evening and *Quiberon* was ordered to pick it up and to continue towing for the night. The steering gear was repaired the next day, but *Weazel*'s race was now run with the BPF at sea. Admiral Rawlings was not willing to have this 'stout-hearted pigmy' in the middle of the Pacific during the typhoon season, and on 22nd sent her back to Eniwetok, escorted by *Whimbrel*, signalling Rear Admiral Fisher 'we find we cannot spare the oil to go on towing our salvage tug about the fuelling area. I see no reason', Admiral Rawlings added, 'why she should not be relied on for mid-week work above Teddington during the summer.'

During the forenoon of 21st, Admiral Halsey, his Chief of Staff Rear Admiral Carney and other members of his staff came alongside *King George V* in the new US destroyer *Frank Knox* and transferred to the British flagship for a conference with Admiral Rawlings; Admiral Vian and Admiral Edelsten also attended. It was a welcome opportunity

---

[1] Matt. 25:7-8. 'Then all those virgins arose, and trimmed their lamps. And the foolish said unto the wise, Give us of your oil; for our lamps are gone out.' Admiral Halsey's reply (possibly apocryphal) was: Foolish – no. Wise – maybe. Virgins – no comment.

for the officers and men of *King George V* to meet their fleet commander, who at once endeared himself to the ship.

The main fuelling was completed on the evening of 21 July but some American groups were still fuelling until early on 23rd and Admiral Rawlings took the chance to top up destroyers from *King George V, Implacable* and *Formidable*. In the afternoon of 23rd the combined fleets set course for the next flying-off position.

On 24 July the American fleet began the final destruction of the surviving major units of the Imperial Japanese Navy, which were lying heavily camouflaged at the naval base of Kure in the Inland Sea. Most of the ships were reduced to the status of floating anti-aircraft batteries and all were totally immobilised by lack of fuel.

The attacks had emotional as well as operational motives. The Japanese must be left with no semblance of a fleet to interfere with OLYMPIC or CORONET, or to use as a bargaining counter in any post-war negotiations. Also, if Russia entered the war against Japan – and American strategic policy at Potsdam was working towards that very consummation – the line of communication to Russia by sea would run between Kamchatka and Hokkaido, a route so exposed that a few Japanese cruisers could dominate it. But lastly, and most important, the annihilation of the Japanese fleet would be the full and final revenge for Pearl Harbour.

Once again, the British fleet was not allowed to take part. This decision was uncharacteristic of Admiral Halsey, and unworthy of the man, but in another much-quoted passage of his memoirs he relates how he reluctantly yielded to his Chief of Staff's insistence that he should forestall a possible post-war claim by the British that they had delivered even a part of the final blow which demolished the Japanese fleet.[1] Admiral Halsey was convinced, apparently against his will, that an all-American attack would be best for American interests. But it was a churlish way to treat an ally who had actually declared war against Japan only a few hours after the attack on Pearl Harbour.

Like *Nagato*, the Japanese ships were lying in positions where they could not be attacked with torpedoes. The American dive-bombers, using variable time-fused bombs, made their attacks through heavy anti-aircraft fire and strong air opposition. They sank the battleship *Hyuga* and the cruiser *Tone*, and badly damaged several other ships including the aircraft carrier *Amagi* which later capsized and sank. The attacks were well co-ordinated with shore-based aircraft. Six hundred

---

[1] *Admiral Halsey's Story*, p. 265.

B-29s from the Marianas bombed aircraft industries and installations around Tokyo, whilst one hundred P.51 fighters from Iwo Jima attacked airfields at Nagoya.

The British Task Force 37 meanwhile attacked subsidiary targets: airfields in north-eastern Shikoku, and shipping in the Inland Sea and at Osaka, where there were some minor Japanese war vessels. For the first time the weather was good enough for the Avengers and fifteen strikes were flown during the day, five of them combined strikes, composed of Avengers, with Seafires, Fireflies and Corsairs. One Seafire and one Avenger were lost while attacking Tokushima, which was one of the most strongly defended airfields in southern Japan, with nearly two hundred anti-aircraft guns. The Seafires, now used confidently as ground-strafing aircraft, had developed techniques for attacks on airfields.

'As we were mostly over the sea, it was the inlets and the green terracing on the hillsides which we noticed first, and the utter peacefulness of it all, except when we went near an airfield, when the scene changed somewhat – I have never seen quite so much 20-mm. and 40-mm. flak! The general sensation of being over Japan was one of foreboding, deep fear. We had heard tales of what the locals did to airmen who got hacked down. We got "in and out" as quickly as we could. We used the "low – pul! up – low" pattern which is still done today, approaching the target area at zero feet all the way in.

'We kept below the radar echo height as long as possible so that we did not give warning of our approach. Near the target we split up and climbed to about 8,000 feet and approached in a sort of "scissors", with aircraft attacking from different angles. Thus we gave the gunners no time at all to get their fingers out before we were gone – *not* to return. Occasionally, when we had twelve or even sixteen aircraft on a raid (all Seafires on air-to-ground strafing) we would all cross over the middle of the enemy airfield. The main hazard was mid-air collision or ricochets from our own bullets (2×20 mm., plus 4×·303s). The angle of dive was as steep (45–60°) as possible (out of the sun if any) from 8,000 to 6,000 feet. We then made our exit at zero feet.'[1]

After Ramrods of Corsairs from *Formidable* and *Victorious* and of Seafires from *Implacable* had attacked airfields at Takamatsu and Komatsushima, the second combined strike of the day chanced upon

---

[1] Lt. Cdr. (now Cdr.) Michael Crosley, then CO of 880 Sq. Seafires in *Implacable*. Letter of 4.6.68.

a Japanese *Kobe* Class escort carrier in Shido Wan, a bay on the coast of Shikoku. This strike, led by the Air Group Leader Cdr. J. C. N. Shrubsole and the CO of 849 Sq. Lt. Cdr. A. J. Griffiths, originally consisted of twenty Avengers, eight Seafires, seven Fireflies and four Corsairs. The strike became separated in bad weather during the climb away from the fleet and only six Avengers, two Fireflies and two Corsairs and none of the Seafires found the target. Nevertheless they scored one direct hit on the carrier, for the loss of a Firefly of 1772 Sq. (*Indefatigable*). The same carrier was attacked again by Corsairs from *Formidable* and a third time by a strike of Avengers and Seafires from *Indefatigable*, who claimed two hits and a near-miss. Thus all four British carriers claimed a share in leaving the carrier, probably *Kaiyo*, with her back broken, and sinking (although *Kaiyo* was also claimed by the Americans). Two Japanese frigates CD No. 4 and CD No. 30 were also sunk and various minor vessels damaged; fifteen enemy aircraft were destroyed on the ground, and thirty damaged. TF 37's aircraft flew 416 sorties that day, for the loss of four aircraft. The combined fleets remained in the operating area for the night, point option being course 060, speed 6 knots.[1]

Strikes continued next day, 25th, against small shipping in the Inland Sea, and against Tokushima airfield. Three of the early strikes were abortive because of the weather and shortly after midday the weather rapidly deteriorated and further strikes were cancelled, after TF 37 had flown 155 offensive sorties in the day.

While the fleets were withdrawing towards the fuelling area, the enemy made a serious attempt to locate them. They began at 1735 with the usual herald – one high-flying unidentified aircraft, obviously searching for the fleet. It evaded the initial interception but was eventually shot down by fighters from TG 38.1 and crashed in flames inside TF 37's destroyer screen. *Tenacious* recovered two Japanese bodies. There were several reports of balloons, mysterious parachutes and 'window' over the fleet; and at 1900, just before landing on, one of *Formidable*'s Hellcats shot down a parachute with a small black box attached to it, which may have been a W/T homing beacon dropped by a snooper.

Some fifteen minutes earlier, the fleet fighter direction officer Captain

---

[1] Point option: an ingenious and successful method of keeping a very large fleet together. An imaginary point moved across the chart at a known course and speed. Ships and task groups could manoeuvre individually at will, provided in general they kept station on point option's course and speed.

E. D. G. Lewin in *Formidable* had noticed on the radar screens a small group of bogeys to the north-east, range ninety-four miles, but closing the fleet. The last daylight CAPS were landing on and Task Force 37 had only four dusk patrol Hellcats from *Formidable* in the air at the time. Despite the scepticism of TG 38.1's direction officers, the Hellcats were directed on to the intruders and intercepted them at 20,000 feet, thirty miles from the fleet. They were four Grace[1] bombers, armed with torpedoes. The Hellcats shot down three and damaged the fourth, which escaped. By now thoroughly convinced, TG 38.1 launched fighters from the night carrier *Bonne Homme Richard* which shot down one of another larger group of the enemy who had worked round to the north of the fleet and were apparently orbiting over the TOMCAT picket. The group was broken up by gunfire from the picket destroyers. A third group turned away at sixty-five miles and made no attack. Enemy air opposition was so light in July and August that this was one of the only two British interception incidents during the entire operation.

Because of changes in the operational programme, the replenishment of 26 July took place seven hundred miles from the position originally planned. Nevertheless, Rear Admiral Fisher had succeeded in placing his faithful little band of peripatetic oilers, escort carriers and miscellaneous support vessels[2] in the right place at more or less the right time. There were four tankers in the party – one more than par – but they brought with them the usual crop of troubles. Only two, *Wave Emperor* and *Cedardale*, had fuelled the fleet before. *Carelia* had been hurriedly converted at Sydney for abeam oiling only, and was now making her nervous début as a fleet tanker. *Eaglesdale* had been repaired in forty-eight hours at Manus, after arriving from Colombo with her speed down to $7\frac{1}{2}$ knots because of engine defects and a foul bottom; she could only fuel ships from one side, and from one hose astern. However, Admiral Rawlings believed that past experience bore out the wisdom of not looking gift-horses in the mouth, and fuelling began at 0900.

Fuelling was not the only problem. The British fleet was short of spare parts and stores of all kinds, and especially radio and radar components. The fleet approached the replenishment area in an atmosphere reminiscent of a 'Bring and Buy Sale'; each ship signalled its most urgent needs and the resulting 'shopping list' was contained

---

[1] Grace: Aichi single-engined torpedo-bomber.

[2] Tankers *Cedardale*, *Carelia*, *Wave Emperor*, *Eaglesdale*; VISS *Glenartney*; Armament Store Issuing Ship (ASIS) *Robert Maersk*; CVEs *Speaker*, *Ruler*, *Striker*; destroyers *Napier*, *Nizam*, *Nepal; Pheasant*, *Crane*, *Redpole*; frigates *Parret* and *Plym*; minesweepers *Whyalla*, *Pirie*, *Launceston*.

in a general signal for what Captain Oliver-Bellasis in *Euryalus* very aptly called 'The Task Force 37 Opportunity Market'. Though pruned of everything but essentials, the 'Market' signal was still a lengthy one. During replenishment periods 'duty picket boat' destroyers were detailed to steam around the fleet and the logistics support group delivering and collecting personnel, staff officers, replacement aircrew, war correspondents, stores, mail and official correspondence. There was also a 'Wells Fargo' destroyer mail service between Task Force 37 and the nearest American Task Group. Going alongside another ship was now a commonplace evolution; between leaving Manus and arriving in Tokyo Bay, *King George V* had ships alongside her at sea on 238 occasions. The destroyer *Quality* went alongside other ships on ninety-five occasions. Other destroyers might well have surpassed that figure.

While replenishing, the fleet learned that the Labour Party had won a landslide victory in the elections at home, the first General Election for ten years. The fruits of pre-war Tory policies had at last been gathered in and not even the presence of Churchill could save the Conservative Party from an electoral disaster. The fleet received the news with mixed feelings. Rightly or wrongly, there was a belief on the messdecks that a Labour Government would 'get the boys home' more quickly after the war was over. Yet there is evidence that many men in the fleet had not appreciated that a change of government also meant a change of Prime Minister. The news of Mr Winston Churchill's departure from 10 Downing Street was a great shock. (When Admiral Rawlings was asked by his personal staff which politician would get his vote, he replied characteristically: 'I'll vote for the least bloody one.')

On 27 July *King George V* embarked ninety-four 14-inch shells and 155 cordite cases from the ammunition ship *Robert Maersk*, having exercised the evolution with empty cases the previous day. The evolution was successful, although *Robert Maersk* was dwarfed by the battleship and her single magnetic compass deviated as much as ten or fifteen degrees because of the heavy ship's presence alongside her. Later the idea was conceived in *King George V* of passing across to *Robert Maersk* a gyro strip repeater on a length of cable. Unfortunately the repeater, like all repeaters, made a faintly perceptible ticking noise. Watched by anxious eyes in the flagship, *Robert Maersk*'s Danish master picked up the foreign object, shook it suspiciously, applied it to his ear, and then firmly put it from him. *Robert Maersk* continued to steer by magnetic.

It was clear that the British tankers could not fuel the whole fleet in the time available and Admiral Rawlings had to ask for American help again. Admiral Halsey agreed at once, and *Newfoundland* and *Achilles* fuelled from the American oiling group TU 30.18.1. 'This brought the number of our unwise virgins to date up to the official five and I tried hard to make myself believe that there would be no further backsliders, but the prospect of the "One day" oiling the following week was coming disturbingly close.'

After fuelling had finished on 27th the Canadian cruiser *Uganda* sailed for Esquimault, via Eniwetok and Pearl Harbour, having been relieved by *Argonaut*.[1] *Striker* and *Nepal* were sailed for Manus, closing Guam en route to fly in press material. Arrangements for transmitting press material had marginally improved since ICEBERG. The normal method was for press copy to be sent back in returning ships of the Logistic Support Group. An attempt was made (in spite of the misgivings of the American operational commanders) to transmit to British stations direct from the operational area. Due to technical difficulties, transmission could not begin until 1700 and all wireless transmission was shut down by order of Commander 3rd Fleet at 1900. In those two hours each day, and by other methods, enough information was passed to keep the British public at home informed – but by no means enough to satisfy individual newspaper editors.

On 28 July the Third Fleet completed the destruction of the Imperial Japanese Navy. By the end of the day the Japanese fleet had virtually ceased to exist. The battleships *Ise* and *Haruna*, the heavy cruiser *Aoba*, the light cruiser *Oyoda* (flagship of the C-in-C Combined Naval Forces), the old heavy cruisers *Iwate* and *Izumo*, and many other lesser units were sunk, and many damaged. The same day seventy-nine B-24 Liberators of the Far Eastern Air Force made an unsolicited and unco-ordinated attack on the Japanese fleet which was 'a mission understandable only as competition with the Third Fleet'.[2] The Liberators achieved four hits on *Aoba*, for the loss of two bombers and flak damage to fourteen more. The Third Fleet lost twenty-seven aircraft.

For the third time the British Fleet was excluded, and attacked instead aircraft and airfields at Akashi, Fukuyama and Sato, shipyards at Harima and Habu, and shipping in the Inland Sea. 260 offensive sorties

---

[1] It was reported that *Uganda*'s return home was a consequence of the 'non-volunteering act'. As a result, her officers and ship's company were not cordially received by the US Navy at Eniwetok and Pearl Harbour.

[2] *The Army Air Forces in World War Two*, Volume V, p. 698.

were flown, in ten individual and four combined strikes. For once there was strong enemy airborne reaction and the fleet lost eight aircraft to flak, or in combat.

At the end of the day Admiral Halsey signalled: 'Mark well the 28 July. To Dumbos and Lifeguard, to CAP and men of the surface team, to the valiant British force on the right flank, well done. For the great flying fighters who fought it out over Japan to a smashing victory I have no words that I can add to the glory of the factual record they wrote with their courage, their blood and lives.' 'A smashing victory' was perhaps overstating the case, but Admiral Rawlings noted: 'A great deal seemed to have happened since twelve days ago when the two Fleets passed the first milestone together.'

No air strikes were planned for 29th and the fleets withdrew eastward in the forenoon. At 0930 *King George V*, with *Urania*, *Undine* and *Ulysses* were detached from the fleet to form TU 37.1.2 and join an American bombardment group (TU 34.8.1) under Rear Admiral J. F. Shafroth, USN, flying his flag in the battleship *South Dakota*, for a bombardment of the industrial town and area of Hammamatsu, on the south-east coast of Honshu.

While the bombarding force were approaching the coast in darkness, *Urania* and *Ulysses* collided in thick fog. *Urania* was only superficially damaged but *Ulysses* reported that she had stopped and, later, that she could proceed only at slow speed. *Urania* was ordered to escort *Ulysses* back to the rendezvous area while Rear Admiral Shafroth generously and promptly offered two of his own destroyers. However, *Ulysses* then reported that her damage was not as serious as was first thought and she was able to proceed.

King George V's assigned target was the innocently named Japanese Musical Instrument Company's Plant No 2, which was actually manufacturing aircraft propellers. This factory and others in that area had recently been heavily bombed by B-29s and production had dropped to 3% of its peak. But production could be resumed, and the factory was still a worthwhile target.

The fog dispersed and the sky cleared to give a brilliant moonlit night. *King George V* fixed her position accurately offshore with a transit bearing between the centre of the target area and Kakezuka lighthouse, east of Hammamatsu, and opened fire at 2319, range 20,075 yards. The spotting aircraft provided by the Americans reported a good opening salvo. One of *King George V*'s officers who was in the Operations Room during the bombardment recalls the moment:

'My job was to ensure that the spotting aircraft, an American Black Widow, was in the correct position over the target before we opened fire and that communications with the aircraft were good. When we fired the first salvo it seemed, as it always does, hours before the fall-of-shot gong rang and long before that Admiral Rawlings was on the telephone waiting to get a report from the spotting aircraft. I warned the pilot that the first salvo was due to arrive, and he almost immediately came back with: "Geezus – smack on the kisser!" '[1]

King George V bombarded for thirty-seven minutes, firing 265 rounds of 14-inch shells. Observers in the flagship could soon see the target area on fire and one of the ship's midshipmen recorded in his journal: 'We could see the target well and truly alight, so much so that it was possible to see the tops of buildings among the flames, as well as surrounding trees.'[2] After a bright start, *King George V*'s shooting deteriorated (possibly because of spotting errors by that same genial Black Widow pilot). Of 179 discovered hits, only seven were on the Japanese Musical Instrument Plant No 2.[3] The American shooting, for the most part, was not a great deal better (*Massachusetts* put nine out of 109 discovered hits on Plant No. 1).

The bombarding group withdrew at 0030' on 30 July. Several bogies were reported but there was no opposition, in the air or from shore batteries. *Undine* had two short engagements, firing by radar, with groups of small craft. These were probably fishing vessels, but may have been suicide craft. *King George V* and her destroyers were detached to rejoin TF 37 at 0430.

The bombardment put the Imperial Government Railway Locomotive Works in Hammamatsu, already heavily bombed from the air, out of action for nearly three months. Two other industrial plants in the area had virtually ceased production before the bombardment. A third was not hit at all. The Tenryu and Bentenjima bridges, carrying the main Tokaido Railway line, also escaped; if they had been destroyed, most of the industry in the Nagoya and Tokyo areas would have come to a halt.

The direct effects of the bombardment were therefore not great. Admiral McCain seemed to have a point when he claimed that the aircraft flying CAPs for the battleships that night could have done more

---

[1] Mr Tom Dyke (ex. Lt. Cdr. RNVR). Letter of 14.8.67.

[2] Mr Derek Parfect (then Midshipman RNVR). Journal for 29.7.45.

[3] *Ships' Bombardments of Japan 1945*, 'Comments and Data of Effectiveness of Ammunition and Accuracy of Firing', Enclosure J, Part IV, Figure 4.

damage to the targets than the battleships themselves. But the bombardment's main effect was more subtle, on enemy civilian morale. Admiral Rawlings believed that naval bombardments had a tremendous effect on the enemy 'who must feel there is no knowing when the next one will come', and post-war interrogations proved that he was right. People of cities which had suffered both admitted they were more afraid of heavy naval bombardment than of aerial high-explosive or incendiary bombing. Air raids were normally heralded by warnings, and stopped when the aircraft flew away. But nobody knew when a bombardment would begin or how long it would last; the battleships might keep it up for hours. Absenteeism in labour forces almost always increased after a bombardment. At Hitachi, bombarded on 17 July, the Yamate Plant stopped production completely for a month because of persistent absenteeism, although only four shells had actually fallen inside the works perimeter. At the Hitachi copper refineries, the output of copper ore after the bombardment dropped sensationally from 40,000 to barely 1,500 tons a month; the miners, reasonably enough, refused to go down into the mines for fear that another bombardment might damage the pumping machinery and flood the mine shafts. However, at two factories, one of them the Wanishi Iron Works, there was a kind of 'London Blitz' spirit; morale actually rose after a bombardment and extra efforts were made to increase production.

Task Force 37's targets for 30 July were airfields in south-western Honshu and shipping at Maizuru and Nagoya Bay. The first combined strike found its targets weathered in, and dropped its bombs by radar. The second sank the frigate *Okinawa* at Maizuru (also claimed by the Americans). 336 sorties were flown: besides *Okinawa*, a large freighter and a transport and several minor vessels were sunk; one *Teretsuki* Class and four other destroyers, four escorts and a freighter were damaged. Six enemy aircraft were destroyed and six damaged. Two Seafires and a Corsair, with their pilots, were lost to flak over their targets.

Implacable, with more aircraft embarked than the other carriers and with a particularly energetic air group, regularly flew the most sorties and consequently ran the risk of having some of her aircraft still in the air after the rest had been recovered. It was not always easy for her to synchronise her landing and launching cycles with the rest of the squadron. On 30 July, this led to an embarrassing situation. Late that afternoon, visibility deteriorated in patches of mist and, in some places, widespread fog; the other carriers had recovered their aircraft, but

Implacable still had her last twelve Seafires airborne and, with the wind in the west, had to steam towards the enemy coast to land them on. It was high time the Task Force retired for the night, but grimly ignoring urgent signals from Admiral Vian, Captain Hughes Hallett stood on towards the Japanese coastline. When the last Seafire had been recovered, *Implacable* was less than sixty miles offshore, in the opening of Tokyo Bay.

'I kept saying to my captain, You must not acknowledge this signal. Fog had come in behind us and I knew it was pretty widespread. Those Seafires, twelve of them, were getting very low on gas. If we'd done the turn, gone back into the fog, out the other side and then turned into the wind, they would have been out of gas. They would have landed up in the sea. I didn't mind the aircraft so much, but how many pilots do you pick up after that sort of thing? The Seafire wasn't a great ditcher. So we kept on and on, and these awful rude signals were coming in. We landed on the Seafires, but Vian never forgave me for that.'[1]

The rest of the Task Force had had to stay whilst *Implacable* sortied into the fog of Tokyo Bay, and there were repercussions for Admiral Vian:

'The British Liaison Officer accommodated in the US Fleet Flagship wrote that the BPF had managed to become separated by over one hundred miles from the US Fleet owing to the inexperience of our Carrier Admiral. This hurt.'[2]

It was a day for embarrassments: that morning *Napier* had reported bubbles and water disturbance outside the screen and, with *Wrangler*, formed a hunter-killer group to investigate. After forty minutes *Napier* somewhat sheepishly signalled that the contact was 'a friendly whale', and the group rejoined.

In the evening while the fleet was retiring, a 'bogey' was detected at eighty miles, closing rapidly from the north. Two Corsairs from *Victorious* intercepted after eighteen minutes and shot down a Dinah.

There was a tight fuelling schedule of only twenty-four hours planned for the next day and so, when the last aircraft had been recovered, Admiral Rawlings requested permission for Task Force 37 to disengage independently and make for the fuelling rendezvous. The

---

[1] Commander (now Admiral Sir Charles) Evans. Conversation of 16.7.68.
[2] *Action This Day*, p. 204.

Logistic Support Group[1] were located by search aircraft early on 31st, and fuelling began at 1000.

The fuelling programme was disrupted almost at once, when it was discovered that the new tanker *Olna* was not ready to pump aviation fuel abeam and *Wave King* was 750 tons of aviation fuel short, having sailed from Sydney in haste. *Wave King*'s new British hoses burst whenever full pressure was put on, and her gear generally was not up to its work. As a last straw, she had been loaded with a disproportionate amount of diesel fuel, instead of boiler furnace fuel. However, several ships were content to accept diesel fuel; it burned well in the furnaces, and it was much better than nothing.

There was a gigantic typhoon swell running, at right angles to the wind, and as the tankers became lighter they began to roll and yaw prodigiously, at times twenty or thirty degrees to either side of their course, while pitching to such an extent that they were showing first the whole of their stem and fore-foot and then their propellers clear of the water. *King George V* embarked a further eighty shells and sixty-four cordite cases from *Robert Maersk* – a valiant effort on *Robert Maersk*'s part, for her ship's company had the greatest difficulty in controlling the heavy weights in the huge swell. To ammunition and refuel at all, the fleet had to keep head to the swell and this unfortunately tended to open the distance to the next American group. TBS communications had to be maintained, and *Achilles* and *Ruler* were stationed as links to relay TBS messages to and from the rest of the Third Fleet. By evening the nearest American group was nearly fifty miles away. *Ruler*, *Achilles*, *Newfoundland* and *Argonaut* were all strung out in a line, acting as TBS links.

The typhoon had passed to the west of Okinawa and into the Sea of Japan and was approaching the China coast along the latitude of 31°N. There was a danger that the storm centre might swing towards the fleet fuelling area but it was later reported heading NNW and clearing the fleet. However, to give the storm as wide a berth as possible, Admiral Halsey ordered all groups to alter to the south at midnight.

The fleets marked time, replenishing and refuelling for the next two days, in a position about two hundred miles west of Iwo Jima. *Formid-*

---

[1] Tankers *Wave Governor, Carelia, Olna, Wave King*; VSIS *Glenartney*; ASIS *Robert Maersk* and *Corinda*; Radar maintenance ship *Arbutus*; CVEs *Chaser, Speaker, Ruler*; *Pheasant, Redpole, Crane*; *Queenborough*; frigates *Odzani, Derg*; *Norman*; *Woodcock*; *Pirie*.

able embarked bombs from *Robert Maersk,* and *Victorious* from *Corinda.* Several ships took on fresh provisions from *Glenartney* – one of the most successful ships in the Fleet Train.

Meanwhile, on the night of 29–30 July, the heavy cruiser *Indianapolis,* on her way to Leyte having delivered material for the atomic bomb to Tinian, was torpedoed by the Japanese submarine I.58. She was unescorted and sank so quickly that no distress message was sent. Her absence was not noticed until she had been overdue at Leyte for more than two days; her survivors were sighted by accident by a patrolling aircraft. Only 318 of her ship's company of nearly 1,200 were picked up. She was the last major Allied warship to be sunk in World War Two.

Fuelling was completed on 2 August and two of the tankers detached to reload. For a short time Admiral Rawlings had the comfortable feeling that the fuel situation was in hand. But at 2000 a signal from Admiral Halsey arrived like a bomb-shell: the next strike would be on 5th, and all ships were to top up destroyers during daylight on 3rd.

This meant that Task Force 37 would have to make do with the fuel already embarked until the next fuelling, which would not be until 8 August. It simply was not possible. In the original programme there had been a sporting chance that TF 37 would contrive to take in enough fuel in one day to keep going but now for the first time there was a possibility that TF 37 would have to miss one day's strike. Rawlings signalled the news to the fleet, urging them to exercise the utmost fuel economy and adding cheerfully that in any case, the tankers on 8th did not hold enough to fill up the fleet.

That night, the nearest American group was seventy miles away; *Argonaut, Newfoundland, Grenville, Black Prince* and *Gambia* were all acting as TBS links. After some 'conservative calculations' it was estimated that the destroyers except 'T' Class would reach the next fuelling position with a comfortable 8 tons in hand. 'T' Class would be burning diesel fuel. *Napier* would be burning cordite.

Admiral Rawlings and his staff were racked by the problem of somehow topping up destroyers with fuel, while still keeping reasonable station with the American fleet. At dawn on 4 August *King George V, Achilles, Newfoundland,* and *Gambia* began furiously fuelling destroyers. By 1015 eight destroyers had been fuelled and a 'fuel remaining' balance struck between the cruisers and destroyers.

At 1330 another signal from Halsey changed the situation yet again. The next strike days would be 8 and 9 August and the fleets would refuel on 6th; 'a disturbing problem had been resolved for this occasion'.

Admiral Halsey had been ordered to withdraw from the operational area because of an imminent 'Special Operation'. This was, of course, the culmination of the Manhattan Project – the first atomic bomb, to be dropped on Hiroshima. Thus, ironically, the British fleet's problems had been temporarily resolved by the atomic bomb. But it was a strange circumstance that Admiral Rawlings, commanding his country's largest fleet, at sea off a hostile coast, at a time when the world was about to enter the nuclear age, should be put in such a position that his chief preoccupation was the 'fuel remaining' reports for three flotillas of destroyers.

Ruler normally provided CAPs over the replenishment area, so that by 5 August the fleet carrier air groups had not flown except on domestic errands for nearly a week. Flying training was therefore carried out that forenoon. The air groups were in a much more robust state of health, mentally and physically, than they had been in ICEBERG. Jaded pilots had been relieved before the operations – which they had not been before ICEBERG – and aircrews now had the satisfaction of knowing they were attacking the Japanese on their home ground. There was a wide and invigorating choice of targets, a great contrast to what one carrier captain called 'the long, drawn-out, stale and arid target features of the Sakishima Gunto'. There had been longer periods of recuperation between strike days, and much shorter periods of waiting 'at readiness' on strike days. Some squadrons were heavily diluted with inexperienced pilots, indeed a common factor of all reminiscences of the BPF is the extreme youth of the aircrews. *Implacable*'s Seafire squadrons included many very young men on their first operational tour and of *Victorious'* forty-four Corsair pilots on leaving Sydney, eleven had completed only a dozen previous deck landings and fifteen had less than 150 hours solo flying on type. Nevertheless, the morale of the air groups was generally magnificent and the whole carrier squadron had 'raised its game' for the occasion. The fighters flew more sorties in eight strike days off Japan than in the entire twenty-four days striking at the Sakishima Gunto, whilst the Avengers' flying effort was 30% greater, even though they were not employed at all on the first two strike days in July. Perhaps the greatest achievement was the manner in which *Indefatigable* and *Implacable* overcame their Seafires' limitations and raised the effectiveness of the Seafire as a fleet fighter by more than threefold, compared with ICEBERG. In the July–August operations Seafires flew twice as many sorties and nearly three times as many hours/aircraft/strike day as in March and April, and for the first time by a British fleet were used consistently in offensive sorties over enemy territory, using overload tanks at long ranges. Seafires flew 1,085 sorties in July and August including 451 strike escort or ground-strafing sorties over Japan. Towards the end, even Admiral Vian softened towards the Seafire.

The fleet met the Logistic Support Group[1] on 6 August and fuelling continued from dawn until evening. Destroyers were topped up the next day.

On 7 August the fleet heard the news of the bomb dropped on Hiroshima. Only a few men in the Pacific theatre knew the true nature of the weapon, but there appear to have been some shrewd guesses in the fleet. Admiral Rawlings records that there was much speculation and considerable dissertations by all and sundry on the theory of atomic energy. For the first time, the men of the fleet lifted their heads from the war and sniffed at the first hint of peace. The lack of enemy air opposition over Japan may have given the aircrews the impression that all was nearly over, but the rest still believed they were faced by a long and hard war. The Japanese had resisted beyond the point of reason on the Central Pacific islands and on Okinawa. What would they do on their own homeland? But now, there was just a chance the war might soon be over.

That evening, when the fleets were on passage to the next flying-off position, *Achilles* detected radar echoes of 'skunks'[2] seventy-five miles to the west. Admiral Halsey sent a force of cruisers and destroyers to engage them but the 'contacts' were mythical, and probably due to anomalous propagation.

It had been suggested that Task Force 37 strike at Hokkaido on 8 and 9 August, to cover TF 38's simultaneous strikes on the Tokyo plain, and Cdr. Le Fanu had transferred to *King George V* on 4th to discuss plans with Admiral Rawlings, who had approved the idea. However, in the meantime, General MacArthur had asked that the next strikes by TF 38 should be at northern Honshu and Hokkaido, where the Japanese were believed to be massing their aircraft.

Dawn on 8 August was foggy and, when the weather closed in further, strikes were cancelled. No CAPs were flown off. Two high-flying enemy aircraft approached the fleet but on orders from Admiral Halsey no ship opened fire and no attempt was made to intercept. The fog con-

---

[1] Tankers *Olna, Wave King, Dingledale, San Amado*; VSIS *Glenartney, Fort Wrangell*; CVEs *Arbiter, Chaser, Ruler*; *Norman, Nizam*; *Pheasant, Crane*, frigate *Barle*; minesweepers *Ballarat* and *Burnie*; hospital ship *Tjitjalengka*.

[2] 'Skunk': unidentified surface ship radar contact.

cealed the fleets and the aircraft flew off to the north, probably without detecting the ships below.

At 0345 on 9 August *Newfoundland* (Flag of Rear Admiral Brind) with *Gambia, Terpsichore, Tenacious* and *Termagant*, formed TU 37.1.8 and joined an American bombarding group TU 34.8.1 commanded by Rear Admiral Shafroth, for a bombardment of the coastal town of Kamaishi, in northern Honshu. The two forces met at 0630, Brind signalling to Shafroth that he hoped he would regard his force as part of his own.

The two forces approached the enemy coast at 22 knots in single line ahead, the British cruisers leading, and deployed for bombardment on a course of 186° at 1145. Bombardment began at 1253 and continued for nearly two hours, until 1447. The force made four bombarding runs, two to the south and two to the north, firing at a mean range of 14,000 yards, but on one occasion closing to within two miles of the coast. The US destroyers steamed off the harbour of Kamaishi to prevent small craft attacking the force.

Hits were scored on warehouses, oil storage tanks, harbour installations and shipping. Spotting aircraft were provided by the US battleships and cruisers and those provided for the British force by *South Dakota* and *Indiana*, in Brind's words, 'performed admirably'. *Newfoundland* fired a total of 329 rounds, *Gambia* 404. The British destroyers were detached to attack targets of opportunity. The opportunities, other than Japan, Brind observed, were not obvious. *Terpsichore* shelled and hit a prominent building on a hill, described as 'the Governor's summer palace', while *Termagant* claimed that she had blocked a coastal road ahead of a pedal cyclist, causing him to swerve into a ditch.

There was some anti-aircraft fire from batteries around Kamaishi and several bogeys were detected as the force retired. They were driven off by the bombarding force – this being the only occasion when any British ships were able to practise their new AA defence methods. One Judy was later reported shot down. The forces withdrew at 1900, parted company at 2300 and Brind's force rejoined the fleet.

Meanwhile, on 9 August, the Task Force air groups swung into action for their first strikes for nearly ten days. It was one of the most intensive and successful day's flying in the BPF's history. Flying began at 0410 and continued through the day; ten individual and four combined strikes were launched and a total of 407 offensive, CAP and photo-reconnaissance sorties flown. Targets were those which should have been attacked the previous day: airfields at Shiogama, Matsushima, Kessenuma, Yamada, Hachinoe and Koriyama were bombed and strafed and rocketed, leaving forty-two enemy aircraft destroyed and twenty-two damaged. Shipping was also attacked, at Onagawa Wan, Kessenuma and Okotsu: two destroyers, an old destroyer, a submarine chaser and various small coasters, junks and launches were sunk, and two other destroyers, a torpedo boat and some small craft probably sunk. Another destroyer, two escort vessels and many small craft were damaged.

Aircrew losses were the heaviest of any day in the operations. Two of *Implacable*'s casualties could only be described as self-inflicted. One Seafire of the first Seafire strike of the day was hit by flak over Matsushima airfield and ditched in the sea close inshore. Japanese picket boats and junks at once put out to capture the pilot, who could be seen floating in his dinghy. They were driven off and set on fire by other Seafires of the strike who remained overhead until the arrival of Hellcats from the Lifeguard submarine CAP. Later in the day, a second Seafire was hit over Matsushima and ditched near the same position as the first. Again, two Seafires from the strike, piloted by S/Lt. P. M. E. Tillett, RNVR, of 801 Sq. and S/Lt. W. H. Squires, RNVR, of 880 Sq., remained on guard overhead. Both outstayed their fuel capacity, lost their way returning to the fleet, and were forced to bale out. Neither was picked up. Meanwhile the two ditched Seafire pilots were recovered close inshore by a US Dumbo aircraft. Thus, by a bitter irony, the two would-be Good Samaritans were lost, whilst their neighbours who fell among thieves were saved.

Victorious had a magnificent day, flying sixty-three offensive Corsair and nineteen Avenger sorties. The total flying time of 378 hours was a ship's record for a single day's operational flying. It was achieved at the cost of S/Lt. S. Newton, RNVR, of 1836 Sq., whose Corsair was last seen over Koriyama airfield, and S/Lt. N. L. Wright, RNVR, of 849 Sq. whose Avenger was badly damaged by flak at Matsushima. Wright attempted a forced landing on the sea, but his wheels were lowered, and the aircraft capsized. The air gunner was picked up by a nearby TOMCAT destroyer, but Wright was killed.

Formidable lost two Corsair pilots. One died in a deck landing crash, his Corsair hitting the round-down while returning from a bombing attack on ships in Onagawa Wan. The other was the leader of that strike, the Senior Pilot of 1841 Sq., and a notable personality in *Formidable*'s air group, Lt. Robert Hampton Gray, RCNVR.

'Hammy' Gray was one of the most aggressive and skilful pilots in the fleet. He had taken part in the attacks on *Tirpitz* in August 1944 and had just won the DSC for his service in ICEBERG. On 12 November 1945 he was posthumously awarded the Victoria Cross for the action in which he lost his life on 9 August, which is best described in the citation: 'For great valour in leading from the aircraft carrier *Formidable* an attack on a Japanese destroyer in Onagawa Wan, in the Japanese Island of Honshu, on 9 August, 1945. In the face of fire from shore batteries and a heavy concentration of fire from some five warships, Lieutenant Gray pressed home his attack, flying very low in order to ensure success. Although he was hit and his aircraft was in flames, he obtained at least one direct hit, sinking the destroyer. Lieutenant Gray has consistently shown a brilliant fighting spirit and most inspiring leadership.' His squadron commander, who knew him well, remembers him warmly:

'He had blond hair – straight and fine – with a fresh boyish complexion. Medium height, and inclined to be plump, with a somewhat rolling gait. I never saw him hurry! His personality can only be described as delightful. He was tremendously warm-hearted, always cheerful and even-tempered – rather easy going, but all these qualities endeared him to everyone. He was modest – not at all the "here's to the next man to die" type. He always enjoyed a party, but never drank too much. He liked to tell us stories of home town life in Nelson B.C. in his mild British Columbian accent, and was unmercifully ribbed about that hick town in the west.'

'[During the *Tirpitz* raid] two or three *Narvik* Class destroyers were anchored at the end of Kaa Fjiord in such a position that they could join in the umbrella or "box" barrage over *Tirpitz*. Hammy's flight was detailed to attack these. We all mounted camera guns and immediately on return to *Formidable* these films were developed and later shown in the Captain's dining room – converted to operations room.

'I shall never forget Hammy's comments when his first film came up, to show him opening fire at the bridge at fairly long range. Then a series of black flashes (it was a negative film) appeared from the AA guns fore and aft. His aim shifted aft and held until, at point blank range flying right down the barrels, only the after guns and a huge black flash filled the screen.

'Hammy turned round to the operator and said "Hey, are you sure you haven't got my film mixed up with someone else's? This is really

Y

giving me the twitch – I shall have to have a very serious talk with that pilot." When assured that it really was his film "Well, all I can say is they make them mighty dumb in Nelson B.C."

'Of course, he went up next day and did exactly the same. Perhaps this is where he acquired his dislike for enemy destroyers, which ended so tragically in Onagawa Wan a year later.

'. . . There were three Ramrods on 9th August. I did the first with 12 aircraft and Hammy the second with 8 aircraft. The first atom bomb had been dropped on 6th and it was very obvious that the end was near. The Captain asked me to "take it easy" and not to take undesirable risks. I passed these instructions to my flight COs and pilots.

'Our orders were to do a round of the airfields (making one pass only at each) to do what damage we could and keep the kamikazes grounded. Hammy's flight happened to pass over Onagawa on their way in and were fired at by this destroyer (which was camouflaged and close inshore) and batteries surrounding it. Several of the Corsairs – but not all – carried a 1000 lb bomb and we always liked to dispose of this as early as possible because it affected the performance for strafing, etc., so Hammy decided that this would be a most suitable target. It has always seemed such a terrible shame to me that this quite unexpected chance should have occurred when the war was virtually over.

'Of course, we did not know it at the time but almost at that moment the second atomic bomb was being dropped on Nagasaki. On the 10th, the final day of operations, we lost another of my best pilots, Alan Maitland [S/Lt. L. A. Maitland, RNVR] making a second strafing pass at one of the airfields – it was a very sad end of the war for us.'[1]

Gray's VC was in a sense the saddest and certainly one of the least-known of the war. The war was so nearly over; the cause for which he gave his life was already won. The award was so little celebrated that nearly a quarter of a century later there were men who had served in the BPF still quite unaware that a member of the fleet had won the Victoria Cross.

Admiral McCain had been ordered not to send air strikes into the Tokyo area but unfortunately, because of the weather, he had to launch aircraft from a position south of a bank of thick fog, which was within range of suicide bombers from the Tokyo airfields. The southerly radar picket destroyers came under almost continual attack throughout the day until, inevitably, one was hit; in the afternoon the US destroyer

[1] R. L. Bigg-Wither (ex-Lt. Cdr. RNVR). Letters of 14.2.69, and 26.2.69.

Borie was badly damaged by a suicider, with forty-nine killed and thirty-four wounded. She was the only Allied ship to be seriously damaged during the July–August operations. Meanwhile, the American CAP shot down several would-be suiciders.

In the midst of the activity of 9th the news was received that Russia had at last declared war on Japan, and that a second atomic bomb had been dropped, on the city of Nagasaki, in Kyushu. This time there could be no holding speculation and rumour in the fleet. Wild fabrications and educated guesses, known in the vernacular as 'buzzes', swept through every ship. Surely, now the war was almost over. Whatever post-war misgivings and heart-searching there may have been, at the time the fleet welcomed the atomic bomb whole-heartedly, as a means of bringing the war to a quick end.

But while the men of the fleet were wondering and rejoicing, one of their fellow servicemen was working as a prisoner-of-war in Nagasaki dockyard only two miles from the ground zero of the explosion:

'I can't make you understand how bright that flash was. It was a blue flash and had a ringing sound. It went through you just like the shock you get from an electric battery. It was terribly hot as well, just like solid heat coming at you. We watched the light changing to a yellow glow. It was like sunlight coming from half a dozen suns instead of one, and there were yellow rainbows following each other rippling up above where the bomb had dropped, and right through the centre there was this column of smoke going up. It was thin at first, changing colours from black to brown, and from brown to white. We watched it forming a mushroom shape. . . .'[1]

To support the Russian offensive, Nimitz ordered the Third Fleet to carry on striking at Japan until 13 August, and possibly after that. Admiral Halsey signalled to the combined fleets that strikes against targets in northern Honshu and Hokkaido on 10 August would proceed as planned, the fleet would fuel on 11th, and strike again on 12th and 13th. He asked Rawlings if his force would be able to take part.

The answer to that, as Admiral Rawlings said, was not easy to give. The proposed targets lay miles to the north and Task Force 37 was to have withdrawn after the strikes of 10th, to replenish and prepare in Sydney for their part in the early stages of OLYMPIC. Fleet train movements, including the tankers', were already under way to carry out this

---

[1] Leading Seaman Thomas H. Evans. Interview with Dick Gregson of the BBC, 11.12.45.

programme. The arrangements could not be changed at a moment's notice. The refitting and replenishing programme in Sydney had been closely planned, and there was no time margin.

However, Admiral Rawlings as always contrived to do a little more. He decided that the British fleet must do its utmost to sustain an all-out effort at this critical time, even if it meant reduced effort for the opening days of OLYMPIC. The Americans had no fuel to spare and Admiral Rawlings knew that, at best, his fleet's contribution could only be small. He replied to Halsey that while the British fleet could not stay the whole course at full strength, he aimed at fielding a full team on 12 August, after which the carriers would have to return to Sydney, but he hoped to keep *King George V* and three 6-inch cruisers for the bombardment planned for 13th – 'provided we can nestle under your CAP'. Even to stay for the bombardment might mean that some of the screening destroyers only reached Manus under tow, but Admiral Rawlings saw no objection to that. At the same time, Admiral Rawlings informed Admiral Fraser at Guam of the revised programme, ending with the eternal heart-cry of the BPF: 'No more oil.' It was a bitter moment for Bernard Rawlings.

Admiral Rawlings also signalled Fisher at Manus to alter his tanker movements to provide for the fuelling on 11th. This was taking risks with the tankers to be available for OLYMPIC. But Admiral Rawlings had made up his mind.

The 10 August was another successful day, with 372 sorties flown, and strikes at shipping at Okkaichi and Onagawa Wan, and airfields at Masuda, Matsushima and Koriyama. The Japanese anti-aircraft gunners were effective to the last; a Corsair, an Avenger and two Fireflies were all lost from one combined strike at Koriyama. The day's score was sixteen enemy aircraft destroyed and thirty-one damaged; two destroyers, two escort vessels, various other ships, locomotives, rolling stock and airfield installations were also damaged. The last strike landed on at 1800 and the fleets withdrew. Admiral Rawlings's hopes for the future then received the unkindest cut of all. *King George V* had long-standing defects in the propulsion machinery on two shafts. These had been aggravated by the steaming of the last few weeks. If *King George V* took part in the bombardment of 13th, and broke down off the enemy coast, she would jeopardise the whole bombarding force. Admiral Rawlings was forced to tell Admiral Halsey that the whole of TF 37 would retire after the strikes of 12th.

At about 2100 that evening the Domei News Agency in Tokyo

announced that Japan had offered to accept the Potsdam terms of surrender.

The fleet met the Logistic Support Group[1] early the next day and began fuelling soon after dawn. In the forenoon Admiral Halsey invited Admiral Rawlings and officers of his staff to a conference on board *Missouri* and, at Le Fanu's prompting, suggested that *King George V* fuel from an American tanker at the same time. At 1030 that morning the two flagships, *Missouri* and *King George V*, were steaming one on each side of the US tanker *Sabine* – 'forming rather a notable sight. It was perhaps another milestone.' The two fleet commanders had an amiable luncheon conference in *Missouri*. Meanwhile, and perhaps almost as important at that stage to the British cause, *Sabine* was pumping more than 1,000 tons of fuel into *King George V*'s tanks (at a rate of 820 tons/hour, more than twice the pumping rate achieved by any British tanker). As Le Fanu said: 'I wasn't listening to the conference, I was listening to the glug-glug-glug as they pumped over the fuel.'[2]

In the event, Task Force 37 did not carry out any more strikes. Another typhoon was approaching and on 11 August Admiral Halsey cancelled the next day's programme. He also warned ships not to drop their guard; the war with Japan was not over and in spite of peace feelers, great vigilance and alertness had to be maintained in case the Japanese repeated their Pearl Harbour tactics (any such operation was quite beyond the Japanese at that time, but 'Pearl Harbour' had now become synonymous in the American fleet with 'treachery').

At 1700 a signal was received from Admiral Fraser which sent Bernard Rawlings's hopes soaring. Admiral Nimitz had accepted a token British force of one battleship, one carrier, two cruisers and necessary destroyer screen to join the Americans for the naval occupation of Japan. Admiral Rawlings knew that the American fuel position was not easy and would remain so for ten days or more. Nevertheless, it seemed to him so unfortunate that so many British ships and the carriers in particular should not be in at the death that his Chief of Staff returned to Commander 3rd Fleet to see if, under the change of circumstances, there were any hopes of more oil becoming available and to say that if there were, he would feel justified in asking that the entire fleet might be retained. But it was not to be. Captain Reid returned with the

---

[1] *Wave Emperor, Olna, San Adolpho, San Amado, San Ambrosio*; VSIS *Fort Wrangell*; CVE *Ruler*; *Pheasant, Crane*; *Findhorn, Usk, Barle*; minesweepers *Burnie, Ballarat, Geraldton, Ipswich*; hospital ship *Tjitjalengka*.

[2] Admiral Sir Michael Le Fanu. Conversation of 26.3.68.

news that matters must stand as arranged. And so, at 1300 on 12 August, Admiral Vian and the bulk of the British Pacific Fleet left for Manus and thence for Sydney.

If the average sailor in the fleet had been asked which he would prefer: to remain at sea off Japan in the typhoon season or to return to Sydney, his answer would have been predictable. But, on second thoughts, there was bitter disappointment in the fleet. The British Pacific Fleet had come so far, and had endured so many handicaps and criticisms to take part in the naval war against Japan; now, lacking a few thousand tons of fuel, it was deprived of its right to be in at the finish. *Victorious'* Engineer Officer has summed up the feelings in his ship and in the fleet:

'It was a sad blow to everyone on board, as we had been in every operation and felt we had a prior right to be present. It may have been intended as a reward by releasing *Victorious* at the earliest moment. But we did not see it that way.'[1]

Nevertheless, Captain Denny reflected that *Victorious* was proud to have operated throughout all the fleet aircraft carrier squadron operations in the Pacific, and that the tedious nursing of her defective rudder, steering gear and centre shaft – a state of affairs aptly described by *Indefatigable* as "with your behind in a poor condition" – should have had their reward.

On their way back, the carriers could be proud that, size for size, they had pulled their weight with the American task groups, as a comparison of British and American carrier operating statistics in July and August shows:

	BRITISH	US
Number of carriers	4	10
Number of light fleet carriers	—	6
Number of strike days[2]	8	13
Aircraft complement	255	1,191
Sorties on strike days	2,615	18,163
Offensive sorties on strike days[3]	1,595	10,678
Number of enemy aircraft destroyed or damaged	347	2,408
Tons of enemy shipping sunk or damaged	356,760	924,000
Offensive sorties/complement aircraft/strike day	1·39	1·39
Enemy aircraft destroyed or damaged/off. sortie	0·21	0·22
Tons of enemy shipping sunk or damaged/off. sortie	224	90
Combat losses as percentage of offensive sorties[4]	2·38	1·61
Operational losses as percentage of offensive sorties	2·0	0·55

British aircraft dropped 517 tons of bombs during the operations and fired fifty-six rockets. Twenty-six pilots, four observers and two air gunners were killed or reported missing. For the number of enemy aircraft destroyed or damaged the British squadrons lost far less aircraft than in ICEBERG and the proportion of operational to combat losses also dropped, as a table of aircraft wastage by cause illustrates:

	Write-Off				Repairable but replaced by CVEs				
	Combat and Flak	Deck Landing	Other	Total	Combat and Flak	Deck Landing	Other	Total	Grand Total
Av	7	3	5	15	1	2	12	15	30
Co	17	9	10	36	4	3	3	10	46
He									
Se	8	22	7	37	1	7	4	12	49
Fi	7	4	2	13	1		2	3	16
TOTAL	39	38	24	101	7	12	21	40	141

The British 'token force' consisted of *King George V*, *Indefatigable*, *Gambia*, *Newfoundland*, *Troubridge*, *Termagant*, *Tenacious*, *Teazer*, *Terpsichore*, *Barfleur*, *Napier*, *Nizam*, *Wakeful* and *Wrangler*. These Admiral Rawlings had chosen 'as representatives of the Empire. The force seemed a little slender but there seemed no reason to give up our position on the right of the line.' The force was designated TG 38.5 and came under the direct command of Admiral McCain, as another Task Group of his Task Force.

On 13 August Admiral Fraser, flying his flag in *Duke of York*, with *Whelp* and *Wager*, left Guam to join the Third Fleet. The Allies had accepted the Japanese surrender, with the proviso that the Emperor would obey the orders of the Supreme Allied Commander. In Halsey's flagship it was not clear whether the next item on the agenda would be a Tokyo strike or a Tokyo landing. Ships were ordered to prepare Marine and Bluejacket armed landing parties. In *King George V* the signal giving TF 38.5's quota was read as '2000'. But there were only enough weapons for 1500. When this was signalled to *Missouri* it was discovered that the figure should have been 200. In view of the pre-

---

[1] Commander (now Vice Admiral Sir Norman) Dalton. Letter of 12.5.68.
[2] Not including 13 and 15 August, when *Indefatigable* launched strikes after the fleet had departed.
[3] 'Offensive sorties' are defined as those against enemy shipping or over enemy territory.
[4] British combat losses were 48% higher than US.

parations already afoot this would obviously have caused great disappointment and Admiral Rawlings asked Admiral Halsey if he could see his way to raise the quota. He at once doubled it.

In *Missouri* the war situation was still unclear but in the early hours of 13 August Admiral Halsey decided to quit interpreting, and strike.

On 13th, Task Force 38 was once more striking at airfields in the Tokyo plain, and claimed 307 enemy aircraft destroyed. *Indefatigable*, now the Commonwealth's sole carrier representative, flew off one morning strike which attacked a chemical factory at Onagawa. A second strike in the afternoon found its targets weathered in and flying was cancelled for the day. The Japanese were now making much more determined attempts to find the Third Fleet. Some twenty-five bogies were detected during the day and twenty-one were shot down. 'Most of these came singly but the precision of the interceptions and the speed at which the bogies were shot down was remarkable. The whole was a most finished performance.'

The British TG 38.5 fuelled from American tankers on 14th and next day returned to fly off what were, at last, the final strikes against Japan. At 0400 *Indefatigable* launched a combined strike of six Avengers, eight Seafires and four Fireflies, which was intercepted by a group of about twelve Zekes. Four Zekes were shot down, four probably shot down and the remainder damaged. Airfields at Hisaruki and Nobara were weathered in but a single Avenger found and bombed a camouflaged factory near Wada.

One Avenger of this strike was hit by flak and its observer, S/Lt. J. A. Bonass, RNVR, of 820 Sq. baled out somewhat prematurely over Tokyo Bay. The aircraft flew on and ditched successfully; the pilot and air gunner were picked up by a destroyer. A Seafire of the escort was also lost to flak, the pilot S/Lt. F. Hockley, RNVR, of 887 Sq. baling out and landing unhurt on Chiba Peninsula east of Tokyo. He was captured and taken to the nearest Japanese army area headquarters. Later that same day he was led out and executed by shooting. The three Japanese officers guilty of the murder were tried as war criminals: Colonel Tamura, and Major Hirano were sentenced to death by hanging, Captain Fujino to fifteen years' imprisonment.[1]

At 0700, on instructions from Admiral Nimitz, all strikes against Japan were cancelled, and at 1100 the news was received that the Japanese had accepted the Allied peace terms. Offensive operations against Japan were to cease.

[1] See also *The Times*, 30 May 1947, and 14 June 1947.

In theory, the war was over. In practice, there were some bizarre incidents to be enacted:

'Everyone was wondering what the Japs would be doing at the last minute and it was no surprise when the radar picket stationed some sixty miles inshore of the fleet reported a large group of unidentified aircraft some eighty miles away. There were a large number of carrier fighters airborne and a section was instructed to investigate this report. I shall never forget listening to the radio fighter wave when this group was intercepted and identified as a miscellaneous collection of enemy aircraft. The leader of the section said "They are flying round in an orbit without apparent offensive intent." Then he said "My God, they're all going into the drink!" and for what seemed like a long time he was counting off the number of aircraft peeling off from the orbit and diving one after the other into the sea. I believe the total was over forty. We learned later that these were the hard core of Kamikaze pilots who, having had their funeral services read over them, reckoned they were officially dead and could not therefore surrender. We did pick up one kamikaze pilot earlier in the operation who was not dressed in normal flying clothing but wrapped in a shroud upon which his funeral sermon had been printed.'[1]

Flag signalling was rarely used by the combined fleets, but Admiral Rawlings made up his mind to signal Japan's defeat by the traditional method and ordered the hoist 'Cease hostilities against Japan' to be flown in the flagship. *King George V*'s upper decks at once became scenes of the wildest jubilation, with men cheering and throwing steel helmets and other equipment overboard in an excess of excitement. Amongst the celebrating crowds could be seen the Gunner (on whose permanent loan list the discarded steel helmets were) urging restraint.

The Gunner was completely vindicated at 1120, when a Judy penetrated to the fleet and dropped two bombs close to *Indefatigable*, the nearest bomb looking in Admiral Rawlings's words, 'like a bloody great grand piano'. The flagship now presented the unusual sight of 'Aircraft warning Flash Red' being hoisted at the rush on one halliard while 'Cease hostilities against Japan' was being hauled down (and hence executed) on another. The Judy was shot down by Corsairs of TG 38.1 and crashed in the sea on *Indefatigable*'s port quarter. Rawlings said ruefully, 'How this aircraft got in so close is not clear'.

Sporadic enemy air activity continued for some hours. Early in the

[1] Dyke. 14.8.67.

afternoon, while Admiral Halsey was broadcasting a moving message to his fleet, TOMCAT and WATCHDOG CAPs shot down two more threatening enemy aircraft – thus complying with the fleet commander's signal: 'It is likely that Kamikazes will attack the fleet as a final fling. Any ex-enemy aircraft attacking the fleet is to be shot down in a friendly manner.'

On 16 August Admiral Rawlings went on board *Missouri* to broadcast to the Third Fleet. The speech was his tribute to the men of the American and British fleets, and his own Nunc Dimittis:

'Admiral Halsey, Flag Officers, Commanding Officers, Officers and Men of the Third Fleet. Yesterday, after hearing Admiral Halsey's inspiring words to the Third Fleet, of which we have the honour to be part, I asked him if I might come to his Flagship to say a few words to you all. I was not sure that with our voice transmission gear, we could carry sufficiently far to reach all units of the Third Fleet, and if I may so put it, I decided to take the bull by the horns and so I asked him if I might come over to speak from his flagship in the centre of his fleet.

'A good deal seems to have happened since March, when I received orders to report for duty to Admiral Nimitz. The words I used then in placing my ships under his orders were that it was "with feelings of great pride and pleasure that the British Pacific Force joins the United States Naval Forces under your command".

'Nothing that has happened since makes me wish to change one word of what I then said; the story of how the two fleets have come together is quite simple and straightforward, which is as things should be among sailors.

'It begins with Task Force 57 as we then were, operating under the orders of Admiral Spruance and we took it as a compliment that he just told us what he wanted and left us to get on with it. We look back on those decisive days in the battle for Okinawa with a feeling of pride. We never met our Admiral but we felt he understood us. Perhaps on the whole it was as well that we were then operating on our own as it gave us the chance to get used to an unaccustomed way of manoeuvring and signalling which was to stand us in good stead later.

'With that behind us we joined the Third Fleet not only with keen anticipation but, I believe, with a little confidence that we knew enough to take our place in the line with the famous fighting Third; and so what Admiral Halsey said yesterday meant much to us.

'The story is, perhaps, reaching its end in the last few days, when we have passed under the direct command of Vice Admiral McCain as Task Group 38.5 and so become an integral part of those fast Carrier Task Forces which have fought their way back from the black days of 1941 to their present victory. It may not perhaps be fantastic to feel that the way our two navies have come together, welded and integrated, may point the manner in which our two great democracies will now move forward together. In their amalgamation, neither Navy, I hope, has lost its own character or individuality. It would be the greatest pity if they did so, for when all is said and done everything in the story of sea warfare shows that character and individuality are in the end the only things that really count. But with them today must go that spirit of co-operation which these months have shown to be within our reach.

'Perhaps I might add that I share to the full with Admiral Halsey the conception that the Navy is still the first line of defence for both our countries, and I believe, also, that the day when either of us abandon his sage advice to keep the naval sword sharp, will bring us nearer to being again attacked by such evil forces as those we have now subdued.

'In so thinking may I quote to you the opening sentence of the message sent by the Board of Admiralty to the British fleet when Germany was broken; it begins – "For the second time since the Battle of Trafalgar sea-power relentlessly applied has preserved and sustained our nation and Commonwealth and led to the decisive defeat of Germany".

'The story of the Third Fleet in which we have been privileged to lend a hand, provides during the last six weeks the perfect picture of the result of sea-power relentlessly applied in the waters of the Pacific.

'Very many of us in both our navies will in the future be returning to civil life. To those who remain may I say that I can conceive of no greater contribution to the future of the world than that our two navies should make a habit of meeting and working together from time to time. Perhaps those of you who will be leaving the sea will help to bring that about.

'But to each one of you, whatever you may feel about that conception, whatever happens and whatever the future holds, I would suggest that each will be able to say to himself "I fought in the Third Fleet under Halsey", and so saying, face up with a greater courage to whatever tomorrow shall bring.'[1]

---

[1] Reproduced by kind permission of Lady Rawlings.

Chapter Eleven

THE END, AND AFTER

'The silence was complete except for the whirring and clicking of cameras, and one could feel that all present at that gathering were struggling to adjust themselves mentally to the fact that they were witnessing the act which put an end to a long and bitter war.'
Admiral Sir Bruce Fraser.

IN cold statistics, the total operational achievement of the surface ships of the BPF was thirty-six air-strike days against the enemy,[1] and four bombardments of enemy territory. Even the most eager British historian could never claim that the British Pacific Fleet played anything more than an ancillary part in the war at sea in the Pacific, although its actions won the admiration and respect of the United States Navy and, incidentally, set the pattern for the shape of the Royal Navy after the war. However, when the war against Japan came to its sudden end, the fleet was the only large, mobile Commonwealth force which was instantly available to safeguard Commonwealth interests in the Pacific. It could be said that the BPF's most valuable services were not military, but political and humanitarian, and were rendered after VJ Day.

Admiral Fraser left Sydney by air for Manus on 4 August. After an eventful trip during which an engine of one aircraft exploded into flames over the Coral Sea and a second aircraft was forced by bad weather to land in Papua, Admiral Fraser arrived on 6th and sailed the same day in *Duke of York*, escorted by *Whelp* and *Wager*, arriving at Guam on 9 August. At 11 o'clock the next day, on *Duke of York*'s quarterdeck, Admiral Fraser on behalf of His Majesty the King invested Fleet Admiral Nimitz as Knight Grand Cross of the Order of the Bath. Admiral Spruance and General Spaatz were present at the ceremony. After a celebratory glass of champagne in Admiral Fraser's cabin,

[1] Four in OUTFLANK, twenty-four in ICEBERG, and eight in the July–August operations off Japan, excluding *Indefatigable*'s two days with TF 38.

Admiral Nimitz was then invited to visit the wardroom, the gunroom and the warrant officers' mess and finally spliced the mainbrace with the ship's company. 'It says much for Admiral Nimitz's stamina that he survived in tolerably good order the ultimate ordeal by camera to which he was subjected before leaving the ship.'[1]

Duke of York sailed from Guam on the morning of 13 August, with the American liaison officer on Admiral Fraser's staff, Captain Julian Wheeler, USN, giving the helm orders at Captain Nicholl's invitation 'to take the British flagship towards peace', and joined the Third Fleet, then some 200 miles south-east of Tokyo, at dawn on 16 August.

The flagship was not greeted with cries of joy by the fleet, indeed there is no doubt *Duke of York* was an unpopular ship; there were incidents when she was taken under fire by potatoes, hurled by the ship's companies of the aircraft carriers, when she passed within shying range. True, *Duke of York* had sunk *Scharnhorst* but the BPF was less concerned with her glamorous past than with her shore-bound present; rightly or wrongly, the fleet believed that the flagship 'never went to sea', and Admiral Fraser took this feeling in the fleet seriously enough to mention it when he addressed *King George V*'s ship's company. (He might have added, though he did not, that he himself had been under fire from the kamikazes long before any of them.)

On the afternoon of 17 August Admiral Fraser transferred to the US destroyer *Taylor* and thence to *Missouri* to invest Admiral Halsey with the Order of Knight of the British Empire. The ceremony took place on the starboard side of No 2 gundeck (on the identical spot where the surrender of Japan was later signed) and it was possibly the first, and only, occasion on which an Order has been bestowed on a foreign Admiral on board his flagship at sea by a British C-in-C.

On 16 August and again on 17th, the Third Fleet indulged in a piece of excusable exhibitionism; the task groups, three American and one British, closed until destroyer screens were one mile apart for high speed manoeuvres in concert as ordered by Admiral Halsey, whilst aircraft overhead took photographs in Operation SNAPSHOT.

Early on 18th, the fleet located the Logistic Support Group[2] and replenishment began at dawn. During the three-day replenishment period the Third Fleet Allied Landing Force was brought to eight hours'

---

[1] Rear Admiral A. D. Nicholl. Letter of 26.8.67.
[2] Tankers *San Adolpho, San Ambrosio, Wave Governor*; CVE *Ruler*; VSIS *Fort Wrangell*; escorts *Pheasant, Odzani, Burnie, Usk, Ipswich, Ballarat. Tjitjalengka* and *Crane* were also in the area.

notice and on 20 August the Commonwealth component embarked by LCM in the US attack transports (APDs) *Barr*, *Sims* and *Pavlic*. The British force, of thirty-seven officers and 499 men (a number which suggested to Admiral Rawlings that some stowaways had crept in) was commanded by Captain Buchanan, RAN, and was composed of RN sailors from the fleet, RAN sailors from *Napier* and *Nizam*, and some 300 Royal Marines from *King George V*, *Gambia* and *Newfoundland* under *King George V*'s senior Royal Marine officer, Major P. L. Norcock. Major Norcock was the third generation of his family to serve in the Royal Marines and by a coincidence was following in the footsteps of his grandfather almost eighty years earlier.

'All 300 Royal Marines were embarked in three US APDs *Barr*, *Pavlic* and *Sims* about 10 days prior to the landing. Our task was to land at dawn on the island of Azuma in the Japanese base and secure the island. We landed operationally, no trouble, and found the island an arsenal of weapons, midget subs, ammunition, oil fuel tanks, etc. A Japanese Lieutenant Commander officially surrendered the island and for the next week we made an inventory of the stores found in the subterranean tunnels which honeycombed the island.

'At some time during this period I remarked that my grandfather, then a Lieutenant of the Royal Marine Light Infantry, had also landed in Yokohama in 1869, almost exactly 80 years before, with a Royal Marine battalion "to see the peace treaty was enforced". Somehow my remark must have come to the ears of Admiral Halsey. When *Missouri*, *KGV* and the rest anchored and the surrender was signed, it was decided to push a small occupying force into Tokyo and Yokohama "to enforce the peace treaty". I suppose Halsey thought a little bit of repetitive history might be a good thing; I was recalled from Azuma, turning over to an American force, rushed on board *KGV*, changed into ceremonial rig with my chaps, picked up the band, landed at Yokohama, and marched through the streets at the slope (with ammunition in our pockets!).'[1]

The escort carrier *Speaker* joined the Support Group on 20 August, with replacement aircraft. As many of her aircraft as possible were flown off at once to *Indefatigable* and *Ruler* while *Speaker* prepared to act as an accommodation ship for repatriated prisoners of war and internees. On 22nd it was the turn of the Third Fleet's aircrews to display themselves, massing over the fleet in swarms while the ships took photographs in Operation TINTYPE.

[1] Colonel P. L. Norcock, Royal Marines, Letter of 20.11.67.

In the meantime, the British ships had been reallocated. *Indefatigable*, with eight destroyers, joined TG 38.3 while *Duke of York*, *King George V*, *Newfoundland*, *Gambia*, and the remaining destroyers joined TG 38.4, being designated TU 38.4.6.

Now occurred a period of anti-climax. The fleets were ready to enter Japanese waters and expected the signal daily, but typhoons were delaying the build-up on Okinawa of the aircraft necessary for the airborne landings in Japan. At sea, the fleets manoeuvred uneasily to avoid the storm centres, topping up destroyers with fuel whenever the opportunity came. On 23rd the signal to carry out Admiral Halsey's plan of entry into Japanese waters was received and the flagships, American and British, formed into 'flagship groups', *Missouri* in TG 30.1, and *Duke of York*, with *Whelp* and *Wager* in TG 30.2. *King George V*, *Newfoundland*, *Gambia*, *Napier* and *Nizam* reformed under their old designation of Task Force 37 which included – to Admiral Rawlings's great pleasure – two American destroyers, *Uhlmann* and *Benham*, under his direct command. But again the entry was delayed.

At last, on 27 August, the first Allied ships anchored in Sagami Wan. Task Force 37, all ships flying the White Ensign at masthead and peak, with *Gambia* flying the New Zealand and *Napier* and *Nizam* the Australian flag at the main, anchored in their berths at 1450. 'It was', as Admiral Rawlings said, 'perhaps rather a small force to represent a large Empire but they had seen many oceans and known several enemies before they had joined their Allies in the Pacific.'

The next day an American patrol boat delivered Private Edgar Campbell of the RASC and Marine John Wynn to *Duke of York*. They had been prisoners of war since the fall of Hong Kong on Christmas Day, 1941. Hearing that the Allied fleet had arrived they had broken camp and walked thirty miles to the beach, only to be bitterly disappointed. All the ships they could see in the bay were new since their capture, with unfamiliar silhouettes, and they had thought the ships were Japanese until a Chesterfield cigarette packet and a Nestlé's chocolate bar wrapper floating in the water had reassured them. They had taken the considerable risk of being mistaken for Japanese saboteurs by attempting to swim out to the ships. They were the first British prisoners of war to be recovered from Japan.

By 29 August minesweepers had cleared sufficient berths off Yokohama and at daylight the flagship groups weighed anchor and proceeded into Tokyo Bay:

'The atmosphere on board was somewhat tense as we half expected that there might be some eleventh hour suicide attacks by the Japanese. However, the only incident on our passage was the transfer, from a small Japanese vessel, of a Japanese pilot and an interpreter. As the pilot was hauled across on the jackstay, all tension was relaxed when one of our sailors sang out "Mr Gieves' man!" '[1]

In the event, the interpreter was little used as 'there was no evidence that he spoke English'.

King George V, with *Quality*, *Napier*, *Nizam* and the hospital ship *Tjitjalengka* (which had arrived at Sagami Wan on 28th) followed the flagship into Tokyo Bay on 30th, anchoring off Yokohama. There was a satisfactory absence of smoke from factory chimneys and the waters of the bay, normally crowded with ships and small craft, were utterly deserted. On that day the Third Fleet Allied Landing Force, commanded by Rear Admiral Badger, USN, and including Major Norcock's party, made their unopposed landings and occupations of Yokosuka and the forts and islands around it and at the entrance to the bay. When *King George V* passed, the White Ensign was already flying over the island known as "Fort Two"; it was echoed by white flags on the shore opposite marking the deserted guns which in the end had proved so useless, and there was not a soul in sight.

Admiral Nimitz arrived in Tokyo Bay on 29 August and hoisted his flag in the battleship *South Dakota*. More Allied ships, commanders and men for the surrender and occupation of Japan were arriving every day, and by the end of the month there were nearly two hundred ships in Tokyo Bay. On 31st there were several Commonwealth arrivals; Rear Admiral Brind (CS 4) flying his flag in *Newfoundland*, with *Gambia*, from Sagami Wan; Commodore J. A. Collins, RAN, commanding TG 70.9, flying his broad pennant in HMAS *Shropshire*, with *Hobart*, *Warramunga* and *Bataan*, from Okinawa; and the British Logistic Support Group[2] from the operating area.

The documents of the surrender of the Japanese Empire were formally signed on board *Missouri* in Tokyo Bay on 2 September. It seems probable that if General MacArthur, Supreme Commander Allied Powers, had had his way the ceremony would have been almost entirely an American performance but Admiral Fraser, at his most

---

[1] Rear Admiral Nicholl. Ibid. Gieves Ltd., of Bond Street, are the well-known naval and military tailors.

[2] Tankers *Wave King*, *Carelia*, *Dingledale*; CVE *Ruler*; VSIS *Fort Wrangell*, escorts *Pheasant*, *Woodcock*, *Crane*, *Ipswich*, *Derg*, *Pirie*, *Cessnock* and *Ballarat*.

persuasive, won permission for a small number of spectators from the Commonwealth ships. The Japanese delegation, led by Mr Mamoru Shigemitsu, the Japanese Foreign Minister, and General Umezu, representing Imperial General Headquarters, were taken out to *Missouri* in the American destroyer *Lansdowne*:

'After the Allied representatives had assembled, the Japanese delegation arrived. As they were seen walking along the deck there was a lot of whispering among the Chinese and I was told afterwards they were noting with satisfaction that Mr Shigemitsu was leaning on ı stick and limping badly. He was still suffering the effects of a bomb thrown at him in Chapei twelve years previously.'[1]

Admiral Fraser was more magnanimous:

'Mr Shigemitsu had been the Japanese Ambassador in London before the war. I had been to many of his parties. I knew him quite well really. Charming old chap. He had a game leg. He was made to stand for quite a long time before this table, while everybody was assembling. I tried to catch his eye, but he didn't look. I felt rather sorry for him.'[2]

Mr Shigemitsu signed 'by command of and on behalf of the Emperor of Japan' and General Umezu 'by command of the Japanese Imperial General Headquarters'. 'The silence was complete except for the whirring and clicking of cameras, and one could feel that all present at that gathering were struggling to adjust themselves mentally to the fact that they were witnessing the act which put an end to a long and bitter war.' General MacArthur then signed on behalf of all the Allied Powers, Admiral Nimitz for the United States, Admiral Fraser for Great Britain, General Sir Thomas Blamey for Australia, Colonel L. M. Cosgrove for Canada, Air Vice Marshal L. M. Isitt for New Zealand, General Hsu Yung-chang for China, General P. Leclerc for France, Admiral C. E. L. Helfrich for the Netherlands, and Lieut. General K. N. Derevyanko for Russia. General Percival, who had surrendered Singapore to the Japanese, and General Jonathan Wainwright, US Army, of Corregidor, were also present.

Admiral Rawlings and Admiral Brind joined General MacArthur behind Admiral Fraser as the C-in-C signed the surrender documents. Admiral Rawlings must have watched with mixed feelings. He in *King George V* had led the fleet into action for the last eight months; Admiral Fraser in *Duke of York* had joined on the day after the war ended. It

[1] Rear Admiral Nicholl. Ibid.
[2] Lord Fraser. Conversation of 12.10.67.

z

was right and correct that the Fleet Commander should represent the fleet and the country at the surrender, but nevertheless there can be no doubt that Admiral Rawlings felt that his position had somehow been usurped.

In signing his name, General MacArthur used several pens, which were later presented to various recipients.[1] Admiral Fraser noticed this:

'When I came to the table I thought, well, I'll do the same. So I brought up Brind and Rawlings. I signed with one pen and handed it to Rawlings. I saw the Americans looking a little blank about this. Afterwards they came along and said, "Look, we're awfully sorry about this, but those pens . . . we can't spare those pens". So poor Rawlings and Brind had to give 'em back again!'[2]

By now, the organisation for repatriating prisoners of war and civilian internees was well under way. At first there was some confusion and lack of liaison (relations between the British and various American authorities were at one time so ill-defined that the services of the escort carrier *Ruler* were simultaneously offered to two separate American commanders). The original Allied plans had been made under the assumptions that the Japanese would still be resisting, that POW camps would be liberated as they came within the Allied zone, and that all ex-POWs would be flown out of Japan. It had not been foreseen that the Japanese would have capitulated completely, that POWs would be breaking out of camps 'to try and find MacArthur', and that many of the airfields in Japan were too small or too badly damaged to be used by large transport aircraft.

The situation was saved by typically quick and decisive action by Admiral Halsey, who established a special repatriation task group (TG 30.6) commanded by Commodore Simpson, USN, and composed of hospital ships, including *Tjitjalengka*, accommodation ships, the cruiser *San Juan*, and landing craft.

On the British side, the Admiralty had already made it clear that the repatriation of POWs was a War Office responsibility. This was unrealistic. There was no properly equipped unit of the British army on the scene nor, by 28 September when repatriation was virtually com-

---

[1] A circumstantial account of the surrender ceremony, full of 'local colour', is in *The Fall of Japan*, by William Craig (Weidenfeld and Nicholson, 1968), Ch. 21. The pens went to General Wainwright, General Percival, West Point Military Academy, US Army Archives, General Courtney Whitney, and Mrs Douglas MacArthur.

[2] Lord Fraser. Ibid.

plete, had any Army officer of field rank been appointed to be responsible for repatriation. However, on 14 August Admiral Fraser had
appointed Admiral Rawlings to be responsible for the co-ordination
of all matters concerning the repatriation of Commonwealth nationals
from Japan, and he was very ably assisted in the event by Commodore
Collins and his Australian task group.

Recovery and repatriation took place in stages: discovery from the
air of the camps and the immediate dropping of food and medical
supplies by parachute; contact on the ground between Allied personnel
and the camps; transport of ex-POWs to Yokohama by road, rail, sea
and air; identification, sorting and 'processing' of POWs and internees;
evacuation by air, or in some cases by sea, from Japan to rehabilitation
centres in Manila; repatriation of POWs and internees to their own
countries (if they so desired it; not all the internees wished to be
repatriated).

Very few of the camps in Japan were known to the International Red
Cross. Many more were identified from the air by USAAF aircraft and
by aircraft of the Third Fleet, which included *Indefatigable* and her
escorting destroyers, remaining at sea to prevent last-minute Japanese
treachery. Several unregistered camps were found by the Third Fleet,
including Okkaichi camp by *Indefatigable*'s aircraft. The fleet was
harassed by typhoons during this period and although the British ships
were comparatively unscathed, some American ships were badly
damaged and suffered casualties in the typhoons.[1]

The first British warship to embark prisoners of war was *Speaker*
(Captain U. H. R. James) who sailed for Manila on 3 September with
473 Commonwealth men on board. Captain James had been instructed
to pass close to the larger ships but when he saw that the decks of every
ship were crammed with men, all bursting to cheer, he took *Speaker*
out of the bay by 'a most tortuous path'.

Speaker's departure from Tokyo Bay was one of the most moving
scenes of the war. 'As she steamed through the British anchorage the
ship's companies of all the British ships gave her a send-off which those
who saw it will never forget. The sight of this small carrier with her
ship's company fallen in for leaving harbour in accordance with naval
custom but with, in addition, these hundreds of ex-prisoners of war

[1] At the height of the storm Rear Admiral Bogan, USN, signalled to *Indefatigable*: 'Are you weathering the typhoon all right?', and there is a legend that
Indefatigable replied 'What typhoon?' In fact, such a reply was considered but
because of the damage suffered by the US ships it was decided that it would be
extremely tactless and was never sent.

ranged on the flight deck cheering like mad and being cheered, brought tears to the eyes and the realisation of what the presence of the great Fleet in Tokyo Bay meant to these men.'

Speaker's passengers[1] were from camps in and around the Tokyo area. But there were scores of other camps far distant from Tokyo and many miles inland. Volunteer 'contact teams' were formed of officers and men from *King George V* and HMAS *Shropshire* to join the American recovery teams and travel into the Japanese interior by any means they could command or commandeer, to meet Commonwealth prisoners of war, carry out preliminary identification, arrange for transport to Yokohama, and where possible to find the whereabouts of unreported camps. The Commonwealth men in the camps were over-joyed to meet men of their own nationalities; the food, medical supplies, tobacco and reading matter dropped into the camps had been American, and the contact teams were the first indication for the men in the camps that the Royal and Commonwealth Navies had played any part in the Pacific war.

When the contact teams arrived some of the prisoners wept, some cheered, some broke down, some 'went a little off the handle'. The contact teams' reception in the camps is best described by a member of one of them, S/Lt. J. D. Harris, of Recovery Team 48:

'To attempt to describe my welcome at any of the camps I liberated would be futile. It was beyond hand-shakes, yarns or cheering, beyond the arrival of the man who would take them away; it was Englishmen meeting Englishmen. The evidence of the return of the way of life they knew, someone from the outside world with the same background, ideals and spirits. This may sound foolish to the reader but should he disbelieve the spirit of it without experiencing it himself then he himself would be the fool.'

In some cases, evacuation was most easily arranged by sea. *Newfound-land, Gambia,* and several destroyers were stored with survivors' kits, blankets, beds, mess-traps, cutlery, cigarettes, chocolate and food from other ships in the fleet and from *City of Dieppe* and *Fort Wrangell.* They were then assigned to TG 30.6 and sailed for various Japanese ports, to embark passengers and bring them back to Tokyo Bay.[2]

---

[1] It was decided, for psychological reasons, that the term 'prisoner of war' should be avoided; 'passenger' was used instead.

[2] The destinations were: *Tenacious* to Hammamatsu; *Wizard* to Hammamatsu and Sendai; *Wakeful* to Sendai; *Barfleur* to Hokkaido; *Gambia* and *Nizam* to Wakayama; *Warramunga* and *Bataan* to Sendai.

In the destroyers, carrying their passengers at top speed to Yokohama, there were some moving and bizarre moments, as Lt. Cdr. R. H. Hodgkinson, commanding *Wizard*, observed:

'An Army medical officer who was amongst the passengers came up to the wardroom for breakfast and put back eight sausages in no time. Two Argyll and Sutherland privates looked rather wistfully at the ship's cat and told me that a fortnight ago it couldn't have got twenty yards along the upper deck with its fur still on.

'My chief impression of the passengers to whom I talked was of their magnificent *esprit de corps* and pride in survival. It had seemed to become a point of honour amongst them not to die. They had been robbed of any possible pride in personal appearance, they had been humiliated and degraded for four years, they could have no pride of craftsmanship, no pride of home. The only thing left for them to revere was their endurance, so they had set it up as their standard, and had settled down to stick anything out.

'In personal appearance they were not too thin, but they had a flabby and fatigued look. They seemed dazed on arrival up the gangway, but after a few minutes their faces broadened into a look of happy relief which they did not lose for the whole voyage.'

The destroyers often arrived in Tokyo Bay at dusk, as the sun was setting behind the sacred mountain of Fuji Yama. 'But it is a different picture from the usual Japanese drawings. It has been a scene which in some ways has reminded one of Dunkirk. Destroyers carrying many hundreds of passengers in all sorts of clothing, crowding all over the upper decks and receiving the tumultuous cheers of all HM Ships as they went by into the inner harbour of Yokohama where the hospital ships were lying.'

The destroyer ship's companies had been strictly warned against 'pumping' their passengers for 'atrocity stories'. But the sailors quickly found that the problem was not to get a passenger to talk about his experiences, but to stop him. After years of humiliation, ill-treatment, near-starvation, forced labour and disease, the passengers were aching to unburden themselves. The inward-looking claustrophobic atmosphere of the camps, the savage punishments, the memories of friends who had died of disease or who had been executed, all these had tended to make the passengers introspective. But once the gates were opened the memories came flooding and men were telling the same story over and over again, to anyone who would listen, or pretend to listen. Some of the passengers were eager and optimistic about the future talking of the families they would return to and the jobs they would get. Others, a few, were 'difficult', resentful of discipline, neglecting their personal hygiene and skilfully evading any suggestion of responsibility (however, they probably owed their survival in the camps to their skill in evasion). But most were in a state of what the ships' medical officers termed 'a deep contentment' – not looking to the future, quite unconcerned about their destinations, just content to be amongst their own countrymen again, and letting events look after themselves.

It was clear that morale in the camps had never wavered. The Japanese had attempted to drive a wedge between the officers and their men, but with almost no success. Humiliation of the officers only increased the respect of their men. Although some camp commandants and guards were undoubtedly sadistic monsters, the passengers bore surprisingly little malice towards the Japanese in general. As one US Marine colonel somewhat cryptically remarked to S/Lt. Harris: 'There are those we'd like to meet again, and those we'd like to meet again.'

Recovered Allied Prisoners of War and Internees (RAPWIs) were received ('processed' in the rather clinical American term) in reception centres at Yokohama, where the hospital and accommodation ships were berthed. A British reception centre under Lt. Cdr. H. R. K. Bates, RNVR, was set up in *Tjitjalengka*. RAPWIs arrived at the reception centres from Atsugi airfield, from Yokohama railway station or by road from local camps, to be welcomed by an American 'swing band', and coffee and doughnuts. 'Processing' consisted of a medical examination, a bath and disinfestation, new clothing and a preliminary intelligence examination. RAPWIs could send ten-word telegrams to their next-of-kin. After this first processing, RAPWIs were flown to the main rehabilitation centres in Manila (although the US Navy preferred to return their own personnel direct to Guam).

In the second week of September typhoons interrupted the air service between Japan and the Philippines and arrangements were made to send some RAPWIs by sea. On 13th the escort carrier *Ruler* (Captain J. Armstrong) embarked 445 passengers who 'ranged from senior Colonels to Chinese babies and included African negroes, Baptist missionaries, Indian school-teachers and a number of miscellaneous Asiatics'. Such a varied passenger list caused a great dislocation and rearrangement of the ship's services and accommodation. Like *Speaker*'s before them, *Ruler*'s officers and ship's company exerted themselves to make their passengers welcome; the sailors had to be restrained from giving away the whole of their Canteen Fund, while the officers undertook to pay the passengers' wine and mess bills. The few aircraft remaining on board were parked rather forlornly at the extreme ends of the flight deck, and the rest of the deck was marked out for games. The hangar had been converted into a vast mess-deck/Dormitory. One lady passenger was heard to describe it as 'a fairy-land' – 'a description', commented Captain Armstrong, 'which had not previously been heard in this ship'. Perhaps the final proof that the war was really over came at six o'clock on the first evening, with the pipe – 'Children to supper'.

On 15 September, *Tjitjalengka* sailed from Yokohama with 436 hospital cases, 382 British and 54 Australians, landing the former at Auckland on 4 October and the latter at Sydney on 12th. At both ports, the patients told their stories to an appalled and fascinated press; their attitude to the Japanese and their thankfulness at shaking the dust of Japan from their feet was best expressed in a Chinese proverb quoted by one erudite passenger to a New Zealand newspaper:

> 'Men without honour,
> Women without virtue,
> Flowers without smell
> And birds without song.'[1]

By 15 September, some 16,500 Allied prisoners of war had been evacuated from Japan, and the work of evacuation was virtually complete by the end of the month, when more than 24,000 prisoners of war and internees had been evacuated.

The work of evacuation, and the Allied occupation which began at the same time was carried out in a country which had been terribly damaged. Yokohama was almost a waste land:

'Devastation was seen everywhere, and the only Japanese visible were a few men and boys hauling timber by means of carts, some drawn by decrepit-looking horses, others by bullocks. A pathetic old man was seen digging his small patch of garden attached to his broken-down shack. The whole scene was one of complete desolation. Large tracts of ground, on which buildings had previously stood, were laid waste and covered with debris and scrap corrugated iron. A good many water mains appeared to have been burst and other public facilities damaged. Dock basins were packed with wrecked craft of all descriptions, and much large timber was floating about, not only in these basins, but in the main harbour as well. Not a single intact building was seen in this

---

[1] *Auckland Star*, 4 October 1945.

area. Everywhere was overgrown with weeds, and the general impression of this dockland area was that the devastation had occurred some long time ago.'[1]

On 4 September, Admiral Fraser went on a tour of Yokohama and Tokyo. 'The damage caused by the American fire raids was indescribable. For seventeen miles there was hardly a building left standing.' Later, Admiral Rawlings and his Chief of Staff Captain Reid also toured the area. 'It was nothing but debris and devastation. All I could see were little humps sticking up amongst the rubble, which I suppose was where a fireproof safe from some office had survived the fire. Otherwise it was flat. I have never seen anything like it in my life.'[2]

More important, politically, than the evacuation of Commonwealth personnel was the swift reoccupation of Commonwealth territories. The BPF had recently been reinforced by the arrival of the battleship *Anson*, the 11th Aircraft Carrier Squadron of four light fleet carriers, *Colossus*, *Glory*, *Vengeance* and *Venerable*, under Rear Admiral C. H. J. Harcourt, the 2nd Cruiser Squadron, including *Bermuda*, and *Belfast* under Rear Admiral R. M. Servaes, and several more destroyers. These ships were available both for repatriation and for the reoccupation task groups which were formed as follows:

Task Group 111.2, for Hong Kong: *Indomitable* (Flag of Admiral Harcourt, A.C.11), *Venerable*, *Swiftsure*, *Euryalus*, HMCS *Prince Robert*, *Kempenfelt*, *Ursa*, *Whirlwind*, *Quadrant*.

Task Group 111.3 for Shanghai: *Bermuda* (flag of Admiral Servaes, C.S.2), *Argonaut*, *Colossus*, *Tyrian*, *Tumult*, *Tuscan*, *Quiberon*.

Task Group 111.4 for Singapore: *Anson* (Rear Admiral Daniel, B.S.1), *Vengeance*, and four destroyers. (This force was not sent to Singapore, but was used eventually to augment the Hong Kong group.)

For the British, the most urgent problem was the reoccupation of Hong Kong. For some time it was not clear whether the entry would be under British or American control; furthermore, Generalissimo Chiang Kai-shek had been given the impression that he would accept the surrender of Hong Kong (and, by implication, absorb Hong Kong into Nationalist China). However, by 15 August it was clear that HM Government intended to reoccupy Hong Kong as a Crown colony and the Americans would not take part; on 27th, after some negotiations, Chiang Kai-shek agreed that Admiral Harcourt would accept the

[1] 'The *Tjitjalengka Times*', 3 September 1945.
[2] Admiral Sir Peter Reid. Conversation of 28.11.67.

surrender of Japanese forces in Hong Kong on behalf of the British Government and himself.

POW contact teams for Hong Kong, Shanghai and Formosa had already been organised and assembled and the task groups for the China Coast sailed from Sydney on 15 August, within two hours of the news that the Japanese had accepted the surrender terms.

The entry into Hong Kong required minesweepers. The BPF's RAN-manned minesweepers had been used as escorts and were scattered all over the operational areas, but there were more Australian minesweepers, just about to begin sweeping in the Tsushima Straits with the Americans. The Australian Commonwealth Naval Board (ACNB) was asked for the loan of them, and they were ordered to concentrate at Subic Bay pending ACNB's approval. Admiral Harcourt's force could not reach Hong Kong before 26 August, and the ACNB was also asked whether Commodore Collins's TG 70.9, then at Subic, could enter Hong Kong until Admiral Harcourt arrived. On 17 August, the ACNB replied that they could not (Commodore Collins's force eventually went to Japan) but the loan of the minesweepers was approved. However, the only BPF ships which could arrive in Hong Kong before Admiral Harcourt were *Maidstone*, the 8th S/M Flotilla submarines, and the Australian minesweepers, all at Subic Bay. This was clearly not a strong enough force, and the reoccupation of Hong Kong had to await Admiral Harcourt's arrival after all. Admiral Harcourt reached Subic Bay on 25 August, collected *Maidstone*, her eight submarines and six Australian minesweepers, and sailed on 27th arriving off Hong Kong on 29 August, where he was joined by Admiral Daniel in *Anson*, with two more destroyers.

Meanwhile Mr F. C. Gimson, who had been Colonial Secretary in the Hong Kong Government before the war, discharged himself from Stanley Camp on 19 August and set up a provisional government on the island. It was due to him, and to the 250 former members of the police and doctors, nurses and technicians from the internment camps that some law and order was restored and there was no looting as there had been in 1941, before the Japanese entered (or as there was soon to be in Singapore, before the British entered). Mr Gimson and his colleagues succeeded so well that by 28 August he was able to broadcast to the world that the British were once more in charge in Hong Kong. The next day Mr Gimson's representative Cdr. D. H. S. Craven, who had been Staff Officer (Operations) in Hong Kong pre-war, flew out from Kaitak airfield to *Indomitable* with information on the state of affairs in the Colony. His arrival on the flagship's flight deck was another moving moment:

'I well remember the moment when he stepped out of the aircraft onto our flight deck, looking very thin and pale, but wonderfully pleased to be with us. He happened to be a man I knew, who had been a well-known amateur jockey in Malta in our younger days.'[1]

Commander Craven had with him a Japanese officer who was later flown back with Admiral Harcourt's instructions for the Japanese commander in Hong Kong. The weather closed in and the Avenger, after searching for Kaitak and *Indomitable*, eventually landed in China; the Japanese officer was only saved from execution by the Avenger's crew, who insisted he was their prisoner.

On 30 August Admiral Harcourt was appointed Commander in Chief, Hong Kong, and Head of the Military Administration which was to relieve Mr Gimson (much against his will). The same day Admiral Harcourt transferred his flag to *Swiftsure* (drawing less water than *Indomitable*) and, preceded by the minesweepers and accompanied by *Euryalus*, *Prince Robert*, *Tuscan*, *Kempenfelt* and two submarines, Admiral Harcourt entered Hong Kong harbour at noon. *Anson*, *Indomitable*, *Maidstone* and the remaining destroyers and submarines remained at sea, in water too deep for mines. Japanese suicide craft were seen to leave their moorings at Lamma Island but aircraft from *Indomitable* sank or dispersed them and the rest were bombed and sunk at their moorings.

Apart from some sporadic sniper fire in Victoria, there was no Japanese resistance. The whole island was occupied by 1 September when all Japanese forces had been removed to the mainland.[2] Captain Eccles, commanding *Indomitable*, who was a Japanese interpreter, began the work of setting up the military administration. Later, Captain H. F. Waight arrived from Manus to organise the restoration of the naval base and dockyard facilities. On 3 September the liner *Empress of Australia* reached Hong Kong with 3,000 RAF personnel (Force SHIELD) on board. They had been on their way to build bases for British long-range bombers on Okinawa, and were now diverted to repair airfields and air facilities in Hong Kong. A week later a convoy arrived

[1] Vice Admiral Sir Norman Parker. Letter of 5.5.68. See also *Half Time*, by Commander Anthony Kimmins (Heinemann, 1947), Chap. 24.
[2] An eye-witness account of the reoccupation of Hong Kong, written by a submarine officer, is in *Dark Seas Above*, by John Frederic Gibson (Blackwoods, 1947), Ch. 29.

carrying the 3rd Commando Brigade, and a squadron of RAF Spitfires (in the escort carrier *Smiter*). On 11 September, Major General F. W. Festing from SEAC took over as Head of the Military Administration from Admiral Harcourt.

On 14 September, *Duke of York* arrived in Hong Kong from Okinawa, flying the flag of the C-in-C BPF, and Admiral Fraser was present at Government House two days later when Major General Okada and Vice Admiral Fujita officially surrendered Hong Kong to Admiral Harcourt.

Admiral Fisher, with the greater part of the Fleet Train, sailed from Manus on 4 September and, on reaching Hong Kong, the Fleet Train set about the task of rehabilitating the Colony with their customary ingenuity and skill in improvisation, well described by the Fleet Train Engineer Officer:

'The crews of the Fleet Train ships included many nationalities and creeds; some of them had to have their meat slaughtered in the traditional ritual way. The meat came with a rubber stamp on it to certify this. Through some unforeseen delay the supply ran out, so to salve religious consciences a certifying stamp was flown up, which was duly impressed on ordinary meat carcases. The people concerned knew all this, but were quite happy about it and accepted it without demur.

'But the main essential was electric power. There was no coal, and wood had been the only fuel available to the Japanese for some time. Most of the trees had been cut down and the better-class houses stripped internally of all timber. The Kowloon power station was running, with one boiler on wood logs giving about 150 Kw. The Japanese had ripped up a land cable from the Taikoo power station and laid it across the harbour to connect to the Kowloon station. I doubt if any of Babcock's designers would have expected to see their boiler being fired by a stream of coolie women walking up a ramp and as they passed dropping a log in the chain-grate stoker. Two submarines went alongside in the dockyard to supply additional power to the island. Unfortunately within a couple of days one of HM Ships dropped her anchor on the cable across the harbour and severed it, so that ended the limited supply to the island from Kowloon.

'Meanwhile we set about converting one of the boilers at Taikoo for oil-burning, much to the consternation of the former operators, now released from Stanley Camp, but we managed to persuade them that we took responsibility for any damage and they left us to it. Starting a 5,000 kW turbo-alternator without any circulating water pump, hoping to get it on the board and then start the circulating pump before the condenser blows up, is quite a game!'[1]

The end of hostilities and the disposition of ships all over the Far East made some reorganisation of the fleet necessary. Admiral Rawlings in *King George V* left Tokyo Bay on 20 September, leaving Admiral Brind in *Newfoundland* as commander of the British task force. At Hong Kong, Admiral Fisher was appointed Flag Officer, British Pacific Fleet, and the ships under his command, Task Force 112, designated in task groups: TG 112.2, Rear Admiral Daniel's force; TG 112.3, Rear Admiral Servaes's force; TG 112.4, the Air Train, under its Commodore (COMAT); and TG 112.5, the British River Patrol, under Captain Love.

On 25 August the Australian Commonwealth Naval Board had asked Admiral Fraser for a cruiser or other large ship to accept the surrender of the Japanese forces in the Bismarcks, the Solomons and New Guinea. TG 111.5 was formed, of the carrier *Glory* and the sloops *Hart* and *Amethyst*. The surrender of the Japanese forces was accepted by General B. A. H. Sturdee of the Australian Army, on *Glory*'s flight deck off Rabaul on 6 September.

All prisoners of war and internees evacuated from Japan had been concentrated in Manila, but the long-term organisation and division of national responsibilities were still somewhat obscure. It was assumed that the Americans would be responsible for all nationals in Japan and Korea, and that the British would be responsible for all nationals in Hong Kong, and for their own nationals in Shanghai, North China and Formosa. (But there were misunderstandings: *Empress of Australia*, with 1,000 civilians on board bound for the United Kingdom, was refused permission to land at Manila although Admiral Fraser had already obtained General MacArthur's special personal permission.) When General MacArthur and the Admiralty were asked for guidance General MacArthur replied somewhat ambiguously, but the Admiralty laid down some details of policy: Hong Kong was to be the collecting and processing centre, and was to take the 'overflow' from Manila; HM Ships were to be used to the maximum for repatriation; and it was also decided that civilian internees were to have the same status and treatment as prisoners of war.

There had also been some doubt whether British ships could enter

[1] Rear Admiral J. G. C. Given. Letter of 12.10.67.

Formosa. After leaving Sydney, Admiral Servaes had left his force (still then TG 111.3) at Leyte while he called on Admiral Kincaid, commander of the US 7th Fleet at Manila. Admiral Fraser had asked Admiral Servaes to take up again with Admiral Kincaid the question of the entry of British ships to ports in Formosa; conditions in POW camps in Formosa were reported to be the worst in the Far East. TG 111.3 left Leyte on 3 September and arrived on Kiirun on 6th. *Bermuda*, *Argonaut* and *Quiberon* entered the harbour while *Colossus* and *Tumult* remained at sea. All moveable POWs had already been embarked in US ships and taken to Manila. The hospital ship *Maunganui* arrived on 8th and evacuated ninety-four sick to Manila. All POWs had been evacuated from Formosa by 9 September. At Manila, *Maunganui* embarked further patients and eventually landed 370 at Auckland in October.

On 11 September Admiral Servaes transferred his flag to *Belfast* and left for Shanghai. The next day POW contact teams were flown into Shanghai in aircraft from *Colossus*. TG 111.3 anchored off the Yangtse Bar on 18th, *Belfast*, *Argonaut* and three destroyers going up river the following day, while *Bermuda* and *Tumult* went to Tsingtao, arriving on 20th. The attitude of the Commander US 7th Fleet and of the Chinese towards Admiral Servaes's force can only be described as unhelpful. The British force was ignominiously berthed out of sight of the main Bund in Shanghai. The Chinese were apparently not aware that British ships had been operating side by side with the Americans and were convinced that the British flag had 'slipped in under the cloak' of the American forces who were there necessarily to continue supplying the Chinese army. However, *Glenearn* left Shanghai for Hong Kong with four hundred internees on 2 October, arriving on 6th, on passage to Ceylon. Admiral Kinkaid had not worked with British forces before and had little knowledge of China (the manner in which his task force, TF 74, later entered Hong Kong gave the greatest offence; TF 74 had all the appearance of an occupying fleet).

Evacuation and repatriation were now in progress all over the Far East. At Macassar 459 British POWs, some of them survivors of *Exeter*, were evacuated in *Maidstone* and arrived in Fremantle on 30 September. Most of the POWs in Korea were evacuated in American ships, but *Colossus* embarked 354 British and Australians, arriving at Manila on 4 October. Seven hundred British, Indian and Dutch were evacuated from Hainan in *Glenearn* and *Gerusalemme* on 18 and 19 September. Ships were leaving Hong Kong in a steady stream: *Oxfordshire* with

321 serious hospital cases for Manila, Brisbane and Sydney; *Empress of Australia* with nine hundred POWs and 1,000 civilians on 12 September; on 18th, *Glengyle* with six hundred British internees, and *Llanstephan Castle* with eight hundred Indian POWs for Madras; on 5 October *Takliwa* with eight hundred Indian POWs, *Highland Monarch* with four hundred internees and 350 Indian POWs, and the hospital ship *Tairea* with 550 Indian POWs.

The main task of repatriation for the British ships was, of course, at Manila. *Implacable* embarked 2,127 British POWs and took them to Canada, arriving at Esquimault on 11 October; *Glory* a further 1,460, including thirty-seven sick and 119 fit Canadians, to Vancouver (it had been decided to repatriate the majority of RAPWIs 'east-about' via North America). *Formidable* arrived at Sydney with 1,200 POWs, mostly Australians, on 13 October,[1] and was followed by *Speaker* with 624 more two days later. On 14 October, *Colossus* embarked two hundred Europeans for Hong Kong and India and *Lothian* 277 Asiatics for Singapore. Small numbers of RAPWIs were carried in ferry escort carriers calling at Manila on passage from Hong Kong to Australia.

The BPF carriers had disembarked their aircraft and aircrews and, with the assistance of Australian dockyards who worked day and night, had been converted to carry large numbers of passengers. Nurses, VADs, and Wrens joined the wardrooms for the passage. For the RAPWIs, feminine company was one of the most effective restoratives: 'Everyone held up their hands in horror, and said, You can't do that, you cannot embark a whole lot of women on a ship, it's never been done before. I said, I can't help it, you're going to do it. These are exceptional circumstances and it shall be done. And it was done.'[2]

Only a few weeks after they had been flying off strikes against the Japanese mainland, the carriers were steaming across the Pacific with their passengers playing deck hockey on the flight deck:

'The reactions of the ex-prisoners-of-war were rather what one would expect, except that I was continually being surprised by the effect some very minor point had on them. One officer confessed that his biggest thrill on the first day was sitting down to lunch at table with a table-cloth on it and using a knife and fork. Another officer, on being offered a drink, said: 'No thanks. I've looked forward to signing a chit again for four years and I'm not going to be robbed of doing that now.' In

---

[1] See *A Formidable Commission* (Seeley Service Ltd., 1946), Chs. 14 and 15.
[2] Vice Admiral Sir Edward Evans Lombe. Conversation of 8.11.67.

general one and all were anxious to talk; but, once started, they nearly always upset themselves by some memory that arose. Another difficulty was their inevitable lack of knowledge of what had occurred. In conversation I mentioned the Madagascar expedition and was met with a blank stare and 'Did we attack it?' A curious feature was the dislike for rain, which I never got to the bottom of. A tropical shower cleared the flight deck like a flash – in fact there was almost a free fight to get through the island doors or down the gun sponson ladders.

'The characteristic that impressed itself on us most of all was their initial desire to do nothing and say nothing. At first they were content as long as they were able to sit down in peace and quiet. If they watched a deck hockey match they hardly cheered or uttered a sound, and one felt a sort of chilled atmosphere. As time passed this attitude completely passed. Community singing, musical PT and eventually deck hockey and deck football began to attract volunteers, and one felt the whole party was slowly coming to life again. This aspect was remarkable to my mind for another reason – they had been in American hands and American camps for weeks and yet they in no way began to come out of their silent reserve until they reached English territory and English people.'[1]

In the immediate post-war period, ships of the fleet transported some 50,000 RAPWIs to various destinations. This total was achieved despite the ending of 'Lease–Lend' contracts, including those for oil fuel, on 21 August.

Meanwhile in South-east Asia after the capture of Rangoon the Japanese armies in Burma were shattered, isolated from each other, and in almost complete retreat. It was important to keep pressure on them and to maintain the Allies momentum towards the reoccupation of Malaya and Singapore. By now the enemy had been so weakened that the date for the assault on Malaya (ZIPPER) was brought forward to August and the intermediate landings at Phuket Island (ROGER) were abandoned. Without the naval anchorage and airfields at Phuket, air support for the assault troops would have to be provided by the fleet at sea and Admiral Mountbatten asked that the four light fleet carriers of the 11th Aircraft Carrier Squadron be retained in the East Indies Fleet for ZIPPER. The British Chiefs of Staff could not agree to this; the carriers were needed for the BPF. However, in May Admiral Mountbatten decided to undertake ZIPPER with the nine escort carriers

[1] *The Naval Review*, Vol. XXXIV, No. 1, February 1946, p. 39.

which would be available to him and detailed planning began on 1 June. Land forces in SEAC were reorganised; a newly formed 12th Army, under Lt. Gen. Stopford, was responsible for all operations in or based on Burma, while the 14th Army, under Lt. Gen. Miles Dempsey, would carry out ZIPPER. Lt. Gen. Slim was promoted General and relieved Lt. Gen. Leese as C-in-C Allied Land Forces South-east Asia (ALFSEA).

During the long retreat from Kohima the Japanese suffered more terrible privations than any other army in recent military history. They lacked food, armour, transport and air cover. All the logistical supports of a modern army were denied them. But, unbelievably, their morale and fighting spirit were intact. 'All armies', said General Slim, 'talk of fighting to the last man and the last round; the Japanese alone did it.'[1] The Japanese in Burma were still capable of one last *coup*, in July. Although half-starved and suffering appalling casualties, Lt. Gen. Sakurai's 28th Army, which had been trapped north of Rangoon, succeeded after a series of battles on the Sittang River in breaking out eastwards over the Pegu mountains, and it was still a military force under proper command when the Japanese surrendered.

The force commanders appointed for ZIPPER were Lt. Gen. O. L. Roberts, commanding 34 Corps who were to carry out the assault, Rear Admiral B. C. S. Martin, Flag Officer Force 'W',[2] and Air Vice Marshal the Earl of Bandon, 224 Group RAF. It was decided that the assault landings were to be made by two divisions on the Morib beaches, south of Port Swettenham. Because of tidal conditions, 27 August and 9 September were the only suitable dates for the landings. Naturally, Admiral Mountbatten strongly preferred the earlier date. But here, once more, external considerations interfered in SEAC affairs. The Navy and the RAF could meet 27 August, but the Army could not, because of the effects of PYTHON – the War Office scheme for repatriating men who had served long periods overseas. Reluctantly, Admiral Mountbatten had to agree to 9 September.

With the war in Europe over and a General Election pending at home, the return of time-expired men from the Far East was a delicate subject, both politically and as far as the Army's morale was concerned. The

---

[1] Field Marshal Sir William Slim, *Courage and other Broadcasts* (Cassell, 1957), p. 164.

[2] 'W', 'X' and 'Y' were the designations of three forces of landing craft each capable of lifting the assault element of one division, promised to SEAC by the Chiefs of Staff, to arrive in March–April 1945. In the event, only part of Force 'W' arrived.

qualifying period of service for return home under the PYTHON scheme had recently been reduced from four years to three years eight months, and had already caused considerable reshuffling of units for ZIPPER. The men who had served longest were naturally the most experienced and battle-hardened; too much dilution with fresh, green troops might jeopardise ZIPPER. However, ALFSEA had reached what was thought to be a satisfactory balance, in spite of PYTHON, when on 7 June the Secretary of State for War Sir James Grigg informed Admiral Mountbatten that on the morrow he would make a speech in the House of Commons in which he would announce that the PYTHON qualifying period in the Far East was to be reduced to three years four months forthwith.

Admiral Mountbatten had only twenty-four hours to frame a reply, but it needed no lengthy staff-work to conclude that the new PYTHON terms disposed of ZIPPER on 9 September. There simply were not in the Far East the physical means, in transport or facilities, to carry out both. There was indeed a saving clause by which men could be retained if their presence was an operational 'necessity', but large-scale use of this clause would be disastrous for morale.

In spite of Admiral Mountbatten's representations, in which he was supported by General Auchinleck, C-in-C India, neither the Secretary of State nor the War Office appeared to realise the full impact of the PYTHON scheme on ZIPPER, nor did they appear to grasp that the new PYTHON terms were totally divorced from the realities of the situation in SEAC. There was not enough shipping available to take home those men who had already been released under the previous PYTHON adjustment. Thus the additional men who were released under the new adjustment would not be returned home any more quickly than before. They could not now take part in operations. But neither could they go home. They would wait idle in India, neither in the war nor out of it, until shipping became available.

On 14 June it was decided to continue with ZIPPER, but on a reduced scale, retaining certain specialist officers and men under the 'operational necessity' clause. In the event, ZIPPER was not put to the test of enemy opposition. Japan had already surrendered and Singapore reoccupied, and it remains for historians to argue whether the landings at Port Swettenham would still have succeeded against determined Japanese resistance.

On 15 August, South-east Asia Command was greatly enlarged, Admiral Mountbatten being ordered to take over responsibility for a

AA

huge area of the south-west Pacific, including Java, Borneo, the Celebes and Dutch New Guinea. The problems of the post-war rehabilitation of the enlarged SEAC, with over 128,000,000 inhabitants, were enormous[1] and the necessary resources did not exist in the theatre. But, as a first step, a large forward base – obviously Singapore – would be needed. By now ZIPPER was at such a stage that it could not be accelerated nor abandoned nor even much changed without causing chaos. However, the 5th Indian Division, part of the ZIPPER follow-up force, was detached from the operation to reoccupy Singapore from the sea (Operation TIDERACE), while an air staging post and advanced naval base for small craft was to be established at Penang, to be occupied by Royal Marines of the East Indies Fleet in Operation JURIST.

Admiral Walker, flying his flag in *Nelson*, sailed from Trincomalee for Penang on 15 August, commanding a force of escort carriers, cruisers and destroyers of the East Indies Fleet and two LSI(L)s, *Princess Beatrix* and *Queen Emma*, with the Royal Marines embarked. His force also included *London* with 120 Marines for Sabang (Operation BEECHAM). Force 155, the 6th, 7th, and 37th Minesweeping Flotillas, sailed from Colombo on 15 and 17 August, to sweep the Malacca Strait. The 3rd Commando Brigade sailed from Bombay on 18th, bound for the reoccupation of Hong Kong, while the 5th Division were embarking at Rangoon for Singapore. It seemed possible that after $3\frac{1}{2}$ years Singapore would once more be in British hands within a few days.

But, as always in SEAC, it was not to be so simple. On 16 August General MacArthur who had been appointed Supreme Commander for the Allied Powers, signalled that the cease-fire instructions would not reach the Japanese in all the war zones of SEAC until 22nd and, so that Admiral Walker's force should not reach Penang prematurely, JURIST was postponed for forty-eight hours. Three days later there was a far more serious delay. General MacArthur ordered that no surrenders were to be signed and no landings made on enemy occupied territory until he had signed the main surrender of Japan in Tokyo, probably at the end of the month.

This placed Admiral Mountbatten and Admiral Power in a very awkward position. Their ships were already at sea and well on their way; to return them to Trincomalee would mean a long delay, at a time when every day that passed meant life or death to the men in the Japanese

---

[1] A full account of the problems and the extraordinary complexity of the post-war situation in SEAC is given in the Supreme Commander's Report to the Combined Chiefs of Staff, Section E, 'Post Surrender Tasks' (HMSO, 1969).

POW camps. The smaller ships could not have turned back into the teeth of the south-west monsoon, then blowing at its height, without risking damage. Admiral Mountbatten and Admiral Power agreed that the ships must somehow remain in the forward area, supporting themselves as best they could. The minesweepers of Force 155 huddled under the lee of Simalur Island, on the west coast of Sumatra, where emergency arrangements were made to supply their crews with food and fresh water. Admiral Walker's force anchored off the Great Nicobar Islands on 20 August, although *Nigeria*, two escort carriers *Stalker* and *Shah* and four destroyers had later to return to Trincomalee for fuel. The 3rd Commando Brigade was called in to Trincomalee and the 5th Indian Division, already embarked, was held at Rangoon.

Preliminary surrender documents to be signed in Rangoon on 28 August would allow entry and minesweeping of enemy-held coastal waters and so Admiral Walker's force sailed the day before, arriving off Penang on 28th. The same day Commodore Poland's force, the cruiser *London* and the destroyer *Raider*, anchored five miles off Sabang. Japanese officers came out to *Nelson* and *London* with assurances that the ships would not be attacked and with details of minefields on the Malayan and Sumatran coasts, in the Malacca Strait and at Singapore. On 30 August minesweeping began at Penang and Sabang, so that they could be entered as soon as the Japanese surrender was signed. Admiral Power, flying his flag in *Cleopatra*, sailed from Colombo on 27 August, called at Sabang on 29th and arrived at Penang on 1 September. The next day Rear Admiral Uzumi (who, incidentally, wore the DSC and Allied Victory Medal for his service in the 1914–18 War) signed the surrender of Penang on board *Nelson*. Royal Marines occupied the island on 3 September and the first Spitfires and Mosquitoes flew in from Rangoon. On 2 September *London*'s Royal Marines occupied Sabang and ceremonially hoisted the British and Dutch flags in the port the next day.

From Penang, *Cleopatra* sailed with the C-in-C on board to join the Singapore occupation force which was then steaming into the Malacca Strait, preceded by the 6th, 7th and 37th Minesweeping Flotillas. A channel was swept through the Japanese minefields on 2 September and the next day *Cleopatra* with HMIS *Bengal* and the 6th and 7th MS Flotillas anchored off Singapore. The convoys carrying the 5th Indian Division and 15th Corps Headquarters from Rangoon and the 3rd Commando Brigade from Bombay arrived on 4th, with *Sussex*, flying the flag of Rear Admiral C. S. Holland, the destroyer *Rotherham*, and

Kedah, the headquarters ship of Rear Admiral J. A. V. Morse, who was to be Flag Officer Malaya. The 3rd Commando Brigade sailed for Hong Kong on 6th.

On the evening of 4 September the surrender of the 77,000 Japanese personnel in Singapore and Johore was signed on board *Sussex*; Lieut. Gen. Itagaki, commanding 7th Area Army, and Vice Admiral Fukudome, commanding the 10th Area Fleet, signed for the Japanese. Admiral Mountbatten was represented by Lieut. Gen. Christison. The first troops of 5th Indian Division disembarked to begin the reoccupation of Singapore at 11 o'clock on 5 September.

The Japanese Navy at the Singapore Naval Base had intimated that they had no intention of surrendering to the British Army. The destroyer *Rotherham* (Captain H. W. Biggs, Captain (D) 11th DF) steamed round the island and arrived off the Naval Base at 0900 on 5th. *Rotherham*'s ship's company were at action stations, in case of treachery, but there was no need for alarm:

'The dockyard was deserted. The Japanese had laid off the work people two or three days previously and there was no one in sight except a small berthing party of Japanese sailors accompanied by the Naval Chief of Staff and a staff officer with a brief-case.'[1]

Captain Biggs set off with the Japanese Chief of Staff for a tour of the Naval Base Area:

'Except for minor bombing damage from US daylight raids, the dockyard and Base area seemed to be in good order – "much better than when we took it over" was the comment of the Japanese Chief of Staff (who spoke good English). I then toured quickly round the north of Singapore Island since this was under Japanese Navy control. It was interesting to note that there was no love lost between the Japanese Navy and Army. The Japanese Army were prohibited from entering the Naval Area (the north half of the island) without prior permission, except along the road to the Johore Causeway which was heavily patrolled by the Navy – as was the demarcation line through the middle of the island – to prevent any infractions.'[2]

Captain Biggs assumed command of the dockyard forthwith and blue-jackets from *Rotherham* were posted on the dockyard gates and perimeter

---

[1] Vice Admiral Sir Hilary Biggs, 'The Return to Singapore Naval Base', in MS, 25.10.67.
[2] Vice Admiral Biggs. Ibid.

patrols (although many armed Japanese remained as sentries because *Rotherham* did not have enough men). The next day a dockyard administration was improvised, Captain Biggs appointing his own wardroom officers to take over the duties of their technical counterparts in the yard; *Rotherham's* Engineer Officer became the Manager of the Engineering Department, the Gunnery Officer (who also happened to be a qualified naval constructor) became Manager of the Constructor's Department, the Torpedo Officer, Senior Electrical Engineer, and the Navigating Officer, Commander of the Yard. Daily conferences were held with the Japanese Naval staff. The Japanese staff work was excellent and *Rotherham's* officers were much impressed:

'On the table were placed many folios of rice paper, maps of Singapore, each folio carefully indexed. It did not matter what was asked for, there seemed to be a map showing all the places where it was stored – 4-inch shells, buckets, motor tyres, we named it, they had it and we could be taken to the stores immediately. As First Lieutenant I was anxious to get fresh vegetables for my ship's company. The Japanese produced a Lieutenant Commander (Farming) who was given my order and quickly disappeared. He turned up again alongside *Rotherham* at eleven o'clock that night with a lorry full of yams and fresh beans – just about enough to victual a whole flotilla. The Lieutenant Commander (Farming) was a surprise to us. Apparently the Japanese had this rank at each base and it was his task to see that captured territory was put to good use in supplying the needs of the troops.'[1]

By that evening the dockyard officers were installed in a mess ashore and were waited on by a large staff of ex-dockyard stewards who had reported for duty. Many of them brought with them their previous British masters' silver, which they had hidden during the Japanese occupation.

Labour was recruited locally, although as yet there was no cashier or accounting staff. The men were paid with a daily rice ration. As each man was paid he was rubber-stamped on his person with an 'HMS Rotherham' date stamp to prevent him 'going round the buoy' for a second ration. By 8 September the build-up of the dockyard was well under way and the naval base buildings rehabilitated for British occupation. Even the grass on the playing fields was cut – by hand, with scissors, by about five hundred Japanese.

The Japanese were to be evacuated from Singapore to Malaya and

[1] Lt. Cdr. Leslie Ellis, RN. Letter of 18.2.68.

their officers had been warned that the men could take only their regulation kit with them. However, this warning had evidently not been passed or had not penetrated to all ranks. When the Japanese assembled they had quantities of suitcases, civilian clothing, and obvious loot – silverware, ornaments, paintings and furnishings. The Japanese were stripped and searched, which caused great resentment amongst them. But *Rotherham*'s officers could not help pointing out the difference between their treatment and the treatment given to British prisoners of war when the Japanese captured Singapore. Afterwards, the civilian internees from the nearby Sime Road camp were given the pick of the loot.

Four small ships, totalling about 3,500 tons, were provided for the evacuation:

'The loading of the four small ships was an eye-opener to those who had not previously seen Japanese logistics in action. Layers of men were put into the hold, on temporary false decking, and every available space in the ships – even the lifeboats – was filled to capacity. Luckily, I had been given two MLs to escort the ships to their destination. I ordered them to take station astern and pick up those who fell over the side during the fifteen-hour trip – which several did.'[1]

On 10 September more British ships and units of the British and Indian Army arrived:

'By now the dockyard was in full peacetime swing and we were able to tell the new arrivals that nothing except food garbage should be placed in the pig swill bins – which made them realise that peace was here again.'[2]

There was one more reminder that peace was here again, in *Rotherham*'s final wind-fall from Singapore dockyard:

'We found a store of tins of "Bluebell" metal polish in cases – 500 tins to a case. I chalked the names of the big ships on the cases and had them despatched to their Commanders. Obviously the Japanese had no use for metal polish, and we had painted our bright-work for the duration. I often wonder what the sailors of those ships had to say when they found themselves at bright-work stations again after so many years. We also discovered a store full of pre-war enamel paint (a First Lieu-

---

[1] Vice Admiral Biggs. Ibid.
[2] Vice Admiral Biggs. Ibid.

tenant's dream) and I quickly restocked our paint store. We painted the ship with enamel paint before we went home and looked like the Royal Yacht.[1]

Meanwhile, the ZIPPER convoys had sailed from Bombay and from Cochin, from Madras and Vizagapatam, from Calcutta and Chittagong and Rangoon, and were converging on the Malayan coast at Port Swettenham.[2] ZIPPER was to be carried through as planned and rehearsed, except that the covering air and sea bombardment had been cancelled. Escorted by *Nelson*, flying the flag of Admiral Walker, and *Richelieu*, the cruisers *Nigeria*, *Cleopatra*, and *Ceylon*, the 21st Aircraft Carrier Squadron of *Royalist* (Commodore Oliver) and the escort carriers *Hunter*, *Stalker*, *Archer*, *Khedive*, *Emperor* and *Pursuer*, and fifteen destroyers, the first D-Day assault convoys arrived off their beaches at first light on 9 September.

The first troops and vehicles landed on the beaches safely and on time, but the landings as a whole did not go well. The first day's unloading fell behind schedule because of a number of factors: the muddy sub-soil only a foot under the sand, the very slight beach gradient, innumerable gullies and channels criss-crossing the beach, and a shallow sand-bar running parallel to the beach about a mile offshore. Vehicles were 'drowned' and landing craft were 'neaped' (i.e. left stranded high and dry at a time of falling tides). From the Navy's point of view, the beaches were as Rear Admiral Martin described them 'a convincing example of the most disadvantageous discharge conditions'. Two Spitfire squadrons, waiting to fly off from the escort carrier *Trumpeter*, wondered whether 'ZIPPER had become slightly un-zipped' and the official historian of 224 Group RAF had some harsh words to describe the conditions on the beaches:

'Conditions on the beaches were chaotic, vehicles drowned in scores as there were no decent exits from the beaches, and roads became choked with ditched tanks which tore up the road surfaces and grass verges. . . . A lack of vehicles ashore made movement of stores an impossible undertaking.'

Port Swettenham and Klang were occupied on the first day, and Kelanang airfield was handed over by the Japanese. Port Dickson was occupied the next day. On 12 September a new beach was opened farther south, at Cape Rachado, where the 23rd Division landed without any of the

---

[1] Lt. Cdr. Ellis. Ibid.　　　　　　　　　　[2] See map, p. 376.

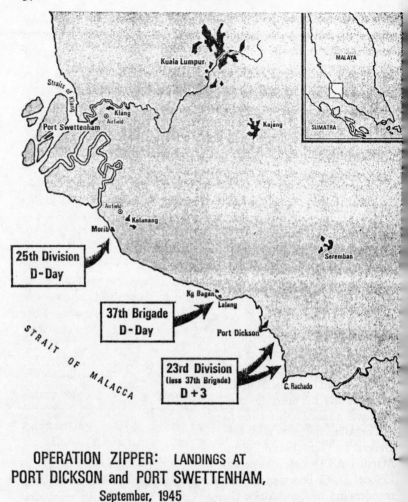

OPERATION ZIPPER: LANDINGS AT PORT DICKSON and PORT SWETTENHAM, September, 1945

difficulties met at Morib. The only incident was the spectacular arrival of one over-enthusiastic LST in the first wave which took the beach at 12 knots and disappeared into the jungle, whence it emerged seven days later – 'a small village having sprung up under its bows'. By the time the beaches were closed, Morib on 25th and Cape Rachado on 28 September, 63,838 troops, 7,337 vehicles and 25,671 tons of stores had been landed over them.

At the time of the ZIPPER landings there were 6,000 Japanese troops only thirty miles away at Kuala Lumpur and it is clear that if they had offered any resistance the assault troops would have been very roughly handled.[1] British troops entered Kuala Lumpur without resistance on 13 September.

On the morning of 12 September Admiral Mountbatten and his Deputy Supreme Commander, Lieut. Gen. R. A. Wheeler, US Army, drove in an open car (their chauffeur was a recently released British prisoner of war) through streets lined with sailors and Royal Marines of the East Indies Fleet to the Municipal Buildings of Singapore City, to accept the surrender of all Japanese forces in South-east Asia. Admiral Mountbatten was met by his three Commanders-in-Chief, Admiral Sir Arthur John Power, General Sir William Slim and Air Chief Marshal Sir Keith Park, and inspected four guards of honour, provided by the Royal Navy, the Royal Air Force, Australian para-troopers and the Indian Army. The massed bands of the ships of the East Indies Fleet played 'Rule Britannia' and the Royal Artillery fired a seventeen-gun salute.

Inside the Municipal Buildings, the entrance hall was hung with the flags of the Allies, and a picture of King George VI and the Royal Arms, hidden in Singapore Museum throughout the war, had been replaced in the main Council Chamber. A British airman stood at the door of the Council chamber and at each of the eight main pillars stood an armed guard representing the Allied nations. Two long tables, six feet apart, had been placed in the middle of the room, one for the Allied delegates and the other for the Japanese. In the centre of the Allies' table was a raised dais for the Supreme Commander.

The Allied delegates were General Wheeler (representing the USA), General Le Clerc (France), Brigadier K. S. Thimayya (India), Air Vice Marshal A. T. Cole (Australia), Major General Feng Yee (China), Colonel D. C. Boorman van Vreedon (Netherlands), the three Com-manders in Chief, and Major General Penney, Director of Intelligence. Behind the Allied delegation sat General Sir Carton de Wiart VC, and Lieut. Gen. C. H. Gairdner (the Prime Minister's and Lord Mount-batten's representatives at Chungking and at General MacArthur's headquarters), Sir Archibald Rowlands (representing the Government of India) and many senior officers of the Navy, Army and Air Force and Supreme Headquarters. In the body of the room and behind the

---

[1] However, post-war assessment showed that the Japanese had only 130,000 troops in the whole of Malaya, and ZIPPER, with a quarter of a million men and full fire support from air and sea, would certainly have succeeded.

Japanese delegation were some four hundred spectators, ex-prisoners of war and officers of the three services, press, film crews and photographers.

The Japanese delegation then entered in silence and took their places at the table opposite the Allies. They were General Itagaki (7th Area Army), General Kimura (Burma Area Army), Lieut. Gen. Nakamura (18th Area Army), Lieut. Gen. Kinoshita (3rd Air Army), Vice Admiral Fukudome (1st Southern Expeditionary Fleet), Vice Admiral Shibata (2nd Southern Expeditionary Fleet) and Lieut. Gen. Numata (Chief of Staff to Field Marshal Count Terauchi).

Admiral Mountbatten addressed the assembly from the dais:

'I have come here today to receive the formal surrender of all the Japanese forces within the South-east Asia Command. I have received the following telegram from the Supreme Commander of the Japanese forces concerned, Field Marshal Count Terauchi:

' "The most important occasion of the formal surrender signing at Singapore draws near, the significance of which is no less great to me than to your Excellency. It is extremely regretful that my ill health prevents me from attending and signing it personally, and that I am unable to pay homage to your Excellency. I hereby notify your Excellency that I have fully empowered General Itagaki, the highest senior general in Japanese armies, and send him on my behalf."

'On hearing of Field Marshal Terauchi's illness, I sent my own doctor, Surgeon Captain Birt, Royal Navy, to examine him, and he certifies that the Field Marshal is suffering from the effects of a stroke. In the circumstances I have decided to accept the surrender from General Itagaki today, but I have warned the Field Marshal that I shall expect him to make his personal surrender to me as soon as he is fit enough to do so.[1]

'In addition to our Naval, Military and Air Forces which we have present in Singapore today, a large fleet is anchored off Port Swettenham and Port Dickson, and a large force started disembarking from them at daylight on 9 September. When I visited the beaches yesterday, men were landing in an endless stream. As I speak there are 100,000 men ashore. This invasion would have taken place on 9 September whether

---

[1] Terauchi made his personal surrender to Lord Mountbatten in Saigon on 30 November, surrendering two swords, a short sword forged in the sixteenth century, which Lord Mountbatten presented to King George VI, and a long sword forged in the thirteenth century. Count Terauchi had suffered a stroke on hearing the news of the capture of Mandalay. He died in 1946.

the Japanese had resisted or not. I wish to make this plain; the surrender today is no negotiated surrender. The Japanese are submitting to superior force, now massed here.'

General Itagaki produced and read his credentials and the Instrument of Surrender. He and Admiral Mountbatten signed eleven copies, one each for the British, American, Chinese, French, Dutch, Australian, Indian and Japanese Governments, and one each for King George VI, Admiral Mountbatten himself, and SEAC records.

Afterwards, Admiral Mountbatten read an Order of the Day[1] from the steps of the Municipal Buildings (simultaneously read to all units in SEAC) and to the strains of 'God Save the King' a Union Jack which had been concealed in Changi Gaol since February 1942 was hoisted at the saluting base. For a few years at least, the British had returned to Singapore.

As in the Pacific theatre, the planning and organisation in SEAC for the repatriation of prisoners of war and internees were overtaken by events. The clandestine Force 136 and 'E' Groups[2] had, for some months before the Japanese surrender, been locating camps in Malaya, Siam and French Indo-China, and where possible, establishing contact with the inmates. RAPWI control staffs had also been set up. But the basic assumption in all planning had been that camps would be liberated over a period of time as territory was recaptured from the enemy. Suddenly, an estimated 125,000 prisoners of war and internees (including those in Java) distributed over a vast area, in some 250 known camps, all required urgent and simultaneous repatriation.

General MacArthur's order forbade actual landings on enemy-held territory but as much as possible was done in SEAC within the letter, if not the spirit, of that prohibition. After the meeting of 27 August in Rangoon to sign the preliminary surrender agreement, Field Marshal Terauchi had instructed his commanders to assist and obey the British reoccupation force commanders:

'As a result of this meeting, at which it had been obvious that the Japanese High Command intended to obey my orders punctiliously, I decided that I did not have to guard against large-scale opposition and that I could now take certain risks. Operations for the recovery of

---

[1] See Appendix E.

[2] Special Operations Executive (SOE) was known in SEAC as Force 136. The 'E' Groups ('Escape and Evasion' Groups) were organised to assist crashed aircrew and escaped prisoners of war to escape from enemy territory.

Allied Prisoners of War and Internees (RAPWI) started on the 28th: when pamphlets were dropped from the air over all known camps, with the object of spreading the news of the Japanese capitulation to the guards and the prisoners themselves (Operation BIRDCAGE). Immediately after this, and in spite of monsoon weather and long ranges, the delivery of stores and relief personnel (Operation MASTIFF) began while "Mercy" ships, loaded with supplies, were sent ahead of our forces, and the supplies were distributed under the guardianship of the Japanese.

'If relief stores and personnel had not been sent in at once, the delay of twelve days imposed on me would have resulted in many more deaths each day among the prisoners. As it was, 950 tons of supplies and some 120 relief personnel were flown into known prison camps in the Command, before any military landings in Malaya took place.'[1]

The first prisoners of war and internees to be recovered were actually flown from Siam to Rangoon on 28 August. Conditions in the camps and the morale of the prisoners are best described in a report written in September by that remarkable woman, Lady Mountbatten, who visited camps in Siam, Malaya, French Indo-China, Sumatra, Java (and later Borneo, Morotai, Manila and Hong Kong) while the recovery operations were under way:

'I went to a large number of camps in Siam, where the death roll in 1942/1943 during the building of the railway into Burma, has been appallingly high (17,000 dead) but the men who came through were in amazingly good spirits, however ill and emaciated they might be. This really applied to every single camp I have seen, and the brave spirits and real "guts" have been unbelievable during all those ghastly years.... No praise can be too high for what the doctors, surgeons and RAMC orderlies have done in the camps . . . even though they had absolutely no medical supplies, drugs or equipment. The way they improvised . . . was quite staggering, extracting drugs from herbs and plants, making surgical and medical equipment out of old bits of tin, glass and bamboo, and setting up, in many camps, entire workshops which really turned out usable stuff.

'I visited camps both in Bangkok and remote parts of Siam, generally conducted by the Japanese who were the only people who knew the

---

[1] Vice Admiral the Earl Mountbatten of Burma. Report to the Combined Chiefs of Staff by the Supreme Allied Commander South-east Asia 1943–1945 (HMSO, 1951), B. Strategy and Operations, p. 184.

locations and the roads, and the surprise of the prisoners of war at seeing, out of the blue, the first white woman for $3\frac{1}{2}$ years, and she stepping out of a Jeep which most of them had never even heard of, and certainly never seen, was truly amazing. . . .

'I spent nearly a week in Sumatra, living in various buildings cheek by jowl with the heavily be-sworded and be-armed Japanese officers . . . the Japanese did what we told them, and we succeeded in doing all the evacuation of British, Australian and Indian prisoners of war from Central and Southern Sumatra by river boat up to the coasts where we got LST and LCI from Singapore to come and fetch them, and a large number also we evacuated by Dakota aircraft from hastily improvised airstrips. The fact that most of the coasts round Sumatra and Java were mined also added to our worries. . . .

'On the whole things went extraordinarily well, and the recovery and repatriation of prisoners of war and civil internees was most successful and speedy, considering the gigantic areas over which they were spread and the endless problems involved, not the least of them the fact that in many places for instance, Sumatra, we had to do the whole of the evacuation of the prisoners of war before we had one single Allied soldier landed, or even the Navy lying off. . . . Luckily, somehow it worked, and there is no doubt that had the war gone on a few more weeks there would have been no prisoners of war in these areas left alive at all. They were absolutely at their last gasp in the Netherlands East Indies areas, and the tragedy is that so many did die in the last few weeks, before the Surrender and even after.'[1]

The problems of repatriating such great numbers over such great distances were indeed endless (some prisoners even said, with a bitter wit, that RAPWI stood for 'Retain All Prisoners of War Indefinitely') but by the end of October over 70,000 prisoners of war and internees had been repatriated from Singapore to India, Australia and the United Kingdom; almost all of them were transported by sea, only about 3,000 being flown out.

One of Japan's main war aims had been first to weaken and finally to remove European colonial influences in the Far East. Paradoxically, this purpose was achieved, although Japan herself was defeated. After the defeat of Japan an irresistible tide of nationalism, often Communist inspired and controlled, swept throughout Asia. The pre-war pattern

[1] *The War against Japan*, by Major General S. Woodburn Kirby, Vol. V (HMSO, 1969), Ch. 23.

of the continent dissolved under the pressures of political change and civil war.

China was accredited with the status of a major power but in fact the country had been in a state of virtual civil war since 1941, and the Communists controlled much of north China. After the war there was a short period of uneasy truce and mutually suspicious parleyings between General Chiang Kai-shek and Mao Tse Tung but, despite the mediations of General Marshall, open civil war broke out once more in 1946, culminating in the great Communist offensive of 1948 and the eventual establishment of a People's Republic on the mainland of China.

One by one the European powers lost their former territories as the structure of colonialism in Asia collapsed. In French Indo-China, Ho Chi Minh proclaimed an independent republic of Vietnam in Hanoi in September 1945. Hurried on by the pre-war attitudes and disastrous diplomacy of the French, and made inevitable at Potsdam by the arbitrary division of the country along the 16th Parallel, giving the north to Chiang Kai-shek, civil war broke out in December 1946, ending in 1954 with the Vietminh general Giap's victory over the French at Dien Bien Phu. In the Dutch East Indies also, an independent state of Indonesia was proclaimed by President Sukarno in August 1945. This republic, too, had eventually to be recognised – after four years of fighting between Indonesian nationalists and British, Indian and latterly, Dutch troops. In Burma, the former Burmese National Army leader General Aung San might have been an Asian political figure to rank with Ho Chi Minh and Sukarno. After he was assassinated in July 1947, an independent Union of Burma was declared the following January, and the country at once plunged into civil war. In Malaya the Chinese, largely Communist-inspired, who had most strongly resisted the Japanese occupation also resisted the civil rule which was re-established in April 1946. After two uneasy years, guerilla warfare began in Malaya in June 1948 and continued sporadically until quelled by General Templer in the mid 1950s.

By another paradox, Japan herself was the most peaceful country in the Far East. The occupying Allied powers under General MacArthur and the occupied Japanese, the winners and the losers, settled down together to make the best of the occupation, showing understanding and magnanimity on one side and a spirit of co-operation on the other.

The great changes occurring in Asia did not penetrate to, or at least did not seem to affect, the decisions of the British Chiefs of Staff Committee. If nothing else, wartime experience in SEAC had surely demonstrated the absolute necessity of a Supreme Commander to exercise overall control of all forces. Admiral Mountbatten strongly recommended that such a commander be retained in peace-time, with a nucleus staff. The proposal was rejected, on the grounds that under a Supreme Commander the individual Navy, Army and RAF C-in-Cs would tend to cultivate their own backyards and neglect larger issues; that the appointment would need too large a staff; and that differences of opinion between the service chiefs were better resolved in London than in the Far East. At the same time, the service chiefs were disposed about the Far East almost as though some wilful attempt was made to cause the maximum fragmentation and minimum liaison. The C-in-C Pacific Fleet had his headquarters at Hong Kong, the C-in-C East Indies Fleet at Trincomalee, while the Army and RAF C-in-Cs had their headquarters at Singapore.

While a Supreme Commander and his organisation still existed in the Far East it might have been thought more economical and convenient to place all British forces and resources in the theatre within that command. In fact, the Pacific Fleet at Hong Kong was an independent command under Admiral Fraser; the difficulties inherent in this arrangement were smoothed, as in 1944, by the close co-operation between Admiral Fraser and Admiral Mountbatten. Hong Kong was excluded from SEAC, Admiral Harcourt being responsible to the British Chiefs of Staff, although SEAC provided ground troops and aircraft and administrative support for forces in the Colony. Thus an anomalous situation developed, where Admiral Mountbatten was administratively responsible for forces he did not control and Admiral Harcourt was operationally responsible for forces he did not administer. Evidently the Chiefs of Staff Committee, like the Bourbons, had forgotten nothing and learned nothing.[1]

The BPF was dispersed and was never reassembled, to Admiral Rawlings's great disappointment. Sadly, and in some ways prophetically, he wrote:

'I have not seen the personal signals, or indeed seen all the official signals, but I am in no two minds about one thing; that the "fading out" of the Task Force and the manner in which this is being done is not only tragic, but is one which I would give much to avoid.

'To me, what is happening to its personnel and its ships seems to

---

[1] The principle of overall command, with the appointment of an equivalent of a Supreme Commander, was re-established in the Far East in 1962.

ignore their feelings, their sentiments and their pride; in so doing quite a lot is being cast away, for that Fleet accomplished something which matters immensely.

'I am not speaking of such enemy they met, nor of the difficulties they overcame, nor of the long periods at sea; I am speaking of that which was from the start our overriding and heaviest responsibility, the fact that we were in a position which was in most ways unique and was in any case decisive; for we could have lowered the good name of the British Navy in American eyes for ever.

'. . . I am not certain that those at home have any idea of what these long operationg periods mean, nor of the strain put on those in the ships, so many of whom, both officers and men, are mere children. I have in my Flagship, for instance, Leading Seamen of 19 and Petty Officers of 21. When I look back on that which this untrained youth has managed to accomplish and to stick out, then I have no fear for the future of the Navy, provided, but only provided, that we handle them with vision and understanding, and that we recognise them for what they were and are – people of great courage who would follow one anywhere, and whose keynote was that the word "impossible" did not exist.

'And so I question the wisdom of dispersing a Fleet in the way in which it is now being done. At the very least there should have been taken home to England a token force somewhat similar to that which was left in the operating area with the American Fleet when the tanker shortage required the withdrawal of the greater part of the Task Force.

'It seems to me that here was a matter which could have been utilised in a dignified and far-reaching manner – the arrival in home waters of ships who had represented the Empire alongside their American allies, and who were present, adding their not ineffective blow, at the annihilation of the Japanese Navy and the defeat of Japan.

'It may well be that the days will come when the Navy will find it hard to get the money it needs. Perhaps then a remembrance of the return and the work of the British Pacific Fleet might have helped to provide a stimulus and an encouragement to wean the public from counter attractions and those more alluringly staged.'

Admiral Rawlings's plea fell on deaf ears. Perhaps, as he suggested, the arrival home of a token force, possibly at the time of the Victory Celebrations in June 1946, might have fixed the British Pacific Fleet more firmly in the public's memory. But it was not to be. In time the fleet quietly faded away, with the result that the Far Eastern fleets may have been the largest assemblies of Commonwealth ships in history but, like the old ladies locked in the lavatory, nobody knew they were there.

As the post-war years passed, the majority of the ships of the British Pacific Fleet were taken out of service, and sent to the breaker's yard, or sold to foreign navies. The last surviving major warship of the BPF in the Royal Navy was the carrier *Victorious* which served, after several refits and modernisations, until the Government defence cuts of 1966.

Yet, in a more subtle way, the fleet did come home. Many British officers remained life-long friends of their American counterparts[1] and still keep their friendships in good repair today, visiting and corresponding whenever possible – even attending the weddings of each other's daughters. Admiral Rawlings himself retired soon after the war – 'to give younger men a chance' – but Fraser, Lambe, who had commanded *Illustrious*, and Le Fanu, who was Halsey's and Spruance's British liaison officer, all became First Sea Lords and many of the 'middle management' officers of the BPF were to become the admirals of the post-war Navy, some of them reaching the Board of Admiralty. Unlike their predecessors of 1939, these officers with Pacific experience were fully accustomed to the idea of a fleet operating at sea for long periods, at long distance from its base, and this was to be particularly fortunate for a Navy which was about to lose almost all its traditional overseas bases. In this sense, the 'forgotten fleet' has been remembered ever since.

[1] After the war, Admiral and Mrs Nimitz stayed with Sir Bernard and Lady Rawlings in Cornwall during a visit to England, and when Admiral Halsey died, the US Navy Department invited Admiral Rawlings to be a pall-bearer. He was greatly touched and honoured, but to his intense disappointment his health was already too bad to allow him to attend the funeral.

Appendices

Appendix A

THE BRITISH PACIFIC FLEET

On VJ DAY, 15 AUGUST 1945

Commander in Chief: Admiral Sir Bruce Fraser, GCB, KBE
Second in Command: Vice Admiral Sir Bernard Rawlings, KCB, KBE
Commanding First Aircraft Carrier Squadron: Vice Admiral Sir Philip Vian, KCB, KBE, DSO
Rear Admiral Fleet Train: Rear Admiral D. B. Fisher, CB, CBE
Commanding Eleventh Aircraft Carrier Squadron: Rear Admiral C. H. J. Harcourt, CB
Commanding Fourth Cruiser Squadron: Rear Admiral E. J. P. Brind, CB, CBE
Commanding Destroyer Flotillas: Rear Admiral J. H. Edelsten, CB, CBE
Commanding Third Cruiser Squadron: Rear Admiral R. M. Servaes, CBE
Vice Admiral (Administration): Vice Admiral C. S. Daniel, CBE, DSO

Battleships
DUKE OF YORK (C-in-C, BPF): Capt. A. D. Nicholl, CBE, DSO
KING GEORGE V (VA 2 in C): Capt. B. B. Schofield, CBE
ANSON: Capt. A. C. G. Madden
HOWE: Capt. H. W. U. McCall, DSO

Fleet Aircraft Carriers
VICTORIOUS: Rear Admiral M. M. Denny, CB, CBE
FORMIDABLE: Capt. W. G. Andrewes, CBE, DSO
INDEFATIGABLE: Capt. Q. D. Graham, CBE, DSO
INDOMITABLE: Capt. J. A. S. Eccles, CBE
IMPLACABLE: Capt. C. C. Hughes-Hallett, CBE

Light Fleet Aircraft Carriers
COLOSSUS: Capt. G. H. Stokes, CB, DSC
GLORY: Capt. A. W. Buzzard, DSO, OBE
VENERABLE: Capt. W. A. Dallmeyer, DSO
VENGEANCE: Capt. D. M. L. Neame, DSO+

Escort Aircraft Carriers
STRIKER: Capt. W. P. Carne
ARBITER: Capt. D. H. Everett, DSO, MBE

CHASER: Capt. R. G. Poole
RULER: Capt. H. P. Currey, OBE
SLINGER: Lt. Cdr. J. G. Hopkins
SPEAKER: Capt. U. H. R. James
VINDEX: Cdr. J. D. L. Williams, DSC
REAPER: Cdr. I. T. Clark, OBE

Cruisers
BERMUDA: Capt. J. S. Bethell, CBE
BELFAST: Capt. R. M. Dick, CBE, DSC
EURYALUS: Capt. R. S. Warne, CBE
GAMBIA (New Zealand manned): Capt. R. A. B. Edwards, CBE
ACHILLES (New Zealand manned): Capt. F. J. Butler, MBE
NEWFOUNDLAND: Capt. R. W. Ravenhill, CBE, DSC
BLACK PRINCE: Capt. G. V. Gladstone
ONTARIO (RCN): Capt. H. T. W. Grant, DSO, RCN
SWIFTSURE: Capt. P. V. McLaughlin
ARGONAUT: Capt. W. P. McCarthy

Fast Minelayers
APOLLO: Capt. L. N. Brownfield
ARIADNE: Capt. F. B. Lloyd, OBE
MANXMAN: Capt. G. Thistleton-Smith, GM

Destroyer Depot Ships
TYNE: Capt. S. Boucher
MONTCLARE: Capt. G. W. Hoare-Smith

Destroyers
QUADRANT: Lt. Cdr. P. C. Hopkins
QUALITY: Cdr. Viscount Jocelyn
QUEENBOROUGH: Cdr. P. L. Saumarez, DSC+
QUIBERON (RAN): Cdr. G. S. Stewart, RAN
QUICKMATCH (RAN): Lt. Cdr. O. H. Becher, DSC+, RAN
QUILLIAM: Lt. J. R. Stephens
NAPIER (RAN manned): Capt. H. J. Buchanan, DSO, RAN
NEPAL (RAN manned): Lt. Cdr. C. J. Stephenson, RAN
NIZAM (RAN manned): Cdr. C. H. Brooks, RAN
NORMAN (RAN manned): Lt. Cdr. J. Plunkett-Cole, RAN
BARFLEUR: Cdr. M. S. Townsend, DSO, OBE, DSC+
TROUBRIDGE: Capt. G. F. Burghard
TEAZER: Lt. Cdr. T. F. Taylor, DSC
TENACIOUS: Lt. Cdr. G. C. Crowley, DSC+
TERMAGANT: Lt. Cdr. D. C. Beatty, DSC+
TERPSICHORE: Cdr. R. T. White, DSO++

TUMULT: Lt. Cdr. A. S. Pomeroy, DSC
TUSCAN: Lt. Cdr. P. B. N. Lewis, DSC
TYRIAN: Cdr. R. H. Mills
TRAFALGAR: Capt. A. F. Pugsley, CB, DSO++
ARMADA: Lt. Cdr. R. A. Fell
CAMPERDOWN: Lt. Cdr. J. J. S. Yorke, DSC+
HOGUE: Cdr. A. St. Clair-Ford, DSO+
GRENVILLE: Capt. R. G. Onslow, DSO+++
ULSTER: Lt. Cdr. R. J. Hanson, DSO, DSC
ULYSSES: Lt. Cdr. B. G. B. Bordes, DSC
UNDINE: Cdr. T. C. Robinson, DSC
UNDAUNTED: Lt. Cdr. C. E. R. Sharp
URANIA: Lt. Cdr. D. H. P. Gardiner, DSC
URCHIN: Lt. Cdr. A. F. Harkness, OBE, DSC, RD, RNR
URSA: Cdr. D. B. Wyburd, DSO, DSC
KEMPENFELT: Capt. E. G. McGregor, DSO
WAGER: Lt. Cdr. R. C. Watkin
WAKEFUL: Lt. Cdr. G. D. Pound, DSC
WESSEX: Lt. Cdr. R. Horncastle
WHELP: Cdr. G. A. F. Norfolk
WHIRLWIND: Cdr. W. A. F. Hawkins, DSO, OBE, DSC+
WIZARD: Lt. Cdr. R. H. Hodgkinson, DSC+
WRANGLER: Lt. Cdr. E. G. Warren
ALGONQUIN (RCN): Lt. Cdr. D. W. Piers, DSC, RCN

Auxiliary Anti-aircraft Ship
PRINCE ROBERT (RCN): Capt. W. B. Creery, RCN

Sloops
ENCHANTRESS: Lt. Cdr. A. J. Clemence, RNR (Command and HQ Ship,
    Escorts)
PHEASANT: Cdr. J. B. Palmer
CRANE: Lt. Cdr. R. G. Jenkins, DSC
REDPOLE: Lt. Cdr. E. J. Lee
WHIMBREL: Lt. Cdr. N. R. Murch
WOODCOCK: Lt. Cdr. S. J. Parsons, DSC
ALACRITY: Lt. Cdr. J. Clutton-Baker, DSC
AMETHYST: Lt. Cdr. N. Scott-Elliott, DSC+
BLACK SWAN: Lt. Cdr. A. D. C. Inglis
ERNE: Lt. Cdr. P. S. Evans
HART: Cdr. H. F. C. Leftwich
HIND: Lt. Cdr. A. D. White, RD, RNR
CYGNET: Lt. Cdr. A. H. Pierce, OBE, RNR
FLAMINGO: Lt. A. Traill, RNR
OPOSSUM: Lt. Cdr. W. F. Hollins
STARLING: Lt. Cdr. G. C. Julian, RNZNVR
STORK: Lt. Cdr. D. E. Mansfield, DSC
WREN: Cdr. S. R. J. Woods, DSC, RD, RNR

Frigates
AVON: Cdr. P. G. A. King, DSC, RD, RNR
FINDHORN: Lt. Cdr. J. P. Burnett, RNVR
PARRET: Lt. Cdr. T. Hood, RNR
HELFORD: Cdr. C. G. Cuthbertson, DSC, RD, RNR
BARLE: Lt. Cdr. J. Duncan, DSC, RNR
DERG: Lt. Cdr. N. B. J. Stapleton, RD, RNR
ODZANI: Lt. Cdr. J. N. Burgess, RANVR
PLYM: Lt. Cdr. A. Foxall, RNR
USK: Lt. Cdr. G. B. Medlycott, RNR
WIDEMOUTH BAY: Lt. Cdr. J. H. MacAlister, RNVR
BIGBURY BAY: Lt. Cdr. G. P. D. Hall, DSC
VERYAN BAY: Lt. J. S. Brownrigg, DSC
WHITESAND BAY: Lt. Cdr. B. C. Longbottom

Submarine Depot Ships
ADAMANT: Capt. B. Bryant, DSO++, DSC
MAIDSTONE, Capt. L. M. Shadwell
BONAVENTURE: Capt. W. R. Fell, OBE, DSC

Submarines
TACITURN: Lt. Cdr. E. T. Stanley, DSO, DSC
TAPIR: Lt. J. C. Y. Roxburgh, DSO, DSC+
TAURUS: Lt. P. E. Newstead, DSC
THOROUGH: Lt. A. G. Chandler, DSC, RNR
THULE: Lt. Cdr. A. C. G. Mars, DSO, DSC
TIPTOE: Lt. R. L. Jay
TOTEM: Lt. Cdr. M. B. St. John, DSC
TRENCHANT: Lt. J. C. Ogle, DSC
TRUMP: Lt. A. A. Catlow
TURPIN: Lt. J. S. Stevens, DSO+, DSC
SCOTSMAN: Lt. A. H. B. Anderson, DSC, RNR
SEASCOUT: Lt. J. W. Kelly
SELENE: Lt. Cdr. H. R. B. Newton, DSC
SIDON: Lt. H. C. Gowan
SLEUTH: Lt. K. H. Martin
SOLENT: Lt. J. D. Martin, DSC
SPEARHEAD: Lt. R. E. Youngman, DSC, RNR
STUBBORN: Lt. A. G. Davies
SUPREME: Lt. T. E. Barlow
SANGUINE: Lt. P. C. S. Pritchard, RNR
SEA DEVIL: Lt. D. W. Mills, DSC
SEANYMPH: Lt. M. I. Usher
SPARK: Lt. D. G. Kent
STYGIAN: Lt. G. S. C. Clarabut, DSO
TERRAPIN: Lt. R. H. H. Brunner, DSC+
TUDOR: Lt. S. A. Porter, DSC
VORACIOUS: Lt. D. R. Wilson, DSC, RANVR

Vox: Lt. W. E. I. Littlejohn, DSC, RANVR
Virtue: Lt. I. G. Raikes, DSC

Fleet Minesweepers
Coquette: Cdr. R. W. D. Thomson, DSC
Rowena: Lt. Cdr. G. C. Hocart, DSC, RNR
Mary Rose: Lt. D. H. Edleston
Moon: Lt. J. B. Lamb, DSC
Providence: Lt. E. G. Mason
Seabear: Lt. Cdr. W. A. C. Harvey, RNR
Thisbe: Cdr. F. A. I. Kirkpatrick
Courier: Cdr. E. S. Jerome, DSO
Felicity: Lt. Cdr. H. R. Richards
Hare: Lt. Cdr. J. K. M. Warde, RNVR
Liberty: Cdr. J. S. Roc, DSC, RNR
Michael: Lt. Cdr. J. D. Jones
Minstrel: Lt. Cdr. E. B. Cutlack, RNR
Wave: Lt. Cdr. D. C. Salter
Welcome: Lt. Cdr. T. Gentle, RNR

RAN Manned Minesweepers
Ballarat: Cdr. N. R. Read, RAN
Bendigo: Lt. W. Jackson, RANVR
Burnie: Lt. Cdr. E. M. Andrewartha, RANR
Goulburn: Lt. E. K. Connor, RANR
Maryborough: Lt. Cdr. M. W. Lancaster, RAN
Toowoomba: Lt. H. F. Goodwin, RANR
Whyalla: Lt. G. L. B. Parry, RANVR
Cessnock: Lt. A. G. Chapman, RANR
Gawler: Lt. Cdr. J. H. P. Dixon, RANR
Geraldton: Cdr. A. J. Travis, RAN
Ipswich: Lt. R. H. Creasy, DSC, RANR
Launceston: Lt. Cdr. E. J. Barron, RANR
Pirie: Lt. C. K. Mackenzie, RANVR
Tamworth: Lt. M. B. Gale, RANR
Wollongong: Lt. J. Hare, RANR
Kalgoorlie: Lt. Cdr. J. S. McBryde, RANR
Lismore: Lt. K. S. Sutherland, RANVR
Cairns: Lt. C. M. Callow, RANVR

Attached Danlayers (Trawlers)
Shillay: Lt. R. P. Rodriguez, RANVR
Trodday: Lt. H. S. Chisholm, RNVR

Aircraft Target Ship
Lewes: Lt. Cdr. M. H. Grylls, SANF(V)

Boom Carriers
FERNMOOR: Lt. Cdr. E. R. Crone, RNR
LEONIAN: Cdr. R. F. Graham, RNR

Landing Ships
LOTHIAN: Capt. G. C. F. Branson, RAN
GLENEARN: Capt. C. A. G. Hutchison, DSO+

Fleet Train Accommodation Ships
AORANGI   LANCASHIRE

Repair and Maintenance Ships
ARTIFEX: Capt. C. C. Flemming
RESOURCE: Capt. D. B. O'Connell, CBE
BERRY HEAD: Cdr. K. M. Drake, RD, RNR
FLAMBOROUGH HEAD: Lt. Cdr. J. F. Denman (Escort Maintenance Ship)
DULLISK COVE: Lt. Cdr. G. B. Herbert-Jones, RD, RNR
ASSISTANCE: Capt. J. H. Young
DILIGENCE: Capt. E. H. Hopkinson, OBE
SPRINGDALE: Lt. J. S. Seal, RNR (Deperming Ship)
KELANTAN: Cdr. S. P. Herivel, OBE, DSC, RNVR (Minesweeper Maintenance Ship)
ARBUTUS (NZ manned): Lt. N. D. Blair, RNZNR (Radio and Radar Repair Ship)

Command Ship, Logistic Supply Group
AIRE: Lt. Cdr. H. I. S. White, RNR (CLSG)

Air Maintenance and Repair Ships
PIONEER (COMAT): Cdre (2nd Cl.) H. S. Murray-Smith
UNICORN: Capt. C. M. Merewether
DEER SOUND: Capt. R. H. Johnson, DSC

Air Store Ships
FORT COLVILLE   FORT LANGLEY

Fleet Oilers

OLNA: Capt. P. L. Williams, RD, RNR	WAVE EMPEROR (RFA)	AASE MAERSK
	WAVE GOVERNOR (RFA)	CARELIA
ARNDALE (RFA)	WAVE KING (RFA)	SAN ADOLFO
BISHOPDALE (RFA)	WAVE MONARCH (RFA)	SAN AMADO
CEDARDALE (RFA)	GREEN RANGER (RFA)	SAN AMBROSIO
DINGLEDALE (RFA)	RAPIDOL (RFA)	DARST CREEK
EAGLESDALE (RFA)	SERBOL (RFA)	GOLDEN MEADOW
		IERE
		LOMA NOVIA

Water Carriers
EMPIRE CREST
BROWN RANGER (RFA)

VACPORT
SEVEN SISTERS

Distilling Ships
BACCHUS (RFA)

STAGPOOL

Net Layer
GUARDIAN: Capt. R. D. Binks, OBE, RD, RNR

Salvage Vessels
KING SALVOR: Lt. R. H. A. Adams, RNVR
SALVESTOR
SALVICTOR: Lt. Cdr. W. J. Harvey, RNR

Hospital Ships
TJITJALENGKA
MAUNGANUI
OXFORDSHIRE

EMPIRE CLYDE
VASNA
GERUSALEMME

Armament Store Carriers and Issuing Ships

CORINDA	KISTNA	THYRA S
DARVEL	PACHECO	GUDRUN MAERSK
HERMELIN	PRINCE DE LIEGE	KOLA
HERON	PRINCESS MARIA PIA	PROME (Mine Issue Ship)
KHETI	ROBERT MAERSK	

Naval Store Carriers and Issuing Ships

GLENARTNEY	BOSPHORUS	HICKORY BURN
FORT WRANGELL	JAARSTROOM	HICKORY DALE
CITY OF DIEPPE	MARUDU	HICKORY GLEN
FORT PROVIDENCE	SAN ANDRES	HICKORY STREAM
	SLESVIG	

Victualling Store Carriers and Issuing Ships
FORT ALABAMA
FORT CONSTANTINE

FORT DUNVEGAN
FORT EDMONTON

Collier
EDNA

Tugs
WEASEL
EMPRESS JOSEPHINE
LARIAT

EMPIRE SAM
INTEGRITY

Floating Docks
AFD 20

AFD 18

Shore Establishments
BEACONSFIELD (Melbourne): Lt. Cdr. M. Gibbs, RNVR
FURNEAUX (Brisbane): Cdr. J. F. Steemson
WOOLOOMOOLOO: Cdr. J. D. Stevenson
GOLDEN HIND (Sydney): Capt. H. B. Crane
PEPYS (Manus): Capt. H. F. Waight, OBE

Appendix B

THE EAST INDIES FLEET

On VJ DAY, 15 AUGUST 1945

Commander in Chief: Admiral Sir Arthur John Power, KCB, CVO
Second in Command: Vice Admiral H. T. C. Walker, CB
Commanding Aircraft Carriers: Vice Admiral C. Moody, CB
Commanding Fifth Cruiser Squadron: Rear Admiral W. R. Patterson, CB, CVO

Battleships
NELSON: Capt. C. Caslon, CBE
RICHELIEU (French): Capt. G. M. J. Du Vignaux, FN

Escort Aircraft Carriers
AMEER: Cdr. P. D. H. R. Pelly, DSO
ATTACKER: Capt. G. F. Renwick
EMPEROR: Capt. Sir Charles Madden, Bt
EMPRESS: Capt. J. R. S. Brown
HUNTER: Capt. A. D. Torlesse
KHEDIVE: Capt. D. H. Magnay
PURSUER: Capt. T. L. Bratt, DSC
SEARCHER: Capt. J. W. Grant, DSO
TROUNCER: Capt. G. A. Rotherham, DSO, OBE
SHAH: Capt. W. J. Yendell
SMITER: Capt. L. G. Richardson
TUMPETER: Capt. C. B. Alers-Hankey, DSC
ACTIVITY: Capt. E. J. R. North, RD, RNR
FENCER: Cdr. A. M. Harris
BEGUM: Capt. C. L. Howe, CBE
STALKER: Capt. L. C. Sinker, DSC

Cruisers
NIGERIA: Capt. H. A. King, DSO
CEYLON: Capt. H. L. Harkness, DSC
CLEOPATRA: Capt. B. I. Robertshaw, CBE

CUMBERLAND: Capt. P. K. Enright
LONDON: Capt. S. L. Bateson
PHOEBE: Capt. S. M. Raw, CBE
SUSSEX: Capt. A. F. de Salis, DSO
ROYALIST: Capt. W. G. Brittain, CBE
GLASGOW: Capt. C. P. Clarke, DSO
JAMAICA: Capt. J. Hughes-Hallett, CB, DSO
NORFOLK: Capt. J. G. Y. Loveband
TROMP (Dutch): Capt. F. Stam, DSO, RNETHN
JACOB VAN HEEMSKERCK (Dutch)

Destroyers
SAUMAREZ: Capt. M. L. Power, CBE, DSO+
VENUS: Cdr. H. G. D. De Chair, DSC+
VERULAM: Lt. Cdr. D. H. R. Bromley, DSC
VIGILANT: Lt. Cdr. L. W. L. Argles, DSC
VIRAGO: Lt. Cdr. A. J. R. White, DSC
VOLAGE: Cdr. L. G. Durlacher, OBE, DSC
MYNGS: Capt. J. H. Allison, DSO+
ZENITH: Lt. Cdr. R. W. B. Lacon, DSC
ZAMBESI: Lt. Cdr. J. M. Palmer
ZEALOUS: Cdr. R. F. Jessel, DSO, DSC
ZEBRA: Lt. Cdr. E. C. Peake
ZEPHYR: Lt. Cdr. C. R. Purse, DSC+
ZEST: Lt. Cdr. R. B. N. Hicks, DSO
ZODIAC: Lt. Cdr. H. R. Rycroft, DSC
CARYSFORT: Cdr. A. L. Hobson
CASSANDRA: Lt. C. C. Anderson
ROEBUCK: Cdr. C. D. Bonham-Carter
ESKIMO: Lt. Cdr. E. N. Sinclair, DSC
TARTAR: Capt. B. Jones, DSO+, DSC
NUBIAN: Lt. Cdr. F. C. Brodrick
PALADIN: Lt. Cdr. H. R. Hewlett, RNVR
PENN: Lt. Cdr. A. H. Diack, DSC+
PETARD: Lt. Cdr. R. L. Caple, DSC
ROTHERHAM: Capt. H. W. Biggs, DSO+
RAPID: Lt. Cdr. F. P. Baker, DSC
RELENTLESS: Lt. Cdr. G. B. Barstow
ROCKET: Lt. Cdr. B. M. D. I'Anson
RACEHORSE: Cdr. G. E. Fardell
RAIDER: Lt. Cdr. J. C. Cartwright, DSC
REDOUBT: Lt. Cdr. F. W. M. Carter, DSC
FARNDALE: Cdr. E. G. Roper, DSO, DSC
BICESTER: Cdr. R. W. F. Northcott, DSO
BLACKMORE: Lt. Cdr. J. S. Kerans
BLEASDALE: Lt. Cdr. T. G. Clarke, DSC, RNVR
BRECON: Lt. Cdr. N. R. H. Rodney
CALPE: Lt. Cdr. N. F. R. Gill, DSC, RNR

CHIDDINGFOLD: Lt. Cdr. F. G. Woods, DSC
COWDRAY: Lt. D. J. Beckley, DSO, DSC
EGGESFORD: Lt. G. H. Evans
TJERK HIDDES (Dutch)
VAN GALEN (Dutch)
LE TRIOMPHANT (French)
CARABINIERE (Italian) (Aircraft Target Ship)

Monitors
ABERCROMBIE: Capt. C. F. H. Churchill, DSC
ROBERTS: Capt. C. B. Tidd

Gunboats
APHIS: Lt. J. E. Dyer, DSC+
COCKCHAFER: Lt. E. A. Tyrer, DSC
SCARAB: Lt. Cdr. B. J. Anderson

Fighter Direction Ships
ULSTER QUEEN: Capt. M. H. J. Bennett, RD, RNR
PALOMARES: Capt. C. L. de H. Bell, DSC, RD, RNR

Destroyer Depot Ship
WOOLWICH: Capt. W. B. Hynes, CBE, DSO
(Destroyer SCOUT – Tender to WOOLWICH)

Submarine Depot and Accommodation Ships
WOLFE: Capt. J. E. Slaughter, DSO
WUCHANG: Lt. Cdr. J. H. L. McCarter, SANF(V)

Submarines
SCORCHER: Lt. K. S. Renshaw, DSC, RNR
SCYTHIAN: Lt. Cdr. C. P. Thode, RNVR
SEADOG: Lt. E. A. Hobson, DSC
SHALIMAR: Lt. W. G. Meeke, MBE, DSC
SIBYL: Lt. H. R. Murray
SPUR: Lt. P. S. Beale
STATESMAN: Lt. R. G. P. Bulkeley
SUBTLE: Lt. B. J. B. Andrew, DSC
THRASHER: Lt. Cdr. M. F. R. Ainslie, DSO, DSC
TORBAY: Lt. Cdr. C. P. Norman, DSO
TRIDENT: Lt. A. R. Profit, DSC
VIGOROUS: Lt. N. R. Wood
VISIGOTH: Lt. C. H. Hammer
VIVID: Lt. J. C. Varley, DSC

Sloops
FALMOUTH: Lt. Cdr. N. E. Cutler
CAUVERY (RIN)
GODAVARI (RIN)
KISTNA (RIN)
ERITREA (Italian)
SHOREHAM: Lt. Cdr. R. J. Tadhunter, RNR
NARBADA (RIN)
SUTLEJ (RIN)
JUMNA (RIN)

Frigates
AWE: Lt. Cdr. H. P. Carse, DSC, RNVR
DART: Lt. Cdr. A. G. Scott, DSC, RNR
EVENLODE: Lt. Cdr. W. F. McAusland, RNVR
INVER: Lt. Cdr. W. R. Seward, RNVR
JED: Lt. Cdr. R. S. Miller, DSC, RD, RNR
KALE: Lt. Cdr. G. W. Houchen, OBE, RD, RNR
LOCHY: Lt. Cdr. W. J. P. Roberts, RN, RNR
LOSSIE: Lt. Cdr. A. F. MacFie, OBE, RD, RNR
ROTHER: Lt. Cdr. B. H. C. Rodgers, DSC, RNVR
TAFF: Lt. Cdr. M. E. Impey, DSO, DSC+
TEVIOT: Lt. D. Welsh
LOCH KATRINE: Lt. Cdr. R. A. Cherry, RNR
LOCH LOMOND: Cdr. S. Darling, DSC++, RANVR
LOCH MORE: Lt. Cdr. R. A. D. Cambridge, DSC, RD, RNR
LOCH QUOICH: Lt. Cdr. J. E. B. Healey, RNVR
LOCH RUTHVEN: Lt. Cdr. R. T. Horan, RNR
LOCH SCAVAIG: Lt. Cdr. C. W. Leadbetter, RNR
LOCH TARBERT: Lt. Cdr. W. S. Thomson, OBE, RNR
NATAL: Lt. Cdr. D. A. Hall, DSC+, SANF(V)
DEVERON: Lt. Cdr. W. P. Bush, DSC+, RNVR
NADDER: Lt. Cdr. P. E. Kitto, RNR
HALLADALE: Lt. Cdr. J. E. Woolfenden, DSC, RD, RNR
NESS: Lt. Cdr. R. S. Steel, RNR
TAY: Lt. Cdr. R. Atkinson, DSC++, RNR
LOCH CRAGGIE: Lt. Cdr. C. L. L. Davies, RNVR
LOCH FYNE: Lt. Cdr. R. F. J. Maberly, RNVR
LOCH GLENDHU: Lt. Cdr. E. G. P. B. Knapton, DSC
LOCH GORM: Lt. Cdr. H. Vernon, RNVR
TEST: Cdr. T. S. L. Fox-Pitt, OBE
BANN: Lt. Cdr. R. H. Jameson, DSC, RNR
SHIEL: Lt. H. P. Crail, DSC, RNR
TRENT: Lt. Cdr. C. D. Smith, DSC, RD, RNR
LOCK ECK: Lt. Cdr. W. McInnes, RNR
LOCH INSH: Lt. Cdr. E. W. C. Dempster, DSC, RNVR
LOCH KILLISPORT: Lt. Cdr. G. Butcher, DSC, RNVR
LOCH ACHRAY: Lt. Cdr. C. J. Alldridge, RNR

Cutters (ex-U.S.C.G.)
BANFF: Lt. Cdr. J. D'A. Nesbitt, RNR
FISHGUARD: Lt. Cdr. C. A. Woods, RNZNVR
GORLESTON: Cdr. J. H. Eaden, DSC++
LULWORTH: Cdr. R. C. S. Woolley, RD, RNR
SENNEN: Lt. B. M. Skinner

Corvettes
FREESIA: Lt. W. L. Hancock, SANF(V)
MEADOWSWEET: Lt. C. G. Jackson, RNR
MONKSHOOD: Lt. O. R. D. Stephen, SANF(V)
ROCKROSE: Lt. E. A. King, RNVR
ROSEBAY: Lt. Cdr. G. R. E. Southwood, RNR
SMILAX: Lt. A. Branson, RNR
SNOWFLAKE: Lt. E. J. Powell, RNR
ASSAM (RIN)
THYME: Lt. Cdr. F. E. Eastman, SANF(V)
TULIP: Lt. J. H. Merriman, RNR
VIOLET: Lt. A. R. J. Tilston, SANF(V)
HONESTY: Lt. M. J. Rowlands, RNVR
JASMINE: Lt. E. C. Leaver, RNR
NIGELLA: Lt. Cdr. J. B. Campbell, RANVR
MAHRATTA (RIN): Lt. J. S. Hough, DSC, RNR
SIND (RIN)

Anti-submarine Patrol Vessels
KALAVATI (RIN)   SONAVATI (RIN)

Fleet Minesweepers
FRIENDSHIP: Cdr. D. L. Johnson
GOZO: Cdr. T. T. Euman
LENNOX: Lt. Cdr. C. H. Walton, RNR
LIGHTFOOT: Lt. Cdr. A. S. Drysdale, RNVR
MELITA: Lt. Cdr. G. R. May, RNR
PELORUS: Lt. Cdr. F. J. Bourjat
PERSIAN: Lt. Cdr. J. L. Woollcombe
POSTILLION: Lt. Cdr. W. E. Halbert, DSC, RNR
PICKLE: Cdr. C. P. F. Brown, DSC+
CHAMELEON: Lt. Cdr. D. P. Richardson, RNVR
PINCHER: Lt. Cdr. C. B. Blake, RNVR
PLUCKY: Lt. Cdr. G. Wallis, RNVR
RECRUIT: Cdr. A. E. Doran, DSC
RIFLEMAN: Lt. Cdr. C. L. Carroll, DSC, RNR
JEWEL: Lt. Cdr. B. A. Breeze, RNVR
SERENE: Lt. Cdr. R. M. Ritchie, DSC, RNVR
BALUCHISTAN (RIN)
BIHAR (RIN)
CARNATIC (RIN)

Deccan (RIN)
Kathiawar (RIN)
Khyber (RIN)
Konkan (RIN)
Kumaon (RIN)
Orissa (RIN)
Oudh (RIN)
Rajputana (RIN)
Rohilkhand (RIN)
Bengal (RIN)
Bombay (RIN)
Punjab (RIN)

Attached Danlayers (Trawlers)
Imersay: Lt. Cdr. J. H. A. Winfield, DSO, RNR
Scaravay: Lt. J. A. Monaghan, RNZNVR
Lingay: Lt. P. W. Jequier, RNVR
Sandray: Lt. J. E. Freestone, RNR

Depot and Repair Ships
Lucia: Capt. G. H. Stapleton
Wayland: Capt. W. G. A. Shuttleworth
Ausonia: Capt. J. M. Scott
Mullion Cove: Cdr. J. E. Evans, DSC, RD, RNR
Caradoc: Capt. A. J. Baker-Cresswell, DSO
Beachy Head: Capt. C. K. Adam, DSO
Corbrae: Lt. Cdr. C. H. Pollock, DSC
Mull of Galloway: Cdr. E. C. Hicks, RN, RNR
Derby Haven: Cdr. T. A. Sergeant, RD, RNR
Gombroon: Cdr. J. E. Fenton, OBE

Surveying Vessels
Challenger: Cdr. C. W. Sabine, OBE
Nguva: Lt. Cdr. C. J. Wood
Virginia: Lt. P. P. O'Sullivan, RNR
White Bear: Lt. Cdr. K. W. Hay, DSC
HDML 1238: Lt. T. E. Powell, RNVR
HDML 1288: S/Lt. W. A. Bailey, RNVR
HDML 1376: Lt. C. M. Ockleford, RNVR

Boom Carriers
Devon City: Cdr. A. McD. Harvey
Ethiopian: Cdr. K. A. S. Phillips, RD, RNR

Anti-U-boat Net Layer
Brittany: Lt. S. R. Berry, RNR

CC

Controlled Minelayers (Trawlers)
DABCHICK: Lt. Cdr. P. E. Martin, RNR
REDSHANK: Lt. L. Punnett, RCNVR
SANDMARTIN

Salvage Vessels
OCEAN SALVOR   SALVIOLA

Landing Ships
BULOLO: Capt. H. R. Conway
LARGS: Capt. A. A. Martin, DSO, DSC++, RD, RNR
KONINGIN EMMA: Cdr. T. L. Alkin, OBE
PRINS ALBERT: Lt. Cdr. E. C. St. A. Coles, RNR
NITH: Lt. Cdr. W. A. Grinham, RNVR
WAVENEY: Lt. Cdr. B. T. Whinney, DSC, RNVR
GLENGYLE: Capt. B. B. Grant, RD, RNR
PERSIMMON: Cdr. W. E. Gelling, DSC, RD, RNR
ROCKSAND: Cdr. H. W. D'Arcy-Evans
SAINFOIN: Cdr. A. Longmuir, DSC, RD, RNR
SANSOVINO: Cdr. A. S. Winton, RD, RNR
SEFTON: Lt. Cdr. F. A. C. Bishop, RD, RNR
PRINSES BEATRIX: Cdr. J. Stretch, RD, RNR
EMPIRE ELAINE (Red Ensign)
HIGHWAY: Cdr. C. Edgecombe, RD, RNR
NORTHWAY: Cdr. K. S. Monro, RD, RNR
DEWDALE (RFA)
ENNERDALE (RFA)
BARPETA (Red Ensign)
LLANSTEPHAN CASTLE (RIN)
GLENROY: Capt. P. M. Archdale

Base and Depot Ships
LANKA (Colombo): Capt. J. F. W. Mudford
HIGHFLYER (Trincomalee): Capt. A. O'Leary, OBE
MARAGA (Addu Atoll): Lt. J. F. Humphreys, DSC, RNVR
LANDGUARD: Lt. R. O. Tyrer, RNVR
MAYINA: Capt. W. R. G. Reid
YING CHOW: Cdr. A. G. D. Bagot
BUSHWOOD: Lt. C. C. Boxall, RNR
SPRINGTIDE: Lt. F. W. Treves, BEM, RNR
TANA (Kilindini): Cdr. Sir P. W. Bowyer-Smyth, Bt
IRONCLAD (Diego Suarez)
SAMBUR (Mauritius): Cdr. W. Pennefather
SANGDRAGON (Seychelles): Cdr. L. P. Lane
SHEBA (Aden): Cdre. E. A. Aylmer, DSC
JUFAIR (Bahrein): Lt. Cdr. J. Irwin, RD, RNR
EUPHRATES (Persian Gulf): Capt. I. W. Whitehorn (Commodore, RNR)
OMAN (Khor Kuwait)

BRAGANZA (Bombay): Capt. A. R. Farquhar, DSC
AMZARI (Vizagapatam): Capt. G. I. S. More, OBE
CHILWA (Calcutta): Lt. R. J. Evans, RNR
CHINKARA (Cochin): Capt. P. C. W. Manwaring
PANGKOR (Bombay): Lt. R. Warren, RNR
RN Base, Madras
TENGRA (Mandapan): Capt. T. N. Sheffield, OBE

Base and Depot Ships, RIN

ADYAR (Madras)	HOOGLI (Calcutta)	VENDURUTHI (Cochin)
CIRCARS (Vizagapatam)	PATUNGA (Chittagong)	MONZE (Karachi)
DALHOUSIE (Bombay)	SITA (Ceylon)	MOTI (Bombay)

RN Air Stations
BAMBARA (Trincomalee): Capt. H. M. Spreckley
BHERNUNDA (Colombo): Capt. A. F. Campbell, OBE
GARUDA (Coimbatore): Capt. E. R. G. Baker
KALUGU (Cochin): Cdr. E. K. Lee, RNVR
RAJALIYA (Puttalam, Ceylon): Cdr. J. C. Cockburn, DSC
UKUSSA (Katukurunda, Ceylon): Capt. J. S. Crawford, DSO
VAIRI (Sular): Cdr. G. R. Brown, DSC
VALLURU (Tambaram, Madras): Capt. H. M. S. Mundy, DSC

Appendix C

AIRCRAFT OF THE BRITISH PACIFIC FLEET

Fighters and Fighter-bombers
GRUMMAN HELLCAT (F.6F). American-built single-seat fighter or fighter-bomber. Six 0·50 calibre machine guns, but capable of being armed with bombs or rockets. Maximum speed, 370 mph. Range 1,500 miles. Endurance 7 hours. Ceiling, 37,000 feet. 1839 Sq. and 1844 Sq. embarked in *Indomitable*. 888 Sq. also employed for photo-reconnaissance.

VOUGHT-SIKORSKY CORSAIR (F.4U). American-built single-seat fighter or fighter-bomber. Four 0·50 calibre machine guns, but capable of being armed with bombs or rockets. Maximum speed, 375 mph. Range, 1,460 miles. Endurance, 6 hours. Ceiling, 34,000 feet. 1830 Sq. and 1833 Sq. embarked in *Illustrious*, 1834 Sq. and 1836 Sq. in *Victorious*, 1841 Sq. and 1842 Sq. in *Formidable*.

VICKERS-ARMSTRONG SUPERMARINE SEAFIRE. British-built single-seat fighter. Two 20-mm. cannon and four 0·303 machine guns. Maximum speed,

CC*

350 mph. Range, 465 miles (without over-load tanks). Endurance, 2 hours 40 minutes. Ceiling, 33,000 feet. 887 Sq. and 894 Sq. embarked in *Indefatigable*, 801 Sq. and 880 Sq. in *Implacable*.

FAIREY FIREFLY. Two-seat fighter-bomber and strike aircraft. Four 20-mm. cannon, plus eight 60-lb rockets or two 1,000-lb bombs. Maximum speed, 290 mph. Range, 1,300 miles. Endurance, 6 hours. Ceiling, 28,000 feet. 1770 Sq. and, later, 1772 Sq. embarked in *Indefatigable*, 1771 Sq. in *Implacable*.

Bomber

GRUMMAN AVENGER (TBF). American-built three-seat bomber, torpedo-bomber, reconnaissance and antisubmarine strike aircraft. Two 0·50 calibre machine guns in wings, one 0·30 calibre in front position and one 0·50 calibre in turret. Four 500-lb bombs or one torpedo. Maximum speed, 230 knots. Range, 1,020 miles. Endurance, 5 hours. Ceiling 24,000 feet. 854 Sq. embarked in *Illustrious*, 849 Sq. in *Victorious*, 857 Sq. in *Indomitable*, 820 Sq. in *Indefatigable*, 848 Sq. in *Formidable*, and 828 Sq. in *Implacable*.

Reconnaissance and Air–Sea Rescue

VICKERS SUPERMARINE WALRUS. Reconnaissance and spotter amphibian. Crew, three. One Vickers machine gun forward, two amidships. Maximum speed, 120 mph. Range, 600 miles. Ceiling, 17,000 feet. Two Walrus normally embarked in one carrier of the squadron.

Appendix D

JAPANESE SHIPPING SUNK BY BRITISH AND NETHERLANDS SUBMARINES IN THE FAR EAST

SEPTEMBER 1944 TO AUGUST 1945

Warships and Naval Vessels

DATE	ENEMY VESSEL	TONS	AREA	SUNK BY
9.9.44	Special S/M Chaser No 8	100	Malacca Strait	*Porpoise* minelay of 8.7.44
23.9.44	U.859	1,600	off Penang	*Trenchant*
6.10.44	Special S/M Chaser No 2	100	Malacca Strait	*Tally Ho*
6.10.44	U.168	1,140	Java Sea	DS *Zwaardvisch*
17.10.44	*Itsu kushima* (Minelayer)	1,970	Java Sea	DS *Zwaardvisch*
4.11.44	Special Minesweeper No 5	615	Malacca Strait	*Terrapin*
20.11.44	Special Minelayer No 4	600	Nicobars	*Tally Ho*
4.3.45	Special S/M Chaser No 5	290	Malacca Strait	*Trenchant* and *Terrapin*

DATE	ENEMY VESSEL		TONS	AREA	SUNK BY
27.3.45	Special Minelayer No 1		500	Malacca Strait	*Porpoise* minelay of 8.7.44
13.4.45	Special Minesweeper No 104		215	Java Sea	*Stygian*
26.4.45	Special Minesweeper No 3		215	Java Sea	*Sleuth, Solent*
25.5.45	Special Minesweeper No 105		215	Java Sea	*Trenchant*
8.6.45	*Ashigara* (Cruiser)		12,700	Banka Strait	*Trenchant*
25.7.45	Patrol Boat No 2 (old destroyer)		750	Java Sea	*Stubborn*

Merchant Vessels over 500 tons (definitely confirmed from enemy records)

DATE	ENEMY VESSEL		TONS	AREA	SUNK BY
2.9.44	*Toso* Maru No 1	Cargo	800	W. Siam	*Strongbow*
5.9.44	*Shiretoko* Maru	Cargo	1,799	Sunda Strait	*Tantivy*
10.9.44	*Takekun* Maru	Tanker	3,029	Penang	*Porpoise* minelay of 8.7.44
18.9.44	*Junyo* Maru	Cargo	5,065	W. Sumatra	*Tradewind*
12.10.44	*Manryo* Maru	Cargo	1,185	Malacca Strait	*Strongbow*
28.10.44	*Sumatra* Maru	Cargo	4,859	Phuket harbour	'Chariots' from *Trenchant*
2.11.44	*Hachijin* Maru	Cargo	1,918	S. China Sea	*Tantalus*
19.11.44	*Nichinan* Maru	Cargo	1,945	Malacca Strait	*Stratagem*
10.12.44	*Shoei* Maru	Cargo	1,985	Sunda Strait	*Stoic*
31.12.44	*Unryu* Maru	Cargo	2,515	Andamans	*Shakespeare*
1.1.45	*Kyokko* Maru	Cargo	593	Mergui	*Tradewind* minelay of 30.10.44
9.1.45	*Shinko* Maru	Converted Gunboat	934	Java Sea	DS O.19
23.1.45	*Hozan* Maru	Tanker	896	E. Sumatra	*Trenchant* minelay of 16.9.44
23.1.45	*Nikkaku* Maru	Cargo	1,946	E. Sumatra	*Trenchant* minelay of 16.9.44
11.2.45	*Nanshin* Maru	Cargo	834	China Sea	*Tradewind*
10.4.45	*Hosei* Maru	Tanker	896	Java Sea	DS O.19
29.4.45	*Takasago* Maru	Tanker	1,116	China Sea	*Tradewind*
25.5.45	*Nittei* Maru	Cargo	1,000	Java Sea	*Thorough*
1.6.45	*Tobi* Maru	Cargo	982	Java Sea	*Tiptoe*

(Between September 1944 and August 1945 British and Dutch submarines carried out 94 patrols in the SEAC area, based on Ceylon, and 79 in the South-west Pacific Area, based on Fremantle or Subic Bay.)

Appendix E

SUPREME ALLIED COMMANDER, SOUTH-EAST ASIA, ADMIRAL LORD LOUIS MOUNTBATTEN

ORDER OF THE DAY, 12 SEPTEMBER 1945

I have today received the surrender of the Supreme Commander of the Japanese forces you have been fighting, and I have accepted this surrender on behalf of all of you.

I wish you all to know the gratitude and the pride that I feel towards every man and woman in this Command today. You beat the Japanese soldier in battle; inflicting six times the amount of deaths that he was able to inflict on you, and chased him out of Burma.

The defeat of Japan last month is the first in her history. For hundreds of years the Japanese have been ruled by a small set of militarists, and they have been taught to look on themselves as a superior race of divine origin. They have been encouraged to be arrogant to foreigners, and to believe that treachery such as they practised at Pearl Harbour is a virtue so long as it results in a Japanese victory. They are finding it very hard to accept defeat, and have not been too proud to try and wriggle out of the terms of their surrender. Field Marshal Count Terauchi, the Supreme Commander of the Japanese forces in this area, is at the present time an ill man, having had a stroke last April; and I therefore decided to accept his surrender through General Itagaki. But I have ordered him to report to me in person as soon as he is strong enough to travel; and you may all rest assured that I shall put up with no evasion or trickery on the part of any defeated Japanese, however important or divine he may consider himself.

I am telling you this because I wish to warn you of the situation you may find when you proceed to liberate the other territories in the Command. In the new areas you will be occupying, the Japanese have not been beaten in battle; they are mostly composed either of troops who have never fought us at all, and so never discovered for themselves that we could lick them; or else of troops who took part in the early days, when we were not strong enough to hold them. So there is every likelihood that they may feel they could have beaten us in battle, if their Emperor had not ordered them to surrender.

You may well find, therefore, that those Japanese who have a fanatical belief in their divine superiority, and who feel that we are too soft to put them in their place will try and behave arrogantly. You are to stand no nonsense from these people. You will have my support in taking the firmest measures against any attempt at obstinacy, impudence, or non-co-operation.

On the other hand, you will find that there are many Japanese who are no more taken in by the preposterous claims of the militarists than you are yourselves. The Japanese, as a nation, had no say whatsoever in their own government, and were perhaps less responsible than any other people for their government's decision to go to war. Many of them therefore have had little desire, for a long time now, to continue the fight, and are only too thankful that it is all over. Prisoners of this kind must be humanely treated, and I will not tolerate any case that is brought to my notice of taking it out on Japanese if they are prepared to be co-operative. In fact I may even consider it necessary to protect them perhaps by separating them from the fanatics among their own countrymen.

It is possible that there will be hopeless cases, who may commit suicide if they are prevented from behaving arrogantly and insultingly towards the Allied troops. This must be their own responsibility; for these are people who can probably never be re-educated, and who have no contribution to make towards building the peaceable, civilised country which Japan must become if she is not to threaten the peace of the world.

The Japanese prisoners, although they will number about half a million, will by no means be your only responsibility. There will be much more which will need doing. You will realise how much when I say that the enlarged South-east Asia Command now includes 1½ million square miles of land, with a population of 128 million people.

For some months to come, only SEAC will be in a position to undertake such vital tasks as repatriating our prisoners of war and civilian internees who number more than one hundred thousand and have the first claim on us. We shall also be removing the half-million Japanese, and we shall have to see about getting the millions of inhabitants in these vast areas properly fed, and given work, and brought back to peacetime conditions. All this will call for a great deal of planning, hard and practical work, initiative and understanding.

I feel sure I can rely on you to do as well in peace as you did in war, and to get down to this gigantic task so that we can all of us return to our homes as soon as is humanely possible, feeling that we have done a good job. In the meantime, I know you will agree that our prisoners of war who have suffered for so long out here must have the first call on shipping space to take them home; but I shall do everything in my power to see that those of you who are due for release and repatriation get home as fast as shipping and the rate of replacements permit.

SELECT BIBLIOGRAPHY

Roy E. Appleman, James M. Burns, Russell H. Gugler and John Stevens: *Okinawa: The Last Battle* (Washington, 1948).

John Ehrman: *Grand Strategy*, Vols. V and VI (HMSO, 1956).

Admiral Sir Bruce Fraser: 'The Contribution of the British Pacific Fleet to the Assault on Okinawa, 1945.' Supplement to the *London Gazette* of 2 June 1948 (HMSO).

Major General S. Woodburn Kirby: *The War against Japan*, Vols. IV and V (HMSO, 1965).

Samuel Eliot Morison: *History of United States Naval Operations in World War Two*, Vol. XIII, 'The Liberation of the Philippines' and Vol. XIV, 'Victory in the Pacific 1945' (Oxford University Press, Vol. XIII 1960, Vol. XIV 1961).

Vice Admiral The Earl Mountbatten of Burma: Report to the Combined Chiefs of Staff by the Supreme Allied Commander, South-east Asia, 1943–1945 (HMSO, 1951); and Section E of the above, 'Post Surrender Tasks' (HMSO, 1969).

Admiral Sir Arthur John Power: 'Naval Operations in the Ramree Area, 19 January – 22 February, 1945', Supplement to the *London Gazette* of 26 April 1948 (HMSO); 'The Carrier-borne Aircraft Attack on Oil Refineries in the Palembang (Sumatra) Area in January, 1945', Supplement to the *London Gazette* of 5 April 1951 (HMSO).

Captain S. W. Roskill: *The War At Sea 1939–1945*, Vol. III, Parts I and II (HMSO, Pt. I 1960, Pt. II 1961).

Captain Donald MacIntyre: *Fighting Admiral* (Evans Bros., 1961).

E. B. Potter and Fleet Admiral Chester W. Nimitz: *The Great Sea War* (Harrap, 1961).

Admiral Sir Philip Vian: *Action This Day* (Muller, 1960).

Index